The Herland Trilogy

by Charlotte Perkins Gilman

Moving the Mountain

Herland

With Her in Ourland

Table of Contents

Biography of Charlotte Perkins Gilman

Charlotte Perkins Gilman (née Perkins) was born on July 3, 1860 in Hartford, Connecticut. She was the daughter of Frederick Beecher Perkins and Mary Wescott Perkins, and had three historic great-aunts: Harriet Beecher Stowe, the author of *Uncle Tom's Cabin*; Isabella Beecher Hooker, a leader in the suffragist movement; and Catharine Beecher, an educator and strong proponent of the education of women. Charlotte was proud of these lofty relations, and they likely influenced her trajectory as a feminist and radical thinker in later life.

Charlotte's father left the family shortly after her birth, and she spent her childhood living in poverty with her mother and older brother, Thomas. The family was forced to move many times, often living with relatives throughout New England. Due to these moves, Charlotte's schooling was extremely scattered; in total, she had only four years of childhood education, spread amongst seven different schools. Still, she was bright and morally principled, deciding while still a teen that her life's work was to help mankind and, indeed, that the purpose of mankind was to improve the human race.

At the age of 17, she began attending the Rhode Island School of Design, and she spent her early adulthood attending classes, painting (both for pleasure and for money), teaching art to young children, and working odd jobs. When she was 23, she married Charles Walter Stetson, despite being deeply uncertain about the idea of marriage. In her autobiography, *The Living of Charlotte Perkins Gilman*, she wrote:

"On the one hand I knew it was normal and right in general, and held that a woman should be able to have marriage and motherhood, and do her work in the world also. On the other hand, I felt strongly that for me it was not right, that the nature of the life before me forbade it, that I ought to forego the more intimate personal happiness for complete devotion to my work."

During the engagement, she felt great foreboding about the pairing, despite having a deep respect for Stetson. She feared that her future husband and children would be miserable and would suffer due to her presence in their life. Still, she went forward with the marriage and became Mrs. Perkins Stetson. She wrote in her autobiography that the two were very happy together, but her depression only grew and her health began to wane.

Ten months after marriage, Charlotte gave birth to her daughter, Katharine. Charlotte and her husband had hoped that her waning spirits and strength would rebound post-birth, but she only deteriorated more. She was not mentally fit enough to care for the child, finding herself crying and shaking if she even tried to dress her daughter; the Stetsons had to ask Charlotte's mother to stay with them and care for Katharine.

About six months after Katharine's birth, Charlotte was urged by her doctor to get a change of scenery. She left home to spend winter with friends in Pasadena. She wrote of this time in her autobiography: "From the moment the wheels began to turn, the train to move, I felt better." She found herself stronger and more mentally sound than she had been in many months; but when winter ended, she returned home and quickly deteriorated into her former condition.

In desperation, Charlotte and her husband consulted a specialist who prescribed her "the rest cure" and advised her to use her brain as little as possible and to never write, draw, or paint. This treatment was extremely hard on Perkins Stetson; she would later describe this period as the closest she ever came to losing her mind. By the end of it, she found herself crawling into closets and playing with a rag baby hung from a doorknob.

Finally, realizing the deleterious effect of the rest treatment and the stark fact that nothing had helped her condition except leaving home, Charlotte and Charles resolved to separate amicably. In 1888, Charlotte and Katharine moved to California, leaving Charles at home in New England.

While she had not done much professional writing up until this point in her life, Perkins Stetson began to write prolifically in California. In her first year in the state, she wrote the story, "The Yellow Wallpaper," based on her experiences with depression and the rest cure. "The Yellow Wallpaper" is her most-recognized work postmortem and has often been described as a semi-autobiographical account of Charlotte's postpartum depression; but, given that her depression began shortly before marriage and continued for over three years post-birth, it seems most likely that Charlotte's disorder was of a different kind. She herself attributed it to "mismarriage." Throughout the rest of her life, she suffered from severe exhaustion, forgetfulness, and mental fatigue; she attributed this to her original episode of "nerve exhaustion" (as her disorder was called at the time) during her first marriage.

Despite her lingering deficiencies, Charlotte continued to write, earning some income by selling poems and articles. These amounts were meager though and were not nearly enough to support her and her daughter. To make ends meet, she also painted cards, taught art classes, gave lessons, worked odd jobs, and, for a while, ran a boarding house. In spite of her hard work, this period was very lean, and she accumulated debts in California that she would spend the rest of her life paying off.

But, in a serendipitous moment, a new source of income came into Charlotte's life—she was asked, quite unexpectedly, to lecture at a Nationalist Club meeting by a stranger she met on the bus; despite having no experience in public speaking, she accepted. The lecture went well, and Charlotte began giving lectures on a weekly basis. Lecturing eventually became her main source of income; it would remain so for most of her life.

Her lectures (and, in fact, her writing) often focused on women's rights and concerns, social evolution, the benefits of socialism (although her socialism was quite different from the version proposed by Marx), and the care and teaching of children. She supported women's suffrage and spoke about it when asked, but was more primarily concerned with women's lack of economic independence.

As her lecturing career took off, her first book, *In This Our World*, was published in 1893. The book of poems was critically acclaimed, but made Charlotte very little money, and she was forced to give up her life in California. Charlotte and her ex-husband agreed that he and his new wife (who, incidentally, was a close friend of Charlotte's and beloved by the whole family) should take Katharine for a while, and Charlotte began a five year stretch of traveling, with no fixed address.

During this time, she traveled all over the continental U.S. and twice to England: once as a delegate to the International Socialist and Labor Congress of 1896 and once to speak at the Quinquennial Congress of The International Council of Women in 1899. Mainly, however, she lectured and preached sermons in the U.S., going where she was requested or where she had friends.

In between speeches, she wrote. It was during this time that she penned her most famous work in her lifetime: *Women and Economics*. The book took only 58 days to write, but achieved great success upon its publishing in 1899. According to the author, it sold well for 25 years but produced only a small income. Still, her reputation as a writer was solidified; the book opened the door for more books, more stories, more editorials, and more lectures.

This long period of wandering ended on June 8, 1900 when Charlotte married her cousin, G.H. Gilman, and settled with him in New York City. Her autobiography is surprisingly sparse about their relationship (and, indeed, does not mention their courtship at all). But what she does say indicates a deep love: "we were married—and lived happy ever after. If this were a novel, now, here's the happy ending." Charlotte changed her name to Charlotte Perkins Gilman (this is the name generally attached to her work now, whether it was written before or after her second marriage), angering her publishers who said it would confuse readers. Whether it confused readers or not is unknown, but Charlotte and her husband would spend the rest of their lives together.

However, it should not be assumed that she traded work for wedded bliss. She published another book shortly after their honeymoon and went on a six-week trip of lecturing and writing in November of that year—less than six months after becoming Mrs. Perkins Gilman. Such trips remained typical for the 22 years she lived in New York. She spoke in a total of 44 states during her lifetime and traveled to Europe three more times. Her daughter was with her on and off through these years, sometimes with Perkins Gilman, sometimes with her father. The author had a deep love and respect for her daughter and never regretted that her child was able to spend time with both pairs of parents and step-parents.

Over time, Charlotte's work slipped in popularity. Her views had always been considered rather radical and had often earned her scorn, but now her work was being rejected in large numbers by editors and publishers. Determined to be heard, she started a self-published monthly magazine in November 1909 called *The Forerunner*. The magazine was all self-written and had between 1,000 and 1,500 subscribers at its peak. She published it through 1916, always lecturing and writing other material concurrently. After ending *The Forerunner*, she tried her hand at writing for a newspaper syndicate, but she struggled to appeal to the general population and only pursued the work for about a year. At that point, her writing slowed down, but her lecturing continued.

In 1922, Charlotte and her husband moved to Norwich Town, Connecticut. There, Perkins Gilman wrote little, feeling that she had said her piece in *The Forerunner*. Her lecturing continued for a while, and she felt that her speaking abilities were strongest during this time. But eventually, the rise of radio quelled popular interest in public speakers and this work, too, dropped off. Her focus in later life shifted to her husband, her garden, and her friends.

In 1932, she was diagnosed with inoperable breast cancer. In her autobiography, she wrote of the diagnosis: "My only distress was for [her husband] Houghton." At his bequest, she tried X-ray treatment, and it helped her for some time. When Houghton unexpectedly passed of a brain hemorrhage in 1934, Perkins Gilman moved back to California to be with her daughter and her grandchildren. Her daughter's step-mother (Perkins Gilman's lifelong friend) came to be with her as her health declined, and they spent the last year of her life together, until Charlotte committed suicide on August 17, 1935, at the age of 75. She wrote in her goodbye letter that she "preferred chloroform to cancer."

Foreword

About *The Forerunner*

In addition to her lecturing and other writing, Charlotte Perkins Gilman self-published a literary magazine, *The Forerunner*, for seven years. The magazine was launched in November 1909 when Perkins Gilman found that public interest in her work had started to wane and her pieces were being rejected with some regularity. Wanting her work published in spite of these challenges, she started the magazine and kept it going until the end of 1916. The periodical had over 1,000 subscribers and circulated as far as Europe, India, and Australia. Issues included installments of novels (like the three novels included here), short stories, poems, book reviews, articles, and more. For a while, Perkins Gilman even wrote advertisements for the magazine, recommending products she liked. Otherwise, it did not contain ads.

The Forerunner proved to be a great undertaking, equal to four books worth of text every year and costing $3,000/year to print. Unfortunately, the work was largely ignored by critics and subscribership never rose above 1,500 persons at a time, so the author was taking a loss on the project, charging $1.00 for a year's subscription or $0.10 per copy. She funded it through additional writing that she sold to other publications.

In the February issue of 1916, Perkins Gilman announced that 1916 was to be the last year of *The Forerunner*. She listed three reasons for the discontinuation: she had successfully said what she needed to say, she believed it incorrect to continue publishing a work that was "insufficiently desired," and she could no longer afford the monetary cost. In her autobiography, she went on to say that she lacked the business acumen necessary for the management of the magazine. For example, a friend of hers once tried to pay her to place an ad in it but, upon sampling his product, Charlotte determined that she did not like it and could not advertise it as such. This attitude, while honorable and undoubtedly in keeping with her established beliefs, contributed to the magazine's inability to support itself.

Compounding the periodical's problems was the fact that many of Charlotte's beliefs were quite controversial for the time—and she did not shy away from any of them in *The Forerunner*. She regularly derided women's fashion, the forced economic dependence of women, the current state and conditions of motherhood (arguing for more specialized childcare), the treatment of African Americans, and capitalism. She suspected that readers who would have bought the magazine if she had only espoused one or two of these views in it were driven away by the sheer number of unpopular opinions.

Still, the work was done for seven years, and it was done well. The readers who wrote Perkins Gilman to renew their subscriptions were often extremely complimentary of the magazine, and Charlotte would publish excerpts of these letters in a section called "Letters from Subscribers." One such excerpt reads:

"I feel now as if I could not do without THE FORERUNNER ever again. It has become a necessity. When I go to the mail box, and find 'only magazines,' I am disappointed, but when I see the big, square envelope, I say, 'Oh, THE FORERUNNER!' and no letter could give me more pleasure. No matter what work I am doing, it usually has to wait until I have at least glanced over the new number. However downcast I may be, it lifts me up, and puts new spirit and pluck into me."

This Edition of *The Herland Trilogy*

"Moving the Mountain," "Herland," and "With Her in Ourland" originally appeared in *The Forerunner* in 1911, 1915, and 1916, respectively. "With Her in Ourland" was explicitly referred to as the sequel to "Herland" in the magazine, but "Moving the Mountain" was not related to either of these stories at the time. Ann J. Lane, a pioneer in Women's Studies, was the first to suggest that the three stories form a trilogy, due to their similar themes; and they have often been grouped together as such in the years since. They have been published in book form, together and separately, in the intervening years and have since come into the public domain.

Due to their public domain status, the works can be published by anyone, in any form. This has often been to their detriment. Editions of the trilogy circulating now, in 2021, are often riddled with: errors not present in the original works, updates to spelling and wordage not disclosed to the reader, a mish-mash of edits from various prior printings, and abridgments and missing text (sometimes ending a chapter mid-sentence). This edition strives to right these wrongs by being as true to the original works, as published in *The Forerunner*, as possible. As such, the following edits have been made (and not made) to the text:

- No sections, sentences, or words have been removed from the text, with the exception of errors. The works have not been abridged in any way from how they appeared in *The Forerunner*.
- Unless obviously and accidentally incorrect, the spelling of words has been maintained. Archaic spellings are not incorrect, simply outdated. To update them would be to rob the reader of the ability

to place the text in time.

- Unless exceedingly confusing or obviously and accidentally incorrect, the original punctuation has been maintained. Charlotte Perkins Gilman had a tendency towards non-standard punctuation but, as any reader knows, a novel is not the same as an essay for English 101, and novelists should be allowed to use punctuation as they please, provided the meaning is clear. The overwhelming majority of punctuation edits corrected misplaced or accidentally excluded quotation marks.

- No antiquated words were replaced with more modern equivalents. The works of Charles Dickens and Jane Austin have been allowed to be received as they were written, and the same should be true for Charlotte Perkins Gilman. However, if an incorrect word was used and the author's intended word was clear, a replacement was made. (This happened most notably with two incorrectly spelled character names.)

- The dinkuses (symbols placed between sections of text to indicate a break) have been standardized across the three books. As the works were published in three different years, the original dinkuses varied.

- The original italics used in the text have been maintained.

- Except where incorrect or overly confusing, paragraph breaks have not been moved from their original locations.

- Most editions of this text include a preface for "Moving the Mountain." Said preface was not a part of *The Forerunner*, but was written for the book version of the tale. Given that the purpose of this edition is to present the stories as they appeared in *The Forerunner*, it is excluded here. The preface did not contain any story elements, but simply asserted Perkins Gilman's belief that the world could change drastically, and for the better, in a very short amount of time.

- Chapters 1 - 8 of "With Her in Ourland" had chapter titles in *The Forerunner*, but chapters 9 - 12 did not. Many later editions of the text have included titles for these chapters. However, since they were not present in *The Forerunner*, they are not present here.

- A mathematical error has been maintained in "Moving the Mountain." The reader is forewarned of the error to prevent confusion, but it has not been corrected.

Moving the Mountain

Chapter I

On a gray, cold, soggy Tibetan plateau stood glaring at one another two white people—a man and a woman.

With the first, a group of peasants; with the second, the guides and carriers of a well-equipped exploring party.

The man wore the dress of a peasant, but around him was a leather belt— old, worn, battered—but a recognizable belt of no Asiatic pattern, and showing a heavy buckle made in twisted initials.

The woman's eye had caught the sunlight on this buckle before she saw that the heavily-bearded face under the hood was white. She pressed forward to look at it.

"Where did you get that belt?" she cried, turning for the interpreter to urge her question.

The man had caught her voice—her words. He threw back his hood and looked at her, with a strange blank look, as of one listening to something far away.

"John!" she cried. "John! My Brother!" He lifted a groping hand to his head, made a confused noise that ended in almost a shout of "Nellie!" reeled and fell backward.

. . . . .

When one loses his mind, as it were, for thirty years, and finds it again; when one wakes up; comes to life; recognizes oneself an American citizen twenty-five years old—

No. This is what I find it so hard to realize. I am not twenty-five; I am fifty-five.

. . . . .

Well, as I was saying, when one comes to life again like this, and has to renew acquaintance with one's own mind, in a sudden swarming rush of hurrying memories—that is a good deal of pressure for a brain so long unused.

But when on top of that, one is pushed headlong into a world immeasurably different from the world one has left at twenty-five—a topsy-turvy world, wherein all one's most cherished ideals are found to be

1

reversed, rearranged, or utterly gone; where strange new facts are accompanied by strange new thoughts and strange new feelings—the pressure becomes terrific.

Nellie has suggested that I write it down, and I think for once she is right. I disagree with her on so many points that I am glad to recognize the wisdom of this idea. It will certainly be a useful process in my re-education; and relieve the mental tension.

So, to begin with my first life, being now in my third—

. . . . .

I am the only son of a Methodist minister of South Carolina. My mother was a Yankee. She died after my sister Ellen was born, when I was seven years old. My father educated me well. I was sent to a small Southern college, and showed such a talent for philology that I specialized in ancient languages, and, after some teaching and the taking of various degrees, I had a wonderful opportunity to join an expedition into India and Tibet. I was eager for a sight of those venerable races, those hoary scriptures, those time-honored customs.

. . . . .

We were traveling through the Himalayas—and the last thing I remember was a night camp, and a six-months-old newspaper from home. We had rejoicingly obtained it from a party we met in the pass.

It was read and re-read by all of us—even the advertisements—even the editorials, and in one of these I learned that Mrs. Eddy had been dead some time and that another religion had burst forth and was sweeping the country, madly taken up by the women. That was my last news item. I suppose it was this reading—and the discussions we had—that made me walk in my sleep that night. That is the only explanation I can give. I know I lay down just as I was—and that's all I know, until Nellie found me.

. . . . .

The party reported me lost. They searched for days, made what inquiry they could. No faintest clue was ever found. Himalayan precipices are very tall, and very sudden.

. . . . .

My sister Nellie was traveling in Tibet and found me, with a party of peasants. She gathered what she could from them, through interpreters. It seems that I fell among these people—literally; bruised, stunned, broken, but not dead. Some merciful—or shall I say unmerciful?—trees had

2

softened the fall and let me down easy, comparatively speaking.

They were good people—Buddhists. They mended my bones and cared for me, and it appears made me quite a chief man, in course of time, in their tiny village. But their little valley was so remote and unknown, so out of touch with any and everything, that no tale of this dumb white man ever reached Western ears. I was dumb until I learned their language, was "as a child of a day," they said—knew absolutely nothing.

They taught me what they knew. I suppose I turned a prayer mill; I suppose I was married—Nellie didn't ask that, and they never mentioned such a detail. Furthermore, they gave so dim an account of where the place was that we don't know now; should have to locate that night's encampment, and then look for a precipice and go down it with ropes.

As I have no longer any interest in those venerable races and time-honored customs, I think we will not do this.

Well, she found me, and something happened. She says I knew her— shouted "Nellie!" and fell down—fell on a stone, too, and hit my head so hard they thought I was dead this time "for sure." But when I "came to" I came all the way, back to where I was thirty years ago; and as for those thirty years—I do not remember one day of them.

Nor do I wish to. I have those filthy Tibetan clothes, sterilized and packed away, but I never want to look at them.

I am back in the real world, back where I was at twenty-five. But now I am fifty-five—

. . . . .

Now, about Nellie. I must go slowly and get this thing straightened out for good and all.

My little sister! I was always fond of her, and she adored me. She looked up to me, naturally; believed everything I told her; minded me like a little dog—when she was a child. And as she grew into girl-hood, I had a strong restraining influence upon her. She wanted to be educated—to go to college—but father wouldn't hear of it, of course, and I backed him up. If there is anything on earth I always hated and despised, it is a strong-minded woman! That is—it *was*. I certainly cannot hate and despise my sister Nellie.

Now it appears that soon after my departure from this life, Father died, very suddenly. Nellie inherited the farm—and the farm turned out to be a mine, and the mine turned out to be worth a good deal of money.

3

So that poor child, having no natural guardian or protector, just set to work for herself—went to college to her heart's content, to a foreign university, too. She studied medicine, practiced a while, then was offered a chair in a college and took it; then—I hate to write it—but she is now president of a college—*a coeducational college*!

"Don't you mean 'dean?'" I asked her.

"No," she said. "There is a dean of the girl's building—but I am the president."

My little sister!

. . . . .

The worst of it is that my little sister is now forty-eight, and I—to all intents and purposes—am twenty-five! She is twenty-three years older than I am. She has had thirty years of world-life which I have missed entirely; and this thirty years, I begin to gather, has covered more changes than an ordinary century or two.

It is lucky about that mine.

"At least I shall not have to worry about money," I said to her when she told me about our increased fortune.

She gave one of those queer little smiles, as if she had something up her sleeve, and said:

"No; you won't have to worry about money."

. . . . .

Having all that medical skill of hers in the background, she took excellent care of me up there on those dreary plains and hills, brought me back to the coast by easy stages, and home on one of those new steamers—but I mustn't stop to describe the details of each new thing I notice!

I have sense enough myself—even if I'm not a doctor—to use my mind gradually, not to swallow too fast, as it were.

Nellie is a little inclined to manage me. I don't know as I blame her. I do feel like a child, sometimes. It is so humiliating not to know little common things such as everybody else knows. Air ships I expected, of course; they had started before I left. They are common enough, all sizes. But water is still the cheaper route—as well as slower.

Nellie said she didn't want me to get home too quick; she wanted time to explain things. So we spent long, quiet hours in our steamer chairs, talking things over.

It's no use asking about the family; there is only a flock of young cousins and "once removed" now; the aunts and uncles are mostly gone. Uncle Jake is left. Nellie grins wickedly when she mentions him.

"If things get too hard on you, John, you can go down to Uncle Jake's and rest up. He and Aunt Dorcas haven't moved an *inch*. They fairly barricade their minds against a new idea—and he ploughs and she cooks up on that little mountain farm just as they always did. People go to see them—"

"Why shouldn't they?" I asked—and she smiled that queer little smile again.

"I mean they go to see them as if they were the Pyramids."

"I see," said I. "I might as well prepare for some preposterous nightmare of a world, like—what was that book of Wells', 'The Sleeper Awakened?'"

"Oh, yes. I remember that book," she answered, "and a lot of others. People were already guessing about things as they might be, weren't they? But what never struck any of them was that the people themselves could change."

"No," I agreed. "You can't alter human nature."

Nellie laughed—laughed out loud. Then she squeezed my hand and patted it.

"You *Dear*! she said. "You precious old Long Lost Brother! When you get too utterly upset and lonesome I'll wear my hair down, put on a short dress and let you boss me awhile—to keep your spirits up. That was just the phrase, wasn't it? 'You can't alter human nature!'" And she laughed again.

There is something queer about Nellie—very queer. It is not only that she is different from my little sister—that's natural; but she is different from any woman of forty-eight I ever saw—from any woman of any age I ever saw.

In the first place, she doesn't look *old*—not at all. Women of forty, in our region, were *old women*, and Nellie's near fifty! Then she isn't—what shall I call it—dependent; not the least in the world. As soon as I became really conscious, and strong enough to be of any use, and began to offer her those little services and attentions due to a woman, I noticed this difference.

She is brisk, firm, assured—not unpleasantly so; I don't mean a thing of that sort; but somehow like—almost like a man! No, I certainly don't mean that. She is not in the least mannish, nor in the least self-assertive; but she

5

takes things so easily—as if she owned them.

. . . . .

I suppose it will be some time before my head is absolutely clear and strong as it used to be. I tire rather easily. Nellie is very reassuring about it. She says it will take about a year to re-establish connections and renew mental processes. She advises me to read and talk only a little every day, to sleep all I can, and not to worry.

"You'll be all right soon, my dear," she says, "and plenty of life before you. You seem to have led a very healthy out-door life. You're really well and strong—and as good-looking as ever."

At least she hasn't forgotten that woman's chief duty is to please.

"And the world is a much better place to be in than it was," she assured me. "Things will surprise you, of course—things I have gotten used to and shall forget to tell you about. But the changes are all good ones, and you'll soon get—acclimated. You're young yet."

That's where Nellie slips up. She cannot help having me in mind as the brave young brother she knew. She forgets that I am an old man now. Finally I told her that.

"Now John Robertson," she said, "that's where you are utterly wrong. Of course, you don't know what we're doing about age—how differently we feel. As a matter of physiology we find that about one hundred and fifty ought to be our natural limit; and that with proper conditions we can easily get to be a hundred now. Ever so many do."

"I don't want to be a hundred," I protested. "I saw a man of ninety-eight once—and never want to be one."

"It's not like that now," she said. "I mean we live to be a hundred and enjoy life still—'keep our faculties,' as they used to put it. Why, the ship's doctor here is eighty-seven."

This surprised me a good deal. I had talked a little with this man, and had thought him about sixty.

"Then a man of a hundred—according to your story—would look like—like—"

"Like Grandpa Ely," she offered.

I remembered my mother's father—a tall, straight, hale old man of seventy-five. He had a clear eye, a firm step, a rosy color in his face. Well, that wasn't so bad a prospect.

6

"I consent to be a hundred—on those terms," I told her.

. . . . .

She talked to me a good bit, in small daily doses, of the more general changes in the world, showed me new maps, even let me read a little in the current magazines.

"I suppose you have a million of these now," I said. "There were thousands when I left!"

"No," she answered. "There are fewer, I believe, but much better."

I turned over the one in my hand. It was pleasantly light and thin, it opened easily, the paper and presswork were of the best, the price was twenty-five cents.

"Is this a cheap one—at a higher price? Or have the best ones come down?"

"It's a cheap one," she told me, "if you mean by that a popular one, and it's cheap enough. They have all of a million subscribers."

"And what's the difference, beyond the paper and print?" I asked.

"The pictures are good."

I looked it through again.

"Yes, very good, much improved. But I don't see anything phenomenal— unless it is the absence of advertisements."

Nellie took it out of my hand and ran it over.

"Just read some of that," she said. "Read this story—and this article—and that."

So I sat reading in the sunny silence, the gulls wheeling and dipping just as they used to, and the wide purple ocean just as changeable—and changeless—as ever.

One of the articles was on an extension of municipal service, and involved so much comment on preceding steps that I found it most enlightening. The other was a recent suggestion in educational psychology, and this too carried a retrospect of recent progress which gave me food for thought. The story was a clever one. I found it really amusing, and only on a second reading did I find what it was that gave the queer flavor to it. It was a story about women, two women who were in business partnership, with their adventures, singly and together.

I looked through it carefully. They were not even girls, they were not

7

handsome, they were not in process of being married—in fact, it was not once mentioned whether they were married or not, ever had been or ever wanted to be. Yet I had found it amusing!

I laid the magazine on my rug-bound knees and meditated. A queer sick feeling came over me—mental, not physical. I looked through the magazine again. It was not what I should have called "a woman's magazine," yet the editor was a woman, most of the contributors were women, and in all the subject matter I began to detect allusions and references of tremendous import.

Presently Nellie came to see how I was getting on. I saw her approaching, a firm brisk figure, well and becomingly dressed, with a tailored trimness and convenience, far indeed from the slim, graceful, yielding girl I had once been so proud to protect and teach.

"How soon do we get in, Lady Manager?" I asked her.

"Day after to-morrow," she answered back promptly—not a word about going to see, or asking anyone!

"Well, ma'am, I want you to sit down here and tell me things—right now. What am I to expect? Are there *no* men left in America?"

She laughed gaily.

"No men! Why, bless you, there are as many men as there are women, and a few more, I believe. Not such an over-plus as there used to be, but some to spare still. We had a million and a-half extra in your day, you know."

"I'm glad to learn we're allowed to live!" said I. "Now tell me the worst— are the men all doing the housework?"

"You call that 'the worst,' do you?" inquired Nellie, cocking her head to one side and looking at me affectionately, and yet quizzically. "Well, I guess it was—pretty near 'the worst!' No dear, men are doing just as many kinds of business as they ever were."

I heaved a sigh of relief and chucked my magazine under the chair.

"I'd begun to think there weren't any men left. And they still wear trousers, don't they?"

She laughed outright.

"Oh, yes. They wear just as many trousers as they did before, too."

"And what do the women wear," I demanded suspiciously.

"Whatever kind of clothing their work demands," she answered.

8

"Their work? What kind of work do they do?"

"All kinds, anything they like."

I groaned and shut my eyes. I could see the world as I left it, with only a small proportion of malcontents, and a large majority of contented and happy homes; and then I saw this awful place I was coming to, with strange, masculine women and subdued men.

"How does it happen that there aren't any on this ship?" I inquired.

"Any what?" asked Nellie.

"Any of these—New Women?"

"Why, there are. They're all new, except Mrs. Talbot. She's older than I am, and rather reactionary."

This Mrs. Talbot was a stiff, pious, narrow-minded old lady, and I had liked her the least of any on board.

"Do you mean to tell me that pretty Mrs. Exeter is—one of this new kind?"

"Mrs. Exeter owns—and manages—a large store, if that is what you mean."

"And those pretty Borden girls?"

"They do house decorating—have been abroad on business."

"And Mrs. Green—and Miss Sandwich?"

"One of them is a hat designer, one a teacher. This is toward the end of vacation, and they're all coming home, you see."

"And Miss Elwell?"

Miss Elwell was quite the prettiest woman on board, and seemed to have plenty of attention—just like the girls I remembered.

"Miss Elwell is a civil engineer," said my sister.

"It's horrid," I said. "It's perfectly horrid! And aren't there any women left?"

"There's Aunt Dorcas," said Nellie, mischievously, "and Cousin Drusilla. You remember Drusilla?"

Chapter II

The day after tomorrow!

I was to see it the day after tomorrow—this strange, new, abhorrent world!

The more I considered what bits of information I had gleaned already, the more I disliked what lay before me. In the first blazing light of returned memory and knowledge, the first joy of meeting my sister, the hope of seeing home again; I had not distinguished very sharply between what was new to my bewildered condition and what was new indeed—new to the world as well as to me. But now a queer feeling of disproportion and unreality began to haunt me.

As my head cleared, and such knowledge as I was now gathering began to help towards some sense of perspective and relation, even my immediate surroundings began to assume a sinister importance.

Any change, to any person, is something of a shock, though sometimes a beneficial one. Changes too sudden, and too great, are hard to bear, for any one. But who can understand the peculiar horror of my unparalleled experience?

Slowly the thing took shape in my mind.

There was the first, irrevocable loss—my life!

Thirty years—*the* thirty years in which a man may really live—these were gone from me forever.

I was coming back; strong to be sure; well enough in health; even, I hoped, with my old mental vigor—*but not to the same world*.

Even the convict who survives thirty years imprisonment, may return at length to the same kind of world he had left so long.

But I! It was as if I had slept, and, in my sleep, they had stolen my world.

I threw off the thought, and started in to action.

Here was a small world—the big steamer beneath me. I had already learned much about her. In the first place, she was not a "steamer," but a thing for which I had no name; her power was electric.

"Oh, well," I thought, as I examined her machinery, "this I might have expected. Thirty years of such advances as we were making in 1910 were sure to develop electric motors of all sorts."

The engineer was a pleasant, gentlemanly fellow, more than willing to talk about his profession and its marvellous advances. The ship was well manned, certainly, though the work required was far less than it used to be, the crew were about as numerous. I had made some acquaintances among the ship's officers—even among the men, who were astonishingly civil and well-mannered—but I had not at first noticed the many points of novelty in their attitude or in my surroundings.

Now I paced the deck and considered the facts I had observed—the perfect ventilation of the vessel, the absence of the smell of cooking and of bilge water, the dainty convenience and appropriate beauty of all the fittings and furnishings, the smooth speed and steadiness of her.

The quarters of the crew I found as remarkable as anything else about the vessel; indeed the forecastle and steerage differed more from what I remembered than from any other part. Every person on board had a clean and comfortable lodging, though there were grades of distinction in size and decoration. But any gentleman could have lived in that "foks'le" without discomfort. Indeed, I soon found that many gentlemen did. I discovered, quite by accident, that one of the crew was a Harvard man. He was not at all loath to talk of it, either—was evidently no black sheep of any sort.

Why had he chosen this work?

Oh, he wanted the experience—it widened life, knowing different trades.

Why was he not an officer then?

He didn't care to work at it long enough—this was only experience work, you see.

I did not see, nor ask, but I inferred, and it gave me again that feeling as if the ground underfoot had wiggled slightly.

Was that old dream of Bellamy's stalking abroad? Were young men portioned out to menial service, willy-nilly?

It was evidently not a universal custom, for some of the sailors were much older men, and long used to the business. I got hold of one who seemed more like the deckhands of old days, though cleaner and more cheerful; a man who was all of sixty.

Yes, he had followed the sea from boyhood. Yes, he liked it, always had liked it, liked it better now than when he was young.

He had seen many changes? I listened carefully, though I asked the question lightly enough.

Changes! He guessed he had. Terbacca was better for one thing—I was relieved to see that men still smoked, and then the jar came again as I remembered that save for this man, and one elderly officer, I had not seen anyone smoking on the vessel.

"How do you account for it?" I asked the old Yankee. "For tobacco's being better?"

He grinned cheerfully.

"Less run on it, I guess," said he. "Young fellers don't seem to smoke no more, and I ain't seen nobody chewin' for—well, for ten years back."

"Is it cheaper as well as better?"

"No, sir, it ain't. It's perishin' high. But then, wages is high, too," he grudgingly admitted.

"Better tobacco and better wages—anything else improved?"

"Yes, sir-ee! Grub's better, by square miles—and 'commodations—an' close. Make better stuff now."

"Well! well!" said I as genially as I knew how. "That's very different from my young days. Then everybody older than I always complained about all manner of things, and told how much better—and cheaper—things were when they were young."

"Yes, 'twas so," he admitted meditatively. "But 'tain't so now. Shoes is better, and tools is better, most things is better, I guess. Seems like water runnin' up hill, don't it, sir?"

It did. I didn't like it. I got away from the old man, and walked by myself— like Kipling's cat.

"Of course, of course!" I said to myself impatiently, "I may as well expect to find everything as much improved from what it was in my time as in, say, sixty years before. That sort of progress goes faster and faster. Things change, but people—"

And here is where I got this creepy sense of unreality.

At first everything was so strange to me, and my sister was so kind and thoughtful, so exquisitely considerate of my feelings and condition, that I had failed to notice this remarkable circumstance—so were the other people! It was like being in a—well, in a house-party of very nice persons. Kind, cheerful, polite—here I suddenly realized that I had not seen a grouchy face; heard an unkind remark; felt, as one does feel through silk and broadcloth, the sense of discontent and disapproval.

There was one, the somewhat hard-faced old lady, Mrs. Talbot, of whom I had hopes. I sought her, and laid myself out to please her by those little attentions which are so grateful to an elderly woman from a young man.

Her accepting these as a commonplace, her somewhat too specific inquiries about my health, suddenly reminded me that I was not a young man—

She talked on while I made again that effort at readjustment which was so hideously hard. Gone in a night—all my young manhood—gone untasted!

"Do you find it difficult to concentrate your attention?" she was saying, a steely eye fixed upon my face.

"I beg your pardon, madam. I fear I do. You were saying—"

"I was saying that you will find many changes when you get back."

"I find them already, Mrs. Talbot. They rather loom up. It *is* sudden, you see."

"Yes, you've been away a long time, I understand. In the far East?"

Mrs. Talbot was the first person who had asked me a question. Evidently hers were the manners of an older generation, and for once I had to admit that the younger generation had improved.

But I recalled the old defensive armor against the old assaults.

"Quite a while," I answered cheerfully, "Quite a while. Now what should you think would impress me most—in the way of change?"

"The women," she answered promptly.

I smiled my gallantest, and replied, bowing:

"I find them still charming."

Her set face broke into a pleased smile.

"You do my heart good!" she cried. "I haven't heard a compliment in fifteen years."

"Good Heavens, madam! what are our men thinking of?"

"It's not the men's fault; it's the women's. They won't have it."

"Are there many of these—new women?"

"There's nothing else—except a few old ones like me."

I hastened to assure her that a woman like her would never be called old—and she looked as pleased as a girl.

13

Presently I excused myself and left her, with relief. It was annoying beyond measure to have the only specimen of the kind of woman I used to like turn out to be personally the kind I never liked.

On the opposite deck, I found Miss Elwell—and for once alone. A retiring back, wearing an aggrieved expression showed that it had not been for long.

"May I join you, Miss Elwell?"

I might. I did. We paced up and down, silent for a bit.

She was a joy to the eye, a lovely, straight, young thing, with a fresh, pure color and eyes of dancing brightness. I spoke of this and that aboard ship— the sea, the weather; and she was so gaily friendly, so sweet and modest, yet wholly frank, that I grew quite happy in her company.

My sister must have been mistaken about her being a civil engineer. She might be a college girl—but nothing worse. And she *was* so pretty!

I devoted myself to Miss Elwell 'till she took herself off, probably to join her—her—it occurred to me that I had seen no one with Miss Elwell.

"Nellie" said I, "for heaven's sake give me the straight of all this. I'm going distracted with the confusion. What has happened to the world? Tell me all. I can bear it—as the extinct novels used to say. But I cannot bear this terrible suspense! Don't you have novels any more?"

"Novels? Oh, yes, plenty; better than ever were written. You'll find it splendidly worth while to read quite a few of them while you're getting oriented.....Well, you want a kind of running, historic sketch?"

"Yes. Give me the outlines—just the heads, as it were. You see, my dear, it is not easy to get readjusted even to the old things, and there are so many new ones—"

We were in our steamer chairs, most people dozing after their midday meal. She reached over and took my hand in hers, and held it tight. It was marvelously comforting, this one live visible link between what was forever past and this uncertain future. But for her, even those old, old days might have flickered and seemed doubtful—I should have felt like one swimming under water and not knowing, which way was up. She gave me solid ground underfoot at any rate. Whatever her place might be in this New World, she had talked to me only of the old one.

In these long, quiet, restful days, she had revived in my mind the pleasant memories of our childhood together; our little Southern home; our patient, restrained Northern mother and the fine education she gave her school-less little ones; our high-minded—and, alas, narrow-minded—father, handsome, courteous, inflexible. Under Nellie's gentle leading, my long unused memory-cells had revived like rain-washed leaves, and my past life had, at last, grown clear and steady.

My college life; my old chum, Granger, who had visited us once; our neighbors and relations; little gold-haired Cousin Drusilla, whom I, in ten years proud seniority, had teased as a baby, played with and tyrannized over as a confiding child, and kissed good-bye—a slim, startled little figure—when I left for Asia.

Nellie had always spoken of things as I remembered them, and avoided adroitly, or quietly refused to discuss, their new aspects.

I think she was right—at first.

"Out with it!" said I. "Come—Have we adopted Socialism?" I braced myself for the answer.

"Socialism? Oh—why, yes. I think we did. But that was twenty years ago."

"And it didn't last? You've proved the impracticable folly of it? You've discarded it?"

I sat up straight, very eager.

"Why, no—" said Nellie. "It's very hard to put these new things into old words—We've got beyond it."

"Beyond Socialism! Not—not—Anarchy?"

"Oh, bless you, no; no indeed! We understand better what socialism meant, that's all. We have more, much more, than it ever asked; but we don't call it that."

I did not understand.

"It's like this," she said. "Suppose you had left a friend in the throes of a long, tempestuous courtship, full of ardor, of keen joy, and keener anticipation. Then, returning, you say to your friend, 'Do you still have courtship?' And he says, 'Why no, I'm married.' It's not that he has discarded it, proved its impracticable folly. He had to have it—he liked it—but he's got beyond it."

"Go on and elucidate," I said. "I don't quite follow your parable."

She considered a bit.

"Well, here's a more direct parallel. Back in the 18th century, the world was wild about Democracy—Democracy was going to do all things for all

15

men. Then, with prodigious struggles, they acquired some Democracy—set it going. It was a good thing. But it took time. It grew. It had difficulties. In the next century, there was less talk about all the heavenly results of Democracy, and more definite efforts to make it work."

This was clearer.

"You mean," I followed her slowly. "That what was called socialism was attained— and you've been improving upon it?"

"Exactly, Brother, 'you are on'—as we used to say. But even that's not the main step."

"No? What else?"

"Only a New Religion."

I showed my disappointment. Nellie watched my face silently. She laughed. She even kissed me.

"John!" said she, "I could make vast sums by exhibiting you to psychologists as an Extinct Species of Mind. You'd draw better than a Woolly Mammoth."

I smiled wryly; and she squeezed my hand. "Might as well make a joke of it, Old Man—you've got to get used to it, and 'the sooner the quicker!'"

"All right—Go ahead with your New Religion."

She sat back in her chair with an expression of amused retrospection.

"I had forgotten," she said, "I had really forgotten. We didn't use to think much of religion, did we?"

"Father did," said I.

"No, not even Father and his kind—they only used it as a—what was the old joke? a patent fire escape! Nobody appreciated Religion!"

"They spent much time and money on it," I suggested.

"*That's* not appreciation!"

"Well, come on with the story. Did you have another Incarnation of any body?"

"You might call it that," Nellie allowed, her voice growing quietly earnest, "We certainly had somebody with an unmistakable Power."

This did not interest me at all. I hated to see Nellie looking so sweetly solemn over her "New Religion." In the not unnatural reaction of a minister's son, rigidly reared, I had had small use for religion of any sort.

16

As a scholar I had studied them all, and felt as little reverence for the ancient ones as for the shifty mushroom crop of new sects and schools of thought with which the country teemed in my time.

"Now, look here, John," said she at length, "I've been watching you pretty closely and I think you're equal to a considerable mental effort—In one way, it *may* be easier for you, just because you've not seen a bit of it— anyhow, you've got to face it—

"Our world has changed in these thirty years, more than the change between what it used to be and what people used to imagine about Heaven. Here is the first thing you've got to do—mentally. You must understand, clearly, in your human consciousness, that the objection and distaste you feel is only in your personal consciousness. Everything *is* better; there is far more comfort, pleasure, peace of mind; a richer swifter growth, a higher happier life in every way; and yet, you won't like it! You won't like it because your—" she seemed to hesitate for a word, now and then; as one trying to translate, "reactions are all turned to earlier conditions. If you can understand this and see over your own personal—attitudes it will not be long before a real convincing *sense* of joy, of life, will follow the intellectual perception that things are better."

"Hold on," I said, "Let me chew on that a little."

"As if," I presently suggested, "as if I'd left a home that was poor and dirty and crowded, with a pair of quarrelsome inefficient parents—drunken and abusive, maybe, and a lot of horrid, wrangling, selfish, little brothers and sisters—and woke up one fine morning in a great clean beautiful house— richly furnished—full of a lot of angels—who were total strangers?"

"Exactly!" she cried. "Hurrah for you, Johnnie, you couldn't have defined it better."

"I don't like it," said I. "I'd rather have my old home and my own family than all the princely palaces and amiable angels you could dream of in a hundred years."

"Mother had an old story-book by a New England author," Nellie quietly remarked, "where somebody said, 'You can't always have your 'druthers'— she used to quote it to me when I was little and complained that things were not as I wanted them. John, dear, please remember that the new people in the new world find it 'like home' and love it far better than we used to. It'll be queer to you, but it's a pleasant commonplace to them. We have found out at last that it is natural to be happy."

She was silent and I was silent; till I asked her "What's the name of your new religion?"

"It hasn't any," she answered.

"Hasn't any? What do they call it? the Believers, I mean?"

"They call it 'Living' and 'Life'—that's all."

"Hm! and what's their specialty?"

Nellie gave a funny little laugh, part sad, part tender, part amused.

"I had no idea it would be so hard to tell you things," she said. "You'll have to just see for yourself, I guess."

"Do go on, Nellie. I'll be good. You were going to tell me, in a nutshell, what had happened—please do."

"The thing that has happened," said she, slowly, "is just this. The world has come alive. We are doing in a pleasant, practical way, all the things which we could have done, at any time before—only we never thought so. The real change is this: we have changed our minds. This happened very soon after you left. Ah! that was a time! To think that you should have missed it!" She gave my hand another sympathetic squeeze and went on. "After that it was only a question of time, of how soon we could do things. And we've been doing them ever since, faster and faster."

This seemed rather flat and disappointing.

"I don't see that you make out anything wonderful—so far. A new Religion which seems to consist only in behaving better; and a gradual improvement of social conditions—all that was going on when I left."

Nellie regarded me with a considering eye.

"I see how you interpret it," she said, "behaving better in our early days was a small personal affair; either a pathetically inadequate failure to do what one could not, or a pharisaic, self-righteous success in doing what one could. All personal—personal!"

"Good behavior has to be a personal affair, hasn't it?" I mildly protested.

"Not by any means!" said Nellie with decision. "That was precisely what kept us so small and bad, so miserably confined and discouraged. Like a lot of well-meaning soldiers imagining that their evolutions were 'a personal affair'—or an orchestra plaintively protesting that if each man played a correct tune of his own choosing, the result would be perfect! Dear! dear! No, *Sir*," she continued with some fierceness, "That's just where we changed our minds! Humanity has come alive, I tell you and we

18

have reason to be proud of our race!"

She held her head high, there was a glad triumphant look in her eyes—not in the least religious. Said she: "You'll see results. That will make it clearer to you than anything I can say. But if I may remark that we have no longer the fear of death—much less of damnation, and no such thing as 'sin'; that the only kind of prison left is called a quarantine—that punishment is unknown but preventive means are of a drastic and sweeping nature such as we never dared think of before—that there is no such thing in the civilized world as poverty—no labor problem—no color problem—no sex problem—almost no disease—very little accident—practically no fires— that the world is rapidly being reforested—the soil improved; the output growing in quantity and quality; that no one needs to work over two hours a day and most people work four—that we have no graft—no adulteration of goods—no malpractice—no crime."

"Nellie," said I, "you are a woman and my sister. I'm very sorry, but I don't believe it."

"I thought you wouldn't," said she. Women always will have the last word.

Chapter III

The blue shore line of one's own land always brings a thrill of the heart; to me, buried exile as I had been, the heart-leap was choking.

Ours was a slow steamer, and we did not stop at Montauk where the mail and the swiftest travelers landed, nor in Jamaica Harbor with the immigrants.

As we swept along the sunny, level spaces of the South shore, Nellie told me how Long Island was now the "Reception Room" of our country, instead of poor, brutal little Ellis Island.

"The shores are still mostly summer places," she said. "One of the most convincing of our early lines of advance was started on the South shore; and there are plenty of Country Clubs, Home Parks and things like that; but the bulk of the island toward the western end is an experiment station in applied sociology."

I was watching the bright shore hungrily. With a glass I could see many large buildings, not too closely set.

"I should think it would spoil the place for homes," I said.

Nellie had a way of listening to my remarks, kindly and pleasantly, but as if I were somehow a long way off and she was trying to grasp what I said.

"In a way it did—at first;" she explained presently, "but even then it meant just as many homes for other people, and now it means so much more!"

She hesitated a moment and then plunged in resolutely.

"You're in for a steady course of instructive remarks from now on. Everybody will be explaining things and bragging about them. We haven't outgrown some of the smaller vices, you see. As to this 'Immigration Problem'—we woke up to this fact among others, that the 'reintegration of peoples' as Ward called it, was a sociological process not possible to stop, but quite possible to assist and to guide to great advantage. And here in America we recognized our own special place—'the melting pot,' you know?"

Yes, I remembered the phrase, I never liked it. Our family were pure English stock, and rightly proud of their descent.

"I begin to see, my dear sister, that while receiving the torrent of instructive remarks you foretell, the way of wisdom for me is steadfastly to withhold my own opinions."

Nellie laughed appreciatively.

"You always had a long head, John. Well, whether you like it or not, our people saw their place and power at last and rose to it. We refuse no one. We have discovered as many ways of utilizing human waste as we used to have for the waste products of coal tar."

"You don't mean to say idiots and criminals?" I protested.

"Idiots, hopeless ones, we don't keep any more," she answered gently. "They are very rare now. The grade of average humanity is steadily rising; and we have the proud satisfaction of knowing we have helped it rise. We organized a permanent 'reception committee' for the whole country, one station here and one in California. Anybody could come—but they had to submit to our handling when they did come."

"We used to have physical examination, didn't we?"

"A rudimentary one. What we have now is Compulsory Socialization."

I stared at her.

"Yes, I know! You are thinking of that geological kind of evolution people used to talk about, and 'you can't alter human nature.' In the first place, we can. In the second place, we do. In the third place, there isn't so much alteration needed as we used to think. Human nature is a pretty good thing. No immigrant is turned loose on the community till he or she is up to a certain standard, and the children we educate."

"We always did, didn't we?"

"Always did? Why brother, we didn't know what the word meant in your time."

"I shall be glad to follow that up," I assured her. "Education was improving even in the old days, I remember. I shall be glad to see the schools."

"Some of them you won't know when you do see them," said Nellie. "On Long Island we have agricultural and industrial stations like—like—I think we had something like it in some of our Western colleges, which it was the fashion to look down upon. We have a graded series of dwellings where the use of modern conveniences is taught to all newcomers."

"Suppose they won't learn? They used to prefer to live like hogs, as I remember."

Again Nellie looked at me as if I were speaking to her from a distance.

"We used to say so—and I suppose we used to think so—some of us. But we know better now. These people are not compelled to come to our country, but if they come they know what they have to do—and they do it. You may have noticed that we have no 'steerage.'"

I had noticed it.

"They have decent surroundings from the first step. They have to be antiseptically clean, they and all their belongings, before entering the ship."

"But what an awful expense!" I ventured.

"Suppose you keep cattle, John, and knew how to fatten and improve them; and suppose your ranch was surrounded by strays—mavericks—anxious to come in. Would you call it 'an expense' to add to your herd?"

"You can't sell people."

"No, but you can profit by their labor."

"That sounds like the same old game. I should think your Socialism would have put an end to that."

"Socialism did not alter the fact that wealth comes by labor," she replied. "All these people work. We provide the opportunity for them, we train them to higher efficiency, especially the children. The very best and wisest of us are proud to serve there—as women used to be proud when they were invited 'to help receive' some personage. We receive Humanity—and introduce it to America. What they produce is used to cover the expense of their training, and also to lay up a surplus for themselves."

"They must produce more than they used to," observed I drily.

"They do," said Nellie.

"You might as well finish this thing up," I said. "Then when people talk to me about immigration, I can look intelligent and say, 'I know about that.' And really, I'm interested. How do you begin with 'em?"

"When they come into Jamaica Harbor they see a great crescent of white piers, each with its gate. We'll go and see it some day—splendid arches with figures on them, like the ones they used to put up for Triumphs. There's the German Gate, and the Spanish Gate, the English Gate, the Italian Gate—and so on. There is welcome in their own language—and instruction in ours. There is physical examination—the most searching and thorough—microscopic—chemical. They have to come up to a certain standard before they are graduated, you see."

"Graduated?"

"Yes. We have a standard of citizenship now—an idea of what people ought to be and how to make them so. Dear me! To think that you don't know about that—"

"I shouldn't think they'd stand for it—all this examination and so on."

"No country on earth offers so much happiness to its people. Nowhere else—yet—is there as good opportunity to be helped up, to have real scientific care, real loving study and assistance! Everybody likes to be made the most of! Everybody—nearly—has the feeling that they might be something better if they had a chance! We give them the chance."

"Then I should think you'd have all creation on your hands at once."

"And depopulate the other nations? They had something to say about that! You see this worked all sorts of ways. In the first place, when we got all the worst and lowest people, that left an average of better ones at home—people who could learn more quickly. When we proved what good stuff human nature was, rightly treated, they all took heart of grace and began to improve their own. Then, as our superior attractions steadily drew off 'the lower classes,' that raised the value of those who remained. They were better paid, better thought of at home. As more and more people came to us, the other nations got rather alarmed, and began to establish counter attractions—to keep their folks at home. Also, many other nations had some better things than we did, you remember. And finally most people love their own country better than any other, no matter how good. No, the balance of population is not seriously altered."

"Still, with such an influx of low-grade people you must have a Malthusian torrent of increasing population on your hands."

Again that odd listening look, her head a little on one side.

"I have to keep remembering," she said. "Have to recall what people wrote and said and thought in the past generation. The idea was that people had to increase like rabbits, and would eat up the food supply, so wars and pestilences and all manner of cruel conditions were necessary to 'keep down the population.' Wasn't that it?"

"You are twenty years out, my dear!" I rejoiced to assure her. "We had largely passed that, and were beginning to worry about the decreasing birth rate—among the more intelligent. It was only the lowest grade that kept on 'like rabbits' as you say. But it's that sort you seem to have been filling in with. I should think it would have materially lowered the average. Or have you, in this new 'forcing system' made decent people out of scrubs?"

"That's exactly what we've done; we've improved the people and lowered

23

the birth-rate at one stroke!"

"They were beginning to talk eugenics when I left."

"This is not eugenics—we have made great advances in that, of course; but the chief factor in this change is a common biological law— 'individuation is in inverse proportion to reproduction,' you know. We individualize the women—develop their personal power, their human characteristics—and they don't have so many children."

"I don't see how that helps unless you have eliminated the brutality of men."

"My dear brother, the brutality of men *lowered* the birthrate—it didn't raise it! One of those undifferentiated peasant women would have a baby every year if she was married to a saint—and she couldn't have more in polyandry—unless it were twins! No, the birthrate was for women to settle—and they have."

"Out of fashion to have children at all?"

"No, John, you needn't sneer. We have better children than ever were born on earth before—and they grade higher every year. But we are approaching a balanced population."

I didn't like the subject, and turned to the clear skyline of the distant city. It towered as of old, but seemed not so close-packed. Not one black cloud—and very few white ones!

"You've ended the smoke nuisance, I'm glad to see. Has steam gone, too?"

"We use electricity altogether in all the cities now," she said. "It occurred to us that to pipe a leaking death into every bedroom; to thread the city with poison, fire and explosion, was foolish."

"'Defective wiring' used to cause both death and conflagration, didn't it?"

"It did," she admitted; "but it is not 'defective' any more."

"Is the coal all gone?"

"No, but we burn it at the mines—by a process which does *not* waste ninety per cent of the energy—and transmit the power."

"For all New York?"

"Oh, no. New York has enough water power, you see. The tide mills are enough for this whole region."

"They solved the tide mill problem, did they?"

24

"Yes. There are innumerable mechanical advances, of course—you'll enjoy them."

We were near enough now to see the city clearly.

"What a splendid water front!" I cried. "Why, this is glorious!"

It surely was. The wide shores swung away, glittering in the pure sunlight. Staten Island lay behind us, a vision of terraced loveliness; the Jersey shore shone clear, no foul pall of oil smoke overhanging; the Brooklyn banks were banks of palaces; and Manhattan itself towered royally before us, all bordered with broad granite piers.

"'Marginal mile after mile of smooth-running granite embankment'" quoted Nellie. "'Broad steps of marble descending for the people to enter the water. White-pillared piers—'"

"Look at the water!" I cried, suddenly. "It's clean!"

"Of course it's clear," she agreed laughingly. "This is a civilized country, I tell you."

I looked and looked. It was blue and bright in the distance; it was a clear, soft green beneath us. I saw a fish leap—

"So far I'm with you, anyhow," said I. "That certainly is a big step—and looks like a miracle. New York harbor *clean!*...How about customs?" I asked as we drew in.

"Gone—clean forgotten—with a lot of other foolishness. The air ships settled that. We couldn't plant custom houses in the air, you see—along ten thousand miles of coast and border."

I was watching the shore. There were plenty of people about, but strangely gay of aspect and bright-colored in raiment. I could see amusement piers— numbers of them—some evidently used as gymnasia, in some there was dancing. Motor cars of all descriptions ran swiftly and quietly about. Air ships large and small floated off, to the north and west mostly. The water was freckled with pleasure boats. I heard singing—and music.

"Some new holiday?" I ventured.

"Not at all," said my sister. "It is afternoon."

She watched me, quizzically.

"It is afternoon," she repeated. "Let that sink in!"

It sank in, slowly.

"Do you mean that no one works in the afternoon?"

"No one—except those who don't work in the morning. Some kinds of work can't stop, of course; but most kinds can. I told you before—no one *has* to work more than two hours a day, most people work four. Why?" She saw my unbelieving stare. "Because we like to. Also because we are ambitious," she went on. "I told you of the gain we've made in 'the civilized world.' Not all of it is civilized. We are still missionarying. And while there is need of help anywhere on earth, most of us work overtime. Also it lays up public capital—we are planning some vast undertakings, and gives a wider margin for vacations."

I was thinking in a hazy way of a world that was not tired, not driven, no nose on any grindstone; of a people who only had to work two hours—and worked four! Yet there was every evidence of increased wealth—

Suddenly Nellie gave a joyous little cry.

"Why, there's Owen!" she waved her veil— "And there's Jerrold and Hallie!" She fairly danced with pleasure.

I could see a big grayish man madly waving his hat down there—and two young folks hopping up and down and flourishing handkerchiefs among many similarly excited.

"Oh, how *good* of him!" she cried. "I never dreamed they'd be here!"

"Nellie," said I sternly. "You never told me you were married!"

"Why should I?" she asked innocently. "You never asked me."

I had not. I had seen that she signed her name "Ellen Robertson," and I knew she was president of a College—how could I imagine her married. Married she evidently was, and even her long-lost brother was forgotten for a moment as the big man engulfed her in his gray overcoat, and the tall son and daughter added their arms to the group.

But it was only a moment, and the big brotherly grasp of my new relation's hand, the cordial nephewly grip, and affectionate niecely kiss gave me a new and unexpected sense of the joys of homecoming.

These were people, real people, as warm and kind and cheery as people ever were; and they greeted me with evident good will. It was "Uncle John" in no time, and Hallie in especial seized upon me as her own.

"I know Mother's got you all broken in by this time," she said. "And that you are prepared for all manner of amazing disclosures. But Mother never told us how handsome you are, Uncle John!"

26

"In vain is the net spread in sight of any bird," murmured young Jerrold mischievously.

"Don't listen to him, Uncle! I am perfectly sincere," she protested, leaning over to hug her mother again, and turning back to me with a confiding smile.

"Why should I doubt such evident good judgment?" said I, and she slipped her hand in mine and squeezed it. Nellie sat there looking as proud and happy and matronly and motherly as anybody could, and a great weight rolled off my heart. Some things were left of my old world anyway.

We talked gaily and excitedly on our way of immediate plans, rolling smoothly along broad open streets. A temporary conclusion was to stop at Hallie's apartment for the time being; and I was conscious of a distinct sense of loss to think of my new-found niece being already married.

"How still it is!" I presently observed. "Is that because it is afternoon, too?"

"Oh, no," they assured me. "We aren't as noisy as we used to be."

"These children don't know anything about what we used to have to put up with," said Owen. "They never were in New York while it was screaming. You see, there are no horses; all surface vehicles are rubber-tired; the minor delivery is pneumatic; and the freight all goes underneath—on those silent monorails."

The great city spread about us, clean as a floor, quiet as a country town by comparison with what I remembered; yet full of the stir and murmur of moving crowds. Everyone we passed or met looked happy and prosperous, and even my inexperienced eye caught a difference in costuming.

"There's no masquerade on, is there?" I asked.

"Oh, no—we all wear what we please, that's all. Don't you like it?" Hallie asked.

Generally there appeared the trim short skirt I had noticed as so appropriate on shipboard; here and there a sort of Florentine gown, long, richly damasked; sometimes a Greekish flow of drapery; the men mostly knicker-bockered. I couldn't deny that it was pleasant to the eye, but it worried me a little none the less.

"There's no hurry, John," said Nellie, always unobtrusively watching me. "Some things you'll just have to get used to."

"Before I wholly accept this sudden new brother," I presently suggested, "I'd like to know his name."

27

"Montrose—Owen Montrose, at your service," he said, bowing his fine head. "Also Jerrold Montrose—and Hallie Robertson!"

"Dear, dear!" I protested. "So it's come to that, has it?"

"It's come to that—and we still love each other!" Nellie cheerfully agreed. "But it isn't final. There's a strong movement on foot to drop hereditary names altogether."

I groaned. "In the name of common humanity, don't tell me anything worse than you have now!"

Hallie's apartment was in a big building, far uptown, overlooking the Hudson.

"I have to live in town nine months of the year, you see, Uncle, on account of my work," she explained rather apologetically.

"Hallie's an official—and awfully proud of it," her brother whispered very loudly.

"Jerrold's only a musician—and pretends to be proud of it!" she retorted. Whereat he forcibly held and kissed her.

I could see no very strong difference between this brother and sister and others I had known—except that they were perhaps unusually affectionate.

It was a big, handsome place. The front windows faced the great river, the rear ones opened on a most unexpected scene of loveliness. A big sheltered garden, every wall-space surrounding it a joy to the eye—rich masses of climbing vines—a few trees—a quiet fountain—beautiful stone seats and winding walks—flowers in profusion—and birds singing.

"We used to have only the song of the tomcat in my time. Have you taught the cat to lie down with the canary—or killed him?"

"There are no animals kept in cities any more—except the birds—and they come and go."

"Mostly sparrows, I suppose?"

"No, the sparrow went with the horse," Owen replied— "And the mouse, the fly and the croton bug went with the kitchen."

I turned with a gesture of despair.

"No homes left?—"

"I didn't say 'home'—I said 'kitchen.' Brace up, old man! We still eat—and better food than you ever dreamed of in your hungriest youth."

"That's a long story," Nellie here suggested. "We mustn't crowd him. Let's get washed and rested a bit, and have some of that food you're boasting of."

They gave me a room with a river window, and I looked out at the broad current, changed only in its lovely clearness, and at the changeless Palisades.

Changeless? I started, and seized the traveling glass still on the strap.

The high cliffs reached away to the northward, still wooded, though sprinkled with buildings; but the more broken section opposite the city was a picture of startling beauty.

The water front was green-parked, white-piered, rimmed with palaces, and the broken slopes terraced and garlanded in rich foliage. White cottages and larger buildings climbed and nestled along the sunny slopes as on the cliffs at Capri—it was a place one would go far to see.

I dropped my eyes to the nearer shore. Again the park, the boulevard, the gracious outlines of fine architecture.

It was beautiful—undeniably beautiful—but a strange world to me. I felt like one at a play. A plain, ordinary American landscape ought not to look like a theatre curtain!

Chapter IV

They called me to supper. "Most of us have our heartiest meal in the middle of the day," my sister said.

"The average man, O Victim of Copious Instruction," added my brother-in-law, "does his work in the morning; the two hours that he has to, or the four that he usually puts in. Eight to twelve, or nine to one, that is the working day for everybody. Then home, rest, a bath maybe, and then— allow me to help you to some of our Improvements!"

I was hungry, and this simple meal looked and smelled most appetizing. There was in particular a large shining covered dish, which, being opened, gave forth so savory a steam as fairly to make my mouth water. A crisp and toothsome bread was by my plate; a hot drink, which they laughingly refused to name, proved most agreeable; a suave, cool salad followed; fruits, some of which were new to me, and most delicate little cakes, closed the meal.

They would not tell me a thing, only saying "Have some more!" and I did. Not till I had eaten, with continuous delight, three helpings from the large dish, did I notice that it stood alone, so to speak.

Nellie followed my eye with her usual prompt intelligence. "Yes," she said, "this is all. But we can send for other things in the twinkling of an eye; what would you like?"

I leaned back in my chair and looked at her reproachfully. "I would like some of that salad—not very much, please! And some of those Burbankian products yonder, and one particularly brown little cake—if I can hold it."

Nellie smiled demurely. "Oh!" she mildly remarked, "I thought for the moment that our little supper seemed scant to you."

I glared at her, retorting, "Now I will not utter the grateful praises that were rising to my lips. I will even try to look critical and dissatisfied," And I did, but they all laughed.

"It's no manner of use, Uncle John," cried my pretty niece, "we saw you eat it."

"'It' indeed!" I protested. "What is this undeniably easy-to-take concoction you have stuffed me with?"

"My esteemed new brother," Owen answered, "we have been considering your case in conclave assembled, and we think it is wiser to feed you for a while and demand by all the rites of hospitality that you eat what is set before you and ask no questions for conscience sake. When you begin to pine, to lose your appetite, to look wan and hollow-eyed, then we may reconsider. Meanwhile we will tell you everything you want to know about food in general, and even some particulars; present dishes always excepted."

"I will now produce information," began Hallie, "my office being that of Food Inspector."

"Her main purpose in bringing you here, Uncle, was to give you food and then talk about it," said Jerrold solemnly. Hallie only made a face at him, and went on:

"We have a magnificent system of production and distribution," she explained, "with a decreasing use of animal foods."

"Was this a vegetarian meal?" I asked in a hollow voice.

"Mostly; but you shall have meat when you want it. Better meat than you used to get, too."

"Cold Storage Meat?"

"Oh, no,—that's long since stopped. The way we manage about meat is this: A proper proportion of edible animals are raised under good conditions—nice, healthy, happy beasts; killed so that they don't know it!—and never kept beyond a certain time limit. You see,—" she paused, looking for the moment like her mother, "the whole food business is changed—you don't realize.—"

"Go ahead and tell me—tell me all—my life at present is that of Rollo, I perceive, and I am most complacent after this meal."

"Uncle, I rejoice in your discovery, I do indeed. You are an uncle after my own heart," said Jerrold.

So my fair niece, looking like any other charming girl in a pretty evening frock, began to expound her specialty. Her mother begged to interrupt for the moment. "Let me recall to him things as they were—which you hardly know, you happy child. Don't forget, John, that when we were young, we did not know what good food was."

I started to protest, but she shook her finger at me.

"No, we didn't, my dear boy. We knew 'what we liked' as the people said at the picture shows; but that did not make it good—good in itself or good for us. The world was ill-fed. Most of the food was below par; a good deal was injurious, some absolutely poison. People sold poison for food in

31

1910—don't forget that! You may remember the row that was beginning to be made about it."

I admitted recalling something of the sort, though it had not particularly interested me at the time.

"Well, that row went on—and gained in force. The women woke up."

"If you have said that once since we met, my dear sister, you've said it forty times. I wish you would make a parenthesis in these food discussions and tell me how, when and why the women woke up."

Nellie looked a little dashed, and Owen laughed outright.

"You stand up for your rights, John!" he said, rising and slapping me on the shoulder, "Let's go in the other room and settle down for a chin, it's our fate."

"Hold him till he sees our housekeeping," said Jerrold. I stood watching, while they rapidly placed our dishes—which I now noticed were very few—in a neat square case which stood on a side table. Everything went in out of sight; paper napkins from the same receptacle wiped the shining table; and then a smooth-running dumbwaiter took it from our sight.

"This is housework," said Nellie, mischievously.

"I refuse to be impressed. Come back to our muttons," I insisted. "You can tell me about your domestic sleight of hand in due season."

So we lounged in the large and pleasant parlor, the broad river before us, rimmed with starry lamps, sparkling everywhere with the lights of tiny pleasure craft, and occasionally the blaze and wash of larger boats. I had a sense of pleasant well being. I had eaten heartily, very heartily, yet was not oppressed. My new-found family pleased me well. The quiet room was beautiful in color and proportion; and as my eyes wandered idly over it I noted how few in number and how harmonious were its contents, giving a sense of peace and spaciousness. The air was sweet—I did not notice then as I did later, that the whole city was sweet-aired now; at least by comparison with what cities used to be. From somewhere came the sound of soft music, real music, grateful to the ear. I stretched myself luxuriously with:

"Now, then, Nellie—let her go—'the women woke up.'"

"Some women were waking up tremendously, before you left, John Robertson, only I dare say you never noticed it. They just kept on, faster and faster, till they all did—about all. There are some Dodos left, even yet, but they don't count—discredited grandmothers!"

"And being awake?" I gently suggested.

"And being awake, they—" She paused for an instant, seeking an expression, and Jerrold's smooth bass voice put in, "They saw their duty and they did it."

"Exactly," his mother agreed, with a proudly loving glance at him, "that's just what they did! And in regard to the food business, they recognized at last that it was their duty to feed the world—and that it was miserably done! So they took hold."

"Now, mother—this is my specialty," Hallie interposed.

"When a person can only talk about one thing—why oppose them?" murmured Jerrold, but she quite ignored him, and reopened her discourse.

"We, that is most of the women, and some of the men, began to seriously study the food question, both from a hygienic and an economic standpoint. I can't tell you that thirty years work in a minute, Uncle John, but here's the way we manage it now. We have learned very definitely what people ought not to eat; and it is not only a punishable, but a punished offense, to sell improper food stuffs."

"How are the people to know?" I ventured.

"The people are not required to know everything. All the food is watched and tested by specialists; what goes into the market is good—all of it."

"By impeccable angelic specialists—like my niece?"

She shook her head at me. "If they were not, the purchaser would spot them at once. You see our food supply is not at the mercy of the millions of ignorant housewives any more. Food is bought and prepared by people who know how—and they have all the means—and knowledge—for expert tests."

"And if the purchaser too was humanly fallible—?"

She cast a pitying glance on me, and her father took the floor for a moment.

"You see, John, in the old time the dealers were mostly poor, and sold cheap and bad stuff to make a little money. The buyers were mostly poor and had to buy the cheap and nasty stuff. Even large manufacturers were under pressure, and had to cheat to make a profit—or thought they had to. Then when we got to inspectors and such like, they were under the harrow, too, and were by no means impeccable. Our big change is this: Nobody is poor now."

"I hear you say that," I answered, "but I can't seem to get it through my head. Have you really divided all the property?"

"John Robertson, I'm ashamed of you!" cried Nellie. "Even in 1910 people knew better than that! People who knew anything!"

"That wasn't necessary," said Owen, "nor desirable. What we have done is this: First, we have raised the productive capacity of the population; second, we have secured their right to our natural resources; third, we have learned to administer business without waste. The wealth of the world grows enormously. It is not what you call 'equally distributed,' but everyone has enough. There is no economic danger any more; there is economic peace."

"And economic freedom?" asked I sharply.

"And economic freedom. People choose the work they like best—and work—freely, more than they have to."

I pondered on this. "Ah, but they *have* to—labor is compulsory."

Owen grinned. "Yes, labor is compulsory—always was. It is compulsory on everyone now. We used to have two sets who wouldn't work—paupers and the idle rich—no such classes left—all busy."

"But—the freedom of the individual—" I persisted.

"Come, come, brother, society always played hob with the freedom of the individuals whenever it saw fit. It killed, imprisoned, fined; it had compulsory laws and regulations; it required people to wear clothes and furnished no clothes for them to wear! If society has a right to take human life, why has it not a right to improve it? No, my dear man," continued Owen (he was evidently launched on *his* specialty now) "society is not somebody else domineering over us! Society is us—taking care of ourselves!"

I took no exception to this, and he began again. "Society, in our young days, was in a state of auto-intoxication. It generated its own poisons, and absorbed them in peaceful, slow suicide. To think!—it seems impossible now—to *think* of allowing anybody to sell bad food!"

"That wasn't the only bad thing they sold," I suggested.

"No, unfortunately. Why, look here—" Owen slid a glass panel in the wall and took out a book.

"That's clever!" I remarked approvingly. "Bookcases built in!"

"Yes, they are everywhere now," said Nellie. "Books—a few of them—are common human necessities. Every home, every room almost, has these little dust-tight, insect-proof wall cases. Concrete construction has helped very much in all such matters."

Owen had found his place, and now poured upon me a concentrated list of the adulterated materials deteriorating the world in that period so slightly referred to as "my day." I noticed with gratitude that Owen said, "When we were young!"

"You never were sure of getting *anything* pure," he said scornfully, "no matter what you paid for it. How we submitted to such rank outrage for so long I cannot imagine! This was taken up very definitely some twenty years ago, by the women mostly."

"Aha—'when the women woke up!'" I cried.

"Yes, just that. It is true that their being mostly mere housewives and seamstresses was a handicap in some ways; but it was a direct advantage in others. They were almost all consumers, you see, not producers. They were not so much influenced by considerations of the profits of the manufacturer as they were by the direct loss to their own pockets and health. Yes," he smiled reminiscently, "there were some pretty warm years while this thing was thrashed out. One of the most successful lines of attack was in the New Food system, though."

"I *will* talk!" cried Hallie. "Here I've inveigled Uncle John up here—and—and fed him to repletion; and have him completely at my mercy, and then you people butt in and do all the talking!"

"Go it, little sister—you're dead right!" agreed Jerrold. "You see, Uncle, it's one thing to restrain and prevent and punish—and another thing to substitute improvements."

"Kindergarten methods?" I ventured.

"Yes, exactly. As women had learned this in handling children, they began to apply it to grown people—the same children, only a little older. Ever so many people had been talking and writing about this food business, and finally some of them got together and really started it."

"One of these co-operative schemes?" I was beginning, but the women looked at me with such pitying contempt that I promptly withdrew the suggestion.

"Not much!" said Nellie disdainfully. "Of course, those co-operative schemes were a natural result of the growing difficulties in our old methods, but they were on utterly wrong lines. No, sir, the new food business was a real business, and a very successful one. The first company

35

began about 1912 or '13, I think. Just some women with a real business sense, and enough capital. They wisely concluded that a block of apartments was the natural field for their services; and that professional women were their natural patrons."

"The unprofessional women—or professional wives, as you might call them—had only their housewifery to preserve their self-respect, you see," put in Owen. "If they didn't do housekeeping for a living, what—in the name of decency—did they do?"

"This was called the Home Service Company," said Hallie. "(I will talk, mother!) They built some unusually attractive apartments, planned by women, to please women; this block was one of the finest designs of their architects—women, too, by the way."

"Who had waked up," murmured Jerrold, unnoticed.

"It was frankly advertised as specially designed for professional women; they looked at it, liked it, and moved in, teachers largely, doctors, lawyers, dressmakers—women who worked."

"Sort of a nunnery?" I asked.

"My dear brother—do you imagine that all working women were orphan spinsters, even in your day?" cried Nellie. "The self-supporting women of that time generally had other people to support, too. Lots of them were married, many were widows with children, even the single ones had brothers and sisters to take care of."

"They rushed in, anyhow," said Hallie. "The place was beautiful and built for enjoyment. There was a nice garden in the middle—"

"Like this one here?" I interrupted. "This is a charming patio. How did they make space for it?"

"New York blocks were not divinely ordained," Owen replied. "It occurred to the citizens at last that they could bisect those 200x800 foot oblongs, and they did. Wide, tree-shaded, pleasant ways run between the old avenues, and the blocks remaining are practically squares."

"You noticed the irregular border of grass and shrubbery as we came up, didn't you, Uncle?" asked Jerrold. "We forgot to speak about it, because we are used to it."

I did recall now that our ride had been not through monotonous, stone-faced, right-angled ravines, but along the pleasant fronts of gracious varying buildings, whose skyline was a pleasure and street line bordered greenly.

"You didn't live here and don't remember, maybe," Owen remarked, "but the regular thing uptown was one of those lean, long blocks, flat-faced and solid, built to the sidewalk's edge. If it was a line of private houses they were bordered with gloomy little stone-paved areas, and ornamented with ash cans and garbage pails. If the avenue end was faced with tall apartments, their lower margin was infested with a row of little shops— meat—fish—vegetable—fruit, with all their litter and refuse and flies, and constant traffic. Now a residence block is a thing of beauty on all sides. The really necessary shops are maintained, but planned for in the building, and made beautiful. Those fly-tainted meat markets no longer exist."

"I *will* talk!" said Hallie, so plaintively that we all laughed, and let her.

"That first one I was telling you about was very charming and attractive. There were arrangements on the top floor for nurseries and child gardens; and the roof was for children all day—evenings the grown-ups had it. Great care was taken by the management in letting this part to the best professionals in child culture.

"There were big rooms, too, for meetings and parties; places for billiards and bowling and swimming—it was planned for real human enjoyment, like a summer hotel."

"But I thought you said this place was for women," I incautiously ventured.

"Oh, Uncle John! And has it never occurred to you that women like to amuse themselves? Or that professional women have men relatives and men friends? There were plenty of men in the building, and plenty more to visit it. They were shown how nice it was, you see. But the chief card was the food and service. This company engaged, at high wages, first-class house-workers, and the residents paid for them by the hour; and they had a food service which was beyond the dreams of—of—homes or boarding houses."

"Your professional women must have been millionaires," I mildly suggested.

"You think so because you do not understand the food business, Uncle John; nobody did in those days. We were so used to the criminal waste of individual housekeeping, with its pitifully low standards, and to monotonous low-grade restaurant meals, with their waste and extortion, that it never occurred to us to estimate the amount of profit there really was in the business. These far-seeing women were pioneers—but not for long! Dozens are claiming first place now, just as the early 'Women's Clubs' used to.

"They established in that block a meal service that was a wonder for excellence, and for cheapness, too; and people began to learn."

I was impressed, but not convinced, and she saw it.

"Look here, Uncle John, I hate to use figures on a helpless listener, but you drive me to it."

Then she reached for the bookcase and produced her evidence; sparingly, but with effect. She showed me that the difference between the expense of hiring separate service, and the same number of people patronizing a service company, was sufficient to reduce expenses to the patrons and leave a handsome payment for the company

Owen looked on, interpreting to my ignorance.

"You never kept house, old man," he said, "nor thought much about it, I expect; but you can figure this out for yourself easily enough. Here were a hundred families, equal to, say, five hundred persons. They hired a hundred cooks, of course; paid them something like six dollars a week— call it five on an average. There's $500 a week, just for cooks—$26,000 a year!

"Now, as a matter of fact (our learned daughter tells us this), ten cooks are plenty for five hundred persons—at the same price would cost $1,300 a year!"

"Ten are plenty, and to spare," said Hallie; "but we pay them handsomely. One chef at $3,000; two next bests at $2,000 each, four thousand; two at $1,000 apiece, two thousand; five at $800, four thousand. That's $13,000—half what we paid before, and the difference in service between a kitchen maid and a scientific artist."

"Fifty per cent saved on wages, and 500 per cent added to skill," Owen continued. "And you can go right on and add 90 per cent saving in fuel, 90 per cent in plant, 50 per cent in utensils, and—how much is it, Hallie, in materials?"

Hallie looked very important.

"Even when they first started, when food was shamefully expensive and required all manner of tests and examinations, the saving was all of 60 per cent. Now it is fully 80 per cent."

"That makes a good deal all told, Uncle John," Jerrold quietly remarked, handing me a bit of paper. "You see, it does leave a margin of profit."

I looked rather helplessly at the figures; also at Hallie.

"It is a shame, Uncle, to hurry you so, but the sooner you get these little matters clear in your head, the better. We have these great food furnishing companies, now, all over the country; and they have market gardens and dairies and so on, of their own. There is a Food Bureau in every city, and a National Food Bureau, with International relations. The best scientific knowledge is used to study food values, to improve old materials and develop new ones; there's a tremendous gain."

"But—do the people swallow things as directed by the government?" I protested. "Is there no chance to go and buy what you want to eat when you want it?"

They rose to their feet with one accord. Jerrold seized me by the hand.

"Come on, Uncle!" he cried. "Now is as good a time as any. You shall see our food department—come to scoff and remain to prey—if you like."

The elevator took us down, and I was led unresistingly among their shining modernities.

"Here is the source of supply," said Owen, showing where the basement supply room connected with a clean, airy subway under the glass-paved sidewalk. "Ice we make, drinking water we distil, fuel is wired to us; but the food stuffs are brought this way. Come down early enough and you would find these arteries of the city flowing steadily with—"

"Milk and honey," put in Jerrold.

"With the milk train, the meat train, the vegetable train, and so on."

"Ordered beforehand?" I asked.

"Ordered beforehand. Up to midnight you may send down word as to the kind of mushrooms you prefer—and no extra charge. During the day you can still order, but there's a trifle more expense—not much. But most of us are more than content to have our managers cater for us. From the home outfit you may choose at any time. There are lists upstairs, and here is the array."

There were but few officials in this part of the great establishment at this hour, but we were politely shown about by a scholarly looking man in white linen, who had been reading as we entered. They took me between rows of glass cases, standing as books do in the library, and showed me the day's baking; the year's preserves; the fragrant, colorful shelves of such fruit and vegetables as were not fresh picked from day to day.

"We don't get today's strawberries till the local ones are ripe," Jerrold told us.

"These are yesterday's, and pretty good yet."

"Excuse me, but those have just come in," said the white-linen person, "this morning's picking, from Maryland."

I tasted them with warm approval. There was a fascinating display of cakes and cookies, some old favorites; some of a new but attractive aspect; and in glass-doored separate ice-chambers, meats, fish, milk, and butter.

"Can people come in here and get what they want, though?" I inquired triumphantly.

"They can, and occasionally they do. But what it will take you some time to realize, John," my sister explained, "is the different attitude of people toward their food. We are all not only well fed—sufficiently fed—but so wisely fed that we seldom think of wanting anything further. When we do we can order from upstairs, come down to the eating room and order, send to the big depots if it is some rare thing, or even come in like this. To the regular purchasers it is practically free."

"And how if you are a stranger—a man in the street?"

"In every city in our land you may go into any eating house and find food as good—and cheap—as this," said Hallie, triumphantly.

Chapter V

While below, they took me into the patio, that quiet inner garden which was so attractive from above. It was a lovely place. The moon was riding high and shone down into it; a slender fountain spray rose shimmering from its carved basin; on the southern-facing wall a great wistaria vine drooped in budding purple, and beds of violets made the air rich with soft fragrance.

Here and there were people walking; and in the shadowy corners sat young couples, apparently quite happy.

"I suppose you don't know the names of one of them," I suggested.

"On the contrary, I know nearly all," answered Hallie. "These apartments are taken very largely by friends and acquaintances. You see, the gardens and roofs are in common; and there are the reading rooms, ballrooms, and so on. It is pleasanter to be friends to begin with, and most of us get to be afterward, if we are not at first."

"But surely there are some disagreeable people left on earth!"

"Yes—but where there is so much more social life, people get together in congenial sets," put in Nellie, "just as we used to in Summer resorts."

"There aren't so many bores and fools as there used to be, John," Owen remarked. "We really do raise better people. Even the old ones have improved; you see, life is so much pleasanter and more interesting."

"We're all healthier, Uncle John, because we're better fed; that makes us more agreeable."

"There's more art in the world to make us happier," said Jerrold. "Hallie thinks it's all due to her everlasting bread and butter. Listen to that now!"

From a balcony up there in the moonlight came a delicious burst of melody; a guitar and two voices; and the refrain was taken up from another window, from one corner of the garden, from the roof; all in smooth accord.

"Your group here must be an operatic one," I suggested; but my nephew answered that it was not, but that music, good music, was so common now, and so well taught, that the average was high in both taste and execution.

We sat late that night, my new family bubbling over with things to say, and filling my mind with a confused sense of new advantages, unexplained and only half believed.

I could not bring myself to accept as commonplace facts the unusual excellences so glibly described, and I suppose my silence showed this as well as what I said, for my sister presently intervened with decision:

"We must all stop this for to-night," she said. "John feels as if he was being forcibly fed—he's got to rest. Then I suggest that to-morrow Owen take him in hand—go off for a tramp, why don't you?—and really straighten out things. You see, there are two distinct movements to consider, the unconscious progress that would have taken place anyway in thirty years, and then the deliberate measures adopted by the 'New Lifers,' and it's rather confusing. I've labored with him all the way home; now I think the man's point of view will help."

. . . . .

Owen was a big man with a strong, wholesome face, and a quizzical little smile of his own. He and I went up the river next morning in a swift motor boat which did not batter the still air with muffled banging as they used to do, and strolled off in the bright Spring sunshine into Palisade Park.

"We've saved all the loveliest of it—for keeps," he said. "Out here, where the grass and trees are just as they used to be, you won't be bothered—and one Expositor will be easier to handle than four at once. Now, shall I talk—or will you ask questions?"

"I'd like to ask a few questions first; then you can expound by the hour. Do give me the long and short of this 'women-waked-up' proposition. What does it mean—to a man?"

Owen stroked his chin.

"No loss," he said at length. "At least, no loss that's not covered by a greater gain. Do you remember the new biological theory in regard to the relative position of the sexes that was beginning to make headway when we were young?"

I nodded. "Ward's theory? Oh, yes. I heard something of it—pretty far-fetched, it seemed to me."

"Far-fetched and dear-bought, but true for all that. You'll have to swallow it. The female *is* the race type; the male *is* her assistant. It's established beyond a peradventure."

I meditated, painfully. I looked at Owen. He had just as happy and proud a look as if he was a real man—not merely an Assistant. I though of Jerrold—nothing cowed about him; of the officers and men on the ship; of such men as I had seen in the street—

42

"I suppose this applies in the main to remote origins?" I suggested at last.

"It holds good all through life—is just as true as it ever was."

"Then—do you mean that women run everything, and men are only helpers?"

"Oh, no; I wasn't talking about human life at all—only about sex. 'Running things' has nothing to do with that. Women run some businesses and are in practically all; but men still do the bulk of the world's work. There is a natural division of labor, after all."

This was pleasant to hear, but he dashed my hopes.

"Men do almost all the violent plain work—digging and hewing and hammering; women, as a class, prefer the administrative and constructive kinds. But all that is open yet, and settling itself gradually, men and women are working everywhere. The big change which Nellie is always referring to means simply that women 'waked up' to a realization of the fact that they were human beings."

"What were they before, pray?"

"Only female beings."

"Female human beings, of course," said I.

"Yes, a little human, but mostly female. Now they are mostly human. It is a great change."

"I don't follow you. Aren't they still wives and mothers?"

"They are still mothers—far more so than they were before, as a matter of fact; but as to being wives—there's a difference."

I was displeased, and showed it.

"Well, is it Polygamy, or Polyandry, or Trial Marriages, or what?"

Owen gazed at me with an expression very like Nellie's.

"There it is," he said. "You can only think about women in some sort of relation to men, of a change in marriage relations as merely a change in kind; whereas what has happened is a change in *degree*. We still have monogamous marriages, on a much purer and more lasting plane than a generation ago; but the word 'wife' does not mean what it used to."

"Go on—I can't follow you at all."

"A 'wife' used to be a possession; 'wilt thou be mine?' said the lover, and the wife was 'his.'"

"Well—whose else is she now?" I asked with some sharpness.

"She does not 'belong' to anyone in that old sense. She is the wife of her husband in that she is his true lover, and that their marriage is legally recorded; but her life and work does not belong to him. He has no right to her 'services' any more. A woman who is in a business—like Hallie, for instance—does not give it up when she marries."

I stopped him. "What! Isn't Hallie married?"

"No—not yet."

"But—that is her flat?"

"Yes; why not?" He laughed at me. "You see, you can't imagine a woman having a home of her own. Hallie is twenty-three. She won't marry for some years, probably; but she has her position and is doing excellent work; it's only a minor inspectorship, but she likes it. Why shouldn't she have a home?"

"Why doesn't she have it with you?"

"Because I like to live with my wife. Her business, and mine, are in Michigan; Hallie's in New York."

"And when she marries she keeps on being an inspector?" I queried.

"Precisely. The man who marries that young woman will have much happiness, but he will not 'own' her, and she will not be his wife in the sense of a servant. She will not darn his socks or cook his meals. Why should she?"

"Will she not nurse his babies?"

"No; she will nurse *her* babies—*their* babies, not 'his' merely."

"And keep on being an inspector?"

"And keep on being an inspector—for four hours a day—in two shifts. Not a bit more difficult than cooking, my dear boy."

"But—she will not be with her children—"

"She will be with her children twenty hours out of the twenty-four—if she wants to. But Hallie's not specially good with children....You see, John, the women have specialized—even in motherhood."

Then he went on at considerable length to show how there had arisen a recognition of far more efficient motherhood than was being given; that those women best fitted for the work had given eager, devoted lives to it and built up a new science of Humaniculture; that no woman was allowed to care for her children without proof of capacity.

"Allowed by whom?" I put in.

"By the other women—the Department of Child Culture, the Government."

"And the fathers—do they submit to this, tamely?"

"No; they cheerfully agree and approve. Absolutely the biggest thing that has happened, some of us think, is that new recognition of the importance of childhood. We are raising better people now."

I was silent for a while, pulling up bits of grass and snapping small sticks into inch pieces.

"There was a good deal of talk about Eugenics, I remember," I said at last, "and—what was that thing? Endowment of Motherhood?"

"Yes—man's talk," Owen explained. "You see, John, we couldn't look at women but in one way—in the old days; it was all a question of sex with us—inevitably, we being males. Our whole idea of improvement was in better breeding; our whole idea of motherhood was in each woman's devoting her whole life to her own children. That turbid freshet of an Englishman, Wells, who did so much to stir his generation, said 'I am wholly feminist'—and he was. He saw women only as females and wanted them endowed as such. He was never able to see them as human beings and amply competent to take care of themselves.

"Now, our women, getting hold of this idea that they really are human creatures, simply blossomed forth in new efficiency. They specialized the food business—Hallie's right about the importance of that—and then they specialized the baby business. All women who wish to, have babies; but if they wish to take care of them they must show a diploma."

I looked at him. I didn't like it—but what difference did that make? I had died thirty years ago, it appeared.

"A diploma for motherhood!" I repeated; but he corrected me.

"Not at all! Any woman can be a mother—if she's normal. I said she had to have a diploma as a child-culturist—quite a different matter."

"I don't see the difference."

"No, I suppose not. I didn't, once," he said. "Any and every mother was supposed to be competent to 'raise' children—and look at the kind of people we raised! You see, we are beginning to learn—just beginning. You

45

needn't imagine that we are in a state of perfection—there are more new projects up for discussion than ever before. We've only made a start. The consequences, so far, are so good that we are boiling over with propositions for future steps."

"Go on about the women," I said. "I want to know the worst and become resigned."

"There's nothing very bad to tell," he continued cheerfully. "When a girl is born she is treated in all ways as if she was a boy; there is no hint made in any distinction between them except in the perfectly open physiological instruction as to their future duties. Children, young humans, grow up under precisely the same conditions. I speak, of course, of the most advanced people—there are still backward places—there's plenty to do yet.

"Then the growing girls are taught of their place and power as mothers—and they have tremendously high ideals. That's what has done so much to raise the standard in men—it came hard, but it worked."

I raised my head with keen interest, remarking, "I've glimpsed a sort of 'iron hand in a velvet glove' back of all this. What did they do?"

Owen looked rather grim for a moment.

"The worst of it was twenty or twenty-five years back. Most of those men are dead. That new religious movement stirred the socio-ethical sense to sudden power; it coincided with the women's political movement, urging measures for social improvement; its enormous spread, both by preaching and literature, lit up the whole community with new facts, ideas and feelings. Health—physical purity—was made a practical ideal. The young women learned the proportion of men with syphilis and gonorrhoea and decided it was wrong to marry them. That was enough. They passed laws in every State requiring a clean bill of health with every marriage license. Diseased men had to die bachelors—that's all."

"And did men submit to legislation like that?" I protested.

"Why not? It was so patently for the protection of the race—of the family—of the women and children. Women were solid for it, of course—and all the best men with them. To oppose it was almost a confession of guilt, and injured a man's chances of marriage."

"It used to be said that any man could find a woman to marry him," I murmured meditatively.

"Maybe he could—once. He certainly cannot now. A man who has one of

46

those diseases is so reported—just like small-pox, you see. Moreover, it is registered against him by the Department of Eugenics—physicians are required to send in lists; any girl can find out."

"It must have left a large proportion of unmarried women."

"It did, at first. And that very thing was of great value to the world. They were wise, conscientious, strong women, you see, and they poured all their tremendous force into social service. Lots of them went into child culture—used their mother-power that way. It wasn't easy for them; it wasn't easy for the left-over men, either!"

"It must have increased prostitution to an awful extent," I said.

Owen shook his head and regarded me quizzically.

"That is the worst of it," he said. "There isn't any."

I sat up. I stood up. I walked up and down. "No prostitution! I—I can't believe it. Why, prostitution is a social necessity, as old as Nineveh!"

Owen laughed outright. "Too late, old man, too late! I know we used to think so. We did use to call it a 'social necessity,' didn't we? Come, now, tell me what necessity it was *to the women.*"

I stopped my march and looked at him.

"To the women," he repeated. "What did they want of prostitution? What good did it do them?"

"Why—why—they made a living at it," I replied, rather lamely.

"Yes, a nice, honorable, pleasant, healthy living, didn't they? With all women perfectly well able to earn an excellent living decently; with all women fully educated about these matters and knowing what a horrible death was before them in this business; with all women brought up like human beings and not like over-sexed female animals, and with all women quite free to marry if they wished to—how many, do you think, would choose that kind of business?

"We never waited for them to choose it, remember! We fooled them and lied to them and dragged them in—and drove them in—forced them in—and kept them as slaves and prisoners. They didn't really enjoy the life; you know that. Why should they go into it if they do not have to; to accommodate us?"

"Do you mean to tell me there are no—wantons—among women?" I demanded.

"No, I don't mean any such thing. There are various kinds of over-developed and morbidly developed women as there are men, and we haven't weeded them out entirely. But the whole thing is now recognized as pathological—cases for medical treatment, or perhaps surgical. Besides, wantonness is not prostitution. Prostitution is a social crime of the worst order. No one thing did more harm. The women stamped it out."

"Legislated us all into morality, did they?" I inquired sarcastically.

"Legislation did a good deal; education did more; the new religion did most; social opinion helped. You remember we men never really tried to legislate against prostitution—we wanted it to go on."

"Why, surely we did legislate against it—and it was of no use!" I protested.

"No, we legislated against the women, but not against the men, or the thing itself. We examined the women, and fined them, and licensed them—and never did anything against the men. Women legislators used very different measures, I assure you."

"I suppose it is for the good of the world," I presently admitted; "but—"

"But you don't quite like to think of men in this new and peculiar position of having to be good!"

"Frankly—I don't. I'm willing to be good, but—I don't like to be given no choice."

"Well, now look at it. As it was, we had one way, according to what we thought was good for us. Rather than lead clean, contented lives at some expense to ourselves in the way of moral and physical control, we deliberately sacrificed an army of women to a horrible life and a more horrible death, and corrupted the blood of the nation. It was on the line of health they made their stand, not on 'morality' alone. Under our new laws it is held a crime to poison another human being with syphilis, just as much as to use prussic acid."

"Nellie said you had no crime now."

"Oh, well, Nellie is an optimist. I suppose she meant the old kinds and definitions; we don't call things 'crimes' any more. And then, really, there is not a hundredth part of the evil done that there used to be. We know more, you see, and have less temptation."

We were silent for a while. I watched a gull float and wheel over the blue water. Big airships flew steadily along certain lines; little ones sailed about on all sides.

One darted over our heads and lit with a soft swoop on an open promontory.

"Didn't they use to buzz?" I asked Owen.

"Of course, just as the first motor boats thumped and banged abominably. We will not stand for unnecessary noise, as we used to."

"How do you stop it? More interference with the individual rights?"

"More recognition of public rights. A bad noise is a nuisance, like a bad smell. We didn't used to mind it much—but the women did. You see, what women like has to be considered now."

"It always was considered!" I broke in with some heat. "The women of America were the most spoiled, pampered lot on earth; men gave up to them in all ways."

"At home, perhaps, but not in public. The city and State weren't run to suit them at all."

"Why should they be? Women belong at home—if they push into a man's world they ought to take the consequences."

Owen stretched his long legs and looked up at the soft, brilliant blue above us.

"Why do you call the world 'man's'?" he asked.

"It *was* man's; it ought to be. Woman's place is in the home. I suppose I sound like ancient history to you?" and I laughed a little shamefacedly.

"We *have* rather lost that point of view," Owen guardedly admitted. "You see—" and then he laughed. "It's no use, John; no matter how we put it to you it's a jar. The world's thought has changed—and you have got to catch up!"

"Suppose I refuse? Suppose I really am unable?"

"We won't suppose it for a moment," he said cheerfully. "Ideas are not nailed down. Just take out what you had and insert some new ones. Women are people—just as much as we are; that's a *fact*, my dear fellow. You'll have to accept it."

"And are men allowed to be people, too?" I asked gloomily.

"Why, of course! Nothing has interfered with our position as human beings; it is only our sex supremacy that we have lost."

"And do you *like* it?" I demanded.

"Some men made a good deal of fuss at first—the old-fashioned kind, and all the worst varieties. But modern men aren't worried in the least over their position...See here, John, you don't grasp this—women are vastly more agreeable than they used to be."

I looked at him in amazement.

"Fact!" he said. "Of course, we loved our own mothers and daughters and sisters, more or less, no matter how they looked or what they did; and when we were 'in love' there was no limit to the glory of 'the beloved object.' But you and I know that women were pretty unsatisfactory in the old days."

I refused to admit it, but he went on calmly:

"The 'wife and mother' was generally a tired, nervous, overworked creature. She soon lost her beauty and vigor, her charm and inspiration. We were forever chasing fine, handsome, highly desirable young girls, and forever reducing them to weary, worn-out women—in the name of love! The gay outsiders were always a fresh attraction—as long as we couldn't have them...See here, John—can't you understand? Our old way of using women wasn't good for them—nor for us, either, by the way—but it simply spoiled the women. They were hopelessly out of the running with us in all human lines; their business was housework, and ours was world work. There was very little real companionship.

"Now, women are intelligent, experienced, well-trained citizens, fully our equals in any line of work they take up, and with us everywhere. It's made the world over!"

"Made it 'feminist' through and through, I suppose!" I groaned.

"Not a bit! It used to be 'masculist' through and through; now it's just *human*. And, see here—women are more attractive, as women, than they used to be."

I stared at this, unbelieving.

"That's true! You see, they are healthy; there's a new standard of physical beauty—very Greek—you must have noticed already the big, vigorous, fresh-colored, free-stepping girls."

I had—even in my brief hours of observation.

"They are far more perfect physically, better developed mentally, with a higher moral sense—yes, you needn't look like that! We used to call them our 'moral superiors' just because they had the one virtue we insisted on— and we never noticed the lack in other lines. Women today are truthful, brave, honest, generous, self-controlled; they are—jollier, more

50

reasonable, more companionable."

"Well, I'm glad to hear that," I rather grudgingly admitted. "I was afraid they would have lost all—charm."

"Yes, we used to feel that way, I remember. Funny! We were convinced on the one hand that there was nothing to a woman but her eternal womanliness, and on the other we were desperately afraid her womanliness would disappear the moment she turned her mind to anything else. I assure you that men love women, in general and in particular, much more than they used to."

I pondered. "But—what sort of home life do you have?"

"Think for a moment of what we used to have—even in a 'happy home.' The man had the whole responsibility of keeping it up—his business life and interests all foreign to her. She had the whole labor of running it—the direct manual labor in the great majority of cases—the management in any case. They were strangers in an industrial sense.

"When he came home he had to drop all his line of thought—and she hers, except that she generally unloaded on him the burden of inadequacy in housekeeping. Sometimes he unloaded, too. They could sympathize and condole—but neither could help the other.

"The whole thing cost like sin, too. It was a living nightmare to lots of men—and women! The only things they had in common were their children and 'social interests.'

"Well—nowadays, in the first place everybody is easy about money. (I'll go into that later.) No woman marries except for love—and good judgment, too; all women are more desirable—more men want to marry them—and that improves the men! You see, a man naturally cares more for women than for anything else in life—and they know it! It's the handle they lift by. That's what has eliminated tobacco."

"Do you mean to say that these women have arbitrarily prevented smoking?" I do not smoke myself, but I was angry nevertheless.

"Not a bit of it, John—not a bit of it. Anybody can smoke who wants to."

"Then why don't they?"

"Because women do not like it."

"What has that to do with it? Can't a man do what he wants to—even if they don't like it?"

"Yes, he can; but it costs too much. Men like tobacco, but they like love better, old man."

"Is it one of your legal requirements for marriage?"

"No, not legal; but women disapprove of tobacco-y lovers, husbands, fathers; they know that the excessive use of it is injurious, and won't marry a heavy smoker. But the main point is that they simply don't like the smell of the stuff, or of the man who uses it—most women, that is."

"But what *difference* does it make? I dare say that most women did not like it before, but surely a man has a right—"

"To make himself a disgusting object to his wife?" Owen interrupted. "Yes, he has a 'right' to. We would have a right to bang on a tin pan, I suppose—or to burn rubber, but he wouldn't be popular!"

"It's tyranny!" I protested.

"Not at all," he said, imperturbably. "We had no idea what a nuisance we used to be, that's all; or how much women put up with that they did not like at all. I asked a woman once—when I was a bachelor—why she objected to tobacco, and she frankly replied that a man who did not smoke was much pleasanter to kiss! She was a very fascinating little widow—I confess it made me think."

"It's the same with liquor, I suppose? Let's get it all told."

"Yes, only more so. Alcoholism was a race evil of the worst sort. I cannot imagine how we put up with it so long."

"Is this spotless world of yours one solid temperance union?"

"Practically. We use some light wines and a little spirits yet, but infrequently—in this country, at least, and Europe is vastly improved.

"But that was a much more serious thing than the other. It wasn't a mere matter of not marrying! They used all kinds of means—But come on— we'll be late to dinner; and dinner, at least, is still a joy, Brother John."

Chapter VI

Out of the mass of information offered by my new family and the pleasant friends we met, together with the books and publications profusely piling around me, I felt it necessary to make a species of digest for my own consideration. This I submitted to Nellie, Owen, and one or two others, adding suggestions and corrections; and thus established in my own mind a coherent view of what had happened.

In the first place, as Owen repeatedly assured me, nothing was *done*—finished—brought to static perfection.

"Thirty years isn't much, you see," he said cheerfully. "I dare say if you'd been here all along you wouldn't think it was such a great advance. We have removed some obvious and utterly unnecessary evils, and cleared the ground for new beginnings; but what we are going to do is the exciting thing!

"Now you think it is so wonderful that we have no poverty. We think it is still more wonderful that a world of even partially sane people could have borne poverty so long."

We naturally discussed this point a good deal, and they brought up a little party of the new economists to enlighten me—Dr. Harkness, sociologist; Mr. Alfred Brown, Department of Production; Mrs. Allerton of the Local Transportation Bureau; and a young fellow named Pike, who had written a little book on "Distinctive Changes of Three Decades," which I found very useful.

"It was such a simple matter, after all, you see," the sociologist explained to me, in an amiable class-room manner.

"Suppose now you were considering the poverty of one family, an isolated family, sir. Now, if this family was poor, it would be due to the limitations of the individual or of the environment. Limitations of the individual would cover inefficiency, false theory of industry, ill-judged division of labor, poor system of production, or misuse of product. Limitation of environment would, of course, apply to climate, soil, natural products, etc. No amount of health, intelligence or virtue could make Iceland rich—if it was completely isolated; nor England, for that matter, owing to the inexorable limitations of that environment.

"Here in this country we have no complaint to make of our natural resources. The soil is capable of sustaining an enormous population. So we have merely to consider the limitations of individuals, transferring our problem from the isolated family to the general public.

"What do we find? All the limitations I enumerated! Inefficiency—nearly every one below par in working power in the generation before last, as well as miserably educated; false theories of industry everywhere—idiotic notions as to what work was 'respectable' and what wasn't, more idiotic notions of payment; worst of all, most idiotic ideas that work was a curse...Might as well call digestion a curse! Dear! Dear! How benighted we were!

"Then there was ill-judged division of labor—almost universal; that evil. For instance, look at this one point; half the workers of the world, nearly, were restricted to one class of labor, and that in the lowest industrial grade."

"He means women, in housework, John," Nellie interpolated. "We never used to think of that as part of our economic problem."

"It was a very serious part," the professor continued, hastily forestalling the evident intention of Mr. Brown to strike in, "but there were many others. The obvious utility of natural specialization in labor seemed scarcely to occur to us. Our system of production was archaic in the extreme; practically *no* system was followed."

"You must give credit to the work of the Department of Agriculture, Dr. Harkness," urged Mr. Brown, "the introduction of new fruits, the improvement of stocks—"

"Yes, yes," agreed Dr. Harkness, "the rudiments were there, of course; but no real grasp of organized productivity. And as to misuse of product— why, my dear Mr. Robertson, it is a wonder anybody had enough to live on in those days, in view of our criminal waste.

"The real turning point, Mr. Robertson, if we can put our finger on one, is where the majority of the people recognized the folly and evil of poverty— and saw it to be a thing of our own making. We saw that our worst poverty was poverty in the stock—that we raised a terrible percentage of poor people. Then we established a temporary Commission on Human Efficiency, away back in 1913 or '14—"

"Thirteen," put in Mr. Pike, who sat back listening to Dr. Harkness with an air of repressed superiority.

"Thank you," said the eminent sociologist courteously. "These young fellows have it all at their fingers' ends, Mr. Robertson. Better methods in education nowadays, far better! As I was saying, we established a Commission on Human Efficiency."

"You will remember the dawning notions of 'scientific management' we began to have in the first decade of the new century," Mrs. Allerton quietly suggested. "It occurred to us later to apply it to ourselves —and we did."

"The Commission found that the majority of human beings were not properly reared," Dr. Harkness resumed, "with a resultant low standard of efficiency—shockingly low; and that the loss was not merely to the individual but to the community. Then Society stretched out a long arm and took charge of the work of humaniculture—began to lift the human standard.

"I won't burden you with details on that line at present; it touched but one cause of poverty after all. The false theory of industry was next to be changed. A few far-seeing persons were already writing and talking about work as an organic social function, but the sudden spread of it came through the new religion."

"*And* the new voters, Dr. Harkness," my sister added.

He smiled at her benevolently. A large, comfortable, full-bearded, rosy old gentleman was Dr. Harkness, and evidently in full enjoyment of his present task.

"Let us never forget the new voters, of course. They have ceased to be thought of as new, Mr. Robertson—so easily does the human mind accept established conditions. The new religion urged work—normal, well-adapted work—as *the* duty of life—as life itself; and the new voters accepted this idea as one woman.

"They were, as a class, used to doing their duty in patient industry, generally distasteful to them; and the opportunity of doing work they liked—with a sense of higher duty added—was universally welcomed."

"I certainly remember a large class of women who practiced no industry at all—no duty, either, unless what they called 'social duties,'" I rather sourly remarked. Mrs. Allerton took me up with sudden heat:

"Yes, there were such, in large numbers, in our great cities particularly; but public opinion was rising against them even as far back as 1910. The more progressive women turned the light on them first, and then men took it up and began to see that this domestic pet was not only expensive and useless but injurious and absurd. I don't suppose we can realize," she continued meditatively, "how complete the change in public opinion is— and how supremely important. In visible material progress we have only followed simple lines, quite natural and obvious, and accomplished what was perfectly possible at any time—if we had only thought so."

"*That's* the point!" Mr. Pike was unable to preserve his air of restraint any longer, and burst forth volubly.

"That was the greatest, the most sudden, the most vital of our changes, sir—the change in the world's thought! Ideas are the real things, sir! Brick and mortar? Bah! We can put brick and mortar in any shape we choose—but we have to choose first! What held the old world back was not facts—not conditions—not any material limitations, or psychic limitations either. We had every constituent of human happiness, sir—except the sense to use them. The channel of progress was obstructed with a deposit of prehistoric ideas. We choked up our children's minds with this mental refuse as we choked our rivers and harbors with material refuse, sir."

Dr. Harkness still smiled. "Mr. Pike was in my class ten years ago," he observed amiably. "I always said he was the brightest young man I had. We are all very proud of Mr. Pike."

Mr. Pike seemed not over pleased with this communication, and the old gentleman went on:

"He is entirely right. Our idiotic ideas and theories were the main causes of poverty after all. The new views on economics—true social economics, not the 'dismal science'; with the blaze of the new religion to show what was right and wrong, and the sudden uprising of half the adult world—the new voters—to carry out the new ideas; these were what changed things! There you have it, Mr. Robertson, in a nutshell—rather a large nutshell, a pericarp, as it were—but I think that covers it."

"We students used always to admire Dr. Harkness' power of easy generalization," said Mr. Pike, in a mild, subacid tone, "but if any ground of inquiry is left to you, Mr. Robertson, I could, perhaps, illuminate some special points."

Dr. Harkness laughed in high good humor, and clapped his whilom pupil on the back.

"You have the floor, Mr. Pike—I shall listen to you with edification."

The young man looked a little ashamed of his small irony, and continued more genially:

"Our first step—or one of our first steps, for we advanced like a strenuous centipede—was to check the birth of defectives and degenerates. Certain classes of criminals and perverts were rendered incapable of reproducing their kind. In the matter of those diseases most injurious to the young, very stringent measures were taken. It was made a felony to infect wife or child knowingly, and a misdemeanor if it were done unknowingly. Physicians were obliged to report all cases of infectious disease, and young girls were clearly taught the consequence of marriage with infected persons. The immediate result was, of course, a great decrease in marriage; but the increase in population was scarce checked at all because of the lowered death rate among children. It was checked a little; but for twenty years now, it has been recovering itself. We increase a little too fast now, but see every hope of a balanced population long before the resources of the world are exhausted."

Mr. Brown seized upon a second moment's pause to suggest that the world's resources were vastly increased also—and still increasing.

"Let Pike rest a moment and get his breath," he said, warming to the subject, "I want to tell Mr. Robertson that the productivity of the earth is gaining every year. Here's this old earth feeding us all—laying golden eggs as it were; and we used to get those eggs by the Caesarian operation! We uniformly exhausted the soil—uniformly! Now a man would no more think of injuring the soil, the soil that feeds him, than he would of hurting his mother. We steadily improve the soil; we improve the seed; we improve methods of culture; we improve everything."

Mrs. Allerton struck in here, "Not forgetting the methods of transportation, Mr. Robertson. There was one kind of old world folly which made great waste of labor and time; that was our constant desire to eat things out of season. There is now a truer sense of what is really good eating; no one wants to eat asparagus that is not of the best, and asparagus cut five or ten days cannot be really good. We do not carry things about unnecessarily; and the carrying we do is swift, easy and economical. For slow freight we use waterways wherever possible—you will be pleased to see the 'all-water routes' that thread the country now. And our roads—you haven't seen our roads yet! We lead the world."

"We used to be at the foot of the class as to roads, did we not?" I asked; and Mr. Pike swiftly answered:

"We did, indeed, sir. But that very need of good roads made easy to us the second step in abolishing poverty. Here was a great social need calling for labor; here were thousands of men calling for employment; and here were we keeping the supply from the demand by main strength—merely from those archaic ideas of ours.

"We had a mass of valuable data already collected, and now that the whole country teemed with new ideals of citizenship and statesmanship, it did not take very long to get the two together."

"We furnished employment for all the women, too," my sister added. "A Social Service Union was formed the country over; it was part of the new religion. Every town has one—men and women. The same spirit that used to give us crusaders and missionaries now gave plenty of enthusiastic workers."

"I don't see yet how you got up any enthusiasm about work," said I.

"It was not work for oneself," Nellie explained. "That is what used to make it so sordid; we used really to believe that we were working each for himself. This new idea was overwhelming in its simplicity—and truth; work is social service—social service is religion—that's about it."

"Not only so," Dr. Harkness added, "it made a three-fold appeal; to the old, deep-seated religious sense; to the new, vivid intellectual acceptance; and to the very wide-spread, wholesome appreciation of a clear advantage.

"When a thing was offered to the world that agreed with every social instinct, that appealed to common sense, that was established by the highest scientific authority, and that had the overwhelming sanction of religion—why the world took to it."

"But it is surely not natural to people to work—much less to like to work!" I protested.

"There's where the change comes in," Mr. Pike eagerly explained. "We used to *think* that people hated work—nothing of the sort! What people hated was too much work, which is death; work they were personally unfit for and therefore disliked, which is torture; work under improper conditions, which is disease; work held contemptible, looked down upon by other people, which is a grievous social distress; and work so ill-paid that no human beings could really live by it."

"Why Mr. Robertson, if you can throw any light on the now inconceivable folly of that time so utterly behind us, we shall be genuinely indebted to you. It was quite understood in your day that the whole world's life, comfort, prosperity and progress depended upon the work done, was it not?"

"Why, of course; that was an economic platitude," I answered.

"Then why were the workers punished for doing it?"

"Punished? What do you mean?"

"I mean just what I say. They were punished, just as we punish criminals—with confinement at hard labor. The great mass of the people were forced to labor for cruelly long hours at dull, distasteful occupations; is not that punishment?"

"Not at all," I said hotly. "They were free at any time to leave an occupation they did not like."

"Leave it for what alternative?"

"To take up another," said I, perceiving that this, after all, was not much of an escape.

"Yes, to take up another under the same heavy conditions, if there was any opening; or to starve—that was their freedom."

"Well, what would you have?" I asked. "A man must work for his living surely."

"Remember your economic platitude, Mr. Robertson," Dr. Harkness suggested. "The whole world's life, comfort, prosperity and progress depends upon the work done, you know. It was not *their* living they were working for; it was the world's."

"That is very pretty as a sentiment," I was beginning; but his twinkling eye reminded that an economic platitude is not precisely sentimental.

"That's where the change came," Mr. Pike eagerly repeated. "The idea that each man had to do it for himself kept us blinded to the fact that it was all social service; that they worked for the world, and the world treated them shamefully—so shamefully that their product was deteriorated, markedly deteriorated."

"You will be continually surprised, Mr. Robertson, at the improvements of our output," remarked Mr. Brown. "We have standards in every form of manufacture, required standards; and to label an article incorrectly is a misdemeanor."

"That was just starting in the pure-food agitation, you remember," my sister put in, "—('with apple juice containing one-tenth of one per cent, of benzoate of soda')."

"And now," Mr. Brown continued, "'all wool' is all wool; if it isn't, you can have the dealer arrested. Silk is silk, nowadays, and cream is cream."

"And 'caveat emptor' is a dead letter?"

"Yes, it is 'caveat vendor' now. You see, selling goods is public service."

"You apply that term quite differently from what it stood for in my memory," said I.

"It used to mean some sort of beneficent statesmanship, at first," Nellie agreed. "Then it spread to various philanthropic efforts and wider grades

59

of government activities. Now it means any kind of world work."

She saw that this description did not carry much weight with me, and added, "Any kind of human work, John; that is, work a man gives his whole time to and does not himself consume, is world work—is social service."

"If a man raises, by his own labor, just enough to feed himself—that is working for himself," Mr. Brown explained, "but if he raises more corn than he consumes, he is serving humanity."

"But he does not give it away," I urged; "he is paid for it."

"Well, you paid the doctor who saved your child's life, but the doctor's work was social service none the less—and the teacher's—anybody's."

"But that kind of work benefits humanity—"

"Yes, and does it not benefit humanity to eat—to have shoes and clothes and houses? John, John, wake up!" Nellie for the first time showed impatience with me. But my brother-in-law extended a protecting arm.

"Now, Nellie, don't hurry him. This thing will burst upon him all at once. Of course, it's glaringly plain, but there was a time when you and I did not see it either."

I was a little sulky. "Well, as far as I gather," and I took out my note book, "people all of a sudden changed all their ideas about everything—and your demi-millennium followed."

"I wish we *could* say that," said Mrs. Allerton. "We are not telling you of our present day problems and difficulties, you see. No, Mr. Robertson, we have merely removed our most obvious and patently unnecessary difficulties, of which poverty was at least the largest.

"What we did, as we have rather confusedly suggested, I'm afraid, was to establish such measures as to insure better births, and vastly better environment and education for every child. That raised the standard of the people, you see, and increased their efficiency. Then we provided employment for everyone, under good conditions, and improved the world in two ways at once."

"And who paid for this universal employment?" I asked.

"Who paid for it before?" she returned promptly.

"The employer, of course."

"Did he? Out of his own private pocket? At a loss to himself."

"Why, of course not," I replied, a little nettled. "Out of the profits of the business."

"And 'the business' was the work done by the employees?"

"Not at all! He did it himself; they only furnished the labor."

"Could he do it alone—without 'labor?' Did he furnish employment as a piece of beneficence, outside of his business—Ah, Mr. Robertson, surely it is clear that unless a man's labor furnished a profit to his employer, he would not be employed. It was on that profit that 'labor' was paid—they paid themselves. They do now, but at a higher rate."

I was annoyed by this clever juggling with the hard facts of business.

"That is very convincing, Mrs. Allerton," I said with some warmth, "but it unfortunately omits certain factors. A lot of laborers could make a given article, of course; but they could not sell it—and that is where the profit comes in. What good would it do the laborer to pile up goods if he could not sell them?"

"And what good would be the ability to sell goods if there were none, Mr. Robertson? Of course, I recognize the importance of transportation; that is my own line of work, but there must be something to transport. As long ago as St. Paul's day it was known that the hand could not say to the foot, 'I have no need of thee.'"

"To cover that ground more easily, Mr. Robertson," Dr. Harkness explained, "just put down in your digest there that Bureaus of Employment were formed all over the country; some at first were of individual initiative, but in a few years' time all were in government management. There was a swift and general improvement in the whole country. The roads became models to the world, the harbors were cleared, canals dug, cities rebuilt, bare hills reforested, the value of our national property doubled and trebled—all owing to the employment of hitherto neglected labor. Out of the general increase of wealth they got their share, of course. And where there is work for everyone, at good wages, there is no poverty; that's clearly seen."

Chapter VII

The country was as astonishing to me as the city—its old beauty added to in every direction. They took me about in motor cars, motor boats and air ships, on foot and on horseback (the only horses now to be found were in the country). And while I speak of horses, I will add that the only dogs and cats I saw, or heard, were in the country, too, and not very numerous at that.

"We've changed our views as to 'pets' and 'domestic animals,'" Nellie said. "We ourselves are the only domestic animals allowed now. Meat eating, as Hallie told you, is decreasing every day; but the care and handling of our food animals improves even more rapidly. Every city has its municipal pastures and dairies, and every village or residence group. By the way, I might as well show you one of those last, and get it clear in your mind."

We were on an air trip in one of the smooth-going, noiseless machines commonly used, which opened a new world of delight to me. This one held two, with the aviator. I had inquired about accidents, and was glad to find that thirty years' practice had eliminated the worst dangers and reared a race of flying men.

"In our educational plan to-day all the children are given full physical development and control," my sister explained. "That goes back to the woman again—the mothers. There was a sort of Hellenic revival—a recognition that it was possible for us to rear as beautiful human beings as walked in Athens. When women were really free of man's selective discrimination they proved quite educable, and learned to be ashamed of their deformities. Then we began to appreciate the human body and to have children reared in an atmosphere of lovely form and color, statues and pictures all about them, and the new stories—Oh! I haven't told you a thing about them, have I?"

"No," I said; "and please don't. I started out to see the country, and your new-fangled 'residence groups,' whatever they may be, and I refuse to have my mind filled up with educational information. Take me on a school expedition another time, please."

"All right," she agreed; "but I can tell you more about the beasts without distracting your mind, I hope. For one thing, we have no longer any menageries."

"What?" I cried. "No menageries! How absurd! They were certainly educational, and a great pleasure to children—and other people."

"Our views of education have changed you see," she replied; "and our views of human relation to the animal world; also our ideas of pleasure. People do not think it a pleasure now to watch animals in pain."

"More absurdity! They were not in pain. They were treated better than when left wild," I hotly replied.

"Imprisonment is never a pleasure," she answered; "it is a terrible punishment. A menagerie is just a prison, not for any offense of the inmates, but to gratify men in the indulgence of grossly savage impulses. Children, being in the savage period of their growth, feel anew the old satisfaction of seeing their huge enemies harmless or their small victims helpless and unable to escape. But it did no human being any good."

"How about the study of these 'victims' of yours—the scientific value?"

"For such study as is really necessary to us, or to them, some laboratories keep a few. Otherwise, the student goes to where the animals live and studies their real habits."

"And how much would he learn of wild tigers by following them about—unless it was an inside view?"

"My dear brother, can you mention one single piece of valuable information for humanity to be found in the study of imprisoned tigers? As a matter of fact, I don't think there are any left by this time; I hope not."

"Do you mean to tell me that your new humanitarianism has exterminated whole species?"

"Why not? Would England be pleasant if the gray wolf still ran at large? We are now trying, as rapidly as possible, to make this world safe and habitable everywhere."

"And how about the hunting? Where's the big game?"

"Another relic of barbarism. There is very little big game left, and very little hunting."

I glared at her, speechless. Not that I was ever a hunter myself, or even wanted to be; but to have that splendid manly sport utterly prevented—it was outrageous! "I suppose this is more of the women's work," I said at length.

She cheerfully admitted it. "Yes, we did it. You see, hunting as a means of livelihood is even lower than private housework—far too wasteful and expensive to be allowed in a civilized world. When women left off using skins and feathers, that was a great blow to the industry. As to the sport, why, we had never greatly admired it, you know—the manly sport of killing things for fun—and with our new power we soon made it undesirable."

I groaned in spirit. "Do you mean to tell me that you have introduced legislation against hunting, and found means to enforce it?"

"We found means to enforce it without much legislation, John."

"As for instance?"

"As for instance, in rearing children who saw and heard the fullest condemnation of all such primitive cruelty. That is another place where the new story-books come in. Why on earth we should have fed our children on silly savagery a thousand years old, just because they liked it, is more than I can see. We were always interfering with their likes and dislikes in other ways. Why so considerate in this? We have a lot of splendid writers now—first-class ones—making a whole lot of new literature for children."

"Do leave out your story books. You were telling me how you redoubtable females coerced men into giving up hunting."

"Mostly by disapproval, consistent and final."

This was the same sort of thing Owen had referred to in regard to tobacco. I didn't like it. It gave me a creepy feeling, as of one slowly surmounted by a rising tide. "Are you—do you mean to tell me, Nellie, that you women are trying to make men over to suit yourselves?"

"Yes. Why not? Didn't you make women to suit yourselves for several thousand years? You bred and trained us to suit your tastes; you liked us small, you liked us weak, you liked us timid, you liked us ignorant, you liked us pretty—what you called pretty—and you eliminated the kinds you did not like."

"How, if you please?"

"By the same process we use—by not marrying them. Then, you see, there aren't any more of that kind."

"You are wrong, Nellie—you're absurdly wrong. Women were naturally that way; that is, womanly women were, and men preferred that kind, of course."

"How do you know women were 'naturally' like that?—without special education and artificial selection, and all manner of restrictions and penalties? Where were any women ever allowed to grow up 'naturally' until now?"

I maintained a sulky silence, looking down at the lovely green fields and forests beneath. "Have you exterminated dogs?" I asked.

"Not yet. There are a good many real dogs left. But we don't make artificial ones any more."

"I suppose you keep all the cats—being women." She laughed.

"No; we keep very few. Cats kill birds, and we need the birds for our farms and gardens. They keep the insects down."

"Do they keep the mice down, too?"

"Owls and night-hawks do, as far as they can. But we attend to the mice ourselves. Concrete construction and the removal of the kitchen did that. We do not live in food warehouses now. There, look! We are coming to Westholm Park; that was one of the first."

In all the beauty spread below me, the great park showed more beautiful, outlined by a thick belt of trees.

We kept our vehicle gliding slowly above it while Nellie pointed things out. "It's about 300 acres," she said. "You can see the woodland and empty part—all that is left wild. That big patch there is pasturage—they keep their own sheep and cows. There are gardens and meadows. Up in the corner is the children's playground, bathing pool, and special buildings. Here is the playground for grown-ups—and their lake. This big spreading thing is the guest house and general playhouse for the folks—ballroom, billiards, bowling, and so on. Behind it is the plant for the whole thing. The water tower you'll see to more advantage when we land. And all around you see the homes; each family has an acre or so."

We dropped softly to the landing platform and came down to the pleasure ground beneath. In a little motor we ran about the place for awhile, that I might see the perfect roads, shaded with arching trees, the endless variety of arrangement, the miles of flowers, the fruit on every side.

"You must have had a good landscape architect to plan this," I suggested.

"We did—one of the best."

"It's not so very unlike a great, first-class summer hotel, with singularly beautiful surroundings."

"No, it's not," she agreed. "We had only the best summer resorts in mind when we began to plan these places. People used to pay heavily in summer to enjoy a place where everything was done to make life smooth and pleasant. It occurred to us at last that we might live that way."

"Who wants to live in a summer hotel all the time? Excuse *me?*"

"O, they don't. The people here nearly all live in 'homes'—the homiest kind—each on its own ground, as you see. Only some unattached ones, and people who really like it, live in the hotel—with transients, of course. Let's call here; I know this family."

She introduced me to Mrs. Masson, a sweet, motherly little woman, rocking softly on her vine-shadowed piazza, a child in her arms. She was eager to tell me about things—most people were, I found.

"I'm a reactionary, Mr. Robertson. I prefer to work at home, and I prefer to keep my children with me, all I can."

"Isn't that allowed nowadays?" I inquired.

"O, yes; if one qualifies. I did. I took the child-culture course, but I do not want to be a regular teacher. My work is done right here, and I can have them as well as not, but they won't stay much."

Even as she spoke the little thing in her arms whispered eagerly to her mother, slipped to the floor, ran out of the gate, her little pink legs fairly twinkling, and joined an older child who was passing.

"They like to be with the others, you see. This is my baby; I manage to hold on to her for part of the day, but she's always running off to The Garden when she can."

"The Garden?"

"Yes; it's a regular Child Garden, where they are cultivated and grow! And they do so love to grow!"

She showed us her pretty little house and her lovely work—embroidery. "I'm so fortunate," she said, "loving home as I do, to have work that's just as well done here."

I learned that there were some thirty families living in the grounds, not counting the hotel people. Quite a number found their work in the necessary activities of the place itself.

"We have a long string of places, you see—from the general manager to the gardeners and dairymen. It is really quite a piece of work, to care for some two hundred and fifty people," Mrs. Masson explained with some pride.

"Instead of a horde of servants and small tradesmen to make a living off these thirty families, we have a small corps of highly trained officers," added Nellie.

"And do you co-operate in housekeeping?" I inquired, meaning no harm, though my sister was quite severe with me for this slip.

"No, *indeed*," protested Mrs. Masson. "I do despise being mixed up with other families. I've been here nearly a year, and I hardly know anyone." And she rocked back and forth, complacently.

"But I thought that the meals were co-operative."

"O, not at *all*—not at *all!* Just see my dining-room! And you must be tired and hungry, now, Mrs. Robertson—don't say no! I'll have lunch in a moment. Excuse me, please."

She retired to the telephone, but we could hear her ordering lunch. "Right away, please; No. 5; no, let me see—No. 7, please. And have you fresh mushrooms? Extra; four plates."

Her husband came home in time for the meal, and she presided just like any other little matron over a pretty table and a daintily served lunch; but it came down from the hotel in a neat, light case, to which the remnants and the dishes were returned.

"O, I wouldn't give up my own table for the world! And my own dishes; they take excellent care of them. Our breakfasts we get all together—see my kitchen!" And she proudly exhibited a small, light closet, where an immaculate porcelain sink, with hot and cold water, a glass-doored "cold closet" and a shining electric stove, allowed the preparation of many small meals.

Nellie smiled blandly as she saw this little lady claiming conservatism in what struck me as being quite sufficiently progressive, while Mr. Masson smiled in proud content.

"I took you there on purpose," she told me later. "She is really quite reactionary for nowadays, and not over popular. Come and see the guest-house."

This was a big, wide-spread concrete building, with terraces and balconies and wide roofs, where people strolled and sat. It rose proudly from its wide lawns and blooming greenery, a picture of peace and pleasure.

"It's like a country club, with more sleeping rooms," I suggested. "But isn't it awfully expensive—the year round?"

"It's about a third cheaper than it would cost these people to live if they kept house. Funny! It took nearly twenty years to prove that organization in housekeeping paid, like any other form of organized labor. Wages have risen, all the work is better done and it costs much less. You can see all that. But what you can't possibly realize is the difference it makes to women. All the change the men feel is in better food, no fret and worry at home, and smaller bills."

"That's something," I modestly suggested.

"Yes, that's a good deal; but to the women it's a thousand times more. The women who liked that kind of work are doing it now, as a profession, for reasonable hours and excellent salaries; and the women who did not like it are now free to do the work they are fitted for and enjoy. This is one of our great additions to the world's wealth—freeing so much productive energy. It has improved our health, too. One of the worst causes of disease is mal-position, you know. Almost everybody used to work at what they did not like—and we thought it was beneficial to character!"

I tried without prejudice to realize the new condition, but a house without a housewife, without children, without servants, seemed altogether empty. Nellie reassured me as to the children, however.

"It's no worse than when they went to school, John, not a bit. If you were here at about 9 A.M. you'd see the mothers taking a morning walk, or ride if it's stormy, to the child-garden, and leaving the babies there, asleep mostly. There are seldom more than five or six real little ones at one time in a group like this."

"Do mothers leave their nursing babies there?"

"Sometimes; it depends on the kind of work they do. Remember they only have to work two hours, and many mothers get ahead on their work and take a year off at baby time. Still, two hours work a day that one enjoys, does not hurt even a nursing mother."

I found it extremely difficult from the first, to picture a world whose working day was but two hours long; or even the four hours they told me was generally given.

"What do people do with the rest of their time; working people, I mean?" I asked.

"The old ones usually rest a good deal, loaf, visit one another, play games, in some cases they travel. Others, who have the working habit ingrained, keep on in the afternoon; in their gardens often; almost all old people love gardening; and those who wish, have one now, you see. The city ones do an astonishing amount of reading, studying, going to lectures, and the theatres. They have a good time."

"But I mean the low rowdy common people—don't they merely loaf and get drunk?"

Nellie smiled at me good humoredly.

"Some of them did, for a while. But it became increasingly difficult to get drunk. You see, their health was better, with sweeter homes, better food and more pleasure; and except for the dipsomaniacs they improved in their tastes presently. Then their children all made a great advance, under the new educational methods; the women had an immense power as soon as they were independent; and between the children's influence and the woman's *and* the new opportunities, the worst men had to grow better. There was always more recuperative power in people than they were given credit for."

"But surely there were thousands, hundreds of thousands, of hoboes and paupers; wretched, degenerate creatures."

Nellie grew sober. "Yes, there were. One of our inherited handicaps was that great mass of wreckage left over from the foolishness and ignorance of the years behind us. But we dealt very thoroughly with them. As I told you before, hopeless degenerates were promptly and mercifully removed. A large class of perverts were incapacitated for parentage and placed where they could do no harm, and could still have some usefulness and some pleasure. Many proved curable, and were cured. And for the helpless residue; blind and crippled through no fault of their own, a remorseful society provides safety, comfort and care; with all the devices for occupation and enjoyment that our best minds could arrange. These are our remaining asylums; decreasing every year. We don't make that kind of people any more."

We talked as we strolled about, or sat on the stone benches under rose bush or grape vine. The beauty of the place grew on me irresistibly. Each separate family could do as they liked in their own yard, under some restriction from the management in regard to general comfort and beauty. I was always ready to cry out about interference with personal rights; but my sister reminded me that we were not allowed to "commit a nuisance" in the old days, only our range of objections had widened. A disagreeable noise is now prohibited, as much as a foul smell; and conspicuously ugly forms and colors, also.

"And who decides—who's your dictator and censor?"

"Our best judges—we elect, recall and change them. But under their guidance we have developed some general sense of beauty. People would complain loudly now of what did not use to trouble them at all."

Then I remembered that I had seen no row of wooden cows in the green meadows, no invitation to "meet me at the fountain," no assailing finger to assure me that my credit was good, no gross cathartic reminders, nothing anywhere to mar the beauty of the landscape; but many a graceful gate, temple-like summer houses crowning the grassy hills, arbors, pergolas, cool seats by stone-rimmed fountains, signs everywhere of the love of beauty and the power to make it.

"I don't see yet how you ever manage to pay for all this extra work everywhere. I suppose in a place like this it comes out of the profit made on food," I suggested.

"No—the gardening expenses of these home clubs come out of the rent."

"And what rent do they have to pay—approximately?"

"I can tell you exactly about this place, because it was opened by a sort of stock company of women, and I was in it for a while. The land cost $100.00 an acre then—$30,000.00. To get it in shape cost $10,000.00, to build thirty of these houses about $4,000.00 apiece—there was great saving in doing it all at one time, the guest-house, furnished, was only $50,000.00, it is very simple, you see; and the general plant and child-garden, and everything else, some $40,000.00 more. I know we raised a capital of $250,000.00, and used it all. The residents pay $600.00 a year for house-rent and $100.00 more for club privileges. That is $28,000.00. We take 4 per cent, and it leaves plenty for taxes and up-keep. Those who have children keep up the child-garden. The hotel makes enough to keep everything going easily, and the food and service departments pay handsomely. Why, if these people had kept on living in New York, it would have cost them altogether at least $8,000.00 a year. Here it just costs them about $2,000.00—and just see what they get for it."

I had an inborn distrust of my sister's figures, and consulted Owen later; also Hallie, who had much detailed knowledge on the subject; and furthermore I did some reading.

There was no doubt about it. The method of living of which we used to be so proud, for which I still felt a deep longing, was abominably expensive. Much smaller amounts, wisely administered, produced better living, and for the life of me I could not discover the cackling herds of people I had been led to expect when such "Utopian schemes" used to be discussed in my youth.

From the broad, shady avenues of this quiet place we looked over green hedges or wire fences thick with honeysuckle and rose, into pleasant home-like gardens where families sat on broad piazzas, swung in hammocks, played tennis, ball, croquet, tether-ball and badminton, just as families used to.

Groups of young girls or young men—or both—strolled under the trees and disported themselves altogether as I remembered them to have done, and happy children frolicked about in the houses and gardens, all the more happily, it would appear, because they had their own place for part of the day.

We had seen the fathers come home in time for the noon meal. In the afternoon most of the parents seemed to think it the finest thing in the world to watch their children learning or playing together, in that amazing Garden of theirs, or to bring them home for more individual companionship. As a matter of fact, I had never seen, in any group of homes that I could recall, so much time given to children by so many parents—unless on a Sunday in the suburbs.

I was very silent on the way back, revolving these things in my mind. Point by point it seemed so vividly successful, so plainly advantageous, so undeniably enjoyed by those who lived there; and yet the old objections surged up continually.

The "noisy crowd all herding together to eat!"—I remembered Mrs. Masson's quiet dining-room—they all had dining-rooms, it appeared. The "dreadful separation of children from their parents!" I thought of all those parents watching with intelligent interest their children's guarded play, or enjoying their companionship at home.

The "forced jumble with disagreeable neighbors!" I recalled those sheltered quiet grounds; each house with its trees and lawn, its garden and its outdoor games.

It was against all my habits, principles, convictions, theories, and sentiments; but there it was, and they seemed to like it. Also, Owen assured me, it paid.

Chapter VIII

After all, it takes time for a great change in world-thought to strike in. That's what Owen insisted on calling it. He maintained that the amazing uprush of these thirty years was really due to the wholesale acceptance and application of the idea of evolution.

"I don't know which to call more important—the new idea, or the new power to use it," he said. "When we were young, practically all men of science accepted the evolutionary theory of life; and it was in general popular favor, though little understood. But the governing ideas of all our earlier time were so completely out of touch with life; so impossible of any useful application, that the connection between belief and behavior was rusted out of us. Between our detached religious ideas and our brutal ignorance of brain culture, we had made ourselves preternaturally inefficient.

"Then—you remember the talk there was about Mental Healing—'Power in Repose'—'The Human Machine'—or was that a bit later? Anyway, people had begun to waken up to the fact that they could do things with their brains. At first they used them only to cure diseases, to maintain an artificial 'peace of mind,' and tricks like that. Then it suddenly burst upon us—two or three important books came along nearly at once, and hosts of articles—that we could use this wonderful mental power every day, to *live* with! That all these scientific facts and laws had an application to life— human life."

I nodded appreciatively. I was getting quite fond of my brother-in-law. We were in a small, comfortable motor boat, gliding swiftly and noiselessly up the beautiful Hudson. Its blue cleanness was a joy. I could see fish— real fish—in the clear water when we were still.

The banks were one long succession of gardens, palaces, cottages and rich woodlands, charming to view.

"It's the *time* that puzzles me more than anything," I said, "even more than the money. How on earth so much could be done in so little time!"

"That's because you conceive of it as being done in one place after another, instead of in every place at once," Owen replied. "If one city, in one year, could end the smoke nuisance, so could all the cities on earth, if they chose to. We chose to, all over the country, practically at once."

"But you speak of evolution. Evolution is the slowest of slow processes. It took us thousands of dragging years to evolve the civilization of 1910, and you show me a 1940 that seems thousands of years beyond that."

72

"Yes; but what you call 'evolution' was that of unaided nature. Social evolution is a distinct process. Below us, you see, all improvements had to be built into the stock—transmitted by heredity. The social organism is open to lateral transmission—what we used to call education. We never understood it. We thought it was to supply certain piles of information, mostly useless; or to develop certain qualities."

"And what do you think it is now?" I asked.

"We know now that *the* social process is to constantly improve and develop society. This has a necessary corollary of improvement in individuals; but the thing that matters most is growth in the social spirit—and body."

"You're beyond me now, Owen."

"Yes; don't you notice that ever since you began to study our advance, what puzzles you most is not the visible details about you, but a changed spirit in people? Thirty years ago, if you showed a man that some one had dumped a ton of soot in his front yard he would have been furious, and had the man arrested and punished. If you showed him that numbers of men were dumping thousands of tons of soot all over his city every year, he would have neither felt nor acted. It's the other way, now."

"You speak as if man had really learned to 'love his neighbor as himself,'" I said sarcastically.

"And why not? If you have a horse, on whose strength you absolutely depend to make a necessary journey, you take good care of that horse and grow fond of him. It dawned on us at last that life was not an individual affair: that other people were essential to our happiness—to our very existence. We are not what they used to call 'altruistic' in this. We do not think of 'neighbors,' 'brothers,' 'others' any more. It is all 'ourself.'"

"I don't follow you—sorry."

Owen grinned at me amiably. "No matter, old chap, you can see results, and will have to take the reasons on trust. Now here's this particular river with its natural beauties, and its unnatural defilements. We simply stopped defiling it—and one season's rain did the rest."

"Did the rains wash away the railroads?"

"Oh, no—they are there still. But the use of electric power has removed the worst evils. There is no smoke, dust, cinders, and a yearly saving of millions in forest fires on the side! Also very little noise. Come and see the way it works now."

73

We ran in at Yonkers. I wouldn't have known the old town. It was as beautiful as Posilipo.

"Where are the factories?" I asked.

"There—and there—and there."

"Why, those are palaces!"

"Well? Why not? Why shouldn't people work in palaces? It doesn't cost any more to make a beautiful building than an ugly one. Remember, we are much richer, now—and have plenty of time, and the spirit of beauty is encouraged."

I looked at the rows of quiet, stately buildings; wide windowed; garden-roofed.

"Electric power there too?" I suggested.

Owen nodded again. "Everywhere," he said. "We store electricity all the time with windmills, water-mills, tide-mills, solar engines—even hand power."

"What!"

"I mean it," he said. "There are all kinds of storage batteries now. Huge ones for mills, little ones for houses; and there are ever so many people whose work does not give them bodily exercise, and who do not care much for games. So we have both hand and foot attachments; and a vigorous man, or woman—or child, for that matter, can work away for half an hour, and have the pleasant feeling that the power used will heat the house or run the motor."

"Is that why I don't smell gasoline in the streets?"

"Yes. We use all those sloppy, smelly things in special places—and apply all the power by electric storage mostly. You saw the little batteries in our boat."

Then he showed me the railroad. There were six tracks, clean and shiney—thick turf between them.

"The inside four are for the special trains—rapid transit and long distance freight. The outside two are open to anyone."

We stopped long enough to see some trains go by; the express at an incredible speed, yet only buzzing softly; and the fast freight; cars seemingly of aluminum, like a string of silver beads.

"We use aluminum for almost everything. You know it was only a question of power—the stuff is endless," Owen explained.

And all the time, on the outside tracks, which had a side track at every station, he told me, ran single coaches or short trains, both passenger and freight, at a comfortable speed.

"All kinds of regular short-distance traffic runs this way. It's a great convenience. But the regular highroads are the best. Have you noticed?"

I had seen from the air-motor how broad and fine they looked, but told him I had made no special study of them.

"Come on—while we're about it," he said; and called a little car. We ran up the hills to Old Broadway, and along its shaded reaches for quite a distance. It was broad, indeed. The center track, smooth, firm, and dustless, was for swift traffic of any sort, and well used. As the freight wagons were beautiful to look at and clean, they were not excluded, and the perfect road was strong enough for any load. There were rows of trees on either side, showing a good growth, though young yet; then a narrower roadway for slower vehicles, on either side a second row of trees, the footpaths, and the outside trees.

"These are only about twenty-five years old. Don't you think they are doing well?"

"They are a credit to the National Bureau of Highways and Arboriculture that I see you are going to tell me about."

"You *are* getting wise," Owen answered, with a smile. "Yes—that's what does it. And it furnishes employment, I can tell you. In the early morning these roads are alive with caretakers. Of course the bulk of the work is done by running machines; but there is a lot of pruning and trimming and fighting with insects. Among our richest victories in that line is the extermination of the gipsy moth—brown tail—elm beetle and the rest."

"How on earth did you do that?"

"Found the natural devourer—as we did with the scale pest. Also by raising birds instead of killing them; and by swift and thorough work in the proper season. We gave our minds to it, you see, at last."

The outside path was a delightful one, wide, smooth, soft to the foot, agreeable in color.

"What do you make your sidewalk of?" I asked.

Owen tapped it with his foot. "It's a kind of semi-flexible concrete—wears well, too. And we color it to suit ourselves, you see. There was no real reason why a path should be ugly to look at."

Every now and then there were seats; also of concrete, beautifully shaped and too heavy to be easily moved. A narrow crack ran along the lowest curve.

"That keeps 'em dry," said Owen.

Drinking fountains bubbled invitingly up from graceful standing basins, where birds drank and dipped in the overflow.

"Why, these are fruit trees," I said suddenly, looking along the outside row.

"Yes, nearly all of them, and the next row are mostly nut trees. You see, the fruit trees are shorter and don't take the sun off. The middle ones are elms wherever elms grow well. I tell you, John, it is the experience of a lifetime to take a long motor trip over the roads of America! You can pick your climate, or run with the season. Nellie and I started once from New Orleans in February—the violets out. We came north with them; I picked her a fresh bunch every day!"

He showed me the grape vines trained from tree to tree in Tuscan fashion; the lines of berry bushes, and the endless ribbon of perennial flowers that made the final border of the pathway. On its inner side were beds of violets, lilies of the valley, and thick ferns; and around each fountain were groups of lilies and water-loving plants.

I shook my head.

"I don't believe it," I said. "I *simply don't believe it!* How could any nation afford to keep up such roads!"

Owen drew me to a seat—we had dismounted to examine a fountain and see the flowers. He produced pencil and paper.

"I'm no expert," he said. "I can't give you exact figures. But I want you to remember that the trees pay. Pay! These roads, hundreds of thousands of miles of them, constitute quite a forest, and quite an orchard. Nuts, as Hallie told you, are in growing use as food. We have along these roads, as beautiful clean shade trees, the finest improved kinds of chestnut, walnut, butternut, pecan—whatever grows best in the locality."

And then he made a number of startling assertions and computations, and showed me the profit per mile of two rows of well-kept nut trees.

"I suppose Hallie has told you about tree farming?" he added.

"She said something about it—but I didn't rightly know what she meant."

"Oh, it's a big thing; it has revolutionized agriculture. As you're sailing over the country now you don't see so many bald spots. A healthy, permanent world has to keep its fur on."

I was impressed by that casual remark, "As you're sailing over the country."

"Look here, Owen, I think I have the glimmer of an idea. Didn't the common use of airships help to develop this social consciousness you're always talking about—this general view of things?"

He clapped me on the shoulder. "You're dead right, John—it did, and I don't believe any of us would have thought to mention it." He looked at me admiringly. "Behold the power of a naturally strong mind—in spite of circumstances! Yes, really that's a fact. You see few people are able to visualize what they have not seen. Most of us had no more idea of the surface of the earth than an ant has of a meadow. In each mind was only a thready fragment of an idea of the world—no real geographic *view*. And when we got flying all over it commonly, it became real and familiar to us—like a big garden.

"I guess that helped on the tree idea. You see, in our earlier kind of agriculture the first thing we did was to cut down the forest, dig up and burn over, plow, harrow, and brush fine—to plant our little grasses. All that dry, soft, naked soil was helplessly exposed to the rain—and the rain washed it steadily away. In one heavy storm soil that it had taken centuries of forest growth to make would be carried off to clog the rivers and harbors. This struck us all at once as wasteful. We began to realize that food could grow on trees as well as grasses; that the cubic space occupied by a chestnut tree could produce more bushels of nutriment than the linear space below it. Of course we have our wheat fields yet, but around every exposed flat acreage is a broad belt of turf and trees; every river and brook is broadly bordered with turf and trees, or shrubs. We have stopped soil waste to a very great extent. Also we make soil—but that is a different matter."

"Hurrying Mother Nature again, eh?"

"Yes, the advance in scientific agriculture is steady. Don't you remember that German professor who raised all kinds of things in water? Just fed them a pinch of chemicals now and then? They said he had a row of trees before his door with their roots in barrels of water—the third generation that had never touched ground! We kept on studying, and began to learn how to put together the proper kind of soil for different kinds of plants. Rock-crushers furnished the basis, then add the preferred constituents and sell, by the bag or the ship load. You can have a radish bed in a box on your window sill, if you like radishes, that will raise you the fattest, sweetest, juiciest, crispiest, tenderest little pink beauties you ever saw— all the year round. No weed seeds in that soil, either."

We rolled slowly back in the green shade. There was plenty of traffic, but all quiet, orderly, and comfortable. The people were a constant surprise to me. They were certainly better looking, even the poorest. And on the faces of the newest immigrants there was an expression of blazing hope that was almost better than the cheery peacefulness of the native born.

Wherever I saw workmen, they worked swiftly, with eager interest. Nowhere did I see the sagging slouch, the slow drag of foot and dull swing of arm which I had always associated with day laborers. We saw men working in the fields—and women, too; but I had learned not to lay my neck on the block too frequently. I knew that my protest would only bring out explanations of the advantage of field work over house work—and that women were as strong as men—or thereabouts. But I was surprised at their eagerness.

"They look as busy as a lot of ants on an ant heap," I said.

"It's their heap, you see," Owen answered. "And they are not tired—that makes a great difference."

"They seem phenomenally well dressed—looks like a scene in an opera. Sort of agricultural uniform?"

"Why not?" Owen was always asking me "why not"—and there wasn't any answer to it. "We used to have hunting suits and fishing suits and yachting suits; now we have farming suits and plumbing suits and so on. It isn't really a uniform, just the natural working out of the best appointed dress for the trade."

Again I held my tongue; not asking how they could afford it, but remembering the shorter hours, the larger incomes, the more universal education.

We got back to Yonkers, put up the car—these things could be hired, I found, for twenty-five cents an hour—and had lunch in a little eating place which bore out Hallie's statement as to the high standard of food everywhere. Our meal was twenty-five cents for each of us. I saw Owen smile at me, but I refused to be surprised. We settled down in our boat again, and pushed smoothly up the river.

"I wish you'd get one thing clear in my mind," I said at last. "Just how did you tackle the liquor question. I haven't seen a saloon—or a drunken man.

Nellie said something about people's not wanting to drink any more—but there were several millions who did want to, thirty years ago, and plenty of people who wanted them to. What were your steps?"

"The first step was to eliminate the self-interest of the dealer—the big business pressure that had to make drunkards. That was done in state after state, within a few years, by introducing government ownership and management. With that went an absolute government guarantee of purity. In five or six years there was no bad liquor sold, and no public drinking places except government ones.

"But that wasn't enough—not by a long way. It wasn't the love of liquor that supported the public house—it was the need of the public house itself."

I stared rather uncertainly.

"The meeting place," he went on. "Men have to get together. We have had public houses as long as we have had private ones, almost. It is a social need."

"A social need with a pretty bad result, it seems to me," I said. "Taking men away from their families, leading to all manner of vicious indulgence."

"Yes, they used to; but that was because only men used them. I said a social need, not a masculine one. We have met it in this way. Whenever we build private houses—if it is the lowest country unit, or the highest city block, we build accommodations for living together.

"Every little village has its Town House, with club rooms of all sorts; the people flock together freely, for games, for talk, for lectures, and plays, and dances, and sermons—it is universal. And in the city—you don't see a saloon on every corner, but you do see almost as many places where you can 'meet a man' and talk with him on equal ground."

"Meet a woman, too?" I suggested.

"Yes; especially, yes. People can meet, as individuals or in groups, freely and frequently, in city or country. But men can not flock by themselves in special places provided for their special vices—without taking a great deal of extra trouble."

"I should think they would take the trouble, then," said I.

"But why? When there is every arrangement made for a natural good time; when you are not overworked, not underfed, not miserable and hopeless. When you can drop into a comfortable chair and have excellent food and drink in pleasant company; and hear good music, or speaking, or reading, or see pictures; or, if you like, play any kind of game; swim, ride, fly, do what you want to, for change and recreation—why long for liquor in a low place?"

"But the men—the real men, people as they were," I insisted. "You had a world full of drinking men who liked the saloon; did you—what do you call it?—eliminate them?"

"A few of them, yes," he replied gravely. "Some preferred it; others, thorough-going dipsomaniacs, we gave hospital treatment and permanent restraint; they lived and worked and were well provided for in places where there was no liquor. But there were not many of that kind. Most men drank under a constant pressure of conditions driving them to it, and the mere force of habit.

"Just remember that the weight and terror of life is lifted off us—for good and all."

"Socialism, you mean?"

"Yes, real socialism. The wealth and power of all of us belongs to all of us now. The Wolf is dead."

"Other things besides poverty drove a man to drink in my time," I ventured.

"Oh, yes—and some men continued to drink. I told you there was liquor to be had—good liquor, too. And other drug habits held on for a while. But we stopped the source of the trouble. The old men died off, the younger ones got over it, and the new ones—that's what you don't realize yet: We make a new kind of people now."

He was silent, his strong mouth set in a kind smile, his eyes looking far up the blue river.

"Well, what comes next? What's done it?" I demanded. "Religion, education, or those everlasting women?"

He laughed outright; laughed till the boat rocked.

"How you do hate to admit that it's their turn, John! Haven't we had full swing—everything in our hands—for all historic time? They have only begun. Thirty years? Why, John, they have done so much in these thirty years that the world's heart is glad at last. You don't know—"

I didn't know. But I did feel a distinct resentment at being treated like an extinct species.

"They have simply stepped on to an eminence men have been all these years building," I said. "We have done all the hard work—the rough work—the dangerous work—are doing it yet, for all I see. We have made it possible for them to live at all! We have made the whole civilization of the world—they just profit by it. And now you speak as if, somehow, they had managed to achieve more than we have!"

Owen considered a while thoughtfully. "What you say is true. We have done a good deal of the work; we did largely make and modify our civilization. But if you read some of the newer histories—" he stopped and looked at me as if I had just happened. "Why you don't know yet, do you? History has been rewritten."

"You speak as if 'history' was a one act play."

"I don't mean it's all done, of course—but we do have now a complete new treatment of the world's history. Each nation its own, some several of them, there's no dead level of agreement, I assure you. But our old androcentric version of life began to be questioned about 1910, I think—and new versions appeared, more and more of them. The big scholars took it up, there was new research work, and now we are not so glib in our assurance that we did it all."

"You're getting pretty close to things I used to know something about," I remarked drily.

"If you knew all that was known, then, you wouldn't know this, John. Don't you remember what Lester Ward calls 'the illusion of the near'—how the most familiar facts were precisely those we often failed to understand? In all our history, ancient and modern, we had the underlying assumption that men were the human race, the people who did things; and that women—were 'their women.'"

"And precisely what have you lately discovered? That Horatio at the bridge was Horatia, after all? That the world was conquered by an Alexandra—and a Napoleona?" I laughed with some bitterness.

"No," said Owen gently, "There is no question about the battles—men did the fighting, of course. But we have learned that 'the decisive battles of history' were not so decisive as we thought them. Man, as a destructive agent did modify history, unquestionably. What did make history, make civilization, was constructive industry. And for many ages women did most of that."

"Did women build the Pyramids? the Acropolis? the Roads of Rome?"

"No, nor many other things. But they gave the world its first start in agriculture and the care of animals; they clothed it and fed it and ornamented it and kept it warm; their ceaseless industry made rich the simple early cultures. Consider—without men, Egypt and Assyria could not have fought—but they could have grown rich and wise. Without women—they could have fought until the last man died alone—if the food held out.

"But I won't bother you with this, John. You'll get all you want out of books better than I can give it. What I set out to say was that the most important influence in weeding out intemperance was that of the women."

I was in a very bad temper by this time, it was disagreeable enough to have this—or any other part of it, true; but what I could not stand was to see that big hearted man speak of it in such a cheerful matter of fact way.

"Have the men of today no pride?" I asked. "How can you stand it—being treated as inferiors—by women?"

"Women stood it for ten thousand years," he answered, "being treated as inferiors—by men."

We went home in silence.

Chapter IX

I learned to understand the immense material prosperity of the country much more easily than its social progress.

The exquisite agriculture which made millions of acres from raw farms and ranches into rich gardens; the forestry which had changed our straggling woodlands into great tree-farms, yielding their steady crops of cut boughs, thinned underbrush, and full-grown trunks; those endless orchard roads, with their processions of workers making continual excursions in their special cars, keeping roadway and bordering trees in perfect order—all this one could see.

There were, of course, far more of the wilder, narrower roads, perfect as to roadbed, but not parked, with all untrimmed nature to travel through.

The airships did make a difference. To look down on the flowing, outspread miles beneath gave a sense of the unity and continuous beauty of our country, quite different from the streak views we used to get. An airship is a moving mountain-top.

The cities were even more strikingly beautiful, in that the change was greater, the contrast sharper. I never tired of wandering about on foot along the streets of cities, and I visited several, finding, as Nellie said, that it took no longer to improve twenty than one; the people in each could do it as soon as they chose to.

But what made them choose? What had got into the people? That was what puzzled me most. It did not show outside, like the country changes, and the rebuilt cities; the people did not look remarkable, though they were different, too. I watched and studied them, trying to analyze the changes that could be seen. Most visible was cleanliness, comfort, and beauty in dress.

I had never dreamed of the relief to the spectator in not seeing any poverty. We were used to it, of course; we had our excuses, religious and economic; we even found, or thought we found, artistic pleasure in this social disease. But now I realized what a nightmare it had been—the sights, the sounds, the smells of poverty—merely to an outside observer.

These people had good bodies, too. They were not equally beautiful, by any means; thirty years, of course, could not wholly return to the normal a race long stunted and overworked. But in the difference in the young generation I could see at a glance the world's best hope, that the "long inheritance" is far deeper than the short.

Those of about twenty and under, those who were born after some of these changes had been made, were like another race. Big, sturdy, blooming creatures, boys and girls alike, swift and graceful, eager, happy, courteous—I supposed at first that these were the children of exceptionally placed people; but soon found, with a heart-stirring sort of shock, that all the children were like that.

Some of the old folk still carried the scars of earlier conditions, but the children were new people.

Then of my own accord I demanded reasons. Nellie laughed sweetly.

"I'm so glad you've come to your appetite," she said. "I've been longing to talk to you about that, and you were always bored."

"It's a good deal of a dose, Nell; you'll admit that. And one hates to be forcibly fed. But now I do want to get an outline, a sort of general idea, of what you do with children. Can you condense a little recent history, and make it easy to an aged stranger?"

"Aged! You are growing younger every day, John. I believe that comparatively brainless life you led in Tibet was good for you. That was all new impression on the brain; the first part rested. Now you are beginning where you left off. I wish you would recognize that."

I shook my head. "Never mind me, I'm trying not to think of my chopped-off life; but tell me how you manufacture this kind of people."

My sister sat still, thinking, for a little. "I want to avoid repetition if possible—tell me just how much you have in mind already." But I refused to be catechised.

"You put it all together, straight; I want to get the whole of it—as well as I can."

"All right. On your head be it. Let me see—first—Oh, there isn't any first, John! We were doing ever so much for children before you left—before you and I were born! It is the vision of all the great child-lovers; that children are people, and the most valuable people on earth. The most important thing to a child is its mother. We made new mothers for them— I guess that is 'first.'

"Suppose we begin this way:

"a. Free, healthy, independent, intelligent mothers.

"b. Enough to live on—right conditions for child-raising.

"c. Specialized care.

84

"d. The new social consciousness, with its religion, its art, its science, its civics, its industry, its wealth, its brilliant efficiency. That's your outline."

I set down these points in my notebook.

"An excellent outline, Nellie. Now for details on 'a.' I will set my teeth till that's over."

My sister regarded me with amused tenderness. "How you do hate the new women, John—in the abstract! I haven't seen you averse to any of them in the concrete!"

At the time I refused to admit any importance to this remark, but I thought it over later—and to good purpose. It was true. I did hate the new kind of human being who loomed so large in every line of progress. She jarred on every age-old masculine prejudice—she was not what woman used to be. And yet—as Nellie said—the women I met I liked.

"Get on with the lesson, my dear," said I. "I am determined to learn and not to argue. What did your omnipresent new woman do to improve the human stock so fast?"

Then Nellie settled down in earnest and gave me all I wanted—possibly more.

"They wakened as if to a new idea, to their own natural duty as mothers; to the need of a high personal standard of health and character in both parents. That gave us a better start right away—clean-born, vigorous children, inheriting strength and purity.

"Then came the change in conditions, a change so great you've hardly glimpsed it yet. No more, never more again, please God, that brutal hunger and uncertainty, that black devil of want and fear. Everybody—everybody—sure of decent living! That one thing lifted the heaviest single shadow from the world, and from the children.

"Nobody is overworked now. Nobody is tired, unless they tire themselves unnecessarily. People live sanely, safely, easily. The difference to children, both in nature and nurture, is very great. They all have proper nourishment, and clothing, and environment—from birth.

"And with that, as advance in special conditions for child-culture, we build for babies now. We, as a community, provide suitably for our most important citizens."

At this point I opened my mouth to say something, but presently shut it again.

"Good boy!" said Nellie. "I'll show you later."

"The next is specialized care. That one thing is enough, almost, to account for it all. To think of all the ages when our poor babies had no benefit at all of the advance in human intelligence!

"We had the best and wisest specialists we could train and hire in every other field of life—and the babies left utterly at the mercy of amateurs!

"Well, I mustn't stop to rage at past history. We do better now. John, guess the salary of the head of the Baby Gardens in a city?"

"Oh, call it a million, and go on," I said cheerfully; which somewhat disconcerted her.

"It's as big a place as being head of Harvard College," she said, "and better paid than that used to be. Our very highest and finest people study for this work. Real geniuses, some of them. The babies, all the babies, mind you, get the benefit of the best wisdom we have. And it grows fast. We are learning by doing it. Every year we do better. 'Growing up' is an easier process than it used to be."

"I'll have to accept it for the sake of argument," I agreed. "It's the last point I care most for, I think. All these new consciousnesses you were so glib about. I guess you can't describe that so easily."

She grew thoughtful, rocking to and fro for a few moments.

"No," she said at length, "it's not so easy. But I'll try. I wasn't very glib, really. I spoke of religion, art, civics, science, industry, wealth, and efficiency, didn't I? Now let's see how they apply to the children.

"This religion—Dear me, John! am I to explain the greatest sunburst of truth that that ever was—in two minutes?"

"Oh, no," I said loftily. "I'll give you five! You've got to try, anyway."

So she tried.

"In place of Revelation and Belief," she said slowly, "we now have Facts and Knowledge. We used to believe in God—variously, and teach the belief as a matter of duty. Now we know God, as much as we know anything else—more than we know anything else—it is The Fact of Life.

"This is the base of knowledge, underlying all other knowledge, simple and safe and sure—and we can teach it to children! The child mind, opening to this lovely world, is no longer filled with horrible or ridiculous old ideas—it learns to know the lovely truth of life."

She looked so serenely beautiful, and sat so still after she said this, that I felt a little awkward.

"I don't mean to jar on you, Nellie," I said. "I didn't know you were so— religious."

Then she laughed again merrily. "I'm not," she said. "No more than anybody is. We don't have 'religious' people any more, John. It's not a separate thing; a 'body of doctrine' and set of observances—it is what all of us have at the bottom of everything else, the underlying basic fact of life. And it goes far, very far indeed, to make the strong good cheer you see in these children's faces.

"They have never been frightened, John. They have never been told any of those awful things we used to tell them. There is no struggle with church-going, no gagging over doctrines, no mysterious queer mess—only life. Life is now open to our children, clear, brilliant, satisfying, and yet stimulating.

"Of course, I don't mean that this applies equally to every last one. The material benefit does, that could be enforced by law where necessary; but this world-wave of new knowledge is irregular, of course. It has spread wider, and gone faster than any of the old religions ever did, but you can find people yet who believe things almost as dreadful as father did!"

I well remembered my father's lingering Calvinism, and appreciated its horrors.

"Our educators have recognized a new duty to children," Nellie went on; "to stand between them and the past. We recognize that the child mind should lift and lead the world; and we feed it with our newest, not our oldest ideas.

"Also we encourage it to wander on ahead, fearless and happy. I began to tell you the other day—and you snubbed me, John, you did really!—that we have a new literature for children, and have dropped the old."

At this piece of information I could no longer preserve the attitude of a patient listener. I sat back and stared at my sister, while the full awfulness of this condition slowly rolled over me.

"Do you mean," I said slowly, "that children are taught nothing of the past?"

"Oh, no, indeed; they are taught about the past from the earth's beginning. In the mind of every child is a clear view of how Life has grown on earth."

"And our own history?"

"Of course; from savagery to to-day—that is a simple story, endlessly interesting as they grow older."

"What do you mean, then, by cutting off the past?"

"I mean that their stories, poems, pictures, and the major part of their instruction deals with the present and future—especially the future. The whole teaching is dynamic—not static. We used to teach mostly facts, or what we thought were facts. Now we teach processes. You'll find out if you talk to children, anywhere."

This I mentally determined to do, and in due course did. I may as well say right here that I found children more delightful companions than they used to be. They were polite enough, even considerate; but so universally happy, so overflowing with purposes, so skillful in so many ways, so intelligent and efficient, that it astonished me. We used to have a sort of race-myth about "happy childhood," but none of us seemed to study the faces of the children we saw about us. Even among well-to-do families, the discontented, careworn, anxious, repressed, or rebellious faces of children ought to have routed our myth forever.

Timid, brow-beaten children, sulky children, darkly resentful; nervous, whining children; foolish, mischievous, hysterically giggling children; noisy, destructive, uneasy children—how well I remembered them.

These new ones had a strange air of being Persons, not subordinates and dependents, but Equals; their limitations frankly admitted, but not cast up at them, and their special powers fully respected. That was it!

I am wandering far ahead of that day's conversation, but it led to wide study among children, analysis, and some interesting conclusions. When I hit on this one I began to understand. Children were universally respected, and they liked it. In city or country, place was made for them; permanent, pleasant, properly appointed place; to use, enjoy, and grow up in. They had their homes and families as before, losing nothing; but they added to this background their own wide gardens and houses, where part of each day was spent.

From earliest infancy they absorbed the idea that home was a place to come out from and go back to; the sweetest, dearest place—for there was mother, and father, and one's own little room to sleep in; but the day hours were to go somewhere to learn and do, to work and play, to grow in.

I branched off from Nellie's startling me with her "new-literature-for-children" idea. She went on to explain it further.

"The greatest artists work for children now, John," she said. "In the child-gardens and child-homes they are surrounded with beauty. I do not mean that we hire painters and poets to manufacture beauty for them; but that painters and poets, architects and landscape artists, designers and decorators of all kinds, love and revere childhood, and delight to work for it.

"Remember that half of our artists are mothers now—a loving, serving, giving spirit has come into expression—a wider and more lasting expression than it was ever possible to put into doughnuts and embroidery! Wait till you see the beauty of our child-gardens!"

"Why don't you call them schools? Don't you have schools?"

"Some. We haven't wholly outgrown the old academic habit. But for the babies there was no precedent, and they do not 'go to school.'"

"You have a sort of central nursery?" I ventured.

"Not necessarily 'central,' John. And we have great numbers of them. How can I make it any way clear to you? See here. Suppose you were a mother, and a very busy one, like the old woman in the shoe; and suppose you had twenty or thirty permanent babies to be provided for. And suppose you were wise and rich—able to do what you wanted to. Wouldn't you build an elaborate nursery for those children? Wouldn't you engage the very best nurses and teachers? Wouldn't you want the cleanest, quietest garden for them to play or sleep in? Of course you would.

"That is our attitude. We have at last recognized babies as a permanent class. They are always here, about a fifth of the population. And we, their mothers, have at last ensured to these, our babies, the best accommodation known to our time. It improves as we learn, of course."

"Mm!" I said. "I'll go and gaze upon these Infant Paradises later—at the sleeping hour, please! But how about that new literature you frightened me with?"

"O why, we have tried to treat their minds as we do their stomachs—putting in only what is good for them. I mean the very littlest, understand. As they grow older they have wider range; we have not expunged the world's past, my dear brother! But we do prepare with all the wisdom, love, and power we have, the mental food for little children. Simple, lovely music is about them always—you must have noticed how universally they sing?"

I had, and said so.

"The coloring and decoration of their rooms is beautiful—their clothes are beautiful—and simple—you've seen that, too?"

"Yes, dear girl. It's because I've seen—and heard—and noticed the surprisingness of the New Child that I sit here fairly guzzling information. Pray proceed to the literature."

"Literature is the most useful of the arts—the most perfect medium for transfer of ideas. We wish to have the first impressions in our children's minds, above all things, true. All the witchery and loveliness possible in presentation—but the things presented are not senseless and unpleasant.

"We have plenty of 'true stories,' stories based on real events and on natural laws and processes; but the viewpoint from which they are written has changed; you'll have to read some to see what I mean. But the major difference is in our stories of the future; our future here on earth. They are good stories, mind, the very best writers make them; good verses and pictures, too. And a diet like that, while it is just as varied and entertaining as the 'once upon a time' kind, leaves the child with a sense that things are going to happen—and he, or she, can help.

"You see, we don't consider anything as done. To you, as a new visitor, we 'point with pride,' but among ourselves we 'view with alarm.' We are just as full of Reformers and Propagandists as ever; and overflowing with plans for improvement.

"These are the main characteristics of the new child literature: Truth and Something Better Ahead."

"I don't like it!" I said firmly. "No wonder you dodged about so long. You've apparently made a sort of pap out of Gradgrind and Rollo, and feed it to these poor babies through a tube."

This time my sister rebelled. She came firmly to my side and pulled my hair—precisely as she used to do forty years ago and more—the few little hairs at the crown which still troubled me in brushing—because of being pulled out straight so often.

"You shall have no more oral instruction, young man," said she. "You shall be taken about and shown things; you shall 'Stop! Look! Listen!' until you admit the advantages I have striven in vain to pump into your resisting intellect—you Product of Past Methods!"

"You're the product of the same methods yourself, my dear," I replied amiably; "but I'm quite willing to be shown—always was something of a Missourian."

No part of my re-education was pleasanter, and I'm sure none was more important, than the next few days. We visited place after place, in different cities, or in the country, and everywhere was the same high standard of health and beauty, of comfort, fun, and visible growth.

I saw babies and wee toddlers by the thousands, and hardly ever heard one cry! Out of that mass of experience some vivid pictures remain in my mind. One was "mother time" in a manufacturing village. There was a big group of mills with waterpower; each mill a beautiful, clean place, light, airy, rich in color; sweet with the flowers about it, where men and women worked their two-hour shifts.

The women took off their work-aprons and slipped into the neighboring garden to nurse their babies. They were in no haste. They were pleasantly dressed and well-fed and not tired.

They were known and welcomed by the women in charge of the child-garden; and each mother slipped into a comfortable rocker and took into her arms that little rosy piece of herself and the man she loved—it was a thing to bring one's heart into one's throat. The clean peace and quiet of it: time enough, the pleasant neighborliness, the atmosphere of contented motherhood, those healthy, drowsy little mites, so busy with their dinner.

Then they put them down, asleep for the most part, kissed them, and strolled back to the pleasant workroom for another two hours.

Specialization used to be a terror, when a whole human being was held down to one motion for ten hours. But specialization hurts nobody when it does not last too long.

In the afternoons some mothers took their babies home at once. Some nursed them and then went out together for exercise or pleasure. The homes were clean and quiet, too; no kitchen work, no laundry work, no self-made clutter and dirt. It looked so comfortable that I couldn't believe my eyes, yet it was just common, everyday life.

As the babies grew old enough to move about, their joys widened. They were kept in rooms of a suitable temperature, and wore practically no clothes. This in itself I was told was one main cause of their health and contentment. They rolled and tumbled on smooth mattresses; pulled themselves up and swung back and forth on large, soft horizontal ropes fastened within reach; delightful little bunches of rose leaves and dimples, in perfect happiness.

Very early they had water to play in; clean, shallow pools, kept at a proper temperature, where they splashed and gurgled in rapture, and learned to swim before they learned to walk, sometimes.

As they grew larger and more competent, their playgrounds were more extensive and varied; but the underlying idea was always clear—safety and pleasure, full exercise and development of every power. There was no quarrelling over toys—whatever they had to play with they all had in abundance; and most of the time they did not have exchangeable objects, but these ropes, pools, sand, clay, and so on; materials common to all, and the main joy was in the use of their own little bodies, is as many ways as was possible.

At any time when they were not asleep a procession of crowing toddlers could be seen creeping up a slight incline, and sliding or rolling triumphantly down the other side. A sort of beautified cellar door, this.

Strange that we always punished children for sliding down unsuitable things and never provided suitable ones. But then, of course, one could not have machinery like this in one brief family. Swings, see-saws, all manner of moving things they had; with building-blocks, of course, and balls. But as soon as it was easy to them they had tools and learned to use them; the major joy of their expanding lives was doing things. I speak of them in an unbroken line, for that was the way they lived. Each stage lapped over into the next, and that natural ambition to be with the older ones and do what they did was the main incentive in their progress.

To go on, to get farther, higher; to do something better and more interesting; this was in the atmosphere; growth, exercise, and joy.

I watched and studied, and grew happy as I did so; which I could see was a gratification to Nellie.

"Aren't they ever naughty?" I demanded one day.

"Why should they be?" she answered. "How could they be? What we used to call 'naughtiness' was only the misfit. The poor little things were in the wrong place—and nobody knew how to make them happy. Here there is nothing they can hurt, and nothing that can hurt them. They have earth, air, fire, and water to play with."

"Fire?" I interrupted.

"Yes, indeed. All children love fire, of course. As soon as they can move about they are taught fire."

"How many burn themselves up?"

"None. Never any more. Did you never hear 'a burnt child dreads the fire'? We said that, but we never had sense enough to use it. No proverb ever said 'a whipped child dreads the fire'! We never safeguarded them, and the poor little things were always getting burned to death in our barbarous 'homes'!"

"Do you arbitrarily burn them all?" I asked. "Have an annual 'branding'?"

"Oh, no; but we allow them to burn themselves—within reason. Come and see."

She showed me a set of youngsters learning Heat and Cold, with basins of water, a row of them; eagerly experimenting with cautious little fingers—very cold, cold, cool, tepid, warm, hot, very hot. They could hardly say the words plain, but learned them all, even when they all had to shut their eyes and the basins were changed about.

Straying from house to house, from garden to garden, I watched them grow and learn. On the long walls about them were painted an endless panorama of human progress. When they noticed and asked questions they were told, without emphasis, that people used to live that way; and grew to this—and this.

I found that as the children grew older they all had a year of travel; each human being knew his world. And when I questioned as to expense, as I always did, Nellie would flatten me with things like this:

"Remember that we used to spend 70 per cent of our national income on the expenses of war, past and present. If we women had done no more than save that, it would have paid for all you see."

Or she would remind me again of the immense sums we used to spend on hospitals and prisons; or refer to the general change in economics, that inevitable socialization of industry, which had checked waste and increased productivity so much.

"We are a rich people, John," she repeated. "So are other nations, for that matter; the world's richer. We have increased our output and lowered our expenses at the same time. One of our big present problems is what to do with our big surplus; we quarrel roundly over that. But meanwhile it is a very poor nation indeed that does not provide full education for its children."

I found that the differences in education were both subtle and profound. The babies' experience of group life, as well as the daily return to family life, gave a sure groundwork for the understanding of civics. Their first impressions included other babies; no child grew up with the intensified self-consciousness we used to almost force upon them.

In all the early years learning was ceaseless and unconscious. They grew among such carefully chosen surroundings as made it impossible not to learn what was really necessary; and to learn it as squirrels learn the trees—by playing and working in them. They learned the simple beginnings of the world's great trades, led by natural interest and desire; gathering by imitation and asked instruction.

I saw nowhere the enforced task; everywhere the eager attention of real interest.

"Are they never taught to apply themselves? To concentrate?" I asked. And for answer she showed me the absorbed, breathless concentration of fresh young minds and busy hands.

"But they soon tire of these things and want to do something else, do they not?"

"Of course. That is natural to childhood. And there is always something else for them to do."

"But they are only doing what they like to do—that is no preparation for a life work surely."

"We find it an excellent preparation for life work. You see, we all work at what we like now. That is one reason we do so much better work."

I had talked on this line before with those who explained the workings of industrial socialism.

"Still, as a matter of education," I urged, "is it not necessary for a child to learn to compel himself to work?"

"Oh, no," they told me; and, to say truth, convincingly showed me. "Children like to work. If any one does not, we know he is sick."

And as I saw more and more of the child-gardens, and sat silently watching for well-spent hours, I found how true this was.

The children had around them the carefully planned stimuli of a genuinely educational environment. The work of the world was there, in words of one syllable, as it were; and among wise, courteous, pleasant people, themselves actually doing something, yet always ready to give information when asked.

First the natural appetite of the young brain, then every imaginable convenience for learning, then the cautiously used accessories to encourage further effort; and then these marvelous teachers—who seemed to like their work, too. The majority were women, and of them nearly all were mothers. It appeared that children had not lost their mothers, as at first one assumed, but that each child kept his own and gained others. And these teaching mothers were somehow more motherly than the average.

Nellie was so pleased when I noticed this. She liked to see me "going to school" so regularly. I was not alone in it, either. There seemed to be numbers of people who cared enough for children to enjoy watching them and playing with them. Nobody was worn out with child care. The parents were not—the nurses and teachers had short shifts—it seemed to be considered a pleasure and an honor to be allowed with the little ones.

And in all this widespread, costly, elaborate, and yet perfectly simple and lovely environment, these little New Persons grew and blossomed with that divine unconsciousness which belongs to children.

They did not know that the best intellects were devoted to their service, they never dreamed what thought and love and labor made these wide gardens, these bright playing-places, these endlessly interesting shops where they could learn to make things as soon as they were old enough. They took it all as life—just Life, as a child must take his first environment.

"And don't you think, John," Nellie said, when I spoke of this, "don't you really think this is a more normal environment for a young human soul than a kitchen? Or a parlor? Or even a nursery?"

I had to admit that it had its advantages. As they grew older there was every chance for specialization. In the first years they gathered the rudiments of general knowledge, and of general activity, of both hand and brain; and from infancy each child was studied, and his growth—or hers—carefully recorded; not by adoring, intimately related love, but by that larger, wiser tenderness of these great child-lovers who had had hundreds of them to study.

They were observed intelligently. Notes were made; the mother and father contributed theirs; in freedom and unconsciousness the young nature developed; never realizing how its environment was altered to fit its special needs.

As the cool, spacious, flower-starred, fruitful forests of this time differed from the tangled underbrush, with crooked, crowded, imperfect trees struggling for growth, that I remembered as "woods"; or from clipped and twisted products of the forcing and pruning process; so did the new child-gardens differ from the old schools.

No wonder children wore so different an aspect. They had the fresh, insatiable thirst for knowledge which has been wisely slaked, but never

95

given the water-torture. As I recalled my own youth, and thought of all those young minds set in rows, fixed open as with a stick between the teeth, and forced to drink, drink, drink till all desire was turned to loathing, I felt a sudden wish to be born again—now!—and begin over.

As an adult observer, I found this rearranged world jarring and displeasing in many ways; but as I sat among the children, played with them, talked with them, became somewhat acquainted with their views of things, I began to see that to them the new world was both natural and pleasant.

When they learned that I was a "leftover" from what to them seemed past ages, I became extremely popular. There was a rush to get near me, and eager requests to tell them about old times—checked somewhat by politeness, yet always eager.

But the cheerful pride with which I began to describe the world as I knew it was considerably dashed by their comments. What I had considered as necessary evils, or as no evils at all, to them appeared as silly and disgraceful as cannibalism; and there grew among them an attitude of chivalrous pity for my unfortunate upbringing which was pretty to see.

"I see no child in glasses!" I suddenly remarked one day.

"Of course not," answered the teacher I stood by. "We use books very little, you see. Education no longer impairs our machinery."

I recalled the Boston school children and the myopic victims of Germany's archaic letterpress; and freely admitted that this was advance. Much of the instruction was oral—much, very much, came through games and exercises; books, I found, were regarded rather as things to consult, like a dictionary, or as instruments of high enjoyment.

"School books"—"text books"—scarcely existed, at least for children. The older ones, some of them, plunged into study with passion; but their eyes were good and their brains were strong; also their general health. There was no "breakdown from overstudy"; that slow, cruel, crippling injury— sometimes death, which we, wise and loving parents of past days, so frequently forced upon our helpless children.

Naturally happy, busy, self-respecting, these grew up; with a wide capacity for action, a breadth of general knowledge which was almost incredible, a high standard of courtesy, and vigorous, well-exercised minds. They were trained to think, I found; to question, discuss, decide; they could reason.

And they faced life with such loving enthusiasm! Such pride in the new accomplishments of the world! Such a noble, boundless ambition to do things, to make things, to help the world still further.

And from infancy to adolescence—all through these years of happy growing—there was nothing whatever to differentiate the boys from the girls! As a rule, they could not be distinguished.

Chapter X

It was this new growth of humanity, which made continuing social progress so rapid and so sure.

These young minds had no rubbish in them. They had a vivid sense of the world as a whole, quite beyond their family "relations." They were marvelously reasonable, free from prejudice; able to see and willing to do. And this spreading tide of hope and courage flowed back into the older minds, as well as forward into the new. I found that people's ideas of youth and age had altered materially. Nellie said it was due to the change in women—but then she laid most things to that. She reminded me that women used to be considered only as females, and were "old" when no longer available in that capacity; but that as soon as they recognized themselves as human beings they put "Grandma" into the background, and "Mother" too; and simply went on working and growing and enjoying life up into the lively eighties—even nineties, sometimes.

"Brains do not cease to function at fifty," she said. "Just because a woman is no longer an object to 'fall in love' with, it does not follow that life has no charms for her. Women today have all that they ever had before, all that was good in it; and more, a thousand times more. When the lives of half the world widen like that it widens the other half too."

This quite evidently had happened.

The average mental standard was higher, the outlook broader. I found many very ordinary people, of course; some whose only attitude toward this wonderful new world was to enjoy its advantages; and even some who grumbled. These were either old persons with bad digestions; or new immigrants from very backward countries.

I traveled about, visiting different places, consulting all manner of authorities, making notes, registering objections. It was all interesting, and grew more so as it seemed less strange. My sense of theatrical unreality gave way to a growing appreciation of the universal beauty about me.

Art, I found, held a very different position from what it used to hold. It had joined hands with life again, was common, familiar, used in all things. There were pictures, many and beautiful, but the great word Art was no longer so closely confined to its pictorial form. It was not narrow, expensive, requiring a special education, but part of the atmosphere in which all children grew, all people lived.

For instance the theatre, which I remember as a two-dollar affair, and mainly vulgar and narrow, was now the daily companion and teacher. The historic instinct with which nearly every child is born was cultivated without check. The little ones played through all their first years of instruction, played the old stone age (most natural to them!), the new stone age, the first stages of industry. Older children learned history that way; and as they reached years of appreciation, special dramas were written for them, in which psychology and sociology were learned without hearing their names.

Those happy, busy, eager young things played gaily through wide ranges of human experience; and when these emotions touched them in later years, they were not strange and awful, but easy to understand.

In every smallest village there was a playhouse, not only in the child-gardens, but for the older people. They each had their dramatic company, as some used to have their bands; had their musical companies too, and better ones.

Out of this universal use of the drama rose freely those of special talent who made it the major business of their lives; and the higher average everywhere gave to these greater ones the atmosphere of real appreciation which a growing art must have.

I asked Nellie how the people managed who lived in the real country— remote and alone.

"We don't live that way any more," she said. "Only some stubborn old people, like Uncle Jake and Aunt Dorcas. You see the women decided that they must live in groups to have proper industrial and educational advantages; and they do."

"Where do the men live?" I asked grimly.

"With the women, of course—Where should they? I don't mean that a person cannot go and live in a hut on a mountain, if he likes; we do that in summer, very largely. It is a rest to be alone part of the time. But living, real human living, requires a larger group than one family. You can see the results."

I could and I did; though I would not always admit it to Nellie; and this beautiful commonness of good music, good architecture, good sculpture, good painting, good drama, good dancing, good literature, impressed me increasingly. Instead of those perpendicular peaks of isolated genius we used to have, surrounded by the ignorantly indifferent many, and the excessively admiring few, those geniuses now sloped gently down to the average on long graduated lines of decreasing ability. It gave to the commonest people a possible road of upward development, and to the most developed a path of connection with the commonest people. The geniuses seemed to like it too. They were not so conceited, not so disagreeable, not so lonesome.

People seemed to have a very good time, even while at work; indeed very many found their work more fun than anything else. The abundant leisure gave a sort of margin to life which was wholly new, to the majority at least. It was that spare time, and the direct efforts of the government in wholesale educational lines, which had accomplished so much in the first ten years.

Owen reminded me of the educational vitality even of the years I knew; of the university extension movement, the lectures in the public schools, the push of the popular magazines; the summer schools, the hundreds of thousands of club women, whose main effort seemed to be to improve their minds.

"And the Press," I said—"our splendid Press."

"That was one of our worst obstacles, I'm sorry to say," he answered.

I looked at him. "O go ahead, go ahead! You'll tell me the public schools were an obstacle next."

"They would have been—if we hadn't changed them," he agreed. "But they were in our hands at least, and we got them rearranged very promptly. That absurd old despotism which kept the grade of teachers down so low, was very promptly changed. We have about five times as many teachers now; fifty times as good; and far better paid; not only in cash, but in public appreciation. Our teachers are 'leading citizens' now—we have elected one President from the School Principalship of a state."

This was news, and not unpleasant.

"Have you elected any Editors?"

"No—but we may soon. They are a new set of men now I can tell you; and women, of course. You remember in our day journalism was frankly treated as a trade; whereas it is visibly one of the most important professions."

"And did you so reform those Editors, so that they became as self-sacrificing as country doctors?"

"O no. But we changed the business conditions. It was the advertising that corrupted the papers—mostly; and the advertisers were only screaming for bread and butter—especially butter. When Socialism reorganized business there was no need to scream."

"But I find plenty of advertising in the papers and magazines."

"Certainly—it is a great convenience. Have you studied it?"

I had to own that I had not; particularly—I never did like advertising.

"You'll find it worth reading. In the first place it's all true."

"How do you secure that?"

"We have made lying to the public a crime—don't you remember? Each community has its Board of Standards; there is a constant effort to improve standards you see, in all products; and expert judgment may always be had, for nothing. If any salesman advertises falsely he loses his job, if he's an official; and is posted, if he's selling as a private individual. When the public is told officially that Mr. Jones is a liar it hurts his trade."

"You have a Government Press?"

"Exactly. The Press is preeminently a public function—it is not and never was a private business—not legitimately."

"But you do have private papers and magazines?"

"Yes indeed, lots of them. Ever so many personal 'organs,' large and small. But they don't carry advertising. If enough people will buy a man's paper to pay him, he's quite free to publish."

"How do you prevent his carrying advertising?"

"It's against the law—like any other misdemeanor. Post Office won't take it—he can't distribute. No, if you want to find out about the latest breakfast food—(and there are a score you never heard of)—or the last improvement in fountain pens or airships—you find it all, clear, short, and reliable, in the hotel paper of every town. There's no such bulk of advertising matter now, you see; not so many people struggling to sell the same thing."

"Is all business socialized?"

"Yes—and no. All the main business is; the big assured steady things that our life depends on. But there is a free margin for individual initiative— and always will be. We are not so foolish as to cut off that supply. We have more inventors and idealists than ever; and plenty of chance for trial. You see the two hours a day which pays board, so to speak, leaves plenty of time to do other work; and if the new thing the man does is sufficiently valuable to enough people, he is free to do that alone. Like the little one-man papers I spoke of. If a man can find five thousand people who will pay a dollar a year to read what he says he's quite as likely to make his living that way."

"Have you no competition at all?"

"Plenty of it. All our young folks are racing and chasing to break the record; to do more work, better work, new work."

"But not under the spur of necessity."

"Why, yes they are. The most compelling necessity we know. They *have* to do it; it is in them and must come out."

"But they are all sure of a living, aren't they?"

"Yes, of course. O, I see! What you meant by necessity was hunger and cold. Bless you, John, poverty was no spur. It was a deadly anaesthetic."

I looked my disagreement, and he went on: "You remember the hideous poverty and helplessness of the old days—did that 'spur' the population to do anything? Don't you see, John, that if poverty had been the splendid stimulus it used to be thought, there wouldn't have been any poverty? Some few exceptional persons triumphed in spite of it, but we shall never know the amount of world loss in the many who did not.

"It was funny," he continued meditatively: "how we went on believing that in some mysterious way poverty 'strengthened character,' 'developed initiative,' 'stimulated industry,' and did all manner of fine things; and never turned our eyes on the millions of people who lived and died in poverty with weakened characters, no initiative, a slow, enforced and hated industry. My word, John, what fools we were!"

I was considering this Government Press he described. "How did you dispose of the newspapers you had?"

"Just as we disposed of the saloons; drove them out of business by underselling them with better goods. The laws against lying helped too."

"I don't see how you can stop people's lying."

"We can't stop their lying in private, except by better social standards; but we can stop public lying, and we have. If a paper published a false statement anyone could bring a complaint; and the district attorney was obliged to prosecute. If a paper pleaded ignorance or misinformation it was let off with a fine and a reprimand the first time, a heavy fine the second time, and confiscation the third time; as being proved by their own admission incompetent to tell the truth! If it was shown to be an intentional falsehood they were put out of business at once."

"That's all very pretty," I said, "and sounds easy as you tell it; but what made people so hot about lying? They didn't used to mind it. The more you tell me of these things the more puzzled I am as to what altered the minds of the people. They certainly had to alter considerably from the kind I remember, to even want all these changes, much more to enforce them."

Owen wasn't much of a psychologist, and said so. He insisted that people had wanted better things, only they did not know it.

"Well—what made them know it?" I insisted. "Now here's one thing, small in a way, but showing a very long step in alteration; people dress comfortably and beautifully; almost all of them. What made them do it?"

"They have more money," Owen began, "more leisure and better education."

But I waved this aside.

"That has nothing to do with it. The people with money and education were precisely the ones who wore the most outrageous clothes. And as to leisure—they spent their leisure in getting up foolish costumes, apparently."

"Women are more intelligent, you see," he began again; but I dismissed this also.

"The intelligence of a Lord Chancellor didn't prevent his wearing a wig! How did people break loose from the force of fashion, I want to know?"

He could not make this clear, and said he wouldn't try.

"You show me all these material changes," I went on; "and I can see that there was no real obstacle to them; but the obstacle that lasted so long was in the people's minds. What moved that? Then you show me this marvellous new education, as resulting in new kinds of people, better people, wiser, freer, stronger, braver; and I can see that at work. But how did you come to accept this new education? You needn't lay it all to the women, as Nellie does. I knew one or two of the most advanced of them in 1910, and they had no such world-view as this. They wore foolish clothes and had no ideas beyond 'Votes for Women'—some of them.

"No sir! I admit that there was potential wealth enough in the earth to support all this ease and beauty; and potential energy in the people to produce the wealth. I admit that it was possible for people to leave off being stupid and become wise—evidently they have done so. But I don't see what made them."

"You go and see Dr. Borderson," said Owen.

Chapter XI

Dr. Borderson, it seemed, held the chair in Ethics at the University. I knew a Borderson once and was very fond of him. Poor Frank! If he was alive he would have more likely reached a prison or a hospital than a professorship. Yet he was brilliant enough. We were great friends in college, and before; let me see—thirty-five years ago. But he was expelled for improper conduct, and went from bad to worse. The last I had heard of him was in a criminal case—but he had run away and disappeared. I well remembered the grief and shame it was to me at the time to see such a promising young life ruined and lost so early.

Thinking of this, I was shown into the study of the great teacher of ethics; and as I shook hands I met the keen brown eyes of—Frank Borderson. He had both my hands and shook them warmly.

"Well, John! It is good to see you again. How well you look! How little you have changed! It's a good world you've come back to, isn't it?"

"You are the most astonishing thing I've seen so far," I replied. "Do you really mean it? Are you—a Professor of Ethics?"

"When I used to be a God-forsaken rascal, eh? Yes, it's really so. I've taught Ethics for twenty years, and gradually pushed along to this position. And I was a good deal farther off than Tibet, old man."

I was tremendously glad to see him. It was more like a touch of the old life than anything I had yet found, except Nellie, of course. We spoke for some time of those years of boyhood; of the good times we had had together, of our common friends.

He kept me to dinner; introduced me to his wife, a woman with a rather sad sweet face, which seemed to bear marks of deep experience; and we settled down for an evening's talk.

"I think you have come to the right person, John; not only because of my special studies, but because of my special line of growth. If I can tell you what changed me, so quickly and so wholly, you won't be much puzzled about the others, eh?"

I fully agreed with him. The boy I knew was clever enough to dismiss all theology, to juggle with philosophy and pick ethics to pieces; but his best friends had been reluctantly compelled to admit that he had "no moral character." He had, to my knowledge, committed a number of unquestionable "sins;" and by hearsay I knew of vices and crimes that followed. And he was Dr. Borderson!

104

"I'll take myself as a sample, Whitman fashion," said he. "There I was when you knew me; conceited, ignorant, clever, self-indulgent, weak, sensual, dishonest. After I was turned out of college I broke a good many laws and nearly all the commandments. What was worse—in one way— was that my 'wages' were being paid me in disease—abominable disease. Also I had two drug habits—alcohol and cocaine. Will you take me as a sample?"

I looked at him. He had not the perfect health I saw so much of in the younger people; but he seemed in no way an invalid; much less a drug victim. His eyes were clear and bright, his complexion good, his hand steady, his manner assured and calm.

"Frank," said I, "you beat anything I've seen yet. You stand absolutely to my mind as an illustration of 'Before Taking' and 'After Taking.' Now in the name of reason tell me what it was you Took!"

"I took a new grip on Life—that's the whole answer. But you want to know the steps; and I'll tell you. The new stage of ethical perception we are in now, or, as you would probably say, this new religion, presents itself to me in this way:

"The business of the universe about us consists in the Transmission of Energy. Some of it is temporarily and partially arrested in material compositions; some is more actively expressed in vegetable and animal form; this stage of expression we call Life. We ourselves, the human animals, were specially adapted for high efficiency in storing and transmitting this energy; and so were able to enter into a combination still more efficient; that is, into social relations. Humanity, man in social relation, is the best expression of the Energy that we know. This Energy is what the human mind has been conscious of ever since it was conscious at all; and calls God. The relation between this God and this Humanity is in reality a very simple one. In common with all other life-forms, the human being must express itself in normal functioning. Because of its special faculty of consciousness, this human engine can feel, see, think, about the power within it; and can use it more fully and wisely. All it has to learn is the right expression of its degree of life-force, of Social Energy." He beamed at me. "I think it's about all there, John."

"You may be a very good Professor of Ethics for these new-made minds; but you don't reach the old kind, not a little bit. To my mind you haven't said anything—yet."

He seemed a little disappointed, but took it mildly. "Perhaps I am a little out of touch. Wait a moment—let me go back and try to take up the old

105

attitude."

He leaned back in his chair and shut his eyes. I saw an expression of pain slowly grow and deepen on his face; and suddenly realized what he was doing.

"Oh, never mind, Frank; don't do it; don't try; I'll catch on somehow."

He seemed not to hear me; but dropped his face in his hands. When he raised it it was calm again. "Now I can make things clearer perhaps," he said. "We had in our minds, thirty years ago, a strange hodge-podge of old and new ideas. What was called God was still largely patterned after the old tribal deity of the Hebrews. Our ideas of 'Sin' were still mostly of the nature of disobedience—wrong only because we were told not to do it. Sin as a personal offence against Somebody, and Somebody very much offended; that was it. We were beginning to see something of Social values too, but not clearly. Our progress was in what we called 'The natural sciences;' and we did not think with the part of our minds wherein we stored religion. Yet there was very great activity and progress in religious thought; the whole field was in motion; the new churches widening and growing in every direction; the older ones holding on like grim death, trying not to change, and changing in spite of themselves; and Ethics being taught indeed, but with no satisfying basis. That's the kind of atmosphere you and I grew up in, John. Now here was I, an ill-assorted team of impulses and characteristics, prejudiced against religion, ignorant of real ethics, and generally going to the devil—as we used to call it! You know how far down I went—or something of it."

"Don't speak of it, Frank!" I said. "That was long ago, forget it, old man!" But he turned toward me a smile of triumph.

"Forget it! I wouldn't forget one step of it, if I could! Why, John; it's because of my intimate knowledge of these down-going steps that I can help other people up them!"

"You looked decidedly miserable just now, all the same, when you were thinking them over."

"Oh, bless you, John, I wasn't thinking of myself at all! I was thinking of the awful state of mind the world was in, and how it suffered! Of all the horror and misery and shame; all that misplaced, unnecessary cruelty we called punishment—the Dark Ages we were still in, in spite of all we had to boast of. However, this new perception came."

I interrupted him.

"What came? Who came? Did you have a new revelation? Who did it?

What do you call it? Nobody seems to be able to give me definite information."

He smiled broadly. "You're a beautiful proof of the kind of mental jumble I spoke of. Knowledge of evolution did not come by a revelation, did it? Or did any one man, or two, give it to us? Darwin and Wallace were not the only minds that helped to see and express that great idea; and many more had to spread it. These great truths break into the world mind through various individuals, and coalesce so that we cannot disconnect them. We have had many writers, preachers, lecturers, who discoursed and explained; this new precept as to the relation between man and God came with such a general sweep that no one even tries to give personal credit for it. These things are not personal—they are world-percepts."

"But every religion has had its Founder, hasn't it?"

"*I* don't call it a religion, my dear fellow! It's a science, like any other science. Ethics is The Science of Human Relation. It is called Applied Sociology—that's all."

"How does a thing like that touch one, personally?" I asked.

"How does any science touch one personally? One studies a science, one teaches a science, one uses a science. That's the point—the *use* of it. Our old scheme of religion was a thing to 'believe,' or 'deny;' it was a sort of shibboleth, a test question one had to pass examination in to get good marks! What I'm telling you about is a general recognition of right behavior; and a general grasp of the necessary power."

"You leave out entirely the emotional side of religion."

"Do I? I did not intend to. You see, we do not distinguish religion from life now, and are apt to forget old terms. You are thinking, I suppose, of the love of God, and man, which we used to preach. We practice it now.

"That Energy I spoke of, when perceived by us, is called Love. Love, the real thing we had in mind when we said 'God is Love,' is beneficent energy. It is the impulse of service, the desire to do, to help, to make, to benefit. That is the 'love' we were told to bestow on one another. Now we do."

"Yes—but what made you do it?—What keeps you up to it?"

"Just nature, John. It is human nature. We used to believe otherwise." He was quiet for a while.

"One of these new doctors got hold of me, when I was about as near the bottom as one can go and get back. Not a priest with a formula, nor a reformer with an exhortation; but a real physician, a soul-doctor, with a passionate enthusiasm for an interesting case. That's what I was, John; not a lost soul; not even a 'sinner;' just 'a case.' Have you heard about these moral sanitariums?"

"Yes—but not definitely."

"Well, as soon as this view of things took hold, they began to want to isolate bad cases, and cure them if they could. And they cured me."

"How, Frank—*how?* What did they tell you that you didn't know before? What did they do to you?"

"Sane, strong, intelligent minds put themselves in connection with mine, John, and shared their strength with me. I was made to feel that my individual failure was no great matter, but that my social duty was; that the whole of my dirty past was as nothing to all our splendid future; that whatever I had done was merely to be forgotten, the sooner the better, and that all life was open before me—all human life; endless, beautiful, profoundly interesting—the game was on, and I was in it.

"John—I wish I could make you feel it. It was as if we had all along had inside us an enormous reservoir of love, human love, that had somehow been held in and soured! This new arrangement of our minds let it out— to our limitless relief and joy. No 'sin'—think of that! Just let it sink in. No such thing as sin....We had, collectively and privately, made mistakes, and done the wrong thing, often. What of it? Of course we had. A growing race *grew that way*.

"Now we are wiser and need not keep on going wrong. We had learned that life was far easier, pleasanter, more richly satisfying when followed on these new lines—and the new lines were not hard to learn. Love was the natural element of social life. Love meant service, service meant doing one's special work well, and doing it for the persons served—of course!

"*All* our mistakes lay in our belated Individualism. You cannot predicate Ethics of individuals. You cannot fulfill any religion as individuals. My fellow creatures took hold of me, you see. That power that was being used so extensively for physical healing in our young days, had become a matter of common knowledge—and use."

"How many of these—moral hygienists—did you have?"

"Scores, hundreds, thousands. We all help one another now. If a person is tired and blue and has lost his grip; if he can't rectify it by change of diet and change of scene, he goes to a moral hygienist as you rightly call it, and gets help. I do a lot of that sort of work."

I meditated awhile, and again shook my head. "I'm afraid it's no use. I can't make it seem credible. I hear what you say and I see what you've done—but I do not get any clear understanding of the process. With people as they were; with all those case-hardened old sinners, all the crass ignorance, the stupidity, the sodden prejudice, the apathy, the selfishness—to make a world like that see reason—in thirty years!—No—I don't get it."

"You are wrong in your premises, John. Human nature is, and was, just as good as the rest of nature. Two things kept us back—wrong conditions, and wrong ideas; we have changed both. I think you forget the sweeping advance in material conditions and its effect on character. What made the well-bred, well-educated, well-meaning, pleasant people we used to know? Good conditions, for them and their ancestors. There were just as pleasant people among the poor and among their millions of children; they had every capacity for noble growth—given the chance. It took no wholesale change of heart to make people want shorter hours, better pay, better housing, food, clothes, amusements. As soon as the shameful pressure of poverty was taken off humanity it rose like a freed spring. Humanity's all right."

"There were some things all wrong," I replied, "that I know. You could not obliterate hereditary disease in ten—or thirty years. You couldn't make clean women of hundreds of thousands of prostitutes. You couldn't turn an invalid tramp into a healthy gentleman."

He stopped me. "We could do better than that," he said; "and we have. I begin to see your central difficulty, John; the difficulty that used to hold us all. You are looking at life as a personal affair—a matter of personal despair or salvation."

"Of course, what else is it?"

"What *else*! Why, that is no part of human life! Human life is social, John; collectively, common, or it isn't human life at all. Hereditary disease looks pretty hopeless when you see one generation or two or three so cursed. But when you realize how swiftly the stream of human life can be cleansed of it, you take a fresh hold. The percentage of hereditary disease has sunk by more than half in thirty years, John, and at its present rate of decrease will be gone, clean gone, in another twenty. Remember that every case is known, and that they are either prevented from transmitting the inheritance, isolated, or voluntarily living single. Diseases from bad conditions we no longer endure, nor diseases from ignorance; those from bacilli we are able to resist or cure; disease was never a permanent thing—only an accident. As for the prostitutes—we thought them 'ruined' because they were no longer suitable for our demands in marriage. As if that was

109

everything! I tell you we opened a way out for them!"

"Namely?"

"Namely all the rest of life! Sex-life isn't everything, John. Not fit to be a mother, we said to them; never mind—there is everything else in the world to be. You may remember, my friend, that thousands of men, as vicious as any prostitutes, and often as diseased, continued to live, to work, and to enjoy. Why shouldn't the women? You haven't ruined your lives, we said to them; only one part. It's a loss, a great loss, but never mind, the whole range of human life remains open to you, the great moving world of service and growth and happiness. If you're sick, you're sick—we'll cure it if possible. If not, you'll die—never mind, we all die—that's nothing."

"Does your new religion call death nothing?"

"Certainly. The fuss we made about death was wholly owing to the old religions; the post-mortem religions, their whole basis was death."

"Hold on a bit. Do you mean to tell me the people aren't afraid of death any more?"

"Not a bit. Why should they be? Every living thing dies; that's part of the living. We do not hide it from children now, we teach it to them."

"Teach death—to children! How horrible!"

"Did you see or hear anything horrible in your educational excursions, John? I know you didn't. No, they learn it naturally; in their gardens; in their autumn and winter songs; in their familiarity with insects and animals. Our children learn life, death, and immortality, from silk-worms; and, then only incidentally. The silk is what they are studying.

"It takes a great many silk-worms to make silk, generations of them. They see them born, live and die, as incidents in silk culture. So we show them how people are born, live and die, in the making of human history. The idea is worked into our new educational literature—and all our literature for that matter. We see human life as a continuous whole now. People are only temporary parts of it. Dying isn't any more trouble than being born.

"People feared death, originally, because it hurt; being chased and eaten was not pleasant. But natural dying does not hurt. Then they were made to fear it by the hell-school of religions. All that is gone by. Our religion rests on life."

"The life of this world or the life eternal?"

"The eternal life of this world, John. We have no quarrel with anyone's

110

belief as to what may happen after death; that is a free field; but the glory and power of our religion is that it rests with assurance on common knowledge of the beautiful facts of life. Here is Humanity, a continuing stream of life. Its line of advance is clear. That which makes Humanity stronger, wiser and happier is evidently what is right for it to do. We do teach it to all our children."

"And they do it?"

"Of course they do it. Why shouldn't they?"

"But our evil tendencies—"

"We don't have evil tendencies, John—and never did. We have earlier and later tendencies; and it is perfectly possible to show the child which is which."

"But surely it is easier to follow the lower impulses than the higher; easier to give way than to strive."

"There's the old misconception, John, that 'striving' idea. We assumed that it was 'natural' to be 'bad' and 'unnatural' to be 'good'—that we had to make special efforts, painful and laborious, to become better. We had not seen, thirty years ago, that social evolution is as 'natural' as the evolution of the horse from the eohippus. If it was easier to be an eohippus than a horse why did the thing change?

"As to that army of 'fallen women' you are so anxious about, they just got up again, that's all, got up and went on. They had only fallen from one position; there was plenty of room left to stand and walk. Why they were not a speck on society compared to the 'fallen men.' Two hundred thousand prostitutes in the city of New York—well? How many patrons? A million, at the least. They kept on doing business, and enjoying life. I tell you, John, all the unnecessary evils of condition in the old days, were as nothing to the unnecessary evils of our foolish ideas! And ideas can be changed in the twinkling of an eye!

"As to your hoboes and bums, that invalid tramp you instanced—I can settle your mind on that point. I was an invalid tramp, John; a drunkard, a cocaine fiend, a criminal, sick, desperate, as bad as they make them."

"Which brings us back to that 'moral sanitarium' I suppose?"

"Yes. I strayed away from it. I keep forgetting my own case. But it is an excellent one for illustration. I was taken hold of with the strong hand, and given a course of double treatment, deep and thorough. By double treatment I mean physical and mental at once; such a complete overhauling and wise care as enabled my exhausted vitality slowly to reassert itself, and at the same time such strong tender cheerful companionship, such well-devised entertainment, such interesting, irresistible instruction— Why, John—put a tramp into Paradise, and there's some hope of him."

I was about to say that tramps did not deserve Paradise, but as I remembered what this man had been, and saw what he was now, I refrained.

He read my mind at once.

"It's not a question of deserve, John. We no longer deal in terms of personal reward or punishment. If I have a bad finger or a bad tooth I save it if I can; not because it deserves it, but because I need it. People who used to be called sinners are now seen to be diseased members of society, and society turns all its regenerative forces on at once. We never used to dream of that flood of power we had at hand—the Regenerative Forces of Society!"

He sat smiling, his fine eyes full of light. "Sometimes we had to amputate," he continued, "especially at first. It is very seldom necessary now."

"You mean you killed the worst people?"

"We killed many hopeless degenerates, insane, idiots, and real perverts, after trying our best powers of cure. But it is really astonishing to see how much can be done with what we used to call criminals, merely by first-class physical treatment. I can remember how strange it seemed to me; having elaborate baths, massage, electric stimulus, perfect food, clean comfortable beds, beautiful clothes, books, music, congenial company, and wonderful instruction. It was very confusing. It went far to rearrange all my ideas."

"If you treat—social invalids—like that, I should think they would 'lie down;' just to remain in hospital forever. Or go out and be bad in order to get back again."

"Oh, no," he said. "A healthy man can't lie around and do nothing very long. Also it is good outside too, remember. Life is good, pleasant, easy. Why on earth should a man want to prowl around at night and steal when he can have all he wants, with less effort, in the daytime? Happy people do not become criminals.

"But I can tell you what treatment like that does to one. It gives a man a new view of human life, of what it is he belongs to. A sense of pride in our common accomplishment, of gratitude for the pleasure he receives, of a natural desire to contribute something. I took this new ethics—it satisfied me, it's reasonable, it's necessary. We make it our basic study now, in all the schools. You must have noticed that?"

Yes, I had noticed it, as I looked back. "But they don't call it that," I said.

"No, they don't call it anything to the children. It is just life; the rules of decent behavior."

We sat silent awhile after this. Things were clearing up a little in my mind.

"A sort of crystallization of chaotic progressive thought into clear diamonds of usable truth—is that about what happened?" I said.

"That's exactly it."

"And a general refutation and clearing out of—of—"

"Of a lot of things we deeply believed—that were not so! That is what was the matter with us, John. Our minds were full of what Mrs. Eddy christened error. I wish I could make you feel what a sunrise it was to the world when we left off believing lies and learned the facts."

"Can you, in a few words, outline a little of your new 'Ethics' to the lay mind?"

"Easily. It is all 'lay' enough. We don't make a separate profession of religion, or a separate science of ethics. Ethics is social hygiene—it teaches how humanity must live in order to be well and strong. We show the child the patent facts of social relation, how all our daily life, our accumulated wealth and beauty and continuing power, rests on common action, on what people do together. Everything about him teaches that. Then we show him the reasons why such and such actions are wrong, what the results are; how to avoid wrong lines of action and adopt right ones. It's no more difficult than teaching any other game, and far more interesting."

I suppose I looked unconvinced, for he added, "Remember we have nature on our side. It is natural for a social animal to develop social instincts; any personal desire which works against the social good is clearly a survival of a lower pre-social period; wrong, in that it is out of place. What we used to call criminals were relics of the past. By artificially maintaining low conditions, such as poverty, individual wealth, we bred low-grade types. We do not breed them any more."

Again we sat silent. I was nursing my knee and sat looking into the fire; the soft shimmering play of rosy light and warmth with which electricity now gave jewels to our rooms.

113

He followed my eyes.

"That clean, safe, beautiful power was always here, John—but we had not learned of it. The power of wind and water and steam were here—before we learned to use them. All this splendid power of human life was here—only we did not know it."

After that talk with Frank Borderson I felt a little clearer in my mind about what had taken place. I saw a good deal of him, and he introduced me to others who were in his line of work. Also I got to know his wife pretty well. She was not so great an authority on ethics as he; but an excellent teacher, widely useful.

One day I said something to her about her lovely spirit, and what she must have been to him—such an uplifting influence.

She laughed outright.

"I'll have to tell you the facts, Mr. Robertson, as part of your instruction. So far from my uplifting him, he picked me out of the gutter, literally, dead drunk in the gutter, the lowest kind of wreck. He made me over. He gave me—Life."

Her eyes shone.

"We work together," she added cheerfully.

They did work together, and evidently knew much happiness. I noted a sort of deep close understanding between them, as in those who have been through the wars in company.

I found Nellie knew about them. "Yes, indeed," she said. "They are devoted to each other, and most united in their work. He was just beginning to try to work, after his own rebuilding; but feeling pretty lonesome. He felt that he had no chance of any personal life, you see, and there were times when he missed it badly. He had no right to marry, of course; that is, with a well woman. And then he found this broken lily—and mended it. There can't be any children, but there is great happiness, you can see that."

"And they are—received?"

"Received?—Oh, I remember! You mean they are invited to dinners and parties. Why, yes."

"Not among the best people, surely?"

"Precisely that, the very best; people who appreciate their wonderful lives."

"Tell me this, Sister; what happened to the Four Hundred—the F.F.V.'s—and the rest of the aristocracy?"

"The same thing that happened to all of us. They were only people, you see. Their atrophied social consciousness was electrified with the new thoughts and feelings. They woke up, too, most of them. Some just died out harmlessly. They were only by-products."

I consulted a rather reactionary old professor of Sociology, Morris Banks; one who had been teaching Political Economy in my youth, and who ought to be able to remember things. I asked him if he would be so good as to show me the dark side of this shield.

"Surely there must have been opposition, misunderstanding, the usual difficulties of new adjustments," I said. "You remember the first years of change—I wish you would give me a clear account of it."

The old man considered awhile: "Take any one state, any one city, or country locality, and study back a little," he said, "and you find the story is about the same. There was opposition and dissent, of course, but it decreased very rapidly. You see the improvements at first introduced were such universal benefits that there could not be any serious complaint.

"By the time we had universal suffrage the women were more than ready for it, full of working plans to carry out, and rich by the experience of the first trials.

"By the time Socialism was generally adopted we had case after case of proven good in Socialistic methods; and also the instructive background of some failures."

"But the big men who ran the country to suit themselves in my time, they didn't give up without a struggle surely? You must have had *some* fighting," I said.

He smiled in cheerful reminiscence. "We had a good deal of noise, if that's what you mean. But there's no fighting to be done, with soldiers, if the soldiers won't fight. Our workingmen declined to shoot or to be shot any longer, and left the big capitalists to see what they could do alone."

"But they had the capital?"

"Not all of it. The revenues of the cities and of the United States Government are pretty considerable, especially when you save the seventy per cent we used to spend on wars past and possible; and the ten or twenty-more that went in waste and graft. With a Socialist State private Capital has no grip!"

115

"Did you confiscate it?"

"Did not have to. The people who were worth anything, swung into line and went to work like other people. Those that weren't were just let alone. Nobody has any respect for them now."

"You achieved Socialism without bloodshed?"

"We did. It did not happen all at once, you see; just spread and spread and proved its usefulness."

Chapter XII

More and more I cut loose from the explanatory guiding strings of my sister and the family; even from the requested information of specialists; and wandered by myself in search of the widening daily acquaintance which alone could make life seem real again.

It was an easy world to wander in. The standard of general courtesy and intelligence of the officials, and of the average passer-by, was as much above what I remembered as the standard in Boston used to be above that of New York.

As most of the business was public business one could study and inquire freely. As much work as could be advantageously localized was so arranged, this saving in transportation. The clothing industry, for instance, instead of being carried on in swarming centers, and then distributed all over the country, formed part of the pleasant everyday work in each community and was mostly in the hands of women.

As a man I could appreciate little of the improved quality of fabrics, save as I noticed their beauty, and that my own clothes wore longer, and both looked and felt more agreeable. But women told me how satisfying it was to know that silk was silk, and wool, wool. This improvement in textile values, with the outgrowing of that long obsession called fashion, reduced the labor of clothes-making materially.

Women's clothes, I found, as I strolled through the stores, were more beautiful, were very delicate and fine, and had a gracious dignity and sanity far removed from the frantic concoctions I remembered in the windows;—shredded patchwork of muslin and lace, necessarily frail and short-lived even as ornaments; never useful, and costing arduous labor in construction, with corresponding expense to the purchaser.

The robes and gowns were a joy to the eye. Some showed less taste than others, naturally, but nowhere was to be seen the shameless ugliness so common in my youth.

Beauty and peace, I found, care, leisure, quietness; plenty of gaiety, too, both in young and old. It struck me that the young people, owing to their wider and sounder upbringing, were more serious; and that older people, owing to their safer, easier lives, were jollier. These sweet-faced, broad-minded young women did not show so much giggling inanity as once seemed necessary to them; and a young man, even a young man in college, did not, therefore, find pleasure in theft, cruelty, gross practical jokes and destruction of property.

As I noted this, I brought myself up with a start. It looked as if Nellie had written it. Surely, when I was in college—and there rose up within me a memory of the crass, wasteful follies that used to be called "pranks" in my time, and considered perfectly natural in young men. I had not minded them in those days. It gave me a queer feeling to see by my own words how my judgment was affected already.

I explored the city from end to end, and satisfied myself that there was no poverty in it; no street that was not clean, no house that was not fit for human habitation. That is, as far as I could judge from an outside view.

Among the masses of people, after their busy mornings, there were vast numbers who used the afternoons for learning, the easy, interesting, endless learning now carried on far and wide. The more they learned the more they wanted to know; and the best minds, free for research work, and upheld in it by the deepening attention of the world, constantly pushed on the boundaries of knowledge.

There were some hospitals yet, but as one to a hundred of what used to be; of higher quality, and fuller usefulness. There were some of what I should have called prisons, though the life inside was not only as comfortable as that without, but administered with a stricter care for the advantage of those within.

There were the moral sanitariums—healthful and beautiful; richly endowed with the world's best methods of improvement, and managed by the world's best people. It made me almost dizzy to try to take in this opposite pole of judgment on the criminal.

Out of town I found that the park-like roads, so generally in use, by no means interfered with the wide stretches of what I used to call "real country." Intensive agriculture took less ground, rather more; and the wide use of food-bearing trees had restored the wooded aspect, so pleasant in every sense.

The small country towns were of special interest to me; I visited scores of them; each differing from the others, all beautiful and clean and busy. They were numerous too; replacing the areas of scattered lonely farmhouses, with these comfortable and pretty groups, each in its home park, with its standard of convenience as high as that in any town.

The smallest group had its power plant, supplying all the houses with heat, light and water; had its child gardens, its Town House and Club House; its workshops and foodshops as necessary as its postoffices.

The Socialized industries ensured employment to every citizen; and provided all the necessaries of life—larger order this than it used to be. Quite above this broad base of social control, the life of the people went on; far freer and more open to individual development than it had ever had a chance to be in the whole history of the world.

This I frankly conceded. I found I was making more concessions in my note-book than I had yet made to either Nellie or Owen. They encouraged me to travel about by myself. In fact, my sister was now about to resume her college position and Owen was going with her.

They both advised me not to settle upon any work for a full year.

"That's little enough time in which to cover thirty," Nellie said, patting my shoulder. "But you're doing splendidly, John. We are proud of you. And there's no hurry. You know there's enough from our mine to enable you to join the 'leisure class'—if you want to!"

I had no idea of doing this, as she well knew, but I did feel it necessary to get myself in some way grafted on to this new world before I took up regular employment. I found that there was not much call for ancient languages in the colleges, even if I had been in touch with the new methods; but there remained plenty of historical work, for which I had now a special fitness. Indeed some of my new scientific friends assured me I could be of the utmost service, with my unique experience.

So I was not worried about what to do, nor under any pressure about doing it. But the more I saw of all these new advantages, the more I was obliged to admit that they were advantages; the more I traveled and read and learned, the more lonesome and homesick I became.

It was a beautiful world, but it was not my world. It was like a beautiful dream, but seemed a dream nevertheless. I could no longer dispute that it was possible for people to be "healthy, wealthy and wise"; and happy, too, visibly happy—here they all were; working and playing and enjoying life as naturally as possible. But they were not the people I used to know; those too were, like Frank Borderson and Morris Banks, changed so that they seemed more unreal than the others.

The beauty and peace and order of the whole thing wore on me. I wanted to hear the roar of the elevated—to smell the foul air of the subway and see the people pile in, pushing and angry; as I still remembered in my visits to New York.

I wanted to see some neglected-looking land, some ragged suburbs, some far-away farmhouse alone under its big elms, with its own barns in odorous proximity, its own cows, boy-driven, running and stumbling home to be milked.

I wanted a newspaper which gave me the excitement of guessing what the truth was; I wanted to see some foolish, crazily dressed, giggling girls; and equally foolish boys, but better dressed and less giggling, given to cigarettes and uproarious "good times."

I was homesick, desperately homesick. So without saying a word to anyone I betook myself to old Slide-face, to see Uncle Jake.

All the way down—and I went by rail—no air travel for this homecoming!—I felt an increasing pleasure in the familiar look of things. The outlines of the Alleghanies had not changed. I would not get out at any town, the shining neatness of the railroad station was enough; but the sleeping cars were a disappointment. The beds were wide, soft, cool, the blankets of light clean wool, the air clear and fresh, the noise and jar almost gone. Oh, well, I couldn't expect to have everything as it used to be, of course.

But when I struck out, on foot, from Paintertown, and began to climb the road that led to my old home, my heart was in my mouth. It was a better road, of course—but I hardly noticed that. All the outlying farms were better managed and the little village groups showed here and there—but I shut my eyes to these things.

The hills were the same—the hills I had grown up among. They couldn't alter the face of the earth much—that was still recognizable. Our own house I did not visit—both father and mother were gone, and the little wooden building replaced by a concrete mining office. Nellie had told me about all this; it was one reason why I had not come back before.

But now I went past our place almost with my eyes shut; and kept on along the road to Uncle Jake's. He had been a rich man, as farmers went, owning the land for a mile or two on every side, owning Slide-face as a matter of fact; and as he made enough from the rich little upland valley where the house stood, to pay his taxes, he owned it still.

The moment I reached his boundary I knew it, unmistakably. A ragged, home-made sign, sagging from its nails, announced "Private Road. No trespassers allowed." Evidently they heeded the warning, for the stony, washed-out roadbed was little traveled.

My heart quite leaped as I set foot on it. It was not "improved" in the least from what I remembered in my infrequent visits. My father and Uncle Jake had "a coldness" between them; which would have been a quarrel, I fancy, if father had not been a minister, so I never saw much of these relations.

Drusilla I remembered well enough, though, a pretty, babyish thing; and Aunt Dorcas's kind, patient, tired smile; and the fruit cakes she made.

Up and up; through the real woods, ragged and thick with dead boughs, fallen trunks and underbrush, not touched by any forester, and finally, around the shoulder of Slide-face, to the farm.

I stood still and drew in a long breath of utter satisfaction. Here was something that had not changed. There was an old negro ploughing, the same negro I remembered, apparently not a day older. It is wonderful how little they do change with years. His wool showed white though, as he doffed his ragged cap and greeted me with cheerful cordiality as Mass' John.

"We all been hearin' about you, Mass' John. We been powerful sorry 'bout you long time, among de heathen," he said. "You folks'll be glad to see you!"

"Well, young man!" said Uncle Jake, with some show of cordiality; "better late than never. We wondered if you intended to look up your country relations."

But Aunt Dorcas put her thin arms around my neck and kissed me, teary kisses with little pats and exclamations. "To think of it! Thirty years among savages! We heard about it from Nellie—she wrote us, of course. Nellie's real good to keep us posted."

"She never comes to see us!" said my Uncle. "Nor those youngsters of hers. We've never had them here but once. They're too 'advanced' for old-fashioned folks."

Uncle Jake's long upper lip set firmly; I remembered that look, as he used to sit in his wagon and talk with mother at our gate, refusing to come in, little sunny-haired Drusilla looking shyly at me from under her sunbonnet the while.

Where was Drusilla? Surely not—that! A frail, weak, elderly, quiet, little woman stood there by Aunt Dorcas, her smooth fine, ash-brown hair drawn tightly back to a flat knot behind; her dull blue calico dress falling starkly about her.

She came forward, smiling, and held out a thin work-worn hand. "We're so glad to see you, Cousin John," she said. "We certainly are."

They made much of me in the old familiar ways I had so thirsted for. The sense of family background, of common knowledge and experience was comforting in the extreme, the very furnishings and clothes as I recalled

121

them. I told them what a joy it was.

This seemed to please Uncle Jake enormously.

"I *thought* you'd do it," he said. "Like to find one place that hasn't been turned upside down by all these new-fangled notions. Dreadful things have been goin' on, John, while you were amongst them Feejees."

I endeavored to explain to him something of the nature and appearance of the inhabitants of Tibet, but it made small impression. Uncle Jake's mind was so completely occupied by what was in it, that any outside fact or idea had small chance of entry.

"They've got wimmin votin' now, I understand," he pursued; "I don't read the papers much, they are so ungodly, but I've heard that. And they've been meddlin' with Divine Providence in more ways than one—but I keep out of it, and so does Aunt Dorcas and the girl here."

He looked around at my Aunt, who smiled her gentle, faithful smile, and at Drusilla, who dropped her eyes and flushed faintly. I suspected her of secret leanings toward the movement of the world outside.

"I don't allow my family off the farm," he went on, "except when we go to meetin', and that's not often. There's hardly an orthodox preacher left, seems to me; but we go up to the Ridge meetin' house sometimes."

"I should think you would find it a little dull—don't you?" I ventured.

Drusilla flashed a grateful look at me.

"Nothing of the sort," he answered. "I was born on this farm, and it's big enough for anybody to be contented on. Your Aunt was born over in Hadley Holler—and she's contented enough. As for Drusilly—" he looked at her again with real affection, "Drusilly's always been a good girl—never made any trouble in her life. Unless 'twas when she pretty near married that heretic minister—eh, Drusilly?"

My cousin did not respond warmly to this sally, but neither did she show signs of grief. I was conscious of a faint satisfaction that she had not married the heretic minister.

They made me very welcome; so welcome indeed that as days passed, Uncle Jake even broached the subject of my remaining there.

"I've got no son," he said, "and a girl can't run the farm. You stay here, John, and keep things goin', and I'll will it to you—what do you say? You ain't married, I see. Just get you a nice girl—if there's any left, and settle down here."

I thanked him warmly, but said I must have time to consider—that I had thought of accepting other work which offered.

He was most insistent about it. "You better stay here, John. Here's pure air and pure food—none of these artificial kickshaws I hear of folks havin' nowadays. We smoke our own hams just as we used to do in my grandfather's time—there's none better. We buy sugar and rice and coffee and such as that; but I grind my own corn in the little mill there on the creek—reckon I'm the only one who uses it now. And your Aunt runs her loom to this day. Drusilly can, too, but she 'lows she hates to do it. Girls aren't what they used to be when I was young!"

It did not seem possible that Uncle Jake had ever been young. His sturdy, stooping frame, his hard, ruddy features were the same at seventy as I remembered them at forty; only the hair, whitened and thinned, was different.

My bedroom was exactly as when I last slept in it, on my one visit to the farm as a boy of fifteen. Drusilla had seemed only a baby then—a slender little five-year old. She had followed me about in silence, with adoring eyes, and I had teased her!—I hated to think of how I had teased her.

The gold in her hair was all dulled and faded, the rose-leaf color of her cheeks had faded, too; and her blue eyes wore a look of weary patience. She worked hard. Her mother was evidently feeble now; and the labor required in that primitive home was considerable.

The old negro brought water from the spring, and milked the cows; but all the care of the dairy, the cooking for the family, the knitting and sewing and mending and the sweeping, scrubbing and washing was in the hands of Aunt Dorcas and Drusilla.

She would make her mother sit down and chat with me, while Uncle Jake smoked his cob pipe, but she herself seemed always at work.

"There's no getting any help nowadays," said my Uncle. "Even if we needed it. Old Joe there stayed on—he was here before I was born. Joe must be eighty or over—there's no telling the age of niggers. But the young ones are too uppity for any use. They want to be paid out of all reason, and treated like white folks at that!"

He boasted that he had never worn a shirt or a pair of socks made off the place. "In my father's time we raised a heap of cotton and sold it. Plenty of niggers then. Now I manage to get enough for my own use, and we spin and weave it on the spot!"

I watched Aunt Dorcas at her wheel and loom, and rubbed my eyes. It was only in the remote mountain regions that these things were done when I was young, and to see it now seemed utterly incredible. But Uncle Jake was proud of it.

"I don't believe there's another wheel agoin' in the whole country," he said. "The mountains ain't what they used to be, John. They've got the trees all grafted up with new kinds of foolishness—nuts and fruit and one thing 'n another—and unheard-of kinds of houses and schools, and play-actin' everywhere. I can't abide it,"

He set his jaw firmly, making the stiff white beard stand out at a sharp angle. "The farm'll keep us for my time," he concluded. "But I should hate to have it all 'reformed' and torn to pieces after I'm gone." And he looked meaningly at me.

I lingered on, still enjoying the sense of family affection; but my satisfaction in the things about me slowly cooling.

A cotton quilt was heavier but not so warm as a woolen blanket. Homespun sheets were durable, doubtless, but not comfortable. The bathing to be done in a small steep-sided china basin, with water poured from a pitcher the outlines of which were more concave than convex, was laborious and unsatisfying.

The relish of that "hog and hominy" and the beaten biscuit, the corn pone, the molasses and pork gravy of my youth wore off as the same viands reappeared on the table from day to day and week to week, and seemed ceaselessly present within me.

It was pleasant to listen to Aunt Dorcas's gentle reminiscences of the past years, of my father and mother in their youth, of my infancy, and Drusilla's. She grieved that she had not more to tell. "I never was one to visit much," she said.

But it was saddening to find that the dear old lady could talk of absolutely nothing else. In all her sixty-eight years she had known nothing else; her father's home and her husband's, alike in their contents and in their labors; her own domestic limitations, and those of her neighbors; and her church paper—taken for forty years, and arbitrarily discontinued by Uncle Jake because it had grown too liberal.

"It never seemed over-liberal to me," she said softly, "and I do miss it. I wouldn't a'believed I'd a missed anything so much. It used to come every week, and I kept more acquainted with what the rest of this circuit was doing. But your Uncle Jake is so set against liberalism!"

I turned to my cousin for some wider exchange of thoughts, and strove with all the remembered arts of my youth, and all the recently acquired wisdom of my present years, to win her confidence.

It was difficult at first. She was shy with the dumb shyness of an animal; not like a wild animal, frankly curious, not like a hunted animal, which runs away and hides; but like an animal in a menagerie, a sullen, hopeless timidity, due to long restriction. Life had slipped by her, all of it, as far as she knew. She had been an "old maid" for twenty-five years—they call them that in these mountains if they are not married at twenty. Her father's domineering ways had discouraged most of the few young men she had known, and he had ruthlessly driven away the only one who came near enough to be dismissed.

Then it was only the housework, and caring for her mother as she grew older. The one pleasure of her own she ever had was in her flowers. She had transplanted wild ones, had now and then been given "a slip" by remote neighbors—in past years; and those carefully nurtured blossoms were all that brought color and sweetness into her gray life.

She did not complain. For a long time I could not get her to talk to me at all about herself, and when she did it was without hope or protest. She had practically no education—only a few years in a country school in childhood, and almost no reading, writing, conversation, any sort of knowledge of the life of the world about her.

And here she lived, meek, patient, helpless, with neither complaint nor desire, endlessly working to make comfortable the parents who must some day leave her alone—to what?

My thirty years in Tibet seemed all at once a holiday compared to this thirty years on an upland farm in the Alleghanies of Carolina. My loss of life—what was it to this loss? I, at least, had never known it, not until I was found and brought back; and she had known it every day and night for thirty years. I had come back at fifty-five, regaining a new youth in a new world. She apparently had had no youth, and now was old—older at forty-five than women of fifty and sixty whom I had met and talked with recently.

I thought of them, those busy, vigorous, eager, active women, of whom no one would ever predict either youth or age; they were just women, permanently, as men were men. I thought of their wide, free lives, their absorbing work and many minor interests; and the big, smooth, beautiful, moving world in which they lived, and my heart went out to Drusilla as to a baby in a well.

"Look here, Drusilla," I said to her at last, "I want you to marry me. We'll go away from here; you shall see something of life, my dear—there's lot of time yet."

She raised those quiet blue eyes and looked at me, a long, sweet, searching look, and then shook her head with gentle finality. "O, no," she said; "Thank you, Cousin John, but I could not do that."

And then, all at once I felt more lonely and out of life than when the first shock met me.

"O, Drusilla!" I begged; "Do—do! Don't you see, if you won't have me nobody ever will? I am all alone in the world, Drusilla—the world has all gone away from me! You are the only woman alive who would understand. Dear cousin—dear little girl—you'll have to marry me—out of pity!" And she did.

. . . . .

Nobody would know Drusilla now. She grew young at a rate that seemed a heavenly miracle. To her the world was like heaven, and, being an angel was natural to her anyway.

I grew to find the world like heaven, too—if only for what it did to Drusilla.

Herland

Chapter I

A Not Unnatural Enterprise

This is written from memory, unfortunately. If I could have brought with me the material I so carefully prepared, this would be a very different story. Whole books full of notes, carefully copied records, firsthand descriptions, and the pictures—that's the worst loss. We had some bird's-eyes of the cities and parks; a lot of lovely views of streets, of buildings, outside and in, and some of those gorgeous gardens, and, most important of all, of the women themselves.

Nobody will ever believe how they looked. Descriptions aren't any good when it comes to women, and I never was good at descriptions anyhow. But it's got to be done somehow; the rest of the world needs to know about that country.

I haven't said where it was for fear some self-appointed missionaries, or traders, or land-greedy expansionists, will take it upon themselves to push in. They will not be wanted, I can tell them that; and will fare worse than we did if they do find it.

It began this way. There were three of us, classmates and friends—Terry O. Nicholson (we used to call him the Old Nick, with good reason), Jeff Margrave, and I, Vandyck Jennings.

We had known each other years and years, and in spite of our differences we had a good deal in common. All of us were interested in science.

Terry was rich enough to do as he pleased. His great aim was exploration. He used to make all kinds of a row because there was nothing left to explore now, only patchwork and filling in, he said. He filled in well enough—he had a lot of talents—great on mechanics and electricity. Had all kinds of boats and motorcars, and was one of the best of our airmen.

We never could have done the thing at all without Terry.

Jeff Margrave was born to be a poet, a botanist—or both—but his folks persuaded him to be a doctor instead. He was a good one, for his age, but his real interest was in what he loved to call "the wonders of science."

As for me, Sociology's my major. You have to back that up with a lot of other sciences, of course. I'm interested in them all.

Terry was strong on facts, geography and meteorology and those; Jeff could beat him any time on biology, and I didn't care what it was they talked about, so long as it connected with human life, somehow. There are few things that don't.

We three had a chance to join a big scientific expedition. They needed a doctor, and that gave Jeff an excuse for dropping his just opening practice; they needed Terry's experience, his machine, and his money; and as for me, I got in through Terry's influence.

The expedition was up among the thousand tributaries and enormous hinterland of a great river, up where the maps had to be made, savage dialects studied, and all manner of strange flora and fauna expected.

But this story is not about that expedition. That was only the merest starter for ours.

. . . . .

My interest was first roused by talk among our guides. I'm quick at languages, know a good many, and pick them up readily. What with that and a really good interpreter we took with us, I made out quite a few legends and folk myths of these scattered tribes.

And as we got farther and farther upstream, in a dark tangle of rivers, lakes, morasses, and dense forests, with here and there an unexpected long spur running out from the big mountains beyond, I noticed that more and more of these savages had a story about a strange and terrible "Woman Land" in the high distance.

"Up yonder," "Over there," "Way up"—was all the direction they could offer, but their legends all agreed on the main point—that there was this strange country where no men lived—only women and girl children.

None of them had ever seen it. It was dangerous, deadly, they said, for any man to go there. But there were tales of long ago, when some brave investigator had seen it—a Big Country, Big Houses, Plenty People—All Women.

Had no one else gone? Yes—a good many—but they never came back. It was no place for men—of that they seemed sure.

I told the boys about these stories, and they laughed at them. Naturally I did myself. I knew the stuff that savage dreams are made of.

But when we had reached our farthest point, just the day before we all had to turn around and start for home again, as the best of expeditions must, in time, we three made a discovery.

The main encampment was on a spit of land running out into the main stream, or what we thought was the main stream. It had the same muddy color we had been seeing for weeks past, the same taste.

I happened to speak of that river to our last guide, a rather superior fellow, with quick, bright eyes.

He told me that there was another river—"over there, short river, sweet water—red and blue."

I was interested in this and anxious to see if I had understood, so I showed him a red and blue pencil I carried, and asked again.

Yes, he pointed to the river, and then to the southwestward. "River—good water—red and blue."

Terry was close by and interested in the fellow's pointing.

"What does he say, Van?"

I told him.

Terry blazed up at once.

"Ask him how far it is."

The man indicated a short journey; I judged about two hours, maybe three.

"Let's go," urged Terry. "Just us three. Maybe we can really find something. May be cinnabar in it."

"May be indigo," Jeff suggested, with his lazy smile.

It was early yet; we had just breakfasted; and leaving word that we'd be back before night, we got away quietly, not wishing to be thought too gullible if we failed, and secretly hoping to have some nice little discovery all to ourselves.

It was a long two hours, nearer three. I fancy the savage could have done it alone much quicker. There was a desperate tangle of wood and water and a swampy patch we never should have found our way across alone. But there was one, and I could see Terry, with compass and notebook, marking directions and trying to place landmarks.

We came after a while to a sort of marshy lake, very big, so that the circling forest looked quite low and dim across it. Our guide told us that boats could go from there to our camp—but "long way—all day."

This water was somewhat clearer than that we had left, but we could not judge well from the margin. We skirted it for another half hour or so, the ground growing firmer as we advanced, and presently we turned the corner of a wooded promontory and saw a quite different country—a sudden view of mountains, steep and bare.

"One of those long easterly spurs," Terry said appraisingly. "May be hundreds of miles from the range. They crop out like that."

Suddenly we left the lake and struck directly toward the cliffs. We heard running water before we reached it, and the guide pointed proudly to his river.

It was short. We could see where it poured down a narrow vertical cataract from an opening in the face of the cliff. It was sweet water. The guide drank eagerly and so did we.

"That's snow water," Terry announced. "Must come from way back in the hills."

But as to being red and blue—it was greenish in tint. The guide seemed not at all surprised. He hunted about a little and showed us a quiet marginal pool where there were smears of red along the border; yes, and of blue.

Terry got out his magnifying glass and squatted down to investigate.

"Chemicals of some sort—I can't tell on the spot. Look to me like dye-stuffs. Let's get nearer," he urged, "up there by the fall."

We scrambled along the steep banks and got close to the pool that foamed and boiled beneath the falling water. Here we searched the border and found traces of color beyond dispute. More—Jeff suddenly held up an unlooked-for trophy.

It was only a rag, a long, raveled fragment of cloth. But it was a well-woven fabric, with a pattern, and of a clear scarlet that the water had not faded. No savage tribe that we had heard of made such fabrics.

The guide stood serenely on the bank, well pleased with our excitement.

"One day blue—one day red—one day green," he told us, and pulled from his pouch another strip of bright-hued cloth.

"Come down," he said, pointing to the cataract. "Woman Country—up there."

Then we were interested. We had our rest and lunch right there and pumped the man for further information. He could tell us only what the others had—a land of women—no men—babies, but all girls. No place for men—dangerous. Some had gone to see—none had come back.

I could see Terry's jaw set at that. No place for men? Dangerous? He looked as if he might shin up the waterfall on the spot. But the guide would not hear of going up, even if there had been any possible method of scaling that sheer cliff, and we had to get back to our party before night.

"They might stay if we told them," I suggested.

But Terry stopped in his tracks. "Look here, fellows," he said. "This is our find. Let's not tell those cocky old professors. Let's go on home with 'em, and then come back—just us—have a little expedition of our own."

We looked at him, much impressed. There was something attractive to a bunch of unattached young men in finding an undiscovered country of a strictly Amazonian nature.

Of course we didn't believe the story—but yet!

"There is no such cloth made by any of these local tribes," I announced, examining those rags with great care. "Somewhere up yonder they spin and weave and dye—as well as we do."

"That would mean a considerable civilization, Van—there couldn't be such a place—and not known about."

"Oh, well, I don't know; what's that old republic up in the Pyrenees somewhere—Andorra? Precious few people know anything about that, and it's been minding its own business for a thousand years. Then there's Montenegro—splendid little state—you could lose a dozen Montenegroes up and down these great ranges."

We discussed it hotly, all the way back to camp. We discussed it, with care and privacy, on the voyage home. We discussed it after that, still only among ourselves, while Terry was making his arrangements.

He was hot about it. Lucky he had so much money—we might have had to beg and advertise for years to start the thing, and then it would have been a matter of public amusement—just sport for the papers.

But T. O. Nicholson could fix up his big steam yacht, load his specially made big motor-boat aboard, and tuck in a "dissembled" biplane without any more notice than a snip in the society column.

We had provisions and preventives and all manner of supplies. His previous experience stood him in good stead there. It was a very complete little outfit.

We were to leave the yacht at the nearest safe port and go up that endless river in our motor, just the three of us and a pilot; then drop the pilot when we got to that last stopping place of the previous party, and hunt up that clear water stream ourselves.

The motor we were going to leave at anchor in that wide shallow lake. It had a special covering of fitted armor, thin but strong, shut up like a clamshell.

"Those natives can't get into it, or hurt it, or move it," Terry explained proudly. "We'll start our flier from the lake and leave the boat as a base to come back to."

"If we come back," I suggested cheerfully.

"'Fraid the ladies will eat you?" he scoffed.

"We're not so sure about those ladies, you know," drawled Jeff. "There may be a contingent of gentlemen with poisoned arrows or something."

"You don't need to go if you don't want to," Terry remarked drily.

"Go? You'll have to get an injunction to stop me!" Both Jeff and I were sure about that.

But we did have differences of opinion, all the long way.

An ocean voyage is an excellent time for discussion. Now we had no eavesdroppers, we could loll and loaf in our deck chairs and talk and talk— there was nothing else to do. Our absolute lack of facts only made the field of discussion wider.

"We'll leave papers with our consul where the yacht stays," Terry planned. "If we don't come back in—say a month—they can send a relief party after us."

"A punitive expedition," I urged. "If the ladies do eat us we must make reprisals."

"They can locate that last stopping place easy enough, and I've made a sort of chart of that lake and cliff and waterfall."

"Yes, but how will they get up?" asked Jeff.

"Same way we do, of course. If three valuable American citizens are lost up there they will follow somehow—to say nothing of the glittering attractions of that fair land—let's call it 'Feminisia,'" he broke off.

"You're right, Terry. Once the story gets out, the river will crawl with expeditions and the airships rise like a swarm of mosquitoes." I laughed as I thought of it. "We've made a great mistake not to let Mr. Yellow Press in on this. Save us! What headlines!"

"Not much!" said Terry grimly. "This is our party. We're going to find that place alone."

"What are you going to do with it when you do find it—if you do?" Jeff asked mildly.

Jeff was a tender soul. I think he thought that country—if there was one, was just blossoming with roses and babies and canaries and tidies—and all that sort of thing.

And Terry, in his secret heart, had visions of a sort of sublimated summer resort—just Girls and Girls and Girls—and that he was going to be—well, Terry was popular among women even when there were other men around, and it's not to be wondered at that he had pleasant dreams of what might happen. I could see it in his eyes as he lay there, looking at the long blue rollers slipping by, and fingering that impressive mustache of his.

But I thought—then—that I could form a far clearer idea of what was before us than either of them.

"You're all off, boys," I insisted. "If there is such a place—and there does seem some foundation for believing it, you'll find it's built on a sort of matriarchal principle—that's all. The men have a separate cult of their own, less socially developed than the women, and make them an annual visit—a sort of wedding call. This is a condition known to have existed—here's just a survival. They've got some peculiarly isolated valley or tableland up there, and their primeval customs have survived. That's all there is to it."

"How about the boys?" Jeff asked.

"Oh, the men take them away as soon as they are five or six, you see."

"And how about this danger theory all our guides were so sure of?"

"Danger enough, Terry, and we'll have to be mighty careful. Women of that stage of culture are quite able to defend themselves and have no welcome for unseasonable visitors."

We talked and talked.

And with all my airs of sociological superiority I was no nearer than any of them.

It was funny though, in the light of what we did find, those extremely clear ideas of ours as to what a country of women would be like. It was no use to tell ourselves and one another that all this was idle speculation. We were idle and we did speculate, on the ocean voyage and the river voyage, too.

"Admitting the improbability," we'd begin solemnly, and then launch out again.

"They would fight among themselves," Terry insisted. "Women always do. We mustn't look to find any sort of order and organization."

"You're dead wrong," Jeff told him. "It will be like a nunnery under an Abbess—a peaceful, harmonious sisterhood."

I snorted derision at this idea.

"Nuns, indeed! Your peaceful sisterhoods were all celibate, Jeff, and under vows of obedience. These are just women, and mothers, and where there's motherhood you don't find sisterhood—not much."

"No, sir—they'll scrap," agreed Terry. "Also we mustn't look for inventions and progress; it'll be awfully primitive."

"How about that cloth mill?" Jeff suggested.

"Oh, cloth! Women have always been spinsters. But there they stop— you'll see."

We joked Terry about his modest impression that he would be warmly received, but he held his ground.

"You'll see," he insisted. "I'll get solid with them all—and play one bunch against another. I'll get myself elected king in no time—whew! Solomon will have to take a back seat!"

"Where do we come in on that deal?" I demanded. "Aren't we Viziers or anything?"

"Couldn't risk it," he asserted solemnly. "You might start a revolution— probably would. No, you'll have to be beheaded, or bowstrung—or whatever the popular method of execution is."

"You'd have to do it yourself, remember," grinned Jeff. "No husky black slaves and mamelukes! And there'd be two of us and only one of you—eh, Van?"

Jeff's ideas and Terry's were so far apart that sometimes it was all I could do to keep the peace between them. Jeff idealized women in the best Southern style. He was full of chivalry and sentiment, and all that. And he was a good boy; he lived up to his ideals.

You might say Terry did, too, if you can call his views about women anything so polite as ideals. I always liked Terry. He was a man's man, very much so, generous and brave and clever; but I don't think any of us in college days was quite pleased to have him with our sisters. We weren't very stringent, heavens no! But Terry was "the limit." Later on—why, of course a man's life is his own, we held, and asked no questions.

But barring a possible exception in favor of a not impossible wife, or of his mother, or, of course, the fair relatives of his friends, Terry's idea seemed to be that pretty women were just so much game and homely ones not worth considering.

It was really unpleasant sometimes to see the notions he had.

But I got out of patience with Jeff, too. He had such rose-colored halos on his women folks. I held a middle ground, highly scientific, of course, and used to argue learnedly about the physiological limitations of the sex.

We were not in the least "advanced" on the woman question, any of us, then.

So we joked and disputed and speculated, and after an interminable journey, we got to our old camping place at last.

It was not hard to find the river, just poking along that side till we came to it, and it was navigable as far as the lake.

When we reached that and slid out on its broad glistening bosom, with that high gray promontory running out toward us, and the straight white fall clearly visible, it began to be really exciting.

There was some talk, even then, of skirting the rock wall and seeking a possible foot-way up, but the marshy jungle made that method look not only difficult but dangerous.

Terry dismissed the plan sharply.

"Nonsense, fellows! We've decided that. It might take months—we haven't got the provisions. No, sir—we've got to take our chances. If we get back safe—all right. If we don't, why, we're not the first explorers to get lost in the shuffle. There are plenty to come after us."

So we got the big biplane together and loaded it with our scientifically compressed baggage—the camera, of course; the glasses; a supply of concentrated food. Our pockets were magazines of small necessities, and we had our guns, of course—there was no knowing what might happen.

Up and up and up we sailed, way up at first, to get "the lay of the land" and make note of it.

Out of that dark green sea of crowding forest this high-standing spur rose steeply. It ran back on either side, apparently, to the far-off white-crowned peaks in the distance, themselves probably inaccessible.

"Let's make the first trip geographical," I suggested. "Spy out the land, and drop back here for more gasoline. With your tremendous speed we can reach that range and back all right. Then we can leave a sort of map on board—for that relief expedition."

"There's sense in that," Terry agreed. "I'll put off being king of Ladyland for one more day."

So we made a long skirting voyage, turned the point of the cape which was close by, ran up one side of the triangle at our best speed, crossed over the base where it left the higher mountains, and so back to our lake by moonlight.

"That's not a bad little kingdom," we agreed when it was roughly drawn and measured. We could tell the size fairly by our speed. And from what we could see of the sides—and that icy ridge at the back end—"It's a pretty enterprising savage who would manage to get into it," Jeff said.

Of course we had looked at the land itself—eagerly, but we were too high and going too fast to see much. It appeared to be well forested about the edges, but in the interior there were wide plains, and everywhere parklike meadows and open places.

There were cities, too; that I insisted. It looked—well, it looked like any other country—a civilized one, I mean.

We had to sleep after that long sweep through the air, but we turned out early enough next day, and again we rose softly up the height till we could top the crowning trees and see the broad fair land at our pleasure.

"Semi-tropical. Looks like a first-rate climate. It's wonderful what a little height will do for temperature." Terry was studying the forest growth.

"Little height! Is that what you call little?" I asked. Our instruments measured it clearly. We had not realized the long gentle rise from the coast perhaps.

"Mighty lucky piece of land, I call it," Terry pursued. "Now for the folks— I've had enough scenery."

So we sailed low, crossing back and forth, quartering the country as we went, and studying it. We saw—I can't remember now how much of this we noted then and how much was supplemented by our later knowledge, but we could not help seeing this much, even on that excited day—a land in a state of perfect cultivation, where even the forests looked as if they were cared for; a land that looked like an enormous park, only it was even more evidently an enormous garden.

"I don't see any cattle," I suggested, but Terry was silent. We were approaching a village.

140

I confess that we paid small attention to the clean, well-built roads, to the attractive architecture, to the ordered beauty of the little town. We had our glasses out, even Terry, setting his machine for a spiral glide, clapped the binoculars to his eyes.

They heard our whirring screw. They ran out of the houses—they gathered in from the fields, swift-running light figures, crowds of them. We stared and stared until it was almost too late to catch the levers, sweep off and rise again; and then we held our peace for a long run upward.

"Gosh!" said Terry, after a while.

"Only women there—and children," Jeff urged excitedly.

"But they look—why, this is a *civilized* country!" I protested. "There must be men."

"Of course there are men," said Terry. "Come on, let's find 'em."

He refused to listen to Jeff's suggestion that we examine the country further before we risked leaving our machine.

"There's a fine landing place right there where we came over," he insisted, and it was an excellent one, a wide, flat-topped rock, overlooking the lake, and quite out of sight from the interior.

"They won't find this in a hurry," he asserted, as we scrambled with the utmost difficulty down to safer footing. "Come on, boys—there were some good lookers in that bunch."

Of course it was unwise of us.

It was quite easy to see afterward that our best plan was to have studied the country more fully before we left our swooping airship and trusted ourselves to mere foot service. But we were three young men. We had been talking about this country for over a year, hardly believing that there was such a place, and now—we were in it.

It looked safe and civilized enough, and among those upturned, crowding faces, though some were terrified enough—there was great beauty—on that we all agreed.

"Come on!" cried Terry, pushing forward. "Oh, come on! Here goes for Herland!"

Chapter II
Rash Advances

Not more than ten or fifteen miles we judged it from our landing rock to that last village. For all our eagerness we thought it wise to keep to the woods and go carefully.

Even Terry's ardor was held in check by his firm conviction that there were men to be met, and we saw to it that each of us had a good stock of cartridges.

"They may be scarce, and they may be hidden away somewhere,—some kind of a matriarchate, as Jeff tells us; for that matter, they may live up in the mountains yonder and keep the women in this part of the country— sort of a national harem! But there are men somewhere—didn't you see the babies?"

We had all seen babies, children big and little, everywhere that we had come near enough to distinguish the people. And though by dress we could not be sure of all the grown persons, still there had not been one man that we were certain of.

"I always liked that Arab saying, 'First tie your camel and then trust in the Lord,'" Jeff murmured; so we all had our weapons in hand, and stole cautiously through the forest. Terry studied it as we progressed.

"Talk of civilization," he cried softly in restrained enthusiasm, "I never saw a forest so petted, even in Germany. Look, there's not a dead bough— the vines are trained—actually! And see here"—he stopped and looked about him, calling Jeff's attention to the kinds of trees.

They left me for a landmark and made a limited excursion on either side.

"Food-bearing, practically all of them," they announced returning. "The rest, splendid hard-wood. Call this a forest? It's a truck farm!"

"Good thing to have a botanist on hand," I agreed. "Sure there are no medicinal ones? Or any for pure ornament?"

As a matter of fact they were quite right. These towering trees were under as careful cultivation as so many cabbages. In other conditions we should have found those woods full of fair foresters and fruit gatherers; but an airship is a conspicuous object, and by no means quiet—and women are cautious.

All we found moving in those woods, as we started through them, were birds, some gorgeous, some musical, all so tame that it seemed almost to contradict our theory of cultivation; at least until we came upon occasional little glades, where carved stone seats and tables stood in the shade beside clear fountains, with shallow bird baths always added.

"They don't kill birds, and apparently they do kill cats," Terry declared. "*Must* be men here. Hark!"

We had heard something; something not in the least like a birdsong, and very much like a suppressed whisper of laughter—a little happy sound, instantly smothered. We stood like so many pointers, and then used our glasses, swiftly, carefully.

"It couldn't have been far off," said Terry excitedly. "How about this big tree?"

There was a very large and beautiful tree in the glade we had just entered, with thick wide-spreading branches that sloped out in lapping fans like a beech, or pine. It was trimmed underneath some twenty feet up, and stood there like a huge umbrella, with circling seats beneath.

"Look," he pursued. "There are short stumps of branches left to climb on. There's someone up that tree, I believe."

We stole near, cautiously.

"Look out for a poisoned arrow in your eye," I suggested; but Terry pressed forward, sprang up on the seat-back, and grasped the trunk. "In my heart, more likely," he answered—"Gee!—Look, boys!"

We rushed close in and looked up. There among the boughs overhead was something—more than one something; that clung motionless close to the great trunk at first, and then, as one and all we started up the tree, separated into three swift-moving figures and fled upwards. As we climbed we could catch glimpses of them scattering above us. By the time we had reached about as far as three men together dared push, they had left the main trunk and moved outwards, each one balanced on a long branch that dipped and swayed beneath the weight.

We paused uncertain. If we pursued further the boughs would break under the double burden. We might shake them off, perhaps, but none of us was so inclined. In the soft dappled light of these high regions, breathless with our rapid climb, we rested awhile, eagerly studying our objects of pursuit; while they in turn, with no more terror than a set of frolicsome children in a game of tag, sat as lightly as so many big bright birds on their precarious perches, and frankly, curiously, stared at us.

"Girls!" whispered Jeff, under his breath, as if they might fly if he spoke aloud.

"Peaches!" added Terry, scarcely louder. "Peacherinos—Apricot-nectarines! Whew!"

They were girls, of course, no boys could ever have shown that sparkling beauty, and yet none of us was certain at first.

We saw short hair, hatless, loose, and shining; a suit of some light firm stuff, the closest of tunics and kneebreeches, met by trim gaiters; as bright and smooth as parrots and as unaware of danger, they swung there before us, wholly at ease, staring as we stared, till first one, and then all of them burst into peals of delighted laughter.

Then there was a torrent of soft talk tossed back and forth; no savage sing-song, but clear musical fluent speech.

We met their laughter cordially, and doffed our hats to them, at which they laughed again, delightedly.

Then Terry, wholly in his element, made a polite speech, with explanatory gestures, and proceeded to introduce us, with pointing finger. "Mr. Jeff Margrave," he said clearly; Jeff bowed as gracefully as a man could in the fork of a great limb. "Mr. Vandyck Jennings"—I also tried to make an effective salute and nearly lost my balance.

Then Terry laid his hand upon his chest—a fine chest he had, too, and introduced himself: he was braced carefully for the occasion and achieved an excellent obeisance.

Again they laughed delightedly, and the one nearest me followed his tactics.

"Celis," she said distinctly, pointing to the one in blue; "Alima"—the one in rose; then, with a vivid imitation of Terry's impressive manner, she laid a firm delicate hand on her gold-green jerkin—"Ellador." This was pleasant, but we got no nearer.

"We can't sit here and learn the language," Terry protested. He beckoned to them to come nearer, most winningly—but they gaily shook their heads. He suggested, by signs, that we all go down together; but again they shook their heads, still merrily. Then Ellador clearly indicated that we should go down, pointing to each and all of us, with unmistakable firmness; and further seeming to imply by the sweep of a lithe arm that we not only go downward, but go away altogether—at which we shook our heads in turn.

"Have to use bait," grinned Terry. "I don't know about you fellows, but I came prepared." He produced from an inner pocket a little box of purple velvet, that opened with a snap—and out of it he drew a long sparkling thing, a necklace of big vari-colored stones that would have been worth a million if real ones. He held it up, swung it, glittering in the sun, offered it first to one, then to another, holding it out as far as he could reach toward the girl nearest him. He stood braced in the fork, held firmly by one hand— the other, swinging his bright temptation, reached far out along the bough, but not quite to his full stretch.

She was visibly moved, I noted, hesitated, spoke to her companions. They chattered softly together, one evidently warning her, the other encouraging. Then, softly and slowly, she drew nearer. This was Alima, a tall long-limbed lass, well-knit and evidently both strong and agile. Her eyes were splendid, wide, fearless, as free from suspicion as a child's who has never been rebuked. Her interest was more that of an intent boy playing a fascinating game than of a girl lured by an ornament.

The others moved a bit farther out, holding firmly, watching. Terry's smile was irreproachable, but I did not like the look in his eyes—it was like a creature about to spring. I could already see it happen—the dropped necklace, the sudden clutching hand—the girl's sharp cry as he seized her and drew her in. But it didn't happen. She made a timid reach with her right hand for the gay swinging thing—he held it a little nearer—then, swift as light, she seized it from him with her left, and dropped on the instant to the bough below.

He made his snatch, quite vainly, almost losing his position as his hand clutched only air; and then, with inconceivable rapidity, the three bright creatures were gone. They dropped from the ends of the big boughs to those below, fairly pouring themselves off the tree, while we climbed downward as swiftly as we could. We heard their vanishing gay laughter, we saw them fleeting away in the wide open reaches of the forest, and gave chase, but we might as well have chased wild antelopes; so we stopped at length somewhat breathless.

"No use," gasped Terry. "They got away with it. My word! The men of this country must be good sprinters!"

"Inhabitants evidently arboreal," I grimly suggested. "Civilized and still arboreal—peculiar people."

"You shouldn't have tried that way," Jeff protested. "They were perfectly friendly, now we've scared them."

But it was no use grumbling, and Terry refused to admit any mistake. "Nonsense," he said. "They expected it. Women like to be run after. Come on, let's get to that town; maybe we'll find them there. Let's see, it was in this direction, and not far from the woods as I remember."

When we reached the edge of the open country we reconnoitered with our field glasses. There it was, about four miles off, the same town we concluded, unless as Jeff ventured, they all had pink houses. The broad green fields and closely cultivated gardens sloped away at our feet, a long easy slant, with good roads winding pleasantly here and there, and narrower paths besides.

"Look at that!" cried Jeff suddenly, "There they go!"

Sure enough, close to the town, across a wide meadow, three bright-hued figures were running swiftly.

"How could they have got that far in this time? It can't be the same ones," I urged. But through the glasses we could identify our pretty tree-climbers quite plainly, at least by costume.

Terry watched them, we all did for that matter, till they disappeared among the houses. Then he put down his glass and turned to us, drawing a long breath. "Mother of Mike, boys—what Gorgeous Girls! To climb like that! to run like that! and afraid of nothing. This country suits me all right. Let's get ahead."

"Nothing venture, nothing have," I suggested, but Terry preferred "'Faint heart ne'er won fair lady.'"

We set forth in the open, walking briskly. "If there are any men, we'd better keep an eye out," I suggested, but Jeff seemed lost in heavenly dreams, and Terry in highly practical plans.

"What a perfect road! What a heavenly country! See the flowers, will you."

This was Jeff, always an enthusiast; but we could agree with him fully.

The road was some sort of hard manufactured stuff, sloped slightly to shed rain, with every curve and grade and gutter as perfect as if it were Europe's best. "No men, eh?" sneered Terry. On either side a double row of trees shaded the footpaths, between the trees bushes or vines, all fruit-bearing, now and then seats and little wayside fountains, everywhere flowers.

"We'd better import some of these ladies and set 'em to parking the United States," I suggested. "Mighty nice place they've got here." We rested a few moments by one of the fountains, tested the fruit that looked ripe, and went on, impressed, for all our gay bravado by the sense of quiet potency which lay about us.

Here was evidently a people highly skilled, efficient, caring for their country as a florist cares for his costliest orchids. Under the soft brilliant blue of that clear sky, in the pleasant shade of those endless rows of trees, we walked unharmed, the placid silence broken only by the birds.

Presently there lay before us at the foot of a long hill the town or village we were aiming for. We stopped and studied it.

Jeff drew a long breath. "I wouldn't have believed a collection of houses could look so lovely," he said.

"They've got architects and landscape gardeners in plenty, that's sure," agreed Terry.

I was astonished myself. You see, I come from California, and there's no country lovelier, but when it comes to towns—! I have often groaned at home to see the offensive mess man made in the face of nature, even though I'm no art sharp, like Jeff. But this place—! It was built mostly of a sort of dull rose colored stone, with here and there some clear white houses; and it lay abroad among the green groves and gardens like a broken rosary of pink coral.

"Those big white ones are public buildings evidently," Terry declared. "This is no savage country, my friend. But no men? Boys, it behooves us to go forward most politely."

The place had an odd look, more impressive as we approached. "It's like an Exposition." "It's too pretty to be true."—"Plenty of palaces, but where are the homes?" "Oh there are little ones enough—but—." It certainly was different from any towns we had ever seen.

"There's no dirt," said Jeff suddenly. "There's no smoke," he added after a little.

"There's no noise," I offered; but Terry snubbed me—"That's because they are laying low for us; we'd better be careful how we go in there."

Nothing could induce him to stay out however, so we walked on.

Everything was beauty, order, perfect cleanness and the pleasantest sense of home over it all. As we neared the center of the town the houses stood thicker, ran together as it were, grew into rambling palaces grouped among parks and open squares, something as college buildings stand in their quiet greens.

And then, turning a corner, we came into a broad paved space and saw before us a band of women standing close together in even order, evidently waiting for us.

147

We stopped a moment, and looked back. The street behind was closed by another band, marching steadily, shoulder to shoulder. We went on, there seemed no other way to do; and presently found ourselves quite surrounded by this close-massed multitude, women, all of them, but—

They were not young. They were not old. They were not, in the girl sense, beautiful, they were not in the least ferocious; and yet, as I looked from face to face, calm, grave, wise, wholly unafraid, evidently assured and determined, I had the funniest feeling—a very early feeling—a feeling that I traced back and back in memory until I caught up with it at last. It was that sense of being hopelessly in the wrong that I had so often felt in early youth when my short legs' utmost effort failed to overcome the fact that I was late to school.

Jeff felt it too, I could see he did. We felt like small boys, very small boys, caught doing mischief in some gracious lady's house. But Terry showed no such consciousness. I saw his quick eyes darting here and there, estimating numbers, measuring distances, judging chances of escape. He examined the close ranks about us, reaching back far on every side, and murmured softly to me, "Every one of 'em over forty as I'm a sinner."

Yet they were not old women. Each was in the full bloom of rosy health, erect, serene, standing sure-footed and light as any pugilist. They had no weapons, and we had, but we had no wish to shoot.

"I'd as soon shoot my Aunts," muttered Terry again. "What do they want with us anyhow? They seem to mean business." But in spite of that business-like aspect, he determined to try his favorite tactics. Terry had come armed with a theory.

He stepped forward, with his brilliant ingratiating smile, and made low obeisance to the women before him. Then he produced another tribute, a broad soft scarf of filmy texture, rich in color and pattern, a lovely thing, even to my eye, and offered it with a deep bow to the tall unsmiling woman who seemed to head the ranks before him. She took it with a gracious nod of acknowledgment, and passed it on to those behind her. He tried again, this time bringing out a circlet of rhine-stones, a glittering crown that should have pleased any woman on earth.

He made a brief address, including Jeff and me as partners in his enterprise, and with another bow presented this.

Again his gift was accepted, and as before, passed out of sight.

"If they were only younger," he muttered between his teeth. "What on earth is a fellow to say to a regiment of old Colonels like this?"

148

In all our discussions and speculations we had always unconsciously assumed that the women, whatever else they might be, would be young. Most men do think that way, I fancy.

"Woman" in the abstract is young, and, we assume, charming. As they get older they pass off the stage, somehow, into private ownership mostly, or out of it altogether. But these good ladies were very much on the stage, and yet any one of them might have been a grandmother.

We looked for nervousness—there was none.

For terror, perhaps—there was none.

For uneasiness, for curiosity, for excitement,—and all we saw was what might have been a vigilance committee of women doctors, as cool as cucumbers, and evidently meaning to take us to task for being there.

Six of them stepped forward now, one on either side of each of us, and indicated that we were to go with them. We thought it best to accede, at first anyway, and marched along, one of these close at each elbow, and the others in close masses before, behind, on both sides.

A large building opened before us, a very heavy thick-walled impressive place, big, and old-looking; of gray stone, not like the rest of the town.

"This won't do!" said Terry to us, quickly. "We mustn't let them get us in this, boys. All together, now—"

We stopped in our tracks. We began to explain, to make signs pointing away toward the big forest—indicating that we would go back to it—at once.

It makes me laugh, knowing all I do now, to think of us three boys— nothing else; three audacious impertinent boys—butting into an unknown country without any sort of a guard or defense. We seemed to think that if there were men we could fight them, and if there were only women—why, they would be no obstacles at all.

Jeff, with his gentle romantic old-fashioned notions of women as clinging vines; Terry, with his clear decided practical theories that there were two kinds of women—those he wanted and those he didn't; Desirable and Undesirable was his demarcation. The last was a large class, but negligible—he had never thought about them at all.

And now here they were, in great numbers, evidently indifferent to what he might think, evidently determined on some purpose of their own regarding him, and apparently well able to enforce their purpose.

149

We all thought hard just then. It had not seemed wise to object to going with them—even if we could have, our one chance was friendliness—a civilized attitude on both sides.

But once inside that building, there was no knowing what these determined ladies might do to us. Even a peaceful detention was not to our minds, and when we named it imprisonment it looked even worse.

So we made a stand, trying to make clear that we preferred the open country. One of them came forward with a sketch of our flier, asking by signs if we were the aerial visitors they had seen.

This we admitted.

They pointed to it again, and to the outlying country, in different directions—but we pretended we did not know where it was—and in truth we were not quite sure, and gave a rather wild indication of its whereabouts.

Again they motioned us to advance, standing so packed about the door that there remained but the one straight path open. All around us and behind they were massed solidly—there was simply nothing to do but go forward—or fight.

We held a consultation.

"I never fought with women in my life," said Terry, greatly perturbed, "But I'm not going in there. I'm not going to be—herded in—as if we were in a cattle chute."

"We can't fight them, of course," Jeff urged. "They're all women, in spite of their nondescript clothes; nice women, too; good strong sensible faces. I guess we'll have to go in."

"We may never get out, if we do," I told them. "Strong and sensible, yes; but I'm not so sure about the good. Look at those faces!"

They had stood at ease, waiting, while we conferred together; but never relaxing their close attention.

Their attitude was not the rigid discipline of soldiers, there was no sense of compulsion about them. Terry's term of a "vigilance committee" was highly descriptive. They had just the aspect of sturdy burghers, gathered hastily to meet some common need or peril, all moved by precisely the same feelings, to the same end.

Never, anywhere before, had I seen women of precisely this quality. Fishwives and market women might show similar strength, but it was coarse and heavy. These were merely athletic, light and powerful. College professors, teachers, writers,—many women showed similar intelligence, but often wore a strained nervous look, while these were as calm as cows, for all their evident intellect.

We observed pretty closely just then, for all of us felt that it was a crucial moment.

The leader gave some word of command and beckoned us on, and the surrounding mass moved a step nearer.

"We've got to decide quick," said Terry.

"I vote to go in," Jeff urged. But we were two to one against him and he loyally stood by us. We made one more effort to be let go, urgent, but not imploring. In vain.

"Now for a rush, boys!" Terry said. "And if we can't break 'em I'll shoot in the air."

Then we found ourselves much in the position of the suffragette trying to get to the Parliament buildings through a triple cordon of London police.

The solidity of those women was something amazing. Terry soon found that it was useless, tore himself loose for a moment, pulled his revolver, and fired upward. As they caught at it, he fired again—we heard a cry—.

Instantly each of us was seized by five women, each holding arm or leg or head; we were lifted like children, straddling helpless children, and borne onward, wriggling indeed, but most ineffectually.

We were borne inside, struggling manfully, but held secure most womanfully, in spite of our best endeavors.

So carried and so held, we came into a high inner hall, gray and bare, and were brought before a majestic gray-haired woman who seemed to hold a judicial position.

There was some talk, not much, among them, and then suddenly there fell upon each of us at once a firm hand holding a wetted cloth before mouth and nose—an order of swimming sweetness—anesthesia.

151

Chapter III

A Peculiar Imprisonment

From a slumber as deep as death, as refreshing as that of a healthy child, I slowly awakened.

It was like rising up, up, up through a deep warm ocean, nearer and nearer to full light and stirring air. Or like the return to consciousness after concussion of the brain. I was once thrown from a horse while on a visit to a wild mountainous country quite new to me, and I can clearly remember the mental experience of coming back to life, through lifting veils of dream. When I first dimly heard the voices of those about me, and saw the shining snow-peaks of that mighty range, I assumed that this too would pass, and I should presently find myself in my own home.

That was precisely the experience of this awakening: receding waves of half-caught swirling vision, memories of home, the steamer, the boat, the airship, the forest—at last all sinking away one after another, till my eyes were wide open, my brain clear, and I realized what had happened.

The most prominent sensation was of absolute physical comfort. I was lying in a perfect bed, long, broad, smooth; firmly soft and level; with the finest linen, some warm light quilt of blanket, and a counterpane that was a joy to the eye. The sheet turned down some fifteen inches, yet I could stretch my feet at the foot of the bed, free but warmly covered.

I felt as light and clean as a white feather. It took me some time to consciously locate my arms and legs, to feel the vivid sense of life radiate from the wakening center to the extremities.

A big room, high and wide, with many lofty windows whose closed blinds let through soft green-lit air; a beautiful room, in proportion, in color, in smooth simplicity; a scent of blossoming gardens outside.

I lay perfectly still, quite happy, quite conscious, and yet not actively realizing what had happened till I heard Terry.

"Gosh!" was what he said.

I turned my head. There were three beds in this chamber, and plenty of room for them.

Terry was sitting up, looking about him, alert as ever. His remark, though not loud, roused Jeff also. We all sat up.

Terry swung his legs out of bed, stood up, stretched himself mightily. He was in a long night-robe, a sort of seamless garment, undoubtedly comfortable—we all found ourselves so covered. Shoes were beside each bed, also quite comfortable and good-looking though by no means like our own.

We looked for our clothes—they were not there, nor anything of all the varied contents of our pockets.

A door stood somewhat ajar; it opened into a most attractive bathroom, copiously provided with towels, soap, mirrors, and all such convenient comforts, with indeed our toothbrushes and combs, our notebooks, and thank goodness, our watches—but no clothes.

Then we made a search of the big room again and found a large airy closet, holding plenty of clothing, but not ours.

"A council of war!" demanded Terry. "Come on back to bed—the bed's all right anyhow. Now then, my scientific friend, let us consider our case dispassionately."

He meant me, but Jeff seemed most impressed.

"They haven't hurt us in the least!" he said. "They could have killed us—or—or anything—and I never felt better in my life."

"That argues that they *are* all women," I suggested, "and highly civilized. You know you hit one in the last scrimmage—I heard her sing out—and we kicked awfully."

Terry was grinning at us. "Do you realize what these ladies have done to us?" he pleasantly inquired. "They have taken away *all* our possessions, *all* our clothes—every stitch. We have been stripped and washed and put to bed like so many yearling babies—by these highly civilized women."

Jeff actually blushed. He had a poetic imagination. Terry had imagination enough, of a different kind. So had I, also different. I always flattered myself I had the scientific imagination, which, incidentally, I considered the highest sort. One has a right to a certain amount of egotism if founded on fact—and kept to one's self—*I* think.

"No use kicking, boys," I said. "They've got us, and apparently they're perfectly harmless. It remains for us to cook up some plan of escape like any other bottled heroes. Meanwhile we've got to put on these clothes—Hobson's choice."

The garments were simple in the extreme, and absolutely comfortable, physically, though of course we all felt like supes in the theater. There was a one-piece cotton undergarment, thin and soft, that reached over the knees and shoulders, something like the one-piece pajamas some fellows wear, and a kind of half-hose, that came up to just under the knee and stayed there—had as elastic top of their own, and covered the edges of the first.

Then there was a thicker variety of union suit, a lot of them in the closet, of varying weights and somewhat sturdier material—evidently they would do at a pinch with nothing further. Then there were tunics, knee length, and some long robes. Needless to say, we took tunics.

We bathed and dressed quite cheerfully.

"Not half bad," said Terry, surveying himself in a long mirror. His hair was somewhat longer than when we left the last barber, and the hats provided were much like those seen on the Prince in the fairy-tale, lacking the plume.

The costume was similar to that which we had seen on all the women, though some of them, those working in the fields, glimpsed by our glasses when we first flew over, wore only the first two.

I settled my shoulders and stretched my arms, remarking: "They have worked out a mighty sensible dress, I'll say that for them." With which we all agreed.

"Now then," Terry proclaimed, "we've had a fine long sleep—we've had a good bath—we're clothed and in our right minds, though feeling like a lot of neuters. Do you think these highly civilized ladies are going to give us any breakfast?"

"Of course they will," Jeff asserted confidently. "If they had meant to kill us, they would have done it before. I believe we are going to be treated as guests."

"Hailed as deliverers, I think," said Terry.

"Studied as curiosities," I told them. "But anyhow, we want food. So now for a sortie!"

A sortie was not so easy.

The bathroom only opened into our chamber, and that had but one outlet, a big heavy door, which was fastened.

We listened.

"There's someone outside," Jeff suggested. "Let's knock."

So we knocked, whereupon the door opened.

Outside was another large room, furnished with a great table at one end, long benches or couches against the wall, some smaller tables and chairs.

All these were solid, strong, simple in structure, and comfortable in use, also, incidentally, beautiful.

This room was occupied by a number of women, eighteen to be exact, some of whom we distinctly recalled.

Terry heaved a disappointed sigh. "The Colonels!" I heard him whisper to Jeff.

Jeff, however, advanced and bowed in his best manner; so did we all, and we were saluted civilly by the tall standing women.

We had no need to make pathetic pantomime of hunger; the smaller tables were already laid with food, and we were gravely invited to be seated. The tables were set for two; each of us found ourselves placed vis-a-vis with one of our hosts, and each table had five other stalwarts nearby, unobtrusively watching. We had plenty of time to get tired of those women!

The breakfast was not profuse, but sufficient in amount and excellent in quality. We were all too good travelers to object to novelty, and this repast with its new but delicious fruit, its dish of large rich-flavored nuts, and its highly satisfactory little cakes, was most agreeable. There was water to drink, and a hot beverage of a most pleasing quality, some preparation like cocoa.

And then and there, willy-nilly, before we had satisfied our appetites, our education began.

By each of our plates lay a little book, a real printed book, though different from ours both in paper and binding, as well, of course, as in type. We examined them curiously.

"Shades of Sauveur!" muttered Terry. "We're to learn the language!"

We were indeed to learn the language, and not only that, but to teach our own. There were blank books with parallel columns, neatly ruled, evidently prepared for the occasion, and in these, as fast as we learned and wrote down the name of anything we were urged to write our own name for it by its side.

The book we had to study was evidently a school-book, one in which children learned to read, and we judged from this, and from their frequent consultation as to methods, that they had had no previous experience in the art of teaching foreigners their language, or of learning any other.

On the other hand, what they lacked in experience, they made up for in genius. Such subtle understanding, such instant recognition of our

155

difficulties, and readiness to meet them, were a constant surprise to us.

Of course, we were willing to meet them halfway. It was wholly to our advantage to be able to understand and speak with them, and as to refusing to teach them—why should we? Later on we did try open rebellion, but only once.

That first meal was pleasant enough, each of us quietly studying his companion, Jeff with sincere admiration, Terry with that highly technical look of his, as of a past master—like a lion-tamer, a serpent charmer, or some such professional. I myself was intensely interested.

It was evident that those sets of five were there to check any outbreak on our part. We had no weapons, and if we did try to do any damage, with a chair, say, why five to one was too many for us, even if they were women; that we had found out to our sorrow. It was not pleasant, having them always around, but we soon got used to it.

"It's better than being physically restrained ourselves," Jeff philosophically suggested when we were alone. "They've given us a room—with no great possibility of escape—and personal liberty—heavily chaperoned. It's better than we'd have been likely to get in a man-country."

"Man-Country! Do you really believe there are no men here, you innocent? Don't you know there must be?" demanded Terry.

"Ye—es," Jeff agreed. "Of course—and yet—"

"And yet—what! Come, you obdurate sentimentalist—what are you thinking about?"

"They may have some peculiar division of labor we've never heard of," I suggested. "The men may live in separate towns, or they may have subdued them—somehow—and keep them shut up. But there must be some."

"That last suggestion of yours is a nice one, Van," Terry protested. "Same as they've got us subdued and shut up! You make me shiver."

"Well, figure it out for yourself, anyway you please. We saw plenty of kids, the first day, and we've seen those girls—"

"Real girls!" Terry agreed, in immense relief. "Glad you mentioned 'em. I declare, if I thought there was nothing in the country but those grenadiers I'd jump out the window."

"Speaking of windows," I suggested, "let's examine ours."

We looked out of all the windows. The blinds opened easily enough, and there were no bars, but the prospect was not reassuring.

This was not the pink-walled town we had so rashly entered the day before. Our chamber was high up, in a projecting wing of a sort of castle, built out on a steep spur of rock. Immediately below us were gardens, fruitful and fragrant, but their high walls followed the edge of the cliff which dropped sheer down, we could not see how far. The distant sound of water suggested a river at the foot.

We could look out east, west, and south. To the southeastward stretched the open country, lying bright and fair in the morning light, but on either side, and evidently behind, rose great mountains.

"This thing is a regular fortress—and no women built it, I can tell you that," said Terry. We nodded agreeingly. "It's right up among the hills—they must have brought us a long way."

"And pretty fast, too," I added.

"We saw some kind of swift moving vehicles the first day," Jeff reminded us. "If they've got motors they *are* civilized."

"Civilized or not, we've got our work cut out for us to get away from here. I don't propose to make a rope of bedclothes and try those walls till I'm sure there is no better way."

We all concurred on this point, and returned to our discussion as to the women.

Jeff continued thoughtful. "All the same, there's something funny about it," he urged. "It isn't just that we don't see any men—but we don't see any signs of them. The—the—reaction of these women is different from any that I've ever met."

"There is something in what you say, Jeff," I agreed. "There is a different—atmosphere."

"They don't seem to notice our being men," he went on. "They treat us—well—just as they do one another. It's as if our being men was a minor incident."

I nodded. I'd noticed it myself. But Terry broke in rudely.

"Fiddlesticks!" he said. "It's because of their advanced age. They're all grandmas, I tell you—or ought to be. Great aunts, anyhow. Those girls were girls all right, weren't they?"

"Yes—" Jeff agreed, still slowly. "But they weren't afraid—they flew up that tree and hid, like school-boys caught out of bounds—not like shy girls."

"And they ran like Marathon winners—you'll admit that, Terry," he added.

Terry was moody as the days passed. He seemed to mind our confinement more than Jeff or I did; and he harped on Alima, and how near he'd come to catching her. "If I had—" he would say, rather savagely, "we'd have had a hostage and could have made terms."

But Jeff was getting on excellent terms with his tutor, and even his guards, and so was I. It interested me profoundly, to note and study the subtle difference between these women and other women, and try to account for them. In the matter of personal appearance, there was a great difference. They all wore short hair, some few inches at most; some curly, some not, all light and clean and fresh-looking.

"If their hair was only long," Jeff would complain, "they would look so much more feminine."

I rather liked it myself, after I got used to it. Why we should so admire "a woman's crown of hair" and not admire a Chinaman's queue is hard to explain, except that we are so convinced that the long hair "belongs" to a woman. Whereas the "mane" in horses, is on both, and in lions, buffalos and such creatures only on the male. But I did miss it—at first.

Our time was quite pleasantly filled. We were free of the garden below our windows, quite long in its irregular rambling shape, bordering the cliff. The walls were perfectly smooth and high, ending in the masonry of the building; and as I studied the great stones I became convinced that the whole structure was extremely old. It was built like the pre-Incan architecture in Peru, of enormous monoliths, fitted as closely as mosaics.

"These folks have a history, that's sure," I told the others. "And *some* time they were fighters—else why a fortress?"

I said we were free of the garden, but not wholly alone in it. There was always a string of those uncomfortably strong women sitting about, always one of them watching us even if the others were reading, playing games, or busy at some kind of handiwork.

"When I see them knit," Terry said, "I can almost call them feminine."

"That doesn't prove anything," Jeff promptly replied. "Scotch shepherds knit—always knitting."

"When we get out—" Terry stretched himself and looked at the far peaks, "when we get out of this and get to where the real women are—the mothers, and the girls—"

"Well, what'll we do then?" I asked, rather gloomily. "How do you know we'll ever get out?"

This was an unpleasant idea, which we unanimously considered, returning with earnestness to our studies.

"If we are good boys and learn our lessons well," I suggested. "If we are quiet and respectful and polite and they are not afraid of us—then perhaps they will let us out. And anyway—when we do escape, it is of immense importance that we know the language."

Personally, I was tremendously interested in that language, and seeing they had books, was eager to get at them, to dig into their history, if they had one.

It was not hard to speak, smooth and pleasant to the ear, and so easy to read and write that I marveled at it. They had an absolutely phonetic system, the whole thing was as scientific as Esparanto yet bore all the marks of an old and rich civilization.

We were free to study as much as we wished, and were not left merely to wander in the garden for recreation but introduced to a great gymnasium, partly on the roof and partly in the story below. Here we learned real respect for our tall guards. No change of costume was needed for this work, save to lay off outer clothing. The first one was as perfect a garment for exercise as need be devised, absolutely free to move in, and, I had to admit, much better looking than our usual one.

"Forty—over forty—some of 'em fifty, I bet—and look at 'em!" grumbled Terry in reluctant admiration.

There were no spectacular acrobatics, such as only the young can perform, but for all-around development they had a most excellent system. A good deal of music went with it, with posture dancing, and sometimes, gravely beautiful processional performances.

Jeff was much impressed by it. We did not know then how small a part of their physical culture methods this really was, but found it agreeable to watch, and to take part in.

Oh yes, we took part all right! It wasn't absolutely compulsory, but we thought it better to please.

Terry was the strongest of us, though I was wiry and had good staying power, and Jeff was a great sprinter and hurdler, but I can tell you those old ladies gave us cards and spades. They ran like deer, by which I mean that they ran not as if it was a performance, but as if it was their natural gait. We remembered those fleeting girls of our first bright adventure, and concluded that it was.

They leaped like deer, too, with a quick folding motion of the legs, drawn up and turned to one side with a sidelong twist of the body. I remembered the sprawling spread-eagle way in which some of the fellows used to come over the line—and tried to learn the trick. We did not easily catch up with these experts, however.

"Never thought I'd live to be bossed by a lot of elderly lady acrobats," Terry protested.

They had games, too, a good many of them, but we found them rather uninteresting at first. It was like two people playing solitaire to see who would get it first; more like a race or a—a competitive examination, than a real game with some fight in it.

I philosophized a bit over this and told Terry it argued against their having any men about. "There isn't a man-size game in the lot," I said.

"But they are interesting—I like them," Jeff objected, "and I'm sure they are educational."

"I'm sick and tired of being educated," Terry protested. "Fancy going to a dame school—at our age. I want to Get Out!"

But we could not get out, and we were being educated swiftly. Our special tutors rose rapidly in our esteem. They seemed of rather finer quality than the guards, though all were on terms of easy friendliness. Mine was named Somel, Jeff's Zava, and Terry's Moadine. We tried to generalize from the names, those of the guards, and of our three girls, but got nowhere.

"They sound well enough, and they're mostly short, but there's no similarity of termination—and no two alike. However, our acquaintance is limited as yet."

There were many things we meant to ask—as soon as we could talk well enough. Better teaching I never saw. From morning to night there was Somel, always on call except between two and four; always pleasant with a steady friendly kindness that I grew to enjoy very much. Jeff said Miss Zava—he would put on a title, though they apparently had none—was a darling, that she reminded him of his Aunt Esther at home; but Terry refused to be won, and rather jeered at his own companion, when we were alone.

"I'm sick of it!" he protested. "Sick of the whole thing. Here we are cooped up as helpless as a bunch of three-year-old orphans, and being taught what they think is necessary—whether we like it or not. Confound their old-maid impudence!"

Nevertheless we were taught. They brought in a raised map of their country, beautifully made, and increased our knowledge of geographical terms; but when we inquired for information as to the country outside, they smilingly shook their heads.

They brought pictures, not only the engravings in the books, but colored studies of plants and trees and flowers and birds. They brought tools and various small objects—we had plenty of "material" in our school.

And, as we made progress, they brought more and more books.

If it had not been for Terry we would have been much more contented, but as the weeks ran into months he grew more and more irritable.

"Don't act like a bear with a sore head," I begged him. "We're getting on finely. Every day we can understand them better, and pretty soon we can make a reasonable plea to be let out—"

"*Let* out!" he stormed. "*Let* out—like children kept after school. I want to Get Out, and I'm going to. I want to find the men of this place and fight!—or the girls—"

"Guess it's the girls you're most interested in," Jeff commented. "What are you going to fight *with*—your fists?"

"Yes—or sticks and stones—I'd just like to!" And Terry squared off and tapped Jeff softly on the jaw—"just for instance," he said.

"Anyhow," he went on, "we could get back to our machine and clear out."

"If it's there—" I cautiously suggested.

"Oh, don't croak, Van! If it isn't there, we'll find our way down somehow—the boat's there, I guess—"

It was hard on Terry, so hard that he finally persuaded us to consider a plan of escape. It was difficult; it was highly dangerous, but he declared that he'd go alone if we wouldn't go with him, and of course we couldn't think of that.

It appeared he had made a pretty careful study of the environment. From our end window that faced the point of the promontory we could get a fair idea of the stretch of wall, and the drop below. Also from the roof we could make out more, and even, in one place, glimpse a sort of path below the wall.

161

"It's a question of three things," he said. "Ropes, agility, and not being seen."

"That's the hardest part," I urged, still hoping to dissuade him. "One or another pair of eyes is on us every minute except at night."

"Therefore we must do it at night," he answered. "That's easy."

"We've got to think that if they catch us we may not be so well treated afterward," said Jeff.

"That's the business risk we must take. I'm going—if I break my neck." There was no changing him.

The rope problem was not easy. Something strong enough to hold a man and long enough to let us down into the garden, and then down over the wall. There were plenty of strong ropes in the gymnasium—they seemed to love to swing and climb on them—but we were never there by ourselves.

We should have to piece it out from our bedding, rugs, and garments, and moreover, we should have to do it after we were shut in for the night, for every day the place was cleaned to perfection by two of our guardians.

We had no shears, no knives, but Terry was resourceful. "These Jennies have glass and china, you see. We'll break a glass from the bathroom and use that. 'Love will find out a way,'" he hummed. "When we're all out of the window, we'll stand three man high and cut the rope as far up as we can reach, so as to have more for the wall. I know just where I saw that bit of path below, and there's a big tree there, too, or a vine or something—I saw the leaves."

It seemed a crazy risk to take, but this was, in a way, Terry's expedition, and we were all tired of our imprisonment.

So we waited for full moon, retired early, and spent an anxious hour or two in the unskilled manufacture of man-strong ropes.

To retire into the depths of the closet, muffle a glass in thick cloth, and break it without noise was not difficult, and broken glass will cut, though not as deftly as a pair of scissors.

The broad moonlight streamed in through four of our windows—we had not dared leave our lights on too long; and we worked hard and fast at our task of destruction.

Hangings, rugs, robes, towels, as well as bed-furniture—even the mattress covers—we left not one stitch upon another, as Jeff put it.

162

Then at an end window, as less liable to observation, we fastened one end of our cable, strongly, to the firm-set hinge of the inner blind, and dropped our coiled bundle of rope softly over.

"This part's easy enough—I'll come last, so as to cut the rope," said Terry.

So I slipped down first, and stood, well braced against the wall; then Jeff on my shoulders, then Terry, who shook us a little as he sawed through the cord above his head. Then I slowly dropped to the ground, Jeff following, and at last we all three stood safe in the garden, with most of our rope with us.

"Good-bye, Grandma!" whispered Terry, under his breath, and we crept softly toward the wall, taking advantage of the shadow of every bush and tree. He had been foresighted enough to mark the very spot, only a scratch of stone on stone, but we could see to read in that light. For anchorage there was a tough, fair-sized shrub close to the wall.

"Now I'll climb up on you two again and go over first," said Terry. "That'll hold the rope firm till you both get up on top. Then I'll go down to the end. If I can get off safely, you can see me and follow—or, say, I'll twitch it three times. If I find there's absolutely no footing—why I'll climb up again, that's all. I don't think they'll kill us."

From the top he reconnoitered carefully, waved his hand, and whispered, "O.K.," then slipped over. Jeff climbed up and I followed, and we rather shivered to see how far down that swaying, wavering figure dropped, hand under hand, till it disappeared in a mass of foliage far below.

Then there were three quick pulls, and Jeff and I, not without a joyous sense of recovered freedom, successfully followed our leader.

Chapter IV

Our Venture

We were standing on a narrow, irregular, all too slanting little ledge, and should doubtless have ignominiously slipped off and broken our rash necks but for the vine. This was a thick-leaved, wide-spreading thing, a little like Amphelopsis.

"It's not *quite* vertical here, you see," said Terry, full of pride and enthusiasm. "This thing never would hold our direct weight, but I think if we sort of slide down on it, one at a time, sticking in with hands and feet, we'll reach that next ledge alive."

"As we do not wish to get up our rope again—and can't comfortably stay here, I approve," said Jeff solemnly.

Terry slid down first—said he'd show us how a Christian meets his death. Luck was with us. We had put on the thickest of those intermediate suits, leaving our tunics behind, and made this scramble quite successfully, though I got a pretty heavy fall just at the end, and was only kept on the second ledge by main force. The next stage was down a sort of "chimney"—a long irregular fissure; and so with scratches many and painful and bruises not a few, we finally reached the stream.

It was darker there, but we felt it highly necessary to put as much distance as possible behind us; so we waded, jumped, and clambered down that rocky river-bed, in the flickering black and white moonlight and leaf shadow, till growing daylight forced a halt.

We found a friendly nut-tree, those large, satisfying, soft-shelled nuts we already knew so well, and filled our pockets.

I see that I have not remarked that these women had pockets in surprising number and variety. They were in all their garments, and the middle one in particular was shingled with them. So we stocked up with nuts till we bulged like a Prussian private in marching order; drank all we could hold, and retired for the day.

It was not a very comfortable place, not at all easy to get at; just a sort of crevice high up along the steep bank; but it was well veiled with foliage and dry. After our exhaustive three or four hours' scramble and the good breakfast food, we all lay down along that crack,—heads and tails, as it were—and slept till the afternoon sun almost toasted our faces.

Terry poked a tentative foot against my head.

"How are you, Van? Alive yet?"

"Very much so," I told him. And Jeff was equally cheerful.

We had room to stretch, if not to turn around; but we could very carefully roll over, one at a time, behind the sheltering foliage.

It was no use to leave there by daylight. We could not see much of the country, but enough to know that we were now at the beginning of the cultivated area, and no doubt there would be an alarm sent out far and wide.

Terry chuckled softly to himself, lying there on that hot narrow little rim of rock. He dilated on the discomfiture of our guards and tutors, making many discourteous remarks.

I reminded him that we had still a long way to go before getting to the place where we'd left our machine, and no probability of finding it there; but he only kicked me, mildly, for a croaker.

"If you can't boost, don't knock," he protested. "I never said 'twould be a picnic. But I'd run away in the Antarctic ice-fields rather than be a prisoner."

We soon dozed off again.

The long rest and penetrating dry heat were good for us, and that night we covered a considerable distance, keeping always in the rough forested belt of land which we knew bordered the whole country. Sometimes we were near the outer edge, and caught sudden glimpses of the tremendous depths beyond.

"This piece of geography stands up like a basalt column," Jeff said. "Nice time we'll have getting down if they have confiscated our machine!" For which suggestion he received summary chastisement.

What we could see inland was peaceable enough, but only moonlit glimpses; by daylight we lay very close. As Terry said, we did not wish to kill the old ladies—even if we could; and short of that they were perfectly competent to pick us up bodily and carry us back, if discovered. There was nothing for it but to lie low, and sneak out unseen if we could do it.

There wasn't much talking done. At night we had our Marathon-obstacle race; we "stayed not for brake and we stopped not for stone," and swam whatever water was too deep to wade and could not be got around; but that was only necessary twice. By day, sleep, sound and sweet. Mighty lucky it was that we could live off the country as we did. Even that margin of forest seemed rich in food-stuffs.

But Jeff thoughtfully suggested that that very thing showed how careful we should have to be, as we might run into some stalwart group of gardeners or foresters or nut-gatherers at any minute. Careful we were, feeling pretty sure that if we did not make good this time we were not likely to have another opportunity; and at last we reached a point from which we could see, far below, the broad stretch of that still lake from which we had made our ascent.

"That looks pretty good to me!" said Terry, gazing down at it. "Now, if we can't find the 'plane, we know where to aim if we have to drop over this wall some other way."

The wall at that point was singularly uninviting. It rose so straight that we had to put our heads over to see the base, and the country below seemed to be a far-off marshy tangle of rank vegetation. We did not have to risk our necks to that extent, however, for at last, stealing along among the rocks and trees like so many creeping savages, we came to that flat space where we had landed; and there, in unbelievable good fortune, we found our machine.

"Covered, too, by jingo! Would you think they had that much sense?" cried Terry.

"If they had that much, they're likely to have more," I warned him, softly. "Bet you the thing's watched."

We reconnoitered as widely as we could in the failing moonlight—moons are of a painfully unreliable nature; but the growing dawn showed us the familiar shape, shrouded in some heavy cloth like canvas, and no slightest sign of any watchman near. We decided to make a quick dash as soon as the light was strong enough for accurate work.

"I don't care if the old thing'll go or not," Terry declared. "We can run her to the edge, get aboard, and just plane down—plop!—beside our boat there. Look there—see the boat!"

Sure enough—there was our motor, lying like a gray cocoon on the flat pale sheet of water.

Quietly but swiftly we rushed forward and began to tug at the fastenings of that cover.

"Confound the thing!" Terry cried in desperate impatience. "They've got it sewed up in a bag! And we've not a knife among us!"

Then, as we tugged and pulled at that tough cloth we heard a sound that made Terry lift his head like a war horse,—the sound of an unmistakable giggle; yes—three giggles.

There they were—Celis, Alima, Ellador,—looking just as they had when we first saw them, standing a little way off from us, as interested, as mischievous as three schoolboys.

"Hold on, Terry—hold on!" I warned. "That's too easy. Look out for a trap."

"Let us appeal to their kind hearts," Jeff urged. "I think they will help us. Perhaps they've got knives."

"It's no use rushing them, anyhow." I was absolutely holding on to Terry. "We know they can out-run and out-climb us."

He reluctantly admitted this; and after a brief parley among ourselves, we all advanced slowly toward them, holding out our hands in token of friendliness.

They stood their ground till we had come fairly near, and then indicated that we should stop. To make sure, we advanced a step or two and they promptly and swiftly withdrew. So we stopped at the distance specified. Then we used their language, as far as we were able, to explain our plight; telling how we were imprisoned, how we had escaped—a good deal of pantomime here and vivid interest on their part—how we had traveled by night and hidden by day, living on nuts—and here Terry pretended great hunger.

I know he could not have been hungry; we had found plenty to eat and had not been sparing in helping ourselves. But they seemed somewhat impressed; and after a murmured consultation they produced from their pockets certain little packages, and with the utmost ease and accuracy tossed them into our hands.

Jeff was most appreciative of this; and Terry made extravagant gestures of admiration, which seemed to set them off, boy-fashion, to show their skill. While we ate the excellent biscuit they had thrown us, and while Ellador kept a watchful eye on our movements, Celis ran off to some distance, and set up a sort of "duck-on-a-rock" arrangement, a big yellow nut on top of three balanced sticks; Alima, meanwhile, gathering stones.

They urged us to throw at it, and we did, but the thing was a long way off, and it was only after a number of failures, at which those elvish damsels laughed delightedly, that Jeff succeeded in bringing the whole structure to the ground. It took me still longer, and Terry, to his intense annoyance, came third.

Then Celis set up the little tripod again, and looked back at us, knocking it down, pointing at it, and shaking her short curls severely. "No," she said. "Bad—wrong!" We were quite able to follow her.

Then she set it up once more, put the fat nut on top, and returned to the others; and there those aggravating girls sat and took turns throwing little stones at that thing, while one stayed by as a setter-up; and they just popped that nut off, two times out of three, without upsetting the sticks. Pleased as Punch they were, too, and we pretended to be, but weren't.

We got very friendly over this game, but I told Terry we'd be sorry if we didn't get off while we could, and then we begged for knives. It was easy to show what we wanted to do, and they each proudly produced a sort of strong clasp-knife from their pockets.

"Yes," we said eagerly, "that's it! Please—" We had learned quite a bit of their language, you see. And we just begged for those knives, but they would not give them to us. If we came a step too near they backed off, standing light and eager for flight.

"It's no sort of use," I said. "Come on—let's get a sharp stone or something—we must get this thing off."

So we hunted about and found what edged fragments we could, and hacked away, but it was like trying to cut sailcloth with a clam-shell.

Terry hacked and dug, but said to us under his breath, "Boys—we're in pretty good condition—let's make a life and death dash and get hold of those girls—we've got to."

They had drawn rather nearer, to watch our efforts, and we did take them rather by surprise; also, as Terry said, our recent training had strengthened us in wind and limb, and for a few desperate moments those girls were scared and we almost triumphant.

But just as we stretched out our hands, the distance between us widened; they had got their pace apparently, and then, though we ran at our utmost speed, and much farther than I thought wise, they kept just out of reach all the time.

We stopped breathless, at last, at my repeated admonitions.

"This is stark foolishness," I urged. "They are doing it on purpose—come back or you'll be sorry."

We went back, much slower than we came, and in truth we were sorry.

As we reached our swaddled machine, and sought again to tear loose its covering, there rose up from all around the sturdy forms, the quiet determined faces we knew so well.

"Oh Lord!" groaned Terry. "The Colonels! It's all up—they're forty to one."

It was no use to fight. These women evidently relied on numbers; not so much as a drilled force, but as a multitude actuated by a common impulse. They showed no sign of fear, and since we had no weapons whatever, and there were at least a hundred of them, standing ten deep about us, we gave in as gracefully as we might.

Of course we looked for punishment; a closer imprisonment, solitary confinement maybe; but nothing of the kind happened. They treated us as truants only; and as if they quite understood our truancy.

Back we went; not under an anesthetic this time, but skimming along in electric motors; enough like ours to be quite recognizable; each of us in a separate vehicle with one able-bodied lady on either side and three facing him.

They were all pleasant enough, and talked to us as much as was possible with our limited powers. And though Terry was keenly mortified, and at first we all rather dreaded harsh treatment, I for one soon began to feel a sort of pleasant confidence, and to enjoy the trip.

Here were my five familiar companions, all good-natured as could be, seeming to have no worse feeling than a mild triumph as of winning some simple game; and even that they politely suppressed.

This was a good opportunity to see the country, too, and the more I saw of it, the better I liked it. We went too swiftly for close observation, but I could appreciate perfect roads, as dustless as a swept floor; the shade of endless lines of trees; the ribbon of flowers that unrolled beneath them; and the rich comfortable country that stretched off and away, full of varied charm.

We rolled through many villages and towns, and I soon saw that the park-like beauty of our first-seen city was no exception. Our swift high-sweeping view from the 'plane had been most attractive, but lacked detail; and in that first day of struggle and capture, we noticed but little; but now we were swept along at an easy rate of some thirty miles an hour and covered quite a good deal of ground.

We stopped for lunch in quite a size-able town, and here, rolling slowly through the streets, we saw more of the population. They had come out to look at us everywhere we had passed, but here were more; and when we

169

went in to eat, in a big garden place, with little shaded tables among the trees and flowers, many eyes were upon us. And everywhere, open country, village, or city—only women. Old women and young women and a great majority who seemed neither young nor old, but just women; young girls, also, though these, and the children, seeming to be in groups by themselves generally, were less in evidence. We caught many glimpses of girls and children in what seemed to be schools or in playgrounds, and so far as we could judge there were no boys. We all looked, carefully. Everyone gazed at us politely, kindly, and with eager interest. No one was impertinent. We could catch quite a bit of the talk, now; and all they said seemed pleasant enough.

Well—before nightfall we were all safely back in our big room. The damage we had done was quite ignored; the beds as smooth and comfortable as before, new clothing and towels supplied. The only thing those women did was to illuminate the gardens at night, and to set an extra watch. But they called us to account next day. Our three tutors, who had not joined in the recapturing expedition, had been quite busy in preparing for us, and now made explanation.

They knew well we would make for our machine; and also that there was no other way of getting down—alive; so our flight had troubled no one; all they did was to call the inhabitants to keep an eye on our movements all along the edge of the forest between the two points. It appeared that many of those nights we had been seen, by careful ladies sitting snugly in big trees by the riverbed, or up among the rocks.

Terry looked immensely disgusted, but it struck me as extremely funny. Here we had been risking our lives, hiding and prowling like outlaws, living on nuts and fruit, getting wet and cold at night, and dry and hot by day, and all the while these estimable women had just been waiting for us to come out.

Now they began to explain, carefully using such words as we could understand. It appeared that we were considered as guests of the country—sort of public wards. Our first violence had made it necessary to keep us safeguarded for a while, but as soon as we learned the language—and would agree to do no harm—they would show us all about the land.

Jeff was eager to reassure them. Of course he did not tell on Terry, but he made it clear that he was ashamed of himself, and that he would now conform. As to the language—we all fell upon it with redoubled energy. They brought us books, in greater numbers, and I began to study them seriously.

170

"Pretty punk literature," Terry burst forth one day, when we were in the privacy of our own room. "Of course one expects to begin on child-stories, but I would like something more interesting now."

"Can't expect stirring romance and wild adventure without men, can you?" I asked. Nothing irritated Terry more than to have us assume that there were no men; but there were no signs of them in the books they gave us, or the pictures.

"Shut up!" he growled. "What infernal nonsense you talk! I'm going to ask 'em outright—we know enough now."

In truth we had been using our best efforts to master the language, and were able to read fluently and to discuss what we read with considerable ease.

That afternoon we were all sitting together on the roof; we three and the tutors gathered about a table; no guards about. We had been made to understand some time earlier that if we would agree to do no violence they would withdraw their constant attendance, and we promised most willingly.

So there we sat, at ease; all in similar dress; our hair, by now, as long as theirs, only our beards to distinguish us. We did not want those beards, but had so far been unable to induce them to give us any cutting instruments.

"Ladies," Terry began, out of a clear sky, as it were, "are there no men in this country?"

"Men?" Somel answered. "Like you?"

"Yes, men," Terry indicated his beard, and threw back his broad shoulders. "Men, real men."

"No," she answered quietly. "There are no men in this country. There has not been a man among us for two thousand years."

Her look was clear and truthful and she did not advance this astonishing statement as if it was astonishing, but quite as a matter of fact.

"But—the people—the children," he protested, not believing her in the least, but not wishing to say so.

"Oh yes," she smiled. "I do not wonder you are puzzled. We are mothers— all of us; but there are no fathers. We thought you would ask about that long ago—why have you not?" Her look was as frankly kind as always; her tone quite simple.

Terry explained that we had not felt sufficiently used to the language, making rather a mess of it, I thought, but Jeff was franker.

"Will you excuse us all," he said, "if we admit that we find it hard to believe? There is no such—possibility—in the rest of the world."

"Have you no kind of life where it is possible?" asked Zava.

"Why, yes—some low forms, of course."

"How low—or how high, rather?"

"Well—there are some rather high forms of insect life in which it occurs. Parthenogenesis, we call it—that means virgin birth."

She could not follow him.

"*Birth*, we know, of course; but what is *virgin*?"

Terry looked uncomfortable, but Jeff met the question quite calmly. "Among mating animals, the term *virgin* is applied to the female who has not mated," he answered.

"Oh, I see. And does it apply to the male also? Or is there a different term for him?"

He passed this over rather hurriedly, saying that the same term would apply, but was seldom used.

"No?" she said. "But one cannot mate without the other surely. Is not each then—virgin—before mating? And, tell me, have you any forms of life in which there is birth from a father only?"

"I know of none," he answered, and I inquired seriously.

"You ask us to believe that for two thousand years there have been only women here, and only girl babies born?"

"Exactly," answered Somel, nodding gravely. "Of course, we know that among other animals it is not so; that there are fathers as well as mothers; and we see that you are fathers, that you come from a people who are of both kinds. We have been waiting, you see, for you to be able to speak freely with us, and teach us about your country, and the rest of the world. You know so much, you see, and we know only our own land."

In the course of our previous studies we had been at some pains to tell them about the big world outside, to draw sketches, maps, to make a globe, even, out of a spherical fruit, and show the size and relation of the countries, and to tell of the numbers of their people. All this had been scant and in outline, but they quite understood.

172

I find I succeed very poorly in conveying the impression I would like to of these women. So far from being ignorant, they were deeply wise—that we realized more and more; and for clear reasoning, for real brain scope and power, they were A No. 1; but there were a lot of things they did not know.

For that matter there were a lot of things Aristotle didn't know.

They had the evenest tempers, the most perfect patience and good nature—one of the things most impressive about them all was the absence of irritability. So far we had only this group to study, but afterward I found it a common trait.

We had gradually come to feel that we were in the hands of friends, and very capable ones at that—but we couldn't form any opinion yet of the general level of these women.

"We want you to teach us all you can," Somel went on, her firm shapely hands clasped on the table before her; her clear quiet eyes meeting ours frankly. "And we want to teach you what we have that is novel and useful. You can well imagine that it is a wonderful event to us, to have men among us—after two thousand years. And we want to know about your women."

What she said about our importance gave instant pleasure to Terry. I could see by the way he lifted his head that it pleased him. But when she spoke of our women—someway I had a queer little indescribable feeling; not like any feeling I ever had before when "women" were mentioned.

"Will you tell us how it came about?" Jeff pursued. "You said 'for two thousand years'—did you have men here before that?"

"Yes," answered Zava.

They were all quiet for a little.

"You should have our full history to read—do not be alarmed—it has been made clear and short—it took us a long time to learn how to write history. Oh, how I should love to read yours!"

She turned with flashing eager eyes, looking from one to the other of us.

"It would be so wonderful—would it not? To compare the history of two thousand years; to see what the differences are—between us, who are only mothers; and you, who are mothers and fathers, too. Of course we see, with our birds, that the father is as useful as the mother, almost; but among insects we find him of less importance, sometimes very little. Is it not so with you?"

"Oh, yes, birds and bugs," Terry said, "but not among animals—have you

173

no animals?"

"We have cats," she said. "The father is not very useful."

"Have you no cattle—sheep—horses?" I drew some rough outlines of these beasts and showed them to her.

"We had, in the very old days, these," said Somel, and sketched with swift sure touches a sort of sheep or llama, "and these"—dogs, of two or three kinds, "that that"—pointing to my absurd but recognizable horse.

"What became of them?" asked Jeff.

"We do not want them any more. They took up too much room—we need all our land to feed our people. It is such a little country, you know."

"Whatever do you do without milk?" Terry demanded incredulously.

"*Milk?* We have milk in abundance—our own."

"But—but—I mean for cooking—for grown people," Terry blundered, while they looked amazed and a shade displeased.

Jeff came to the rescue. "We keep cattle for their milk, as well as for their meat," he explained. "Cow's milk is a staple article of diet—there is a great milk industry—to collect and distribute it."

Still they looked puzzled. I pointed to my outline of a cow. "The farmer milks the cow," I said, and sketched a milk pail, the stool, and in pantomime showed the man milking. "Then it is carried to the city and distributed by milkmen—everybody has it at the door in the morning."

"Has the cow no child?" asked Somel earnestly.

"Oh, yes, of course, a calf, that is."

"Is there milk for the calf and you, too?"

It took some time to make clear to those three sweet-faced women the process which robs the cow of her calf, and the calf of its true food; and the talk led us into a further discussion of the meat business. They heard it out, looking very white, and presently begged to be excused.

Chapter V

A Unique History

It is no use for me to try to piece out this account with adventures. If the people who read it are not interested in these amazing women and their history, they will not be interested at all.

As for us,—three young men to a whole landful of women—what could we do? We did get away, as described, and were peacefully brought back again without, as Terry complained, even the satisfaction of hitting anybody.

There were no adventures because there was nothing to fight. There were no wild beasts in the country and very few tame ones. Of these I might as well stop to describe the one common pet of the country. Cats, of course. But such cats!

What do you suppose these lady Burbanks had done with their cats? By the most prolonged and careful selection and exclusion they had developed a race of cats that did not sing! That's a fact. The most those poor dumb brutes could do was to make a kind of squeak when they were hungry or wanted the door open; and, of course, to purr, and make the various mother-noises to their kittens.

Moreover, they had ceased to kill birds. They were rigorously bred to destroy mice and moles and all such enemies of the food supply; but the birds were numerous and safe.

While we were discussing birds, Terry asked them if they used feathers for their hats, and they seemed amused at the idea. He made a few sketches of our women's hats, with plumes and quills and those various tickling things that stick out so far; and they were eagerly interested, as at everything about our women.

As for them, they said they only wore hats for shade when working in the sun; and those were big light straw hats, something like those used in China and Japan. In cold weather they wore caps or hoods.

"But for decorative purposes—don't you think they would be becoming?" pursued Terry, making as pretty a picture as he could of a lady with a plumed hat.

They by no means agreed to that, asking quite simply if the men wore the same kind. We hastened to assure her that they did not—drew for them our kind of headgear.

"And do no men wear feathers in their hats?"

"Only Indians," Jeff explained, "savages, you know." And he sketched a war-bonnet to show them.

"And soldiers," I added, drawing a military hat with plumes.

They never expressed horror or disapproval, nor indeed much surprise—just a keen interest. And the notes they made!—miles of them!

But to return to our pussy-cats. We were a good deal impressed by this achievement in breeding, and when they questioned us—I can tell you we were well pumped for information—we told of what had been done for dogs and horses and cattle, but that there was no effort applied to cats, except for show purposes.

I wish I could represent the kind, quiet, steady, ingenious way they questioned us. It was not just curiosity—they weren't a bit more curious about us than we were about them, if as much. But they were bent on understanding our kind of civilization and their lines of interrogation would gradually surround us and drive us in till we found ourselves up against some admissions we did not want to make.

"Are all these breeds of dogs you have made useful?" they asked.

"Oh—useful! Why, the hunting dogs and watch-dogs and sheep-dogs are useful—and sled-dogs of course!—and ratters, I suppose, but we don't keep dogs for their *usefulness*. The dog is 'the friend of man,' we say—we love them."

That they understood. "We love our cats that way. They surely are our friends, and helpers too. You can see how intelligent and affectionate they are."

It was a fact. I'd never seen such cats, except in a few rare instances. Big, handsome silky things, friendly with everyone and devotedly attached to their special owners.

"You must have a heartbreaking time drowning kittens," we suggested. But they said: "Oh, no! You see we care for them as you do for your valuable cattle. The fathers are few compared to the mothers, just a few very fine ones in each town; they live quite happily in walled gardens and the houses of their friends. But they only have a mating season once a year."

"Rather hard on Thomas, isn't it?" suggested Terry.

"Oh, no—truly! You see, it is many centuries that we have been breeding the kind of cats we wanted. They are healthy and happy and friendly, as you see. How do you manage with your dogs? Do you keep them in pairs, or segregate the fathers, or what?"

Then we explained that—well, that it wasn't a question of fathers exactly; that nobody wanted a—a mother dog; that, well, that practically all our dogs were males—there was only a very small percentage of females allowed to live.

Then Zava, observing Terry with her grave sweet smile, quoted back at him: "Rather hard on Thomas, isn't it? Do they enjoy it—living without mates? Are your dogs as uniformly healthy and sweet-tempered as our cats?"

Jeff laughed, eyeing Terry mischievously. As a matter of fact we began to feel Jeff something of a traitor—he so often flopped over and took their side of things; also his medical knowledge gave him a different point of view somehow.

"I'm sorry to admit," he told them, "that the dog, with us, is the most diseased of any animal—next to man. And as to temper—there are always some dogs who bite people—especially children."

That was pure malice. You see, children were the—the *raison d'etre* in this country. All our interlocutors sat up straight at once. They were still gentle, still restrained, but there was a note of deep amazement in their voices.

"Do we understand that you keep an animal—an unmated male animal—that bites children? About how many are there of them, please?"

"Thousands—in a large city," said Jeff, "and nearly every family has one in the country."

Terry broke in at this. "You must not imagine they are all dangerous—it's not one in a hundred that ever bites anybody. Why, they are the best friends of the children—a boy doesn't have half a chance that hasn't a dog to play with!"

"And the girls?" asked Somel.

"Oh—girls—why they like them too," he said, but his voice flatted a little. They always noticed little things like that, we found later.

Little by little they wrung from us the fact that the friend of man, in the city, was a prisoner; was taken out for his meager exercise on a leash; was liable not only to many diseases but to the one destroying horror of rabies, and, in many cases, for the safety of the citizens, had to go muzzled. Jeff maliciously added vivid instances he had known or read of injury and death from mad dogs.

They did not scold or fuss about it. Calm as judges, those women were. But they made notes; Moadine read them to us.

"Please tell me if I have the facts correct," she said. "In your country—and in others too?"

"Yes," we admitted, "in most civilized countries."

"In most civilized countries a kind of animal is kept which is no longer useful—"

"They are a protection," Terry insisted. "They bark if burglars try to get in."

Then she made notes of "burglars" and went on: "because of the love which people bear to this animal."

Zava interrupted here. "Is it the men or the women who love this animal so much?"

"Both!" insisted Terry.

"Equally?" she inquired.

And Jeff said, "Nonsense, Terry—you know men like dogs better than women do—as a whole."

"Because they love it so much—especially men. This animal is kept shut up, or chained."

"Why?" suddenly asked Somel. "We keep our father cats shut up because we do not want too much fathering; but they are not chained—they have large grounds to run in."

"A valuable dog would be stolen if he was let loose," I said. "We put collars on them, with the owner's name, in case they do stray. Besides, they get into fights—a valuable dog might easily be killed by a bigger one."

"I see," she said. "They fight when they meet—is that common?" We admitted that it was.

"They are kept shut up, or chained." She paused again, and asked, "Is not a dog fond of running? Are they not built for speed?" That we admitted, too, and Jeff, still malicious, enlightened them further.

"I've always thought it was a pathetic sight, both ways—to see a man or a woman taking a dog to walk—at the end of a string."

"Have you bred them to be as neat in their habits as cats are?" was the next

178

question. And when Jeff told them of the effect of dogs on sidewalk merchandise and the streets generally, they found it hard to believe.

You see, their country was as neat as a Dutch kitchen, and as to sanitation—but I might as well start in now with as much as I can remember of the history of this amazing country before further description.

And I'll summarize here a bit as to our opportunities for learning it. I will not try to repeat the careful, detailed account I lost; I'll just say that we were kept in that fortress a good six months all told; and after that, three in a pleasant enough city where—to Terry's infinite disgust—there were only "Colonels" and little children—no young women whatever. Then we were under surveillance for three more—always with a tutor or a guard or both. But those months were pleasant because we were really getting acquainted with the girls. That was a chapter!—or will be—I will try to do justice to it.

We learned their language pretty thoroughly—had to; and they learned ours much more quickly and used it to hasten our own studies.

Jeff, who was never without reading matter of some sort, had two little books with him, a novel and a little anthology of verse; and I had one of those pocket encyclopedias—a fat little thing, bursting with facts. These were used in our education—and theirs. Then as soon as we were up to it, they furnished us with plenty of their own books, and I went in for the history part—I wanted to understand the genesis of this miracle of theirs.

And this is what happened, according to their records:

As to geography—at about the time of the Christian era this land had a free passage to the sea. I'm not saying where, for good reasons. But there was a fairly easy pass through that wall of mountains behind us, and there is no doubt in my mind that these people were of Aryan stock, and were once in contact with the best civilization of the old world. They were "white," but somewhat darker than our northern races because of their constant exposure to sun and air.

The country was far larger then, including much land beyond the pass, and a strip of coast. They had ships, commerce, an army, a king—for at that time they were what they so calmly called us—a bi-sexual race.

What happened to them first was merely a succession of historic misfortunes such as have befallen other nations often enough. They were decimated by war, driven up from their coastline till finally the reduced population with many of the men killed in battle, occupied this hinterland, and defended it for years, in the mountain passes. Where it was open to

179

any possible attack from below they strengthened the natural defenses so that it became unscalably secure, as we found it.

They were a polygamous people, and a slave-holding people, like all of their time; and during the generation or two of this struggle to defend their mountain home they built the fortresses, such as the one we were held in, and other of their oldest buildings, some still in use. Nothing but earthquakes could destroy such architecture,—huge solid blocks, holding by their own weight. They must have had efficient workmen and enough of them in those days.

They made a brave fight for their existence, but no nation can stand up against what the steamship companies call "an act of God." While the whole fighting force was doing its best to defend their mountain pathway, there occurred a volcanic outburst, with some local tremors, and the result was the complete filling up of the pass,—their only outlet. Instead of a passage, a new ridge, sheer and high, stood between them and the sea; they were walled in, and beneath that wall lay their whole little army. Very few men were left alive, save the slaves; and these now seized their opportunity, rose in revolt, killed their remaining masters even to the youngest boy, killed the old women too, and the mothers, intending to take possession of the country with the remaining young women and girls.

But this succession of misfortunes was too much for those infuriated virgins. There were many of them, and but few of these would-be masters, so the young women, instead of submitting, rose in sheer desperation and slew their brutal conquerors.

This sounds like Titus Andronicus, I know, but that is their account. I suppose they were about crazy—can you blame them?

There was literally no one left on this beautiful high garden land but a bunch of hysterical girls and some older slave women.

That was about two thousand years ago.

At first there was a period of sheer despair. The mountains towered between them and their old enemies, but also between them and escape. There was no way up or down or out—they simply had to stay there. Some were for suicide, but not the majority. They must have been a plucky lot, as a whole, and they decided to live—as long as they did live. Of course they had hope, as youth must, that something would happen to change their fate.

So they set to work, to bury the dead, to plow and sow, to care for one another.

Speaking of burying the dead, I will set down while I think of it, that they had adopted cremation in about the thirteenth century, for the same reason that they had left off raising cattle—they could not spare the room. They were much surprised to learn that we were still burying—asked our reasons for it, and were much dissatisfied with what we gave. We told them of the belief in the resurrection of the body, and they asked if our God was not as well able to resurrect from ashes as from long corruption. We told them of how people thought it repugnant to have their loved ones burn, and they asked if it was less repugnant to have them decay. They were inconveniently reasonable, those women.

Well—that original bunch of girls set to work to clean up the place and make their living as best they could. Some of the remaining slave women rendered invaluable service, teaching such trades as they knew. They had such records as were then kept, all the tools and implements of the time, and a most fertile land to work in.

There were a handful of the younger matrons who had escaped slaughter, and a few babies were born after the cataclysm—but only two boys, and they both died.

For five or ten years they worked together, growing stronger and wiser and more and more mutually attached, and then the miracle happened—one of these young women bore a child. Of course they all thought there must be a man somewhere, but none was found. Then they decided it must be a direct gift from the gods, and placed the proud mother in the Temple of Maaia—their Goddess of Motherhood—under strict watch. And there, as years passed, this wonder-woman bore child after child, five of them—all girls.

I did my best, keenly interested as I have always been in sociology and social psychology, to reconstruct in my mind the real position of these ancient women. There were some five or six hundred of them, and they were harem-bred; yet for the few preceding generations they had been reared in the atmosphere of such heroic struggle that the stock must have been toughened somewhat. Left alone in that terrific orphanhood, they had clung together, supporting one another and their little sisters, and developing unknown powers in the stress of new necessity. To this pain-hardened and work-strengthened group, who had lost not only the love and care of parents, but the hope of ever having children of their own, there now dawned the new hope.

Here at last was Motherhood, and though it was not for all of them personally, it might—if the power was inherited—found here a new race.

181

It may be imagined how those five Daughters of Maaia, Children of the Temple, Mothers of the Future—they had all the titles that love and hope and reverence could give—were reared. The whole little nation of women surrounded them with loving service, and waited, between a boundless hope and an equally boundless despair, to see if they too would be mothers.

And they were! As fast as they reached the age of twenty-five they began bearing. Each of them, like her mother, bore five daughters. Presently there were twenty-five New Women, Mothers in their own right, and the whole spirit of the country changed from mourning and mere courageous resignation to proud joy. The older women, those who remembered men, died off; the youngest of all the first lot of course died too, after a while, and by that time there were left one hundred and fifty-five parthenogenetic women, founding a new race.

They inherited all that the devoted care of that declining band of original ones could leave them. Their little country was quite safe. Their farms and gardens were all in full production. Such industries as they had were in careful order. The records of their past were all preserved, and for years the older women had spent their time in the best teaching they were capable of, that they might leave to the little group of sisters and mothers all they possessed of skill and knowledge.

There you have the start of Herland! One family, all descended from one mother! She lived to be a hundred years old; lived to see her hundred and twenty-five great-granddaughters born; lived as Queen-Priestess-Mother of them all; and died with a nobler pride and a fuller joy than perhaps any human soul has ever known—she alone had founded a new race!

The first five daughters had grown up in an atmosphere of holy calm, of awed watchful waiting, of breathless prayer. To them the longed-for Motherhood was not only a personal joy, but a nation's hope. Their twenty-five daughters in turn, with a stronger hope, a richer, wider outlook, with the devoted love and care of all the surviving population, grew up as a holy sisterhood, their whole ardent youth looking forward to their great office. And at last they were left alone; the white-haired First Mother was gone, and this one family, five sisters, twenty-five first cousins, and a hundred and twenty-five second cousins, began a new race.

Here you have human beings, unquestionably, but what we were slow in understanding was how these ultra-women, inheriting only from women, had eliminated not only certain masculine characteristics, which of course we did not look for, but so much of what we had always thought essentially feminine.

The tradition of men as guardians and protectors had quite died out. These stalwart virgins had no men to fear and therefore no need of protection. As to wild beasts—there were none in their sheltered land.

The power of mother-love, that maternal instinct we so highly laud, was theirs of course, raised to its highest power; and a sister-love which, even while recognizing the actual relationship, we found it hard to credit.

Terry, incredulous, even contemptuous, when we were alone, refused to believe the story. "A lot of traditions as old as Herodotus—and about as trustworthy!" he said. "It's likely women—just a pack of women—would have hung together like that! We all know women can't organize—that they scrap like anything—are frightfully jealous."

"But these New Ladies didn't have anyone to be jealous of, remember," drawled Jeff.

"That's a likely story," Terry sneered.

"Why don't you invent a likelier one?" I asked him. "Here *are* the women—nothing but women, and you yourself admit there's no trace of a man in the country." This was after we had been about a good deal.

"I'll admit that," he growled. "And it's a big miss, too. There's not only no fun without 'em—no real sport—no competition; but these women aren't *womanly*. You know they aren't."

That kind of talk always set Jeff going; and I gradually grew to side with him. "Then you don't call a breed of women whose one concern is Motherhood—womanly?" he asked.

"Indeed I don't," snapped Terry. "What does a man care for motherhood—when he hasn't a ghost of a chance at fatherhood? And besides—what's the good of talking sentiment when we are just men together? What a man wants of women is a good deal more than all this 'motherhood'!"

We were as patient as possible with Terry. He had lived about nine months among the Colonels when he made that outburst; and with no chance at any more strenuous excitement than our gymnastics gave us—save for our escape fiasco. I don't suppose Terry had ever lived so long with neither Love, Combat, nor Danger to employ his superabundant energies, and he was irritable. Neither Jeff nor I found it so wearing. I was so much interested intellectually that our confinement did not wear on me; and as for Jeff, bless his heart!—he enjoyed the society of that tutor of his almost as much as if she had been a girl—I don't know but more.

As to Terry's criticism, it was true. These women, whose essential distinction of Motherhood was the dominant note of their whole culture, were strikingly deficient in what we call "femininity." This led me very promptly to the conviction that those "feminine charms" we are so fond of are not feminine at all, but mere reflected masculinity—developed to please us because they had to please us—and in no way essential to the real fulfillment of their great process. But Terry came to no such conclusion.

"Just you wait till I get out!" he muttered.

Then we both cautioned him. "Look here, Terry, my boy! You be careful! They've been mighty good to us—but do you remember the anesthesia? If you do any mischief in this virgin land, beware of the vengeance of the Maiden Aunts! Come, be a man! It won't be forever."

To return to the history:

They began at once to plan and built for their children, all the strength and intelligence of the whole of them devoted to that one thing. Each girl, of course, was reared in full knowledge of her Crowning Office, and they had, even then, very high ideas of the molding powers of the mother, as well as those of education.

Such high ideals as they had! Beauty, Health, Strength, Intellect, Goodness—for those they prayed and worked.

They had no enemies; they themselves were all sisters and friends; the land was fair before them, and a great future began to form itself in their minds.

The religion they had to begin with was much like that of old Greece—a number of gods and goddesses; but they lost all interest in deities of war and plunder, and gradually centered on their Mother Goddess altogether. Then, as they grew more intelligent, this had turned into a sort of Maternal Pantheism.

Here was Mother Earth, bearing fruit. All that they ate was fruit of motherhood, from seed or egg or their product. By motherhood they were born and by motherhood they lived—life was, to them, just the long cycle of motherhood.

But very early they recognized the need of improvement as well as of mere repetition, and devoted their combined intelligence to that problem—how to make the best kind of people. First this was merely the hope of bearing better ones, and then they recognized that however the children differed at birth, the real growth lay later—through education.

Then things began to hum.

As I learned more and more to appreciate what these women had accomplished, the less proud I was of what we, with all our manhood, had done.

You see, they had had no wars. They had had no kings, and no priests, and no aristocracies. They were sisters, and as they grew, they grew together; not by competition, but by united action.

We tried to put in a good word for competition, and they were keenly interested. Indeed, we soon found, from their earnest questions of us, that they were prepared to believe our world must be better than theirs. They were not sure; they wanted to know; but there was no such arrogance about them as might have been expected.

We rather spread ourselves, telling of the advantages of competition: how it developed fine qualities; that without it there would be "no stimulus to industry." Terry was very strong on that point.

"No stimulus to industry," they repeated, with that puzzled look we had learned to know so well. "*Stimulus? To Industry?* But don't you *like* to work?"

"No man would work unless he had to," Terry declared.

"Oh, no *man!* You mean that is one of your sex distinctions?"

"No, indeed!" he said hastily. "No one, I mean, man or woman, would work without incentive. Competition is the—the motor power, you see."

"It is not with us," they explained gently, "so it is hard for us to understand. Do you mean, for instance, that with you no mother would work for her children without the stimulus of competition?"

No, he admitted that he did not mean that. Mothers, he supposed, would of course work for their children in the home; but the world's work was different—that had to be done by men, and required the competitive element.

All our teachers were eagerly interested.

"We want so much to know—you have the whole world to tell us of, and we have only our little land! And there are two of you—the two sexes—to love and help one another. It must be a rich and wonderful world. Tell us—what is the work of the world, that men do—which we have not here?"

"Oh, everything," Terry said grandly. "The men do everything, with us." He squared his broad shoulders and lifted his chest. "We do not allow our women to work. Women are loved—idolized—honored—kept in the home to care for the children."

"What is 'the home'?" asked Somel a little wistfully.

But Zava begged: "Tell me first, do *no* women work, really?"

"Why, yes," Terry admitted. "Some have to, of the poorer sort."

"About how many—in your country?"

"About seven or eight million," said Jeff, as mischievous as ever.

Chapter VI

Comparisons Are Odious

I had always been proud of my country, of course. Everyone is. Compared with the other lands and other races I knew, the United States of America had always seemed to me, speaking modestly, as good as the best of them.

But just as a clear-eyed, intelligent, perfectly honest and well-meaning child will frequently jar one's self-esteem by innocent questions, so did these women, without the slightest appearance of malice or satire, continually bring up points of discussion which we spent our best efforts in evading.

Now that we were fairly proficient in their language, had read a lot about their history, and had given them the general outlines of ours, they were able to press their questions closer.

So when Jeff admitted the number of "women wage earners" we had, they instantly asked for the total population, for the proportion of adult women, and found that there were but twenty million or so at the outside.

"Then at least a third of your women are—what is it you call them—wage earners? And they are all *poor*. What is *poor*, exactly?"

"Ours is the best country in the world as to poverty," Terry told them. "We do not have the wretched paupers and beggars of the older countries, I assure you. Why, European visitors tell us we don't know what poverty is."

"Neither do we," answered Zava. "Won't you tell us?"

Terry put it up to me, saying I was the sociologist, and I explained that the laws of nature require a struggle for existence, and that in the struggle the fittest survive, and the unfit perish. In our economic struggle, I continued, there was always plenty of opportunity for the fittest to reach the top, which they did, in great numbers, particularly in our country; that where there was severe economic pressure the lowest classes of course felt it the worst, and that among the poorest of all the women were driven into the labor market by necessity.

They listened closely, with the usual note-taking.

"About one-third, then, belong to the poorest class," observed Moadine gravely. "And two-thirds are the ones who are—how was it you so beautifully put it?—'loved, honored, kept in the home to care for the children.' This inferior one-third have no children, I suppose?"

Jeff—he was getting as bad as they were—solemnly replied that, on the contrary, the poorer they were, the more children they had. That too, he explained, was a law of nature: "Reproduction is in inverse proportion to individuation."

"These 'laws of nature,'" Zava gently asked, "are they all the laws you have?"

"I should say not!" protested Terry. "We have systems of law that go back thousands and thousands of years—just as you do, no doubt," he finished politely.

"Oh no," Moadine told him. "We have no laws over a hundred years old, and most of them are under twenty. In a few weeks more," she continued, "we are going to have the pleasure of showing you over our little land, and explaining everything you care to know about. We want you to see our people."

"And I assure you," Somel added, "that our people want to see you."

Terry brightened up immensely at this news, and reconciled himself to the renewed demands upon our capacity as teachers. It was lucky that we knew so little, really, and had no books to refer to, else I fancy we might all be there yet, teaching those eager-minded women about the rest of the world.

I'd better try to give a little synopsis of what part of the world knowledge they had developed, and what they had not. The wonder was that they knew so much.

As to geography, they had the tradition of the Great Sea, beyond the mountains; and they could see for themselves the endless thick-forested plains below them—that was all. But from the few records of their ancient condition—not "before the flood" with them, but before that mighty quake which had cut them off so completely—they were aware that there were other peoples and other countries.

In geology they were quite ignorant.

As to anthropology, they had those same remnants of information about other peoples, and the knowledge of the savagery of the occupants of those dim forests below. Nevertheless, they had inferred (marvelously keen on inference and deduction their minds were!) the existence and development of civilization in other places, much as we infer it on other planets.

When our biplane came whirring over their heads in that first scouting flight of ours, they had instantly accepted it as proof of the high development of Some Where Else, and had prepared to receive us as cautiously and eagerly as we might prepare to welcome visitors who came "by meteor" from Mars.

Of history—outside their own—they knew nothing, of course, save for their ancient traditions.

Of astronomy they had a fair working knowledge—that is a very old science; and with it, a surprising range and facility in mathematics.

Physiology they were quite familiar with. Indeed, when it came to the simpler and more concrete sciences, wherein the subject matter was at hand and they had but to exercise their minds upon it, the results were surprising. They had worked out a chemistry, a botany, a physics, with all the blends where a science touches an art, or merges into an industry, to such fullness of knowledge as made us feel like schoolchildren.

Also we found this out, as soon as we were free of the country, and by further study and question—that what one knew, all knew, to a very considerable extent.

I talked later with little mountain girls from the fir-dark valleys away up at their highest part, and with sunburned plains-women, and agile foresters, all over the country, as well as those in the towns, and everywhere there was the same high level of intelligence. Some knew far more than others about one thing—they were specialized, of course; but all of them knew more about everything—that is, about everything the country was acquainted with—than is the case with us.

We boast a good deal of our "high level of general intelligence" and our "compulsory public education," but in proportion to their opportunities they were far better educated than our people.

With what we told them, from what sketches and models we were able to prepare, they constructed a sort of working outline to fill in as they learned more.

A big globe was made, and our uncertain maps, helped out by those in that precious year-book thing I had, were tentatively indicated upon it.

They sat in eager groups, masses of them who came for the purpose, and listened while Jeff roughly ran over the geologic history of the earth, and showed them their own land in relation to the others. Out of that same pocket reference book of mine came facts and figures which were seized upon and placed in right relation with unerring acumen.

Even Terry grew interested in this work. "If we can keep this up they'll be having us lecture to all the girls' schools and colleges—how about that?"

he suggested to us. "Don't know as I'd object to being an Authority to such audiences."

They did, in fact, urge us to give public lectures later, but not to the hearers or with the purpose we expected.

What they were doing with us was like—like—well, say like Napoleon extracting military information from a few illiterate peasants. They knew just what to ask, and just what use to make of it; they had mechanical appliances for disseminating information almost equal to ours at home; and by the time we were led forth to lecture, our audiences had thoroughly mastered a well arranged digest of all we had previously given to our teachers, and were prepared with such notes and questions as might have intimidated a University Professor.

They were not audiences of girls, either. It was some time before we were allowed to meet the young women.

. . . . .

"Do you mind telling what you intend to do with us?" Terry burst forth one day, facing the calm and friendly Moadine with that funny half-blustering air of his. At first he used to storm and flourish quite a good deal, but nothing seemed to amuse them more; they would gather around and watch him as if it was an exhibition, politely, but with evident interest. So he learned to check himself, and was almost reasonable in his bearing— but not quite.

She announced smoothly and evenly: "Not in the least. I thought it was quite plain. We are trying to learn of you all we can, and to teach you what you are willing to learn of our country."

"Is that all?" he insisted.

She smiled a quiet enigmatic smile: "That depends."

"Depends on what?"

"Mainly on yourselves," she replied.

"Why do you keep us shut up so closely?"

"Because we do not feel quite safe in allowing you at large where there are so many young women."

Terry was really pleased at that. He had thought as much, inwardly; but he pushed the question. "Why should you be afraid? We are gentlemen."

She smiled that little smile again, and asked: "Are 'gentlemen' always

190

safe?"

"You surely do not think that any of us," he said it with a good deal of emphasis on the "us," "would hurt your young girls?"

"Oh no," she said quickly, in real surprise. "The danger is quite the other way. They might hurt you. If, by any accident, you did harm any one of us, you would have to face a million mothers."

He looked so amazed and outraged that Jeff and I laughed outright, but she went on gently.

"I do not think you quite understand yet. You are but men, three men, in a country where the whole population are mothers—or are going to be. Motherhood means to us something which I cannot yet discover in any of the countries of which you tell us. You have spoken"—she turned to Jeff, "of Human Brotherhood as a great idea among you, but even that I judge is far from a practical expression?"

Jeff nodded rather sadly. "Very far—" he said.

"Here we have Human Motherhood—in full working use," she went on. "Nothing else except the literal sisterhood of our origin, and the far higher and deeper union of our social growth.

"The children in this country are the one center and focus of all our thoughts. Every step of our advance is always considered in its effect on them—on the race. You see, we are *Mothers*," she repeated, as if in that she had said it all.

"I don't see how that fact—which is shared by all women—constitutes any risk to us," Terry persisted. "You mean they would defend their children from attack. Of course. Any mothers would. But we are not Savages, my dear Lady; we are not going to hurt any mother's child."

They looked at one another and shook their heads a little, but Zava turned to Jeff and urged him to make us see—said he seemed to understand more fully than we did. And he tried.

I can see it now, or at least much more of it, but it has taken me a long time, and a good deal of honest intellectual effort.

What they call Motherhood was like this:

They began with a really high degree of social development, something like that of Ancient Egypt or Greece. Then they suffered the loss of everything masculine, and supposed at first that all human power and safety had gone too. Then they developed this virgin birth capacity. Then, since the prosperity of their children depended on it, the fullest and subtlest co-ordination began to be practised.

I remember how long Terry balked at the evident unanimity of these women—the most conspicuous feature of their whole culture. "It's impossible!" he would insist. "Women cannot cooperate—it's against nature."

When we urged the obvious facts he would say: "Fiddlesticks!" or "Hang your facts—I tell you it can't be done!" And we never succeeded in shutting him up till Jeff dragged in the hymenoptera.

"'Go to the ant, thou sluggard'—and learn something," he said triumphantly. "Don't they co-operate pretty well? You can't beat it. This place is just like an enormous ant-hill—you know an ant-hill is nothing but a nursery. And how about bees? Don't they manage to cooperate and love one another?

'As the birds do love the Spring,
Or the bees their careful king,'

as that precious Constable had it. Just show me a combination of male creatures, bird, bug, or beast, that works as well, will you? Or one of our masculine countries where the people work together as well as they do here! I tell you, women are the natural co-operators, not men!"

Terry had to learn a good many things he did not want to.

To go back to my little analysis of what happened:—

They developed all this close inter-service in the interests of their children. To do the best work they had to specialize, of course; the children needed spinners and weavers, farmers and gardeners, carpenters and masons, as well as mothers.

Then came the filling up of the place. When a population multiplies by five every thirty years it soon reaches the limits of a country, especially a small one like this. They very soon eliminated all the grazing cattle—sheep were the last to go, I believe. Also they worked out a system of intensive agriculture surpassing anything I ever heard of, with the very forests all reset with fruit- or nut-bearing trees.

Do what they would, however, there soon came a time when they were confronted with the problem of "the pressure of population" in an acute form. There was really crowding, and with it, unavoidably, a decline in standards.

And how did those women meet it?

192

Not by a "struggle for existence" which would result in an everlasting writhing mass of underbred people trying to get ahead of one another; some few on top, temporarily; many constantly crushed out underneath, a hopeless substratum of paupers and degenerates, and no serenity or peace for anyone—no possibility for really noble qualities among the people at large.

Neither did they start off on predatory excursions to get more land from somebody else, or to get more food from somebody else, to maintain their struggling mass.

Not at all. They sat down in council together and thought it out. Very clear, strong thinkers they were. They said: "With our best endeavors this country will support about so many people, with the standard of peace, comfort, health, beauty, and progress we demand. Very well. That is all the people we will make."

. . . . .

There you have it. You see, they were Mothers, not in our sense of helpless involuntary fecundity, forced to fill and overfill the land, every land, and then see their children suffer, sin, and die, fighting horribly with one another; but in the sense of Conscious Makers of People. Mother love with them was not a brute passion, a mere "instinct," a wholly personal feeling; it was—A Religion.

It included that limitless feeling of sisterhood, that wide unity in service, which was so difficult for us to grasp. And it was National, Racial, Human—Oh, I don't know how to say it.

We are used to seeing what we call "a mother" completely wrapped up in her own pink bundle of fascinating babyhood, and taking but the faintest theoretic interest in anybody else's bundle, to say nothing of the common needs of *all* the bundles. But these women were working all together at the grandest of tasks—they were Making People—and they made them well.

There followed a period of "negative Eugenics" which must have been an appalling sacrifice. We are commonly willing to "lay down our lives" for our country, but they had to forego Motherhood for their country—and it was precisely the hardest thing for them to do.

When I got this far in my reading I went to Somel for more light. We were as friendly by that time as I had ever been in my life with any woman. A mighty comfortable soul she was, giving one the nice smooth mother-feeling a man likes in a woman, and yet giving also the clear intelligence and dependableness I used to assume to be masculine qualities. We had talked volumes already.

"See here," said I. "Here was this dreadful period when they got far too thick, and decided to limit the population. We have a lot of talk about that among us, but your position is so different that I'd like to know a little more about it.

"I understand that you make Motherhood the highest Social Service—a Sacrament, really; that it is only undertaken once, by the majority of the population; that those held unfit are not allowed even that; and that to be encouraged to bear more than one child is the very highest Reward and Honor in the power of the State."

(She interpolated here that the nearest approach to an aristocracy they had was to come of a line of "Over-Mothers"—those who had been so honored.)

"But what I do not understand, naturally, is how you prevent it. I gathered that each woman had five. You have no tyrannical husbands to hold in check—and you surely do not destroy the unborn—"

The look of ghastly horror she gave me I shall never forget. She started from her chair, pale, her eyes blazing.

"Destroy the unborn—!" she said in a hard whisper. "Do men do that in your country?"

"Men!" I began to answer, rather hotly, and then saw the gulf before me. None of us wanted these women to think that *our* women, of whom we boasted so proudly, were in any way inferior to them. I am ashamed to say that I equivocated. I told her of certain criminal types of women—perverts, or crazy, who had been known to commit infanticide. I told her, truly enough, that there was much in our land which was open to criticism, but that I hated to dwell on our defects until they understood us and our conditions better.

And, making a wide detour, I scrambled back to my question of how they limited the population.

As for Somel, she seemed sorry, a little ashamed even, of her too clearly expressed amazement. As I look back now, knowing them better, I am more and more and more amazed as I appreciate the exquisite courtesy with which they had received over and over again statements and admissions on our part which must have revolted them to the soul.

She explained to me, with sweet seriousness, that as I had supposed, at first each woman bore five children; and that, in their eager desire to build

194

up a nation, they had gone on in that way for a few centuries, till they were confronted with the absolute need of a limit. This fact was equally plain to all—all were equally interested.

They were now as anxious to check their wonderful power as they had been to develop it; and for some generations gave the matter their most earnest thought and study.

"We were living on rations before we worked it out," she said. "But we did work it out. You see, before a child comes to one of us there is a period of utter exaltation—the whole being is uplifted and filled with a concentrated desire for that child. We learned to look forward to that period with the greatest caution. Often our young women, those to whom motherhood had not yet come, would voluntarily defer it. When that deep inner demand for a child began to be felt she would deliberately engage in the most active work, physical and mental; and even more important, would solace her longing by the direct care and service of the babies we already had."

She paused. Her wise sweet face grew deeply, reverently tender.

"We soon grew to see that mother-love has more than one channel of expression. I think the reason our children are so—so fully loved, by all of us, is that we never—any of us—have enough of our own."

This seemed to me infinitely pathetic, and I said so. "We have much that is bitter and hard in our life at home," I told her, "but this seems to me piteous beyond words—a whole nation of starving mothers!"

But she smiled her deep contented smile, and said I quite misunderstood.

"We each go without a certain range of personal joy," she said, "but remember—we each have a million children to love and serve—*our* children."

It was beyond me. To hear a lot of women talk about "our children"! But I suppose that is the way the ants and bees would talk—do talk, maybe.

That was what they did, anyhow.

When a woman chose to be a mother, she allowed the child-longing to grow within her till it worked its natural miracle. When she did not so choose she put the whole thing out of her mind, and fed her heart with the other babies.

Let me see—with us, children—minors, that is—constitute about three-fifths of the population; with them only about one-third, or less. And precious—! No sole heir to an Empire's throne, no solitary millionaire baby, no only child of middle-aged parents, could compare as an idol with these Herland children.

But before I start on that subject I must finish up that little analysis I was trying to make.

They did effectually and permanently limit the population, in numbers, so that the country furnished plenty for the fullest, richest life for all of them: plenty of everything, including room, air, solitude even.

And then they set to work to improve that population in quality—since they were restricted in quantity. This they had been at work on, uninterruptedly, for some fifteen hundred years. Do you wonder they were nice people?

Physiology, hygiene, sanitation, physical culture—all that line of work had been perfected long since. Sickness was almost wholly unknown among them, so much so that a previously high development in what we call the "science of medicine" had become practically a lost art. They were a clean-bred, vigorous lot, having the best of care, the most perfect living conditions always.

When it came to psychology—there was no one thing which left us so dumbfounded, so really awed, as the everyday working knowledge—and practice—they had in this line. As we learned more and more of it, we learned to appreciate the exquisite mastery with which we ourselves, strangers of alien race, of unknown opposite sex, had been understood and provided for from the first.

With this wide, deep, thorough knowledge, they had met and solved the problems of education in ways some of which I hope to make clear later. Those nation-loved children of theirs compared with the average in our country as the most perfectly cultivated, richly developed roses compare with—tumbleweeds. Yet they did not *seem* "cultivated" at all—it had all become a natural condition.

And this people, steadily developing in mental capacity, in will power, in social devotion, had been playing with the arts and sciences—as far as they knew them, for a good many centuries now with inevitable success.

Into this quiet lovely land, among these wise, sweet, strong women, we in our easy assumption of superiority, had suddenly arrived; and now, tamed and trained to a degree they considered safe, we were at last brought out to see the country, to know the people.

Chapter VII

Our Growing Modesty

Being at last considered sufficiently tamed and trained to be trusted with scissors, we barbered ourselves as best we could. A close-trimmed beard is certainly more comfortable than a full one. Razors, naturally, they could not supply.

"With so many old women you'd think there'd be some razors," sneered Terry. Whereat Jeff pointed out that he never before had seen such complete absence of facial hair on women.

"Looks to me as if the absence of men made them more feminine in that regard, anyhow," he suggested.

"Well, it's the only one then," Terry reluctantly agreed. "A less feminine lot I never saw. A child apiece doesn't seem to be enough to develop what I call motherliness."

Terry's idea of motherliness was the usual one, involving a baby in arms, or "a little flock about her knees," and the complete absorption of the mother in said baby or flock. A motherliness which dominated society, which influenced every art and industry, which absolutely protected all childhood, and gave to it the most perfect care and training, did not seem motherly—to Terry.

We had become well used to the clothes. They were quite as comfortable as our own; in some ways more so; and undeniably better looking. As to pockets they left nothing to be desired. That second garment was fairly quilted with pockets. They were most ingeniously arranged, so as to be convenient to the hand, and not inconvenient to the body, and were so placed as at once to strengthen the garment and add decorative lines of stitching.

In this, as in so many other points we had now to observe, there was shown the action of a practical intelligence, coupled with fine artistic feeling, and, apparently, untrammeled by any injurious influences.

Our first step of comparative freedom was a personally conducted tour of the country. No pentagonal bodyguard now! Only our special tutors, and we got on famously with them. Jeff said he loved Zava like an aunt—"only jollier than any aunt I ever saw"; Somel and I were as chummy as could be—the best of friends; but it was funny to watch Terry and Moadine. She was patient with him, and courteous, but it was like the patience and courtesy of some great man, say a skilled, experienced diplomat, with a schoolgirl. Her grave acquiescence with his most preposterous expression of feeling; her genial laughter, not only with, but, I often felt, at him—though impeccably polite; her innocent questions, which almost invariably led him to say more than he intended—Jeff and I found it all amusing to watch.

He never seemed to recognize that quiet background of superiority. When she dropped an argument he always thought he had silenced her; when she laughed he thought it tribute to his wit.

I hated to admit to myself how much Terry had sunk in my esteem. Jeff felt it too, I am sure; but neither of us admitted it to the other. At home we had measured him with other men, and, though we knew his failings, he was by no means an unusual type. We knew his virtues too, and they had always seemed more prominent than the faults. Measured among women—our women at home, I mean—he had always stood high. He was visibly popular. Even where his habits were known, there was no discrimination against him; in some cases his reputation for what was felicitously termed "gaiety" seemed a special charm.

But here, against the calm wisdom and quiet restrained humor of these women, with only that blessed Jeff and my inconspicuous self to compare with, Terry did stand out rather strong.

As "a man among men," he didn't; as a man among—I shall have to say, "females," he didn't; his intense masculinity seemed only fit complement to their intense femininity. But here he was all out of drawing.

Moadine was a big woman, with a balanced strength that seldom showed. Her eye was as quietly watchful as a fencer's. She maintained a pleasant relation with her charge, but I doubt if many, even in that country, could have done as well.

He called her "Maud," amongst ourselves, and said she was "a good old soul, but a little slow"; wherein he was quite wrong. Needless to say, he called Jeff's teacher "Java," and sometimes "Mocha," or plain "Coffee"; when specially mischievous, "Chicory," and even "Postum." But Somel rather escaped this form of humor, save for a rather forced "Some 'ell."

"Don't you people have but one name?" he asked one day, after we had been introduced to a whole group of them, all with pleasant, few-syllabled strange names, like the ones we knew.

"Oh yes," Moadine told him. "A good many of us have another, as we get on in life—a descriptive one. That is the name we earn. Sometimes even that is changed, or added to, in an unusually rich life. Such as our present

Land Mother—what you call President or King, I believe. She was called Mera, even as a child; that means 'thinker.' Later there was added Du—Du-Mera—the wise thinker, and now we all know her as O-du-mera—great and wise thinker. You shall meet her."

"No surnames at all then?" pursued Terry, with his somewhat patronizing air. "No family name?"

"Why no," she said. "Why should we? We are all descended from a common source—all one 'family' in reality. You see, our comparatively brief and limited history gives us that advantage at least."

"But does not each mother want her own child to bear her name?" I asked.

"No—why should she? The child has its own."

"Why for—for identification—so people will know whose child she is."

"We keep the most careful records," said Somel. "Each one of us has our exact line of descent all the way back to our dear First Mother. There are many reasons for doing that. But as to every one knowing which child belongs to which mother—why should she?"

Here, as in so many other instances, we were led to feel the difference between the purely maternal and the paternal attitude of mind. The element of personal pride seemed strangely lacking.

"How about your other works?" asked Jeff. "Don't you sign your names to them—books and statues and so on?"

"Yes, surely, we are all glad and proud to. Not only books and statues, but all kinds of work. You will find little names on the houses, on the furniture, on the dishes sometimes. Because otherwise one is likely to forget, and we want to know to whom to be grateful."

"You speak as if it were done for the convenience of the consumer—not the pride of the producer," I suggested.

"It's both," said Somel. "We have pride enough in our work."

"Then why not in your children?" urged Jeff.

"But we have! We're magnificently proud of them," she insisted.

"Then why not sign 'em?" said Terry triumphantly.

Moadine turned to him with her slightly quizzical smile. "Because the finished product is not a private one. When they are babies, we do speak of them, at times, as 'Essa's Lato,' or 'Novine's Amel'; but that is merely descriptive and conversational. In the records, of course, the child stands

199

in her own line of mothers; but in dealing with it personally it is Lato, or Amel, without dragging in its ancestors."

"But have you names enough to give a new one to each child?"

"Assuredly we have, for each living generation."

Then they asked about our methods, and found first that "we" did so and so, and then that other nations did differently. Upon which they wanted to know which method has been proved best—and we had to admit that so far as we knew there had been no attempt at comparison, each people pursuing its own custom in the fond conviction of superiority, and either despising or quite ignoring the others.

With these women the most salient quality in all their institutions was reasonableness. When I dug into the records to follow out any line of development, that was the most astonishing thing—the conscious effort to make it better.

They had early observed the value of certain improvements; had easily inferred that there was room for more; and took the greatest pains to develop two kinds of minds—the critic and inventor. Those who showed an early tendency to observe, to discriminate, to suggest, were given special training for that function; and some of their highest officials spent their time in the most careful study of one or another branch of work, with a view to its further improvement.

In each generation there was sure to arrive some new mind to detect faults and show need of alterations; and the whole corps of inventors was at hand to apply their special faculty at the point criticized, and offer suggestions.

We had learned by this time not to open a discussion on any of their characteristics without first priming ourselves to answer questions about our own methods; so I kept rather quiet on this matter of conscious improvement. We were not prepared to show our way was better.

There was growing in our minds, at least in Jeff's and mine, a keen appreciation of the advantages of this strange country and its management. Terry remained critical. We laid most of it to his nerves. He certainly was irritable.

The most conspicuous feature of the whole land was the perfection of its food supply. We had begun to notice from that very first walk in the forest, the first partial view from our 'plane. Now we were taken to see this mighty garden, and shown its methods of culture.

The country was about the size of Holland, some ten or twelve thousand square miles. One could lose a good many Hollands along the forest-smothered flanks of those mighty mountains. They had a population of about three million—not a large one, but quality is something. Three million is quite enough to allow for considerable variation, and these people varied more widely than we could at first account for.

Terry had insisted that if they were parthenogenetic they'd be as alike as so many ants or aphids; he urged their visible differences as proof that there must be men—somewhere.

But when we asked them, in our later, more intimate conversations, how they accounted for so much divergence without cross-fertilization, they attributed it partly to the careful education, which followed each slight tendency to differ, and partly to the law of mutation. This they had found in their work with plants, and fully proven in their own case.

Physically they were more alike than we, as they lacked all morbid or excessive types. They were tall, strong, healthy, and beautiful as a race, but differed individually in a wide range of feature, coloring, and expression.

"But surely the most important growth is in mind—and in the things we make," urged Somel. "Do you find your physical variation accompanied by a proportionate variation in ideas, feelings, and products? Or, among people who look more alike, do you find their internal life and their work as similar?"

We were rather doubtful on this point, and inclined to hold that there was more chance of improvement in greater physical variation.

"It certainly should be," Zava admitted. "We have always thought it a grave initial misfortune to have lost half our little world. Perhaps that is one reason why we have so striven for conscious improvement."

"But acquired traits are not transmissible," Terry declared. "Weissman has proved that."

They never disputed our absolute statements, only made notes of them.

"If that is so, then our improvement must be due either to mutation, or solely to education," she gravely pursued. "We certainly have improved. It may be that all these higher qualities were latent in the original mother; that careful education is bringing them out; and that our personal differences depend on slight variations in prenatal condition."

"I think it is more in your accumulated culture," Jeff suggested. "And in the amazing psychic growth you have made. We know very little about methods of real soul culture—and you seem to know a great deal."

Be that as it might, they certainly presented a higher level of active intelligence, and of behavior, than we had so far really grasped. Having known in our lives several people who showed the same delicate courtesy and were equally pleasant to live with, at least when they wore their "company manners," we had assumed that our companions were a carefully chosen few. Later we were more and more impressed that all this gentle breeding was breeding; that they were born to it, reared in it, that it was as natural and universal with them as the gentleness of doves or the alleged wisdom of serpents.

As for the intelligence, I confess that this was the most impressive and, to me, most mortifying, of any single feature of Herland. We soon ceased to comment on this or other matters which to them were such obvious commonplaces as to call forth embarrassing questions about our own conditions.

This was nowhere better shown than in that matter of food supply, which I will now attempt to describe.

Having improved their agriculture to the highest point, and carefully estimated the number of persons who could comfortably live on their square miles; having then limited their population to that number, one would think that was all there was to be done; but they had not thought so. To them the country was a unit—it was Theirs. They themselves were a unit, a conscious group; they thought in terms of the community. As such, their time-sense was not limited to the hopes and ambitions of an individual life. Therefore, they habitually considered and carried out plans for improvement which might cover centuries.

I had never seen, had scarcely imagined, human beings undertaking such a work as the deliberate replanting of an entire forest area with different kinds of trees. Yet this seemed to them the simplest common-sense, like a man's plowing up an inferior lawn and reseeding it. Now every tree bore fruit—edible fruit, that is. In the case of one tree, in which they took especial pride, it had originally no fruit at all—that is, none humanly edible—yet was so beautiful that they wished to keep it. For nine hundred years they had experimented, and now showed us this particularly lovely graceful tree, with a profuse crop of nutritious seeds.

That trees were the best food plants they had early decided, requiring far less labor in tilling the soil, and bearing a larger amount of food for the same ground space; also doing much to preserve and enrich the soil.

Due regard had been paid to seasonable crops, and their fruit and nuts, grains and berries, kept on almost the year through.

On the higher part of the country, near the backing wall of mountains, they had a real winter with snow. Toward the southeastern point, where there was a large valley with a lake whose outlet was subterranean, the climate was like that of California, and citrus fruits, figs, and olives grew abundantly.

What impressed me particularly was their scheme of fertilization. Here was this little shut-in piece of land where one would have thought an ordinary people would have been starved out long ago or reduced to an annual struggle for life. These careful culturists had worked out a perfect scheme of refeeding the soil with all that came out of it. All the scraps and leavings of their food, plant waste from lumber work or textile industry; all the solid matter from the sewage, properly treated and combined; everything which came from the earth went back to it.

The practical result was like that in any healthy forest; an increasingly valuable soil was being built, instead of the progressive impoverishment so often seen in the rest of the world.

When this first burst upon us we made such approving comments that they were surprised that such obvious common sense should be praised; asked what our methods were; and we had some difficulty in—well, in diverting them, by referring to the extent of our own land, and the—admitted—carelessness with which we had skimmed the cream of it.

At least we thought we had diverted them. Later I found that besides keeping a careful and accurate account of all we told them, they had a sort of skeleton chart, on which the things we said and the things we palpably avoided saying were all set down and studied. It really was child's play for those profound educators to work out a painfully accurate estimate of our conditions—in some lines. When a given line of observation seemed to lead to some very dreadful inference they always gave us the benefit of the doubt, leaving it open to further knowledge. Some of the things we had grown to accept as perfectly natural, or as belonging to our human limitations, they literally could not have believed; and, as I have said, we had all of us joined in a tacit endeavor to conceal much of the social status at home.

"Confound their grandmotherly minds!" Terry said. "Of course they can't understand a Man's World! They aren't human—they're just a pack of Fe-Fe-Females!" This was after he had to admit their parthenogenesis.

"I wish our grandfatherly minds had managed as well," said Jeff. "Do you really think it's to our credit that we have muddled along with all our poverty and disease and the like? They have peace and plenty, wealth and beauty, goodness and intellect. Pretty good people, I think!"

"You'll find they have their faults too," Terry insisted; and partly in self-defense, we all three began to look for those faults of theirs. We had been very strong on this subject before we got there—in those baseless speculations of ours.

"Suppose there are," Jeff had put it, over and over. "What'll they be like?"

And we had been cocksure as to the inevitable limitations, the faults and vices, of a lot of women. We had expected them to be given over to what we called "feminine vanity"—"frills and furbelows," and we found they had evolved a costume more perfect than the Chinese dress; richly beautiful when so desired, always useful, of unfailing dignity and good taste.

We had expected a dull submissive monotony, and found a daring social inventiveness far beyond our own, and a mechanical and scientific development fully equal to ours.

We had expected pettiness, and found a social consciousness besides which our nations looked like quarreling children—feebleminded ones at that.

We had expected jealousy, and found a broad sisterly affection, a fair-minded intelligence, to which we could produce no parallel.

We had expected hysteria, and found a standard of health and vigor, a calmness of temper, to which the habit of profanity, for instance, was impossible to explain—we tried it.

All these things even Terry had to admit, but he still insisted that we should find out the other side pretty soon.

"It stands to reason, doesn't it?" he argued. "The whole thing's deuced unnatural—I'd say impossible if we weren't in it. And an unnatural condition's sure to have unnatural results. You'll find some awful characteristics—see if you don't! For instance—we don't know yet what they do with their criminals—their defectives—their aged. You notice we haven't seen any! There's got to be something!"

I was inclined to believe that there had to be something, so I took the bull by the horns—the cow, I should say!—and asked Somel.

"I want to find some flaw in all this perfection," I told her flatly. "It simply isn't possible that three million people have no faults. We are trying our best to understand and learn—would you mind helping us by saying what, to your minds, are the worst qualities of this unique civilization of yours?"

We were sitting together in a shaded arbor, in one of those eating-gardens of theirs. The delicious food had been eaten, a plate of fruit still before us. We could look out on one side over a stretch of open country, quietly rich and lovely; on the other, the garden, with tables here and there, far apart enough for privacy. Let me say right here that with all their careful "balance of population" there was no crowding in this country. There was room, space, a sunny breezy freedom everywhere.

Somel set her chin upon her hand; her elbow on the low wall beside her, and looked off over the fair land.

"Of course we have faults—all of us," she said. "In one way you might say that we have more than we used to—that is, our standard of perfection seems to get farther and farther away. But we are not discouraged, because our records do show gain—considerable gain.

"When we began—even with the start of one particularly noble mother— we inherited the characteristics of a long race-record behind her. And they cropped out from time to time—alarmingly. But it is—yes, quite six hundred years since we have had what you call a 'criminal.'

"We have, of course, made it our first business to train out, to breed out, when possible, the lowest types."

"Breed out?" I asked. "How could you—with parthenogenesis?"

"If the girl showing the bad qualities had still the power to appreciate social duty, we appealed to her, by that, to renounce motherhood. Some of the few worst types were, fortunately, unable to reproduce. But if the fault was in a disproportionate egotism—then the girl was sure she had the right to have children; even that hers would be better than others."

"I can see that," I said. "And then she would be likely to rear them in the same spirit."

"That we never allowed," answered Somel quietly.

"Allowed?" I queried. "Allowed a mother to rear her own children?"

"Certainly not," said Somel, "unless she was fit for that supreme task."

This was rather a blow to my previous convictions.

"But I thought motherhood was for each of you—"

"Motherhood—yes, that is, maternity, to bear a child. But education is our highest art, only allowed to our highest artists."

"Education?" I was puzzled again. "I don't mean education. I mean by motherhood not only child-bearing, but the care of babies."

"The care of babies involves education, and is entrusted only to the most fit," she repeated.

"Then you separate mother and child!" I cried in cold horror, something of Terry's feeling creeping over me, that there must be something wrong among these many virtues.

"Not usually," she patiently explained. "You see, almost every woman values her maternity above everything else. Each girl holds it close and dear, an exquisite joy, a crowning honor, the most intimate, most personal, most precious thing. That is, the child-rearing has come to be with us a culture so profoundly studied, practised with such subtlety and skill, that the more we love our children the less we are willing to trust that process to unskilled hands—even our own."

"But a mother's love—" I ventured.

She studied my face, trying to work out a means of clear explanation.

"You told us about your dentists," she said, at length, "those quaintly specialized persons who spend their lives filling little holes in other persons' teeth—even in children's teeth sometimes."

"Yes?" I said, not getting her drift.

"Does mother-love urge mothers—with you—to fill their own children's teeth? Or to wish to?"

"Why no—of course not," I protested. "But that is a highly specialized craft. Surely the care of babies is open to any woman—any mother!"

"We do not think so," she gently replied. "Those of us who are the most highly competent fulfill that office; and a majority of our girls eagerly try for it—I assure you we have the very best."

"But the poor mother—bereaved of her baby—"

"Oh no!" she earnestly assured me. "Not in the least bereaved. It is her baby still—it is with her—she has not lost it. But she is not the only one to care for it. There are others whom she knows to be wiser. She knows it because she has studied as they did, practised as they did, and honors their real superiority. For the child's sake, she is glad to have for it this highest care."

I was unconvinced. Besides, this was only hearsay; I had yet to see the motherhood of Herland.

Chapter VIII

The Girls of Herland

At last Terry's ambition was realized. We were invited, always courteously and with free choice on our part, to address general audiences and classes of girls.

I remember the first time—and how careful we were about our clothes, and our amateur barbering. Terry, in particular, was fussy to a degree about the cut of his beard, and so critical of our combined efforts that we handed him the shears and told him to please himself. We began to rather prize those beards of ours; they were almost our sole distinction among those tall and sturdy women, with their cropped hair and sexless costume. Being offered a wide selection of garments, we had chosen according to our personal taste, and were surprised to find, on meeting large audiences, that we were the most highly decorated, especially Terry.

He was a very impressive figure, his strong features softened by the somewhat longer hair—though he made me trim it as closely as I knew how; and he wore his richly embroidered tunic with its broad, loose girdle with quite a Henry V air. Jeff looked more like—well, like a Huguenot Lover; and I don't know what I looked like, only that I felt very comfortable. When I got back to our own padded armor and its starched borders I realized with acute regret how comfortable were those Herland clothes.

We scanned that audience, looking for the three bright faces we knew; but they were not to be seen. Just a multitude of girls; quiet, eager, watchful, all eyes and ears to listen and learn.

We had been urged to give, as fully as we cared to, a sort of synopsis of world history, in brief, and to answer questions.

"We are so utterly ignorant, you see," Moadine had explained to us. "We know nothing but such science as we have worked out for ourselves, just the brain work of one small half-country; and you, we gather, have helped one another all over the globe, sharing your discoveries, pooling your progress. How wonderful, how supremely beautiful your civilization must be!"

Somel gave a further suggestion.

"You do not have to begin all over again, as you did with us. We have made a sort of digest of what we have learned from you, and it has been eagerly absorbed, all over the country. Perhaps you would like to see our outline?"

We were eager to see it, and deeply impressed. To us, at first, these women, unavoidably ignorant of what to us was the basic commonplace of knowledge, had seemed on the plane of children, or of savages. What we had been forced to admit, with growing acquaintance, was that they were ignorant as Plato and Aristotle were, but with a highly developed mentality quite comparable to that of Ancient Greece.

Far be it from me to lumber these pages with an account of what we so imperfectly strove to teach them. The memorable fact is what they taught us, or some faint glimpse of it. And at present, our major interest was not at all in the subject matter of our talk, but in the audience.

Girls—hundreds of them—eager, bright-eyed, attentive young faces; crowding questions, and, I regret to say, an increasing inability on our part to answer them effectively.

Our special guides, who were on the platform with us, and sometimes aided in clarifying a question; or, oftener, an answer; noticed this effect, and closed the formal lecture part of the evening rather shortly.

"Our young women will be glad to meet you," Somel suggested, "to talk with you more personally, if you are willing?"

Willing! We were impatient and said as much, at which I saw a flickering little smile cross Moadine's face. Even then, with all those eager young things waiting to talk to us, a sudden question crossed my mind: "What was their point of view? What did they think of us?" We learned that later.

Terry plunged in among those young creatures with a sort of rapture; somewhat as a glad swimmer takes to the sea. Jeff, with a rapt look on his high-bred face, approached as to a sacrament. But I was a little chilled by that last thought of mine, and kept my eyes open. I found time to watch Jeff, even while I was surrounded by an eager group of questioners—as we all were—and saw how his worshipping eyes, his grave courtesy, pleased and drew some of them; while others, rather stronger spirits they looked to be, drew away from his group to Terry's or mine.

I watched Terry with special interest, knowing how he had longed for this time, and how irresistible he had always been at home. And I could see, just in snatches, of course, how his suave and masterful approach seemed to irritate them; his too-intimate glances were vaguely resented, his compliments puzzled and annoyed. Sometimes a girl would flush, not with drooped eyelids and inviting timidity, but with anger and a quick lift of the head. Girl after girl turned on her heel and left him, till he had but a small ring of questioners, and they, visibly, were the least "girlish" of the lot.

I saw him looking pleased at first, as if he thought he was making a strong impression; but, finally, casting a look at Jeff, or me, he seemed less pleased—and less.

As for me, I was most agreeably surprised. At home I never was "popular." I had my girl friends, good ones, but they were friends—nothing else. Also they were of somewhat the same clan, not "popular" in the sense of swarming admirers. But here, to my astonishment, I found my crowd was the largest.

I have to generalize, of course, rather telescoping many impressions; but the first evening was a good sample of the impression we made. Jeff had a following, if I may call it that, of the more sentimental—though that's not the word I want. The less practical, perhaps; the girls who were artists of some sort, ethicists, teachers—that kind.

Terry was reduced to a rather combative group; keen, logical, inquiring minds; not overly sensitive; the very kind he liked least; while, as for me—I became quite cocky over my general popularity.

Terry was furious about it. We could hardly blame him.

"Girls!" he burst forth, when that evening was over and we were by ourselves once more. "Call those *girls*!"

"Most delightful girls, I call them," said Jeff, his blue eyes dreamily contented.

"What do *you* call them?" I mildly inquired.

"Boys! Nothing but boys, most of 'em. A stand-offish, disagreeable lot at that. Critical, impertinent youngsters. No girls at all."

He was angry and severe, not a little jealous, too, I think. Afterward, when he found out just what it was they did not like, he changed his manner somewhat and got on better. He had to. For, in spite of his criticism, they were girls, and, furthermore, all the girls there were! Always excepting our three!—with whom we presently renewed our acquaintance.

When it came to courtship, which it soon did, I can of course best describe my own—and am least inclined to. But of Jeff I heard somewhat; he was inclined to dwell reverently and admiringly, at some length, on the exalted sentiment and measureless perfection of his Celis; and Terry—Terry made so many false starts and met so many rebuffs, that by the time he really settled down to win Alima, he was considerably wiser. At that, it was not smooth sailing. They broke and quarreled, over and over; he would rush

209

off to console himself with some other fair one—the other fair one would have none of him—and he would drift back to Alima, becoming more and more devoted each time.

She never gave an inch. A big, handsome creature, rather exceptionally strong even in that race of strong women, with a proud head and sweeping level brows that lined across above her dark eager eyes like the wide wings of a soaring hawk.

I was good friends with all three of them but best of all with Ellador, long before that feeling changed, for both of us.

From her, and from Somel, who talked very freely with me, I learned at last something of the viewpoint of Herland toward its visitors.

Here they were, isolated, happy, contented, when the booming buzz of our biplane tore the air above them.

Everybody heard it—saw it—for miles and miles; word flashed all over the country; and a council was held in every town and village.

And this was their rapid determination:

"From another country. Probably men. Evidently highly civilized. Doubtless possessed of much valuable knowledge. May be dangerous. Catch them if possible; tame and train them if necessary This may be a chance to re-establish a bi-sexual state for our people."

They were not afraid of us—three million highly intelligent women—or two million, counting only grown-ups—were not likely to be afraid of three young men. We thought of them as "Women," and therefore timid; but it was two thousand years since they had had anything to be afraid of, and certainly more than one thousand since they had outgrown the feeling.

We thought—at least Terry did—that we could have our pick of them. They thought—very cautiously and farsightedly—of picking us, if it seemed wise.

All that time we were in training they studied us, analyzed us, prepared reports about us, and this information was widely disseminated all about the land.

Not a girl in that country had not been learning for months as much as could be gathered about our country, our culture, our personal characters. No wonder their questions were hard to answer. But I am sorry to say, when we were at last brought out and—exhibited (I hate to call it that, but that's what it was), there was no rush of takers. Here was poor old Terry fondly imagining that at last he was free to stray in "a rosebud garden of girls"—and behold! the rosebuds were all with keen appraising eye, studying us.

They were interested, profoundly interested, but it was not the kind of interest we were looking for.

To get an idea of their attitude you have to hold in mind their extremely high sense of solidarity. They were not each choosing a lover, they hadn't the faintest idea of love—sex-love, that is. These girls—to each of whom motherhood was a lode-star, and that motherhood exalted above a mere personal function, looked forward to as the highest social service, as the sacrament of a lifetime; were now confronted with an opportunity to make the great step of changing their whole status, of reverting to their earlier bi-sexual order of nature.

Beside this underlying consideration there was the limitless interest and curiosity in our civilization; purely impersonal; and held by an order of mind beside which we were like—schoolboys.

It was small wonder that our lectures were not a success; and none at all that our, or at least Terry's, advances were so ill received. The reason for my own comparative success was at first far from pleasing to my pride.

"We like you the best," Somel told me, "because you seem more like us."

"More like a lot of women!" I thought to myself disgustedly; and then remembered how little like "women," in our derogatory sense, they were. She was smiling at me, reading my thought.

"We can quite see that we do not seem like—women—to you. Of course, in a bi-sexual race the distinctive feature of each sex must be intensified. But surely there are characteristics enough which belong to People, aren't there? That's what I mean about you being more like us—more like People. We feel at ease with you."

Jeff's difficulty was his exalted gallantry. He idealized women, and was always looking for a chance to "protect" or to "serve" them. These needed neither protection nor service. They were living in peace and power and plenty; we were their guests, their prisoners, absolutely dependent.

Of course we could promise whatsoever we might of advantages, if they would come to our country; but the more we knew of theirs, the less we boasted.

Terry's jewels and trinkets they prized as curios; handed them about, asking questions as to workmanship, not in the least as to value; and discussed not ownership, but which museum to put them in.

When a man has nothing to give a woman, is dependent wholly on his personal attraction, his courtship is under limitations.

They were considering these two things: the advisability of making the Great Change; and the degree of personal adaptability which would best serve that end.

Here we had the advantage of our small personal experience with those three fleet forest girls; and that served to draw us together.

As for Ellador: Suppose you come to a strange land and find it pleasant enough; just a little more than ordinarily pleasant; and then you find rich farmland, and then gardens, gorgeous gardens; and then palaces full of rare and curious treasures—incalculable, inexhaustible, and then—mountains—like the Himalayas, and then the sea.

I liked her that day she balanced on the branch before me and named the trio. I thought of her most. Afterward I turned to her like a friend when we met for the third time, and continued the acquaintance. While Jeff's ultra-devotion rather puzzled Celis, really put off their day of happiness, while Terry and Alima quarreled and parted—re-met and re-parted, Ellador and I grew to be close friends.

We talked and talked. We took long walks together. She showed me things, explained them, interpreted much that I had not understood. Through her sympathetic intelligence I became more and more comprehending of the spirit of the people of Herland; more and more appreciative of its marvelous inner growth as well as outer perfection.

I ceased to feel a stranger, a prisoner. There was a sense of understanding, of identity, of purpose. We discussed—everything. And, as I traveled farther and farther, exploring the rich, sweet soul of her, my sense of pleasant friendship became but a broad foundation for such height, such breadth, such interlocked combination of feeling, as left me fairly blinded with the wonder of it.

As I've said, I had never cared very much for women, nor they for me— not Terry-fashion. But this one—

At first I never even thought of her "in that way," as the girls have it. I had not come to the country with any Turkish-harem intentions; and I was no woman-worshipper like Jeff. I just liked that girl "as a friend," as we say. That friendship grew like a tree. She was *such* a good sport! We did all kinds of things together; she taught me games and I taught her games, and we raced and rowed and had all manner of fun, as well as higher comradeship.

Then, as I got on farther, the palace and treasures and snowy mountain ranges opened up. I had never known there could be such a human being. So—great. I don't mean talented. She was a forester—one of the best; but it was not that gift I mean. When I say *great*, I mean great—big, all through. If I had known more of those women, as intimately, I should not have found her so unique; but even among them she was noble. Her mother was an Over-Mother—and her grandmother, too, I heard later.

So she told me more and more of her beautiful land; and I told her as much, yes, more than I wanted to, about mine; and we became inseparable. Then this deeper recognition came and grew. I felt my own soul rise and lift its wings, as it were. Life got bigger. It seemed as if I understood—as I never had before—as if I could Do things—as if I too could grow—if she would help me. And then It came—to both of us, all at once.

A still day—on the edge of the world, their world. The two of us, gazing out over the far dim forest-land below, talking of heaven and earth and human life, and of my land and other lands and what they needed and what I hoped to do for them—

"If you will help me," I said.

She turned to me, with that high, sweet look of hers, and then, as her eyes rested in mine and her hands too—then suddenly there blazed out between us a farther glory, instant, overwhelming—quite beyond any words of mine to tell.

Celis was a blue-and-gold-and-rose person; Alma, black-and-white-and-red, a blazing beauty. Ellador was brown; hair dark and soft, like a seal coat; clear brown skin with a healthy red in it; brown eyes—all the way from topaz to black velvet they seemed to range—splendid girls, all of them.

They had seen us first of all, far down in the lake below; and flashed the tidings across the land even before our first exploring flight. They had watched our landing, flitted through the forest with us, hidden in that tree and—I shrewdly suspect—giggled on purpose.

They had kept watch over our hooded machine, taking turns at it; and when our escape was announced, had followed along-side for a day or two, and been there at the last, as described. They felt a special claim on us—called us "their men"—and when we were at liberty to study the land and people, and be studied by them, their claim was recognized by the wise leaders.

But I felt, we all did, that we should have chosen them among millions, unerringly.

And yet "the path of true love never did run smooth"; this period of courtship was full of the most unsuspected pitfalls.

Writing this as late as I do, after manifold experiences both in Herland and, later, in my own land, I can now understand and philosophize about what was then a continual astonishment and often a temporary tragedy.

The "long suit" in most courtships is sex attraction, of course. Then gradually develops such comradeship as the two temperaments allow. Then, after marriage, there is either the establishment of a slow-growing, widely based friendship; the deepest, tenderest, sweetest of relations, all lit and warmed by the recurrent flame of love; or else that process is reversed, love cools and fades, no friendship grows, the whole relation turns from beauty to ashes.

Here everything was different. There was no sex-feeling to appeal to, or practically none. Two thousand years' disuse had left very little of the instinct; also we must remember that those who had at times manifested it as atavistic exceptions were often, by that very fact, denied motherhood.

Yet while the mother process remains, the inherent ground for sex-distinction remains also; and who shall say what long-forgotten feeling, vague and nameless, was stirred in some of these mother hearts by our arrival?

What left us even more at sea in our approach was the lack of any sex-tradition. There was no accepted standard of what was "manly" and what was "womanly."

When Jeff said, taking the fruit basket from his adored one, "A woman should not carry anything," Celis said, "Why?" with the frankest amazement. He could not look that fleet-footed, deep-chested young forester in the face and say, "Because she is weaker." She wasn't. One does not call a race-horse weak because it is visibly not a cart horse.

He said, rather lamely, that women were not built for heavy work.

She looked out across the fields to where some women were working, building a new bit of wall, out of large stones; looked back at the nearest town with its woman-built houses; down at the smooth, hard road we were walking on; and then at the little basket he had taken from her.

"I don't understand," she said quite sweetly. "Are the women in your country so weak that they could not carry such a thing as that?"

"It is a convention," he said. "We assume that motherhood is a sufficient burden—that men should carry all the others."

"What a beautiful feeling!" she said, her blue eyes shining.

"Does it work?" asked Alima, in her keen, swift way. "Do all men in all countries carry everything? Or is it only in yours?"

"Don't be so literal," Terry begged lazily. "Why aren't you willing to be worshipped and waited on? We like to do it."

"You don't like to have us do it to you," she answered.

"That's different," he said, annoyed; and when she said, "Why is it?" he quite sulked, referring her to me, saying, "Van's the philosopher."

Ellador and I talked it all out together; so that we had an easier experience of it when the real miracle-time came. Also, between us, we made things clearer to Jeff and Celis. But Terry would not listen to reason.

He was madly in love with Alima. He wanted to take her by storm, and nearly lost her forever.

You see, if a man loves a girl who is in the first place young and inexperienced; who in the second place is educated with a background of cave-man tradition, a middle-ground of poetry and romance, and a foreground of unspoken hope and interest all centering upon the one Event; and who has, furthermore, absolutely no other hope or interest worthy of the name—why, it is a comparatively easy matter to sweep her off her feet with a dashing attack. Terry was a past master in this process. He tried it here, and Alima was so affronted, so repelled, that it was weeks before he got near enough to try again.

The more coldly she denied him, the hotter his determination; he was not used to real refusal. The approach of flattery she dismissed with laughter; gifts and such "attentions" we could not bring to bear; pathos and complaint of cruelty stirred only a reasoning inquiry. It took Terry a long time.

I doubt if she ever accepted her strange lover as fully as did Celis and Ellador theirs; he had hurt and offended her too often; there were reservations.

But I think Alima retained some faint vestige of long-descended feeling which made Terry more possible to her than to others; and that she had made up her mind to the experiment and hated to renounce it.

However it came about, we all three at length achieved full understanding, and solemnly faced what was to them a step of measureless importance, a grave question as well as a great happiness; to us a strange, new joy.

Of marriage as a ceremony they knew nothing. Jeff was for bringing them to our country for the religious and the civil ceremony, but neither Celis nor the others would consent.

"We can't expect them to want to go with us—yet," said Terry sagely. "Wait a bit, boys. We've got to take 'em on their own terms—if at all." This, in rueful reminiscence of his repeated failures.

"But our time's coming," he added cheerfully. "These women have never been mastered, you see—" This, as one who had made a discovery.

"You'd better not try to do any mastering if you value your chances," I told him seriously; but he only laughed, and said, "Every man to his trade!"

We couldn't do anything with him. He had to take his own medicine.

If the lack of tradition of courtship left us much at sea in our wooing, we found ourselves still more bewildered by lack of tradition of matrimony.

And here again, I have to draw on later experience, and as deep an acquaintance with their culture as I could achieve, to explain the gulfs of difference between us.

Two thousand years of one continuous culture with no men. Back of that, only traditions of the harem. They had no exact analogue for our word "home," any more than they had for our Roman-based "family."

They loved one another with a practically universal affection; rising to exquisite and unbroken friendships; and broadening to a devotion to their country and people for which our word "patriotism" is no definition at all.

Patriotism, red hot, is compatible with the existence of a neglect of national interests, a dishonesty, a cold indifference to the suffering of millions. Patriotism is largely pride, and very largely combativeness. Patriotism generally has a chip on its shoulder.

This country had no other country to measure itself by—save the few poor savages far below, with whom they had no contact.

They loved their country because it was their nursery, playground, and workshop; theirs and their children's. They were proud of it as a workshop; proud of their record of ever-increasing efficiency; they had made a pleasant garden of it, a very practical little heaven; but most of all they valued it—and here it is hard for us to understand them—as a cultural environment for their children.

That, of course, is the keynote of the whole distinction—their children.

From those first breathlessly guarded, half-adored race mothers, all up the ascending line; they had this dominant thought of building up a great race through the children.

All the surrendering devotion our women have put into their private families, these women put into their country and race. All the loyalty and service men expect of wives, they gave, not singly to men, but collectively to one another.

And the mother instinct, with us so painfully intense, so thwarted by conditions, so concentrated in personal devotion to a few; so bitterly hurt by death, disease, or barrenness, and even by the mere growth of the children, leaving the mother alone in her empty nest—all this feeling with them flowed out in a strong, wide current, unbroken through the generations, deepening and widening through the years, including every child in all the land.

With their united power and wisdom, they had studied and overcome the "diseases of childhood"—their children had none.

They had faced the problems of education and so solved them that their children grew up as naturally as young trees; learning through every sense; taught continuously but unconsciously—never knowing they were being educated.

In fact, they did not use the word as we do. Their idea of education was the special training they took, when half grown up, under experts. Then the eager young minds fairly flung themselves on their chosen subjects; and acquired with an ease, a breadth, a grasp, at which I never ceased to wonder.

But the babies and little children never felt the pressure of that "forcible feeding" of the mind that we call education. Of this, more later.

Chapter IX

Our Relations and Theirs

What I'm trying to show here is that with these women the whole relationship of life counted in a glad, eager growing-up to join the ranks of workers in the line best loved; a deep, tender reverence for one's own mother—too deep for them to speak of freely—and beyond that, the whole, free, wide range of sisterhood, the splendid service of the country, and friendships.

To these women we came, filled with the ideas, convictions, traditions, of our culture; and undertook to rouse in them the emotions which—to us—seemed proper.

However much, or little, of true sex-feeling there was between us, it phrased itself in their minds in terms of friendship, the one purely personal love they knew, and of ultimate parentage. Visibly we were not mothers, nor children, nor compatriots; so, if they loved us, we must be friends.

That we should pair off together in our courting days was natural to them; that we three should remain much together, as they did themselves, was also natural. We had as yet no work, so we hung about them in their forest tasks; that was natural, too.

But when we began to talk about each couple having "homes" of our own, they could not understand it.

"Our work takes us all around the country," explained Celis. "We cannot live in one place all the time."

"We are together now," urged Alima, looking proudly at Terry's stalwart nearness. (This was one of the times when they were "on," though presently "off" again.)

"It's not the same thing at all," he insisted. "A man wants a home of his own, with his wife and family in it."

"Staying in it? All the time?" asked Ellador. "Not imprisoned, surely!"

"Of course not! Living there,—naturally," he answered.

"What does she do there—all the time?" Alima demanded. "What is her work?"

Then Terry patiently explained again that our women did not work,—with reservations.

"But what do they do—if they have no work?" she persisted.

"They take care of the home—and the children."

"At the same time?" asked Ellador.

"Why yes. The children play about, and the mother has charge of it all. There are servants, of course."

It seemed so obvious, so natural to Terry, that he always grew impatient; but the girls were honestly anxious to understand.

"How many children do your women have?" Alima had her note-book out now, and a rather firm set of lip. Terry began to dodge.

"There is no set number, my dear," he explained. "Some have more, some have less."

"Some have none at all," I put in mischievously.

They pounced on this admission; and soon wrung from us the general fact that those women who had the most children had the least servants, and those who had the most servants had the least children.

"There!" triumphed Alima. "One or two or no children, and three or four servants. Now what do those women *do?*"

We explained as best we might. We talked of "social duties," disingenuously banking on their not interpreting the words as we did; we talked of hospitality, entertainment, and various "interests." All the time we knew that to these large-minded women whose whole mental outlook was so collective, the limitations of a wholly personal life were inconceivable.

"We cannot really understand it," Ellador concluded. "We are only half a people. We have our woman-ways and they have their man-ways and their both-ways. We have worked out a system of living which is, of course, limited. They must have a broader, richer, better one. I should like to see it."

"You shall, dearest," I whispered.

. . . . .

"There's nothing to smoke," complained Terry. He was in the midst of a prolonged quarrel with Alima, and needed a sedative. "There's nothing to drink. These blessed women have no pleasant vices. I wish we could get out of here!"

This wish was vain. We were always under a certain degree of watchfulness. When Terry burst forth to tramp the streets at night he always found a "Colonel" here or there; and when, on an occasion of fierce though temporary despair, he had plunged to the cliff edge with some vague view to escape, he found several of them close by. We were free—but there was a string to it.

"They've no unpleasant ones, either," Jeff reminded him.

"Wish they had!" Terry persisted. "They've neither the vices of men, nor the virtues of women—they're neuters!"

"You know better than that. Don't talk nonsense," said I, severely.

I was thinking of Ellador's eyes when they gave me a certain look; a look she did not at all realize.

Jeff was equally incensed. "I don't know what 'virtues of women' you miss. Seems to me they have all of them."

"They've no modesty," snapped Terry. "No patience, no submissiveness; none of that natural yielding which is woman's greatest charm."

I shook my head pityingly. "Go and apologize and make friends again, Terry. You've got a grouch, that's all. These women have the virtue of humanity, with less of its faults than any folks I ever saw. As for patience—they'd have pitched us over the cliffs the first day we lit among 'em, if they hadn't that."

"There are no—distractions," he grumbled. "Nowhere a man can go and cut loose a bit. It's an everlasting parlor and nursery."

"And workshop," I added. "And school, and office, and laboratory, and studio, and theater, and—home."

"Home!" he sneered. "There isn't a home in the whole pitiful place."

"There isn't anything else, and you know it," Jeff retorted hotly. "I never saw, I never dreamed of such universal peace and good will and mutual affection."

"Oh, well, of course, if you like a perpetual Sunday-school, it's all very well. But I like Something Doing. Here it's all done."

There was something to this criticism. The years of pioneering lay far behind them. Theirs was a civilization in which the initial difficulties had long since been overcome. The untroubled peace, the unmeasured plenty, the steady health, the large good will and smooth management which ordered everything, left nothing to overcome. It was like a pleasant family in an old established, perfectly-run country place.

I liked it because of my eager and continued interest in the sociological achievements involved. Jeff liked it as he would have liked such a family and such a place anywhere.

Terry did not like it because he found nothing to oppose, to struggle with, to conquer.

"Life is a struggle, has to be," he insisted. "If there is no struggle, there is no life—that's all."

"You're talking nonsense—masculine nonsense," the peaceful Jeff replied. He was certainly a warm defender of Herland. "Ants don't raise their myriads by a struggle, do they? Or the bees?"

"Oh, if you go back to insects—and want to live in an ant-hill—! I tell you the higher grades of life are reached only through struggle—combat. There's no Drama here. Look at their plays! They make me sick."

He rather had us there. The drama of the country was—to our taste—rather flat. You see, they lacked the sex motive; and, with it, jealousy. They had no interplay of warring nations; no aristocracy and its ambitions; no wealth and poverty opposition.

I see I have said little about the economics of the place; it should have come before; but I'll go on about the drama now.

They had their own kind. There was a most impressive array of pageantry, of processions, a sort of grand ritual, with their arts and their religion broadly blended. The very babies joined in it. To see one of their great annual festivals, with the massed and marching stateliness of those great mothers; the young women brave and noble, beautiful and strong; and then the children, taking part as naturally as ours would frolic round a Christmas tree—it was overpowering in the impression of joyous, triumphant life.

They had begun at a period when the drama, the dance, music, religion, and education were all very close together; and instead of developing them in detached lines, they had kept the connection. Let me try again to give, if I can, a faint sense of the difference in the life-view—the background and basis on which their culture rested.

Ellador told me a lot about it. She took me to see the children, the growing girls, the special teachers. She picked out books for me to read; she always seemed to understand just what I wanted to know, and how to give it to me.

While Terry and Alima struck sparks and parted,—he always madly drawn to her and she to him—she must have been, or she'd never have stood the way he behaved—Ellador and I had already a deep, restful feeling, as if we'd always had one another. Jeff and Celis were happy; there was no question of that; but it didn't seem to me as if they had the good times we did.

Well, here is the Herland child facing life—as Ellador tried to show it to me. From the first memory, they knew Peace, Beauty, Order, Safety, Love, Wisdom, Justice, Patience, and Plenty. By "plenty" I mean that the babies grew up in an environment which met their needs; just as young fawns might grow up in dewy forest glades and brook-fed meadows. And they enjoyed it as frankly and utterly as the fawns would.

They found themselves in a big bright lovely world, full of the most interesting and enchanting things to learn about and to do. The people everywhere were friendly and polite. No Herland child ever met the overbearing rudeness we so commonly show to children. They were People, too, from the first; the most precious part of the nation.

In each step of the rich experience of living, they found the instance they were studying widen out into contact with an endless range of common interests. The things they learned were *related*, from the first; related to one another, and to the national prosperity.

"It was a butterfly that made me a forester," said Ellador. "I was about eleven years old, and I found a big purple and green butterfly on a low flower. I caught it, very carefully, by the closed wings, as I had been told to do, and carried it to the nearest insect teacher—" (I made a note there to ask her what on earth an insect teacher was) "to ask her its name. She took it from me with a little cry of delight. 'Oh, you blessed child,' she said. 'Do you like obernuts?' Of course I liked obernuts, and said so. It is our best food-nut, you know. 'This is a female of the obernut moth,' she told me, 'they are almost gone. We have been trying to exterminate them for centuries. If you had not caught this one, it might have laid eggs enough to raise worms enough to destroy thousands of our nut trees—thousands of bushels of nuts,—and make years and years of trouble for us.'

"Everybody congratulated me. The children all over the country were told to watch for that moth, if there were any more. I was shown the history of the creature, and account of the damage it used to do, and of how long and hard our foremothers had worked to save that tree for us. I grew a foot, it seemed to me, and determined then and there to be a forester."

This is but an instance; she showed me many. The big difference was that whereas our children grow up in private homes and families, with every effort made to protect and seclude them from a dangerous world; here they grew up in a wide, friendly world, and knew it for theirs, from the first.

Their child-literature was a wonderful thing. I could have spent years following the delicate subtleties, the smooth simplicities, with which they had bent that great art to the service of the child mind.

We have two life cycles: the man's and the woman's. To the man there is growth, struggle, conquest, the establishment of his family, and as much further success in gain or ambition, as he can achieve.

To the woman, growth, the securing of a husband, the subordinate activities of family life; and afterward such "social" or charitable interests as her position allows.

Here was but one cycle, and that a large one.

The child entered upon a broad open field of life, in which motherhood was the one great personal contribution to the national life, and all the rest the individual share in their common activities. Every girl I talked to, at any age above babyhood, had her cheerful determination as to what she was going to be when she grew up.

What Terry meant by saying they had "no modesty" was, that this great life-view had no shady places; they had a high sense of personal decorum, but no shame—no knowledge of anything to be ashamed of.

Even their shortcomings and misdeeds in childhood never were presented to them as sins; merely as errors and misplays—as in a game. Some of them, who were palpably less agreeable than others or who had a real weakness or fault, were treated with cheerful allowance, as a friendly group at whist would treat a poor player.

Their religion, you see, was maternal; and their ethics, based on the full perception of evolution, showed the principle of growth and the beauty of wise culture. They had no theory of the essential opposition of good and evil; life to them was Growth; their pleasure was in growing, and their duty also.

With this background, with their sublimated mother-love, expressed in terms of widest social activity; every phase of their work was modified by its effect on the national growth. The language itself they had deliberately clarified, simplified, made easy and beautiful, for the sake of the children.

This seemed to us a wholly incredible thing; first, that any nation should have the foresight, the strength, and the persistence to plan and fulfill such a task; and second, that women should have had so much initiative. We have assumed, as a matter of course, that women had none; that only the man, with his natural energy and impatience of restriction, would ever invent anything.

Here we found that the pressure of life upon the environment develops in the human mind its inventive reactions, regardless of sex; and further, that a fully awakened motherhood plans and works without limit, for the good of the child.

That the children might be most nobly born, and reared in an environment calculated to allow the richest, freest growth, they had deliberately remodeled and improved the whole state.

I do not mean in the least that they stopped at that; any more than a child stops at childhood. The most impressive part of their whole culture beyond this perfect system of child-rearing, was the range of interests and associations open to them all, for life. But in the field of literature I was most struck, at first, by the child-motive.

They had the same gradation of simple repetitive verse and story that we are familiar with, and the most exquisite, imaginative tales; but where, with us, these are the dribbled remnants of ancient folk myths, and primitive lullabies, theirs were the exquisite work of great artists; not only simple and unfailing in appeal to the child-mind, but *true*, true to the living world about them.

To sit in one of their nurseries for a day was to change one's views forever as to babyhood. The youngest ones, rosy fatlings in their mothers' arms, or sleeping lightly in the flower-sweet air, seemed natural enough, save that they never cried. I never heard a child cry in Herland, save once or twice at a bad fall; and then people ran to help, as we would at a scream of agony from a grown person.

Each mother had her year of Glory; the time to love and learn, living closely with her child; nursing it proudly, often for two years or more. This perhaps was one reason for their wonderful vigor.

But after the baby-year the mother was not so constantly in attendance, unless, indeed, her work was among the little ones. She was never far off, however, and her attitude toward the co-mothers, whose proud child-service was direct and continuous, was lovely to see.

As for the babies—a group of those naked darlings playing on short velvet grass, clean-swept; or rugs as soft; or in shallow pools of bright water; tumbling over with bubbling joyous baby laughter—it was a view of infant happiness such as I had never dreamed.

The babies were reared in the warmer part of the country, and gradually acclimated to the cooler heights as they grew older.

Sturdy children of ten and twelve played in the snow as joyfully as ours do; there were continuous excursions of them, from one part of the land to another, so that, to each child, the whole country might be home.

It was all theirs, waiting for them to learn, to love, to use, to serve; as our own little boys plan to be "a big soldier," or "a cowboy," or whatever pleases their fancy; and our little girls plan for the kind of home they mean to have, or how many children; these planned, freely and gaily with much happy chattering; of what they would do for the country when they were grown.

It was the eager happiness of the children and young people which first made me see the folly of that common notion of ours—that if life was smooth and happy people would not enjoy it. As I studied these youngsters, vigorous, joyous, eager little creatures, and their voracious appetite for life, it shook my previous ideas so thoroughly that they have never been re-established. The steady level of good health gave them all that natural stimulus we used to call "animal spirits"—an odd contradiction in terms. They found themselves in an immediate environment which was agreeable and interesting, and before them stretched the years of learning and discovery, the fascinating, endless process of education.

As I looked into these methods and compared them with our own, my strange uncomfortable sense of race-humility grew apace.

Ellador could not understand my astonishment. She explained things kindly and sweetly, but with some amazement that they needed explaining, and with sudden questions as to how we did it that left me meeker than ever.

I betook myself to Somel one day, carefully not taking Ellador. I did not mind seeming foolish to Somel—she was used to it.

"I want a chapter of explanation," I told her. "You know my stupidities by heart, and I do not want to show them to Ellador—she thinks me so wise!"

She smiled delightedly. "It is beautiful to see," she told me, "this new wonderful love between you. The whole country is interested, you know—how can we help it!"

I had not thought of that. We say: "All the world loves a lover," but to have a couple of million people watching one's courtship—and that a difficult one—was rather embarrassing.

"Tell me about your theory of education," I said. "Make it short and easy. And, to show you what puzzles me, I'll tell you that in our theory great stress is laid on the forced exertion of the child's mind; we think it is good for him to overcome obstacles."

"Of course it is," she unexpectedly agreed. "All our children do that—they love to."

That puzzled me again. If they loved to do it, how could it be educational?

"Our theory is this," she went on carefully. "Here is a young human being. The mind is as natural a thing as the body, a thing that grows, a thing to use and enjoy. We seek to nourish, to stimulate, to exercise the mind of a child as we do the body. There are the two main divisions in education— you have those, of course?—the things it is necessary to know, and the things it is necessary to do."

"To do? Mental exercises, you mean?"

"Yes. Our general plan is this: in the matter of feeding the mind, of furnishing information, we use our best powers to meet the natural appetite of a healthy young brain; not to overfeed it, to provide such amount and variety of impressions as seem most welcome to each child. That is the easiest part. The other division is in arranging a properly graduated series of exercises which will best develop each mind; the common faculties we all have, and most carefully, the especial faculties some of us have. You do this also, do you not?"

"In a way," I said rather lamely. "We have not so subtle and highly developed a system as you, not approaching it; but tell me more. As to the information—how do you manage? It appears that all of you know pretty much everything—is that right?"

This she laughingly disclaimed. "By no means. We are, as you soon found out, extremely limited in knowledge. I wish you could realize what a ferment the country is in over the new things you have told us; the passionate eagerness among thousands of us to go to your country and learn—learn—learn! But what we do know is readily divisible into common knowledge and special knowledge. The common knowledge we have long since learned to feed into the minds of our little ones with no waste of time or strength; the special knowledge is open to all, as they desire it. Some of us specialize in one line only; but most take up several; some for their regular work, some to grow with."

"To grow with?"

"Yes; when one settles too close in one kind of work there is a tendency to atrophy in the disused portions of the brain. We like to keep on learning, always."

"What do you study?"

"As much as we know of the different sciences. We have, within our limits, a good deal of knowledge of anatomy, physiology, nutrition—all that pertains to a full and beautiful personal life. We have our botany and chemistry, and so on; very rudimentary, but interesting; our own history, with its accumulating psychology."

"You put psychology with history—not with personal life?"

"Of course. It is ours; it is among and between us, and it changes with the succeeding and improving generations. We are at work, slowly and carefully, developing our whole people along these lines. It is glorious work—splendid! To see the thousands of babies improving, showing stronger clearer minds, sweeter dispositions, higher capacities—don't you find it so in your country?"

This I evaded flatly. I remembered the cheerless claim that the human mind was no better than in its earliest period of savagery, only better informed—a statement I had never believed.

"We try most earnestly for two powers," Somel continued. "The two that seem to us basically necessary for all noble life: a clear, far-reaching judgment, and a strong well-used will. We spend our best efforts, all through childhood and youth, in developing these faculties, individual judgment and will."

"As part of your system of education, you mean?"

"Exactly. As the most valuable part. With the babies, as you may have noticed, we first provide an environment which feeds the mind without tiring it; all manner of simple and interesting things to do, as soon as they are old enough to do them; physical properties, of course, come first. But as early as possible, going very carefully, not to tax the mind, we provide choices, simple choices, with very obvious causes and consequences. You've noticed the games?"

I had. The children seemed always playing something; or else, sometimes, engaged in peaceful researches of their own. I had wondered at first when they went to school, but soon found that they never did—to their knowledge. It was all education but no schooling.

"We have been working for some sixteen hundred years, devising better and better games for children," continued Somel.

I sat aghast. "Devising games?" I protested. "Making up new ones, you mean?"

"Exactly," she answered. "Don't you?"

Then I remembered the kindergarten, and the "material" devised by Signora Montessori, and guardedly replied: "To some extent." But most of our games, I told her, were very old—came down from child to child, along the ages, from the remote past.

"And what is their effect?" she asked. "Do they develop the faculties you wish to encourage?"

Again I remembered the claims made by the advocates of "sports," and again replied guardedly that that was, in part, the theory.

"But do the children *like* it?" I asked. "Having things made up and set before them that way? Don't they want the old games?"

"You can see the children," she answered. "Are yours more contented— more interested—happier?"

Then I thought, as in truth I never had thought before, of the dull, bored children I had seen, whining: "What can I do now?"; of the little groups and gangs hanging about; of the value of some one strong spirit who possessed initiative and would "start something"; of the children's parties and the onerous duties of the older people set to "amuse the children," also of that troubled ocean of misdirected activity we call "mischief," the foolish, destructive, sometimes evil things done by unoccupied children.

"No," said I grimly. "I don't think they are."

The Herland child was born not only into a world carefully prepared, full of the most fascinating materials and opportunities to learn, but into the society of plentiful numbers of teachers, teachers born and trained, whose business it was to accompany the children along that, to us, impossible thing—the royal road to learning.

There was no mystery in their methods. Being adapted to children it was at least comprehensible to adults. I spent many days with the little ones, sometimes with Ellador, sometimes without, and began to feel a crushing pity for my own childhood, and for all others that I had known.

The houses and gardens planned for babies had in them nothing to hurt— no stairs, no corners, no small loose objects to swallow, no fire—just a babies paradise. They were taught, as rapidly as feasible, to use and control their own bodies, and never did I see such sure-footed, steady-handed, clear-headed little things. It was a joy to watch a row of toddlers learning to walk, not only on a level floor, but, a little later, on a sort of rubber rail raised an inch or two above the soft turf or heavy rugs, and falling off with shrieks of infant joy, to rush back to the end of the line and try again. Surely we have noticed how children love to get up on something and walk along it! But we have never thought to provide that simple and inexhaustible form of amusement and physical education for the young.

Water they had, of course, and could swim even before they walked. If I feared at first the effects of a too intensive system of culture, that fear was dissipated by seeing the long sunny days of pure physical merriment and natural sleep in which these heavenly babies passed their first years. They never knew they were being educated. They did not dream that in this association of hilarious experiment and achievement they were laying the foundation for that close beautiful group feeling into which they grew so firmly with the years. This was education for citizenship.

Chapter X

Their Religions and Our Marriages

It took me a long time, as a man, a foreigner, and a species of Christian—I was that as much as anything—to get any clear understanding of the religion of Herland.

Its deification of motherhood was obvious enough; but there was far more to it than that; or, at least, than my first interpretation of that.

I think it was only as I grew to love Ellador more than I believed anyone could love anybody, as I grew faintly to appreciate her inner attitude and state of mind, that I began to get some glimpses of this faith of theirs.

When I asked her about it, she tried at first to tell me, and then, seeing me flounder, asked for more information about ours. She soon found that we had many, that they varied widely, but had some points in common. A clear methodical luminous mind had my Ellador, not only reasonable, but swiftly perceptive.

She made a sort of chart, superimposing the different religions as I described them, with a pin run through them all, as it were; their common basis being a Dominant Power or Powers, and some Special Behavior, mostly taboos, to please or placate. There were some common features in certain groups of religions, but the one always present was this Power, and the things which must be done or not done because of it. It was not hard to trace our human imagery of the Divine Force up through successive stages of bloodthirsty, sensual, proud, and cruel gods of early times to the conception of a Common Father with its corollary of a Common Brotherhood.

This pleased her very much and when I expatiated on the Omniscience, Omnipotence, Omnipresence, and so on of our God, and of the loving kindness taught by his Son, she was much impressed.

The story of the Virgin birth naturally did not astonish her, but she was greatly puzzled by the Sacrifice, and still more by the Devil, and the theory of Damnation.

When in an inadvertent moment I said that certain sects had believed in infant damnation—and explained it—she sat very still indeed.

"They believed that God was Love—and Wisdom—and Power?"

"Yes—all of that."

Her eyes grew large, her face ghastly pale.

"And yet that such a God could put little new babies to burn—for eternity?" She fell into a sudden shuddering and left me, running swiftly to the nearest Temple.

Every smallest village had its Temple, and in those gracious retreats sat wise and noble women, quietly busy at some work of their own until they were wanted, always ready to give comfort, light, or help, to any applicant.

Ellador told me afterward how easily this grief of hers was assuaged, and seemed ashamed of not having helped herself out of it.

"You see, we are not accustomed to horrible ideas," she said, coming back to me rather apologetically. "We haven't any. And when we get a thing like that into our minds it's like—oh, like red pepper in your eyes. So I just ran to her blinded and almost screaming, and she took it out so quickly—so easily!"

"How?" I asked, very curious.

"'Why, you blessed child,' she said, 'you've got the wrong idea altogether. You do not have to think that there ever was such a God—for there wasn't. Or such a happening—for there wasn't. Nor even that this hideous false idea was believed by anybody. But only this—that people who are utterly ignorant will believe anything—which you certainly knew before.'

"Anyhow," pursued Ellador, "she turned pale for a minute when I first said it."

This was a lesson to me. No wonder this whole nation of women was peaceful and sweet in expression—they had no horrible ideas.

"Surely you had some when you began," I suggested.

"Oh, yes, no doubt. But as soon as our religion grew to any height at all we left them out of course."

From this, as from many other things, I grew to see what I finally put in words.

"Have you no respect for the past? For what was thought and believed by your foremothers?"

"Why, no," she said. "Why should we? They are all gone. They knew less than we do. If we are not beyond them, we are unworthy of them—and unworthy of the children who must go beyond us."

This set me thinking in good earnest. I had always imagined—simply from hearing it said, I suppose—that women were by nature conservative. Yet these women, quite unassisted by any masculine spirit of enterprise, had

231

ignored their past and built daringly for the future.

Ellador watched me think. She seemed to know pretty much what was going on in my mind.

"It's because we began in a new way, I suppose. All our folks were swept away at once, and then, after that time of despair, came those wonder children—the first. And then the whole breathless hope of us was for *their* children—if they should have them. And they did! Then there was the period of pride and triumph till we grew too numerous; and after that, when it all came down to one child apiece, we began to really work—to make better ones."

"But how does this account for such a radical difference in your religion?" I persisted.

She said she couldn't talk about the difference very intelligently, not being familiar with other religions, but that theirs seemed simple enough. Their great Mother Spirit was to them what their own motherhood was—only magnified beyond human limits. That meant that they felt beneath and behind them an upholding, unfailing, serviceable love—perhaps it was really the accumulated mother-love of the race they felt—but it was a Power.

"Just what is your theory of worship?" I asked her.

"Worship? What is that?"

I found it singularly difficult to explain. This Divine Love which they felt so strongly did not seem to ask anything of them—"any more than our mothers do," she said.

"But surely your mothers expect honor, reverence, obedience, from you. You have to do things for your mothers, surely?"

"Oh, no," she insisted, smiling, shaking her soft brown hair. "We do things *from* our mothers—not *for* them. We don't have to do things *for* them— they don't need it, you know. But we have to live on—splendidly— because of them; and that's the way we feel about God."

I meditated again. I thought of that "God of Battles" of ours, that "Jealous God," that "Vengeance is mine" God. I thought of our world-nightmare— Hell.

"You have no theory of eternal punishment then, I take it?"

Ellador laughed. Her eyes were as bright as stars, and there were tears in them, too, she was so sorry for me.

"How could we?" she asked, fairly enough. "We have no punishments in life, you see, so we don't imagine them after death."

"Have you *no* punishments? Neither for children nor criminals—such mild criminals as you have?" I urged.

"Do you punish a person for a broken leg or a fever? We have preventive measures, and cures; sometimes we have to 'send the patient to bed,' as it were; but that's not a punishment—it's only part of the treatment," she explained.

Then studying my point of view more closely, she added: "You see, we recognize, in our human motherhood, a great tender limitless uplifting force—patience and wisdom and all subtlety of delicate method. We credit God—our idea of God—with all that and more. Our mothers are not angry with us—why should God be?"

"Does God mean a person to you?"

This she thought over a little. "Why—in trying to get close to it in our minds we personify the idea, naturally; but we certainly do not assume a Big Woman somewhere, who is God. What we call God is a Pervading Power, you know, an Indwelling Spirit, something inside of us that we want more of. Is your God a Big Man?" she asked innocently.

"Why—yes, to most of us, I think. Of course we call it an Indwelling Spirit just as you do, but we insist that it is Him, a Person, and a Man—with whiskers."

"Whiskers? Oh yes—because you have them! Or do you wear them because He does?"

"On the contrary, we shave them off—because it seems cleaner and more comfortable."

"Does He wear clothes—in your idea, I mean?"

I was thinking over the pictures of God I had seen,—rash advances of the devout mind of man, representing his Omnipotent Deity as an Old Man in a flowing robe, flowing hair, flowing beard, and in the light of her perfectly frank and innocent questions this concept seemed rather unsatisfying.

I explained that the God of the Christian world was really the ancient Hebrew God, and that we had simply taken over the patriarchal idea—that ancient one which quite inevitably clothed its thought of God with the attributes of the patriarchal ruler, the grandfather.

233

"I see," she said eagerly, after I had explained the genesis and development of our religious ideals. "They lived in separate groups, with a male head, and he was probably a little—domineering?"

"No doubt of that," I agreed.

"And we live together without any 'head,' in that sense—just our chosen Leaders—that *does* make a difference."

"Your difference is deeper than that," I assured her. "It is in your common motherhood. Your children grow up in a world where everybody loves them. They find life made rich and happy for them by the diffused love and wisdom of all mothers. So it is easy for you to think of God in the terms of a similar diffused and competent love. I think you are far nearer right than we are."

"What I cannot understand," she pursued carefully, "is your preservation of such a very ancient state of mind. This patriarchal idea you tell me is thousands of years old?"

"Oh yes—four, five, six thousand—ever so many."

"And you have made wonderful progress in those years—in other things?"

"We certainly have. But religion is different. You see our religions come from behind us, and are initiated by some great teacher who is dead. He is supposed to have known the whole thing and taught it, finally. All we have to do is Believe—and Obey."

"Who was the great Hebrew teacher?"

"Oh—there it was different. The Hebrew religion is an accumulation of extremely ancient traditions, some far older than their people, and grew by accretion down the ages. We consider it inspired—'the Word of God.'"

"How do you know it is?"

"Because it says so?"

"Does it say so in as many words? Who wrote that in?"

I began to try to recall some text that did say so, and could not bring it to mind.

"Apart from that," she pursued, "what I cannot understand is why you keep these early religious ideas so long. You have changed all your others, haven't you?"

"Pretty generally," I agreed. "But this we call 'revealed religion,' and think it is final. But tell me more about these little Temples of yours," I urged.

234

"And these Temple Mothers you run to."

Then she gave me an extended lesson in applied religion, which I will endeavor to concentrate.

They developed their central theory of a Loving Power, and assumed that its relation to them was motherly—that it desired their welfare and especially their development. Their relation to it, similarly, was filial, a loving appreciation and a glad fulfillment of its high purposes. Then, being nothing if not practical, they set their keen and active minds to discover the kind of conduct expected of them. This worked out in a most admirable system of ethics. The principle of Love was universally recognized—and used.

Patience, gentleness, courtesy, all that we call "good breeding," was part of their code of conduct. But where they went far beyond us was in the special application of religious feeling to every field of life. They had no ritual, no little set of performances called "divine service," save those glorious pageants I have spoken of, and those were as much educational as religious, and as much social as either. But they had a clear established connection between everything they did—and God. Their cleanliness, their health, their exquisite order, the rich peaceful beauty of the whole land, the happiness of the children, and above all the constant progress they made—all this was their religion.

They applied their minds to the thought of God, and worked out the theory that such an Inner Power demanded Outward Expression. They lived as if God was real and at work within them.

As for those little Temples everywhere—some of the women were more skilled, more temperamentally inclined, in this direction, than others. These, whatever their work might be, gave certain hours to the Temple Service, which meant being there with all their love and wisdom and trained thought, to smooth out rough places for anyone who needed it. Sometimes it was a real grief, very rarely a quarrel, most often a perplexity; even in Herland the human soul had its hours of darkness. But all through the country their best and wisest were ready to give help.

If the difficulty was unusually profound, the applicant was directed to someone more specially experienced in that line of thought.

Here was a religion which gave to the searching mind a rational basis in life, the concept of an immense Loving Power working steadily out through them, toward good. It gave to the "soul" that sense of contact with the inmost force, of perception of the uttermost purpose, which we always crave. It gave to the "heart" the blessed feeling of being loved, loved and *understood.* It gave clear, simple, rational directions as to how we should live—and why. And for ritual it gave, first those triumphant group demonstrations, when with a union of all the arts, the revivifying combination of great multitudes moved rhythmically with march and dance, song and music, among their own noblest products and the open beauty of their groves and hills. Second, it gave these numerous little centers of wisdom where the least wise could go to the most wise and be helped.

"It is beautiful!" I cried enthusiastically. "It is the most practical, comforting, progressive religion I ever heard of. You *do* love one another—you *do* bear one another's burdens—you *do* realize that a little child is a type of the kingdom of heaven. You are more Christian than any people I ever saw. But—how about Death? And the Life Everlasting? What does your religion teach about Eternity?"

"Nothing," said Ellador. "What is Eternity?"

What indeed? I tried, for the first time in my life, to get a real hold on the idea.

"It is—never stopping."

"Never stopping?" She looked puzzled.

"Yes, life, going on forever."

"Oh—we see that, of course. Life does go on forever, all about us."

"But eternal life goes on *without dying.*"

"The same person?"

"Yes, the same person, unending, immortal." I was pleased to think that I had something to teach from our religion, which theirs had never promulgated.

"Here?" asked Ellador. "Never to die—here?" I could see her practical mind heaping up the people, and hurriedly reassured her.

"Oh no, indeed, not here—hereafter. We must die here, of course, but then we 'enter into eternal life.' The soul lives forever."

"How do you know?" she inquired.

"I won't attempt to prove it to you," I hastily continued. "Let us assume it to be so. How does this idea strike you?"

Again she smiled at me, that adorable, dimpling, tender, mischievous, motherly smile of hers. "Shall I be quite, quite honest?"

236

"You couldn't be anything else," I said, half gladly and half a little sorry. The transparent honesty of these women was a never-ending astonishment to me.

"It seems to me a singularly foolish idea," she said calmly. "And if true, most disagreeable."

Now I had always accepted the doctrine of personal immortality as a thing established. The efforts of inquiring Spiritualists, always seeking to woo their beloved ghosts back again, never seemed to me necessary. I don't say I had ever seriously and courageously discussed the subject with myself even; I had simply assumed it to be a fact. And here was the girl I loved, this creature whose character constantly revealed new heights and ranges far beyond my own, this superwoman of a super-land, saying she thought immortality foolish! She meant it, too.

"What do you *want* it for?" she asked.

"How can you *not* want it!" I protested. "Do you want to go out like a candle? Don't you want to go on and on—growing and—and—being happy, forever?"

"Why, no," she said. "I don't in the least. I want my child—and my child's child—to go on—and they will. Why should *I* want to?"

"But it means Heaven!" I insisted. "Peace and Beauty and Comfort and Love—with God." I had never been so eloquent on the subject of religion. She could be horrified at Damnation, and question the justice of Salvation, but Immortality—that was surely a noble faith.

"Why, Van," she said, holding out her hands to me. "Why Van—darling! How splendid of you to feel it so keenly. That's what we all want, of course—Peace and Beauty, and Comfort and Love—with God! And Progress too, remember; Growth, always and always. That is what our religion teaches us to want and to work for, and we do!"

"But that is *here*," I said, "only for this life on earth."

"Well? And do not you in your country, with your beautiful religion of love and service have it here, too—for this life—on earth?"

. . . . .

None of us were willing to tell the women of Herland about the evils of our own beloved land. It was all very well for us to assume them to be necessary and essential, and to criticize—strictly among ourselves—their all-too-perfect civilization, but when it came to telling them about the failures and wastes of our own, we never could bring ourselves to do it.

Moreover, we sought to avoid too much discussion, and to press the subject of our approaching marriage.

Jeff was the determined one on this score.

"Of course they haven't any marriage ceremony or service, but we can make it a sort of Quaker wedding, and have it in the Temple—it is the least we can do for them."

It was. There was so little, after all, that we could do for them. Here we were, penniless guests and strangers, with no chance even to use our strength and courage—nothing to defend them from or protect them against.

"We can at least give them our names," Jeff insisted.

They were very sweet about it, quite willing to do whatever we asked, to please us. As to the names, Alima, frank soul that she was, asked what good it would do.

Terry, always irritating her, said it was a sign of possession. "You are going to be Mrs. Nicholson," he said. "Mrs. T. O. Nicholson. That shows everyone that you are my wife."

"What is a 'wife' exactly?" she demanded, a dangerous gleam in her eye.

"A wife is the woman who belongs to a man," he began.

But Jeff took it up eagerly: "And a husband is the man who belongs to a woman. It is because we are monogamous, you know. And marriage is the ceremony, civil and religious, that joins the two together—'until death do us part,'" he finished, looking at Celis with unutterable devotion.

"What makes us all feel foolish," I told the girls, "is that here we have nothing to give you—except, of course, our names."

"Do your women have no names before they are married?" Celis suddenly demanded.

"Why, yes," Jeff explained. "They have their maiden names—their father's names, that is."

"And what becomes of them?" asked Alima.

"They change them for their husbands', my dear," Terry answered her.

"Change them? Do the husbands then take the wives' 'maiden names'?"

"Oh, no," he laughed. "The man keeps his own and gives it to her, too."

"Then she just loses hers and takes a new one—how unpleasant! We won't

238

do that!" Alima said decidedly.

Terry was good-humored about it. "I don't care what you do or don't do so long as we have that wedding pretty soon," he said, reaching a strong brown hand after Alima's, quite as brown and nearly as strong.

"As to giving us things—of course we can see that you'd like to, but we are glad you can't," Celis continued. "You see, we love you just for yourselves—we wouldn't want you to—to pay anything. Isn't it enough to know that you are loved personally—and just as men?"

Enough or not, that was the way we were married. We had a great triple wedding in the biggest Temple of all, and it looked as if most of the nation was present. It was very solemn and very beautiful. Someone had written a new song for the occasion, nobly beautiful, about the New Hope for their people—the New Tie with other lands—Brotherhood as well as Sisterhood, and, with evident awe, Fatherhood.

Terry was always restive under their talk of fatherhood. "Anybody'd think we were High Priests of—of Philoprogenitiveness!" he protested. "These women think of *nothing* but children, seems to me! We'll teach 'em!"

He was so certain of what he was going to teach, and Alima so uncertain in her moods of reception, that Jeff and I feared the worst. We tried to caution him—much good that did. The big handsome fellow drew himself up to his full height, lifted that great chest of his, and laughed.

"There are three separate marriages," he said. "I won't interfere with yours—nor you with mine."

So the great day came, and the countless crowds of women, and we three bridegrooms without any supporting "best men," or any other men to back us up, felt strangely small as we came forward.

Somel and Zava and Moadine were on hand; we were thankful to have them, too—they seemed almost like relatives.

There was a splendid procession, wreathing dances, the new Anthem I spoke of, and the whole great place pulsed with feeling—the deep awe, the sweet hope, the wondering expectation of a new miracle.

"There has been nothing like this in the country since our Motherhood began!" Somel said softly to me, while we watched the symbolic marches. "You see, it is the dawn of a new era. You don't know how much you mean to us. It is not only Fatherhood—that marvelous dual parentage to which we are strangers—the miracle of union in life-giving—but it is Brotherhood. You are the rest of the world. You join us to our kind—to all

239

the strange lands and peoples we have never seen. We hope to know them—to love and help them—and to learn of them. Ah! You cannot know!"

. . . . .

Thousands of voices rose in the soaring climax of that great Hymn of The Coming Life. By the great Altar of Motherhood, with its crown of fruit and flowers, stood a new one, crowned as well. Before the Great Over-Mother of the Land and her ring of High Temple Counsellors, before that vast multitude of calm-faced mothers and holy-eyed maidens, came forward our own three chosen ones, and we, three men alone in all that land, joined hands with them and made our marriage vows.

Chapter XI

Our Difficulties

We say, "Marriage is a lottery"; also "Marriages are made in Heaven"—but this is not so widely accepted as the other.

We have a well-founded theory that it is best to marry "in one's class," and certain well-grounded suspicions of international marriages, which seem to persist in the interests of social progress, rather than in those of the contracting parties.

But no combination of alien races, of color, of caste, or creed, was ever so basically difficult to establish as that between us, three modern American men, and these three women of Herland.

It is all very well to say that we should have been frank about it beforehand. We had been frank. We had discussed—at least Ellador and I had—the conditions of The Great Adventure, and thought the path was clear before us. But there are some things one takes for granted, supposes are mutually understood, and to which both parties may repeatedly refer without ever meaning the same thing.

The differences in the education of the average man and woman are great enough, but the trouble they make is not mostly for the man; he generally carries out his own views of the case. The woman may have imagined the conditions of married life to be different; but what she imagined, was ignorant of, or might have preferred, did not seriously matter.

I can see clearly and speak calmly about this now, writing after a lapse of years, years full of growth and education, but at the time it was rather hard sledding for all of us—especially for Terry. Poor Terry! You see, in any other imaginable marriage among the peoples of the earth, whether the woman were black, red, yellow, brown, or white; whether she were ignorant or educated, submissive or rebellious, she would have behind her the marriage tradition of our general history. This tradition relates the woman to the man. He goes on with his business, and she adapts herself to him and to it. Even in citizenship, by some strange hocus-pocus, that fact of birth and geography was waved aside, and the woman automatically acquired the nationality of her husband.

Well—here were we, three aliens in this land of women. It was small in area, and the external differences were not so great as to astound us. We did not yet appreciate the differences between the race-mind of this people and ours.

In the first place, they were a "pure stock" of two thousand uninterrupted years. Where we have some long connected lines of thought and feeling, together with a wide range of differences, often irreconcilable, these people were smoothly and firmly agreed on most of the basic principles of their life; and not only agreed in principle, but accustomed for these sixty-odd generations to act on those principles.

This is one thing which we did not understand—had made no allowance for. When in our pre-marital discussions one of those dear girls had said: "We understand it thus and thus," or "We hold such and such to be true," we men, in our own deep-seated convictions of the power of love, and our easy views about beliefs and principles, fondly imagined that we could convince them otherwise. What we imagined, before marriage, did not matter any more than what an average innocent young girl imagines. We found the facts to be different.

It was not that they did not love us; they did, deeply and warmly. But there are you again—what they meant by "love" and what we meant by "love" were so different.

Perhaps it seems rather cold-blooded to say "we" and "they," as if we were not separate couples, with our separate joys and sorrows, but our positions as aliens drove us together constantly. The whole strange experience had made our friendship more close and intimate than it would ever have become in a free and easy lifetime among our own people. Also, as men, with our masculine tradition of far more than two thousand years, we were a unit, small but firm, against this far larger unit of feminine tradition.

I think I can make clear the points of difference without a too painful explicitness. The more external disagreement was in the matter of "the home," and the housekeeping duties and pleasures we, by instinct and long education, supposed to be inherently appropriate to women.

I will give two illustrations, one away up, and the other away down, to show how completely disappointed we were in this regard.

For the lower one, try to imagine a male ant, coming from some state of existence where ants live in pairs, endeavoring to set up housekeeping with a female ant from a highly developed ant-hill. This female ant might regard him with intense personal affection, but her ideas of parentage and economic management would be on a very different scale from his. Now, of course, if she was a stray female in a country of pairing ants, he might have had his way with her; but if he was a stray male in an anthill—!

For the higher one, try to imagine a devoted and impassioned man trying to set up housekeeping with a lady Angel, a real wings-and-harp-and-halo

Angel, accustomed to fulfilling Divine missions all over interstellar space. This Angel might love the man with an affection quite beyond his power of return or even of appreciation, but her ideas of service and duty would be on a very different scale from his. Of course, if she was a stray Angel in a country of men, he might have had his way with her; but if he was a stray man among Angels—!

Terry, at his worst, in a black fury for which, as a man, I must have some sympathy, preferred the ant simile. More of Terry and his special troubles later. It was hard on Terry.

Jeff—well, Jeff always had a streak that was too good for this world! He's the kind that would have made a saintly priest in earlier times. He accepted the Angel theory, swallowed it whole, tried to force it on us—with varying effect. He so worshipped Celis, and not only Celis, but what she represented; he had become so deeply convinced of the almost supernatural advantages of this country and people, that he took his medicine like a—I cannot say "like a man," but more as if he wasn't one.

Don't misunderstand me for a moment. Dear old Jeff was no milksop or molly-coddle either. He was a strong, brave, efficient man, and an excellent fighter when fighting was necessary. But there was always this angel streak in him. It was rather a wonder, Terry being so different, that he really loved Jeff as he did; but it happens so sometimes, in spite of the difference—perhaps because of it.

As for me, I stood between. I was no such gay Lothario as Terry, and no such Galahad as Jeff. But for all my limitations I think I had the habit of using my brains in regard to behavior rather more frequently than either of them. I had to use brain-power now, I can tell you.

The big point at issue between us and our wives was, as may easily be imagined, in the very nature of the relation.

"Wives! Don't talk to me about wives!" stormed Terry. "They don't know what the word means."

Which is exactly the fact—they didn't. How could they? Back in their prehistoric records of polygamy and slavery there were no ideals of wifehood as we know it, and since then no possibility of forming such.

"The only thing they can think of about a man is *Fatherhood!*" said Terry in high scorn. "*Fatherhood!* As if a man was always wanting to be a *father!*"

This also was correct. They had their long, wide, deep, rich experience of Motherhood, and their only perception of the value of a male creature as such, was for Fatherhood.

Aside from that, of course, was the whole range of personal love; love which as Jeff earnestly phrased it "passeth the love of women!" It did, too. I can give no idea—either now, after long and happy experience of it, or as it seemed then, in the first measureless wonder—of the beauty and power of the love they gave us.

Even Alima—who had a more stormy temperament than either of the others, and who, heaven knows, had far more provocation—even Alima was patience and tenderness and wisdom personified to the man she loved, until he—but I haven't got to that yet.

. . . . .

These, as Terry put it, "alleged or so-called wives" of ours, went right on with their profession as foresters. We, having no special learnings, had long since qualified as assistants. We had to do something, if only to pass the time, and it had to be work—we couldn't be playing forever.

This kept us out of doors with those dear girls, and more or less together— too much together sometimes.

These people had, it now became clear to us, the highest, keenest, most delicate sense of personal privacy, but not the faintest idea of that "solitude a deux" we are so fond of. They had, every one of them, the "two rooms and a bath" theory realized. From earliest childhood each had a separate bedroom with toilet conveniences, and one of the marks of coming of age was the addition of an outer room in which to receive friends.

Long since we had been given our own two rooms apiece, and as being of a different sex and race, these were in a separate house. It seemed to be recognized that we should breathe easier if able to free our minds in real seclusion.

For food we either went to any convenient eating-house, ordered a meal brought in, or took it with us to the woods, always and equally good. All this we had become used to and enjoyed—in our courting days.

After marriage there arose in us a somewhat unexpected urge of feeling that called for a separate house; but this feeling found no response in the hearts of those fair ladies.

"We *are* alone, dear," Ellador explained to me with gentle patience. "We are alone in these great forests; we may go and eat in any little summer-house—just we two, or have a separate table anywhere—or even have a separate meal in our own rooms. How could we be aloner?"

This was all very true. We had our pleasant mutual solitude about our work, and our pleasant evening talks in their apartments or ours; we had, as it were, all the pleasures of courtship carried right on; but we had no sense of—perhaps it may be called possession.

"Might as well not be married at all," growled Terry. "They only got up that ceremony to please us—please Jeff, mostly. They've no real idea of being married."

I tried my best to get Ellador's point of view, and naturally I tried to give her mine. Of course what we, as men, wanted to make them see was that there were other, and as we proudly said "higher," uses in this relation than what Terry called "mere parentage." In the highest terms I knew I tried to explain this to Ellador.

"Anything higher than for mutual love to hope to give life, as we did?" she said. "How is it higher?"

"It develops love," I explained. "All the power of beautiful permanent mated love comes through this higher development."

"Are you sure?" she asked gently. "How do you know that it was so developed? There are some birds who love each other so that they mope and pine if separated, and never pair again if one dies, but they never mate except in the mating season. Among your people do you find high and lasting affection appearing in proportion to this indulgence?"

It is a very awkward thing, sometimes, to have a logical mind.

Of course I knew about those monogamous birds and beasts too, that mate for life and show every sign of mutual affection, without ever having stretched the sex relationship beyond its original range. But what of it?

"Those are lower forms of life!" I protested. "They have no capacity for our higher feelings. Of course they are faithful and affectionate, and apparently happy—but Oh, my dear! my dear!—what can they know of such a love as draws us together? Why, to touch you—to be near you—to come closer and closer—to lose myself in you—surely you feel it too, do you not?"

I came nearer. I seized her hands.

Her eyes were on mine, tender, radiant, but steady and strong. There was something so powerful, so large and changeless, in those eyes that I could not sweep her off her feet by my own emotion as I had unconsciously assumed would be the case.

It made me feel as, one might imagine, a man might feel who loved a

245

goddess—not a Venus, though! She did not resent my attitude, did not repel it, did not in the least fear it, evidently. There was not a shade of that timid withdrawal or pretty resistance which are so—provocative.

"You see, dearest," she said, "you have to be patient with us. We are not like the women of your country. We are Mothers, and we are People, but we have not specialized in this line."

"We" and "we" and "we"—it was so hard to get her to be personal. And, as I thought that, I suddenly remembered how we were always criticizing *our* women for *being* so personal.

Then I did my earnest best to picture to her the sweet intense joy of married lovers, and the result in higher stimulus to all creative work.

"Do you mean," she asked quite calmly, as if I was not holding her cool firm hands in my hot and rather quivering ones, "that with you, when people marry, they go right on doing this in season and out of season, with no thought of children at all?"

"They do," I said, with some bitterness. "They are not mere parents. They are men and women, and they love each other."

"How long?" asked Ellador, rather unexpectedly.

"How long?" I repeated, a little dashed. "Why as long as they live."

"There is something very beautiful in the idea," she admitted, still as if she were discussing life on Mars. "This climactic expression, which, in all the other life-forms, has but the one purpose, has with you become specialized to higher, purer, nobler uses. It has—I judge from what you tell me—the most ennobling effect on character. People marry, not only for parentage, but for this exquisite interchange—and, as a result, you have a world full of continuous lovers, ardent, happy, mutually devoted, always living on that high tide of supreme emotion which we had supposed to belong only to one season and one use. And you say it has other results, stimulating all high creative work. That must mean floods, oceans of such work, blossoming from this intense happiness of every married pair! It is a beautiful idea!"

She was silent, thinking.

So was I.

She slipped one hand free, and was stroking my hair with it in a gentle motherly way. I bowed my hot head on her shoulder and felt a dim sense of peace, a restfulness which was very pleasant.

246

"You must take me there someday, darling," she was saying. "It is not only that I love you so much, I want to see your country—your people—your mother—" she paused reverently. "Oh, how I shall love your mother!"

I had not been in love many times—my experience did not compare with Terry's. But such as I had was so different from this that I was perplexed, and full of mixed feelings: partly a growing sense of common ground between us, a pleasant rested calm feeling, which I had imagined could only be attained in one way; and partly a bewildered resentment because what I found was not what I had looked for.

It was their confounded psychology! Here they were with this profound highly developed system of education so bred into them that even if they were not teachers by profession they all had a general proficiency in it— it was second nature to them.

And no child, stormily demanding a cookie "between meals," was ever more subtly diverted into an interest in house-building than was I when I found an apparently imperative demand had disappeared without my noticing it.

And all the time those tender mother eyes, those keen scientific eyes, noting every condition and circumstance, and learning how to "take time by the forelock" and avoid discussion before occasion arose.

I was amazed at the results. I found that much, very much, of what I had honestly supposed to be a physiological necessity was a psychological necessity—or so believed. I found, after my ideas of what was essential had changed, that my feelings changed also. And more than all, I found this—a factor of enormous weight—these women were not provocative. That made an immense difference.

The thing that Terry had so complained of when we first came—that they weren't "feminine," they lacked "charm," now became a great comfort. Their vigorous beauty was an aesthetic pleasure, not an irritant. Their dress and ornaments had not a touch of the "come-and-find-me" element.

Even with my own Ellador, my wife, who had for a time unveiled a woman's heart and faced the strange new hope and joy of dual parentage, she afterward withdrew again into the same good comrade she had been at first. They were women, *plus*, and so much plus that when they did not choose to let the womanness appear, you could not find it anywhere.

I don't say it was easy for me; it wasn't. But when I made appeal to her sympathies I came up against another immovable wall. She was sorry, honestly sorry, for my distresses, and made all manner of thoughtful suggestions, often quite useful, as well as the wise foresight I have mentioned above, which often saved all difficulty before it arose; but her sympathy did not alter her convictions.

"If I thought it was really right and necessary, I could perhaps bring myself to it, for your sake, dear; but I do not want to—not at all. You would not have a mere submission, would you? That is not the kind of high romantic love you spoke of, surely? It is a pity, of course, that you should have to adjust your highly specialized faculties to our unspecialized ones."

Confound it! I hadn't married the nation, and I told her so. But she only smiled at her own limitations and explained that she had to "think in we's."

Confound it again! Here I'd have all my energies focused on one wish, and before I knew it she'd have them dissipated in one direction or another, some subject of discussion that began just at the point I was talking about and ended miles away.

It must not be imagined that I was just repelled, ignored, left to cherish a grievance. Not at all. My happiness was in the hands of a larger, sweeter womanhood than I had ever imagined. Before our marriage my own ardor had perhaps blinded me to much of this. I was madly in love with, not so much what was there, as with what I supposed to be there. Now I found an endlessly beautiful undiscovered country to explore, and in it the sweetest wisdom and understanding. It was as if I had come to some new place and people, with a desire to eat at all hours, and no other interests in particular; and as if my hosts, instead of merely saying: "You shall not eat," had presently aroused in me a lively desire for music, for pictures, for games, for exercise, for playing in the water, for running some ingenious machine; and, in the multitude of my satisfactions, I forgot the one point which was not satisfied, and got along very well until meal-time.

One of the cleverest and most ingenious of these tricks was only clear to me many years after, when we were so wholly at one on this subject that I could laugh at my own predicament then. It was this: You see, with us, women are kept as different as possible and as feminine as possible. We men have our own world, with only men in it; we get tired of our ultra-maleness and turn gladly to the ultra-femaleness. Also, in keeping our women as feminine as possible, we see to it that when we turn to them we find the thing we want always in evidence. Well, the atmosphere of this place was anything but seductive. The very numbers of these human women, always in human relation, made them anything but alluring. When, in spite of this, my hereditary instincts and race-traditions made me long for the feminine response in Ellador, instead of withdrawing so that I should want her more, she deliberately gave me a little too much of her

248

society—always de-feminized, as it were. It was awfully funny, really.

Here was I, with an Ideal in mind, for which I hotly longed, and here was she, deliberately obtruding in the foreground of my consciousness a Fact— a fact which I coolly enjoyed, but which actually interfered with what I wanted. I see now clearly enough why a certain kind of man, like Sir Almroth Wright, resents the professional development of women. It gets in the way of the sex ideal; it temporarily covers and excludes femininity.

Of course, in this case, I was so fond of Ellador my friend, of Ellador my professional companion, that I necessarily enjoyed her society on any terms. Only—when I had had her with me in her de-feminine capacity for a sixteen-hour day, I could go to my own room and sleep without dreaming about her.

The Witch! If ever anybody worked to woo and win and hold a human soul, she did, great Superwoman that she was. I couldn't then half comprehend the skill of it, the wonder. But this I soon began to find: that under all our cultivated attitude of mind toward women, there is an older, deeper, more "natural" feeling; the restful reverence which looks up to the Mother sex.

So we grew together in friendship and happiness, Ellador and I, and so did Jeff and Celis.

When it comes to Terry's part of it, and Alima's, I'm sorry—and I'm ashamed. Of course I blame her somewhat. She wasn't as fine a psychologist as Ellador, and what's more, I think she had a far-descended atavistic trace of more marked femaleness, never apparent till Terry called it out. But when all that is said, it doesn't excuse him. I hadn't realized to the full Terry's character—I couldn't, being a man.

The position was the same as with us, of course, only with these distinctions: Alima, a shade more alluring, and several shades less able as a practical psychologist; Terry, a hundredfold more demanding—and proportionately less reasonable.

Things grew strained very soon between them. I fancy at first, when they were together, in her great hope of parentage and his keen joy of conquest—that Terry was inconsiderate. In fact, I know it, from things he said.

"You needn't talk to me," he snapped at Jeff one day, just before our weddings. "There never was a woman yet that did not enjoy being *mastered.* All your pretty talk doesn't amount to a hill o' beans—I *know.*" And Terry would hum:

"I've taken my fun where I found it. I've rogued and I've ranged in my time,"
and
"The things that I learned from the yellow and black, They 'ave helped me a 'eap with the white."

. . . . .

Jeff turned sharply and left him at the time. I was a bit disquieted myself.

Poor old Terry! The things he'd learned didn't help him a heap in Herland. His idea was To Take—he thought that was the way. He thought, he honestly believed, that women like it. Not the women of Herland! Not Alima!

I can see her now—one day in the very first week of their marriage, setting forth to her day's work with long determined strides and hard-set mouth, and sticking close to Ellador. She didn't wish to be alone with Terry—you could see that.

But the more she kept away from him, the more he wanted her—naturally.

He made a tremendous row about their separate establishments; tried to keep her in his rooms, tried to stay in hers. But there she drew the line sharply.

He came away one night, and stamped up and down the moonlit road, swearing under his breath. I was taking a walk that night too, but I wasn't in his state of mind. To hear him rage you'd not have believed that he loved Alima at all—you'd have thought that she was some quarry he was pursuing, something to catch and conquer.

I think that, owing to all those differences I spoke of, they soon lost the common ground they had at first, and were unable to meet sanely and dispassionately. I fancy too—this is pure conjecture—that he had succeeded in driving Alima beyond her best judgment, her real conscience; and that after that her own sense of shame, the reaction of the thing, made her bitter perhaps.

They quarrelled, really quarrelled, and after making it up once or twice, they seemed to come to a real break—she would not be alone with him at all. And perhaps she was a bit nervous, I don't know, but she got Moadine to come and stay next door to her. Also, she had a sturdy assistant detailed to accompany her in her work.

Terry had his own ideas, as I've tried to show. I daresay he thought he had a right to do as he did. Perhaps he even convinced himself that it would be better for her. Anyhow, he hid himself in her bedroom one night...

The women of Herland have no fear of men. Why should they have? They are not timid in any sense. They are not weak; and they all have strong trained athletic bodies. Othello could not have extinguished Alima with a pillow, as if she were a mouse.

Terry put in practice his pet conviction that a woman loves to be mastered, and by sheer brute force, in all the pride and passion of his intense masculinity, he tried to master this woman.

It did not work. I got a pretty clear account of it later from Ellador, but what we heard at the time was the noise of a tremendous struggle, and Alima calling to Moadine. Moadine was close by and came at once; one or two more strong grave women followed.

Terry dashed about like a madman; he would cheerfully have killed them—he told me that, himself—but he couldn't. When he swung a chair over his head one sprang in the air and caught it, two threw themselves bodily upon him and forced him to the floor; it was only the work of a few moments to have him tied hand and foot, and then, in sheer pity for his futile rage, to anaesthetize him.

. . . . .

Alima was in a cold fury. She wanted him killed—actually.

There was a trial before the local Over-Mother, and this woman, who did not enjoy being mastered, stated her case.

In a court in our country he would have been held quite "within his rights," of course. But this was not our country, it was theirs. They seemed to measure the enormity of the offense by its effect upon a possible fatherhood, and he scorned even to reply to this way of putting it.

He did let himself go once, and explained in definite terms that they were incapable of understanding a man's needs, a man's desires, a man's point of view. He called them neuters, epicenes, bloodless, sexless creatures. He said they could of course kill him—as so many insects could—but that he despised them nonetheless.

And all those stern grave mothers did not seem to mind his despising them, not in the least.

It was a long trial, and many interesting points were brought out as to their views of our habits, and after a while Terry had his sentence. He waited, grim and defiant. The sentence was: "You must go home!"

Chapter XII

Expelled

We had all meant to go home again. Indeed we had *not* meant—not by any means—to stay as long as we had. But when it came to being turned out, dismissed, sent away for bad conduct, we none of us really liked it.

Terry said he did. He professed great scorn of the penalty and the trial, as well as all the other characteristics of "this miserable half-country." But he knew, and we knew, that in any "whole" country we should never have been as forgivingly treated as we had been here.

"If the people had come after us according to the directions we left, there'd have been quite a different story!" said Terry. We found out later why no reserve party had arrived. All our careful directions had been destroyed in a fire. We might have all died there and no one at home have ever known our whereabouts.

Terry was under guard now, all the time, known as unsafe, convicted of what was to them an unpardonable sin.

He laughed at their chill horror. "Parcel of old maids!" he called them. "They're all old maids—children or not. They don't know the first thing about Sex."

When Terry said *Sex, sex* with a very large *S*, he meant the male sex, naturally; its special values, its profound conviction of being "the life force," its cheerful ignoring of the true life process, and its interpretation of the other sex solely from its own point of view.

I had learned to see these things very differently since living with Ellador; and as for Jeff, he was so thoroughly Herlandized that he wasn't fair to Terry, who fretted sharply in his new restraint.

Moadine, grave and strong, as sadly patient as a mother with a degenerate child, kept steady watch on him, with enough other women close at hand to prevent an outbreak. He had no weapons, and well knew that all his strength was of small avail against those grim, quiet women.

We were allowed to visit him freely, but he had only his room, and a small high-walled garden to walk in, while the preparations for our departure were under way.

Three of us were to go: Terry, because he must; I, because two were safer for our flyer, and the long boat trip to the coast; Ellador, because she would not let me go without her.

If Jeff had elected to return, Celis would have gone too—they were the most absorbed of lovers; but Jeff had no desire that way.

"Why should I want to go back to all our noise and dirt, our vice and crime, our disease and degeneracy?" he demanded of me privately. We never spoke like that before the women. "I wouldn't take Celis there for anything on earth!" he protested. "She'd die! She'd die of horror and shame to see our slums and hospitals. How can you risk it with Ellador? You'd better break it to her gently before she really makes up her mind."

Jeff was right. I ought to have told her more fully than I did, of all the things we had to be ashamed of. But it is very hard to bridge the gulf of as deep a difference as existed between our life and theirs. I tried to.

"Look here, my dear," I said to her. "If you are really going to my country with me, you've got to be prepared for a good many shocks. It's not as beautiful as this—the cities, I mean, the civilized parts—of course the wild country is."

"I shall enjoy it all," she said, her eyes starry with hope. "I understand it's not like ours. I can see how monotonous our quiet life must seem to you, how much more stirring yours must be. It must be like the biological change you told me about when the second sex was introduced—a far greater movement, constant change, with new possibilities of growth."

I had told her of the later biological theories of sex, and she was deeply convinced of the superior advantages of having two, the superiority of a world with men in it.

"We have done what we could alone; perhaps we have some things better in a quiet way, but you have the whole world—all the people of the different nations—all the long rich history behind you—all the wonderful new knowledge. Oh, I just can't wait to see it!"

What could I do? I told her in so many words that we had our unsolved problems, that we had dishonesty and corruption, vice and crime, disease and insanity, prisons and hospitals; and it made no more impression on her than it would to tell a South Sea Islander about the temperature of the Arctic Circle. She could intellectually see that it was bad to have those things; but she could not *feel* it.

We had quite easily come to accept the Herland life as normal, because it was normal—none of us make any outcry over mere health and peace and happy industry. And the abnormal, to which we are all so sadly well acclimated, she had never seen.

The two things she cared most to hear about, and wanted most to see, were these: the beautiful relation of marriage and the lovely women who were mothers and nothing else; beyond these her keen, active mind hungered eagerly for the world life.

"I'm almost as anxious to go as you are yourself," she insisted, "and you must be desperately homesick."

I assured her that no one could be homesick in such a paradise as theirs, but she would have none of it.

"Oh, yes—I know. It's like those little tropical islands you've told me about, shining like jewels in the big blue sea—I can't wait to see the sea! The little island may be as perfect as a garden, but you always want to get back to your own big country, don't you? Even if it is bad in some ways?"

Ellador was more than willing. But the nearer it came to our really going, and to my having to take her back to our "civilization," after the clean peace and beauty of theirs, the more I began to dread it, and the more I tried to explain.

Of course I had been homesick at first, while we were prisoners, before I had Ellador. And of course I had, at first, rather idealized my country and its ways, in describing it. Also, I had always accepted certain evils as integral parts of our civilization and never dwelt on them at all. Even when I tried to tell her the worst, I never remembered some things—which, when she came to see them, impressed her at once, as they had never impressed me. Now, in my efforts at explanation, I began to see both ways more keenly than I had before; to see the painful defects of my own land, the marvelous gains of this.

In missing men we three visitors had naturally missed the larger part of life, and had unconsciously assumed that they must miss it too. It took me a long time to realize—Terry never did realize—how little it meant to them. When we say *men, man, manly, manhood,* and all the other masculine derivatives, we have in the background of our minds a huge vague crowded picture of the world and all its activities. To grow up and "be a man," to "act like a man"—the meaning and connotation is wide indeed. That vast background is full of marching columns of men, of changing lines of men, of long processions of men; of men steering their ships into new seas, exploring unknown mountains, breaking horses, herding cattle, ploughing and sowing and reaping, toiling at the forge and furnace, digging in the mine, building roads and bridges and high cathedrals, managing great businesses, teaching in all the colleges, preaching in all the churches; of men everywhere, doing everything—The World.

And when we say *Women*, we think *Female*—the sex.

But to these women, in the unbroken sweep of this two-thousand-year-old feminine civilization, the word *woman* called up all that big background, so far as they had gone in social development; and the word *man* meant to them only *male*—the sex.

Of course we could *tell* them that in our world men did everything; but that did not alter the background of their minds. That man, "the male," did all these things was to them a statement, making no more change in the point of view than was made in ours when we first faced the astounding fact—to us—that in Herland women were "the world."

We had been living there more than a year. We had learned their limited history, with its straight, smooth, upreaching lines, reaching higher and going faster up to the smooth comfort of their present life. We had learned a little of their psychology, a much wider field than the history, but here we could not follow so readily. We were now well used to seeing women not as females but as people; people of all sorts, doing every kind of work.

This outbreak of Terry's, and the strong reaction against it, gave us a new light on their genuine femininity. This was given me with great clearness by both Ellador and Somel. The feeling was the same, sick revulsion and horror, such as would be felt at some climactic blasphemy.

They had no faintest approach to such a thing in their minds, knowing nothing of the custom of marital indulgence among us. To them the one high purpose of Motherhood had been for so long the governing law of life, and the contribution of the father, though known to them, so distinctly another method to the same end, that they could not, with all their effort, get the point of view of the male creature whose desires quite ignore parentage and seek only for what we euphoniously term "the joys of love."

When I tried to tell Ellador that women too felt so, with us, she drew away from me, and tried hard to grasp intellectually what she could in no way sympathize with.

"You mean—that with you—love between man and woman expresses itself in that way—without regard to motherhood? To parentage, I mean," she added carefully.

"Yes, surely. It is Love we think of—the deep sweet love between two. Of course we want children, and children come—but that is not what we think about."

"But—but—it seems so against nature!" she said. "None of the creatures we know do that. Do other animals—in your country?"

"We are not animals!" I replied with some sharpness. "At least we are something more—something higher. This is a far nobler and more beautiful relation, as I have explained before. Your view seems to us rather—shall I say, practical? Prosaic? Merely a means to an end! With us—Oh, my dear girl—cannot you see? Cannot you feel? It is the last, sweetest, highest consummation of mutual love."

She was impressed visibly. She trembled in my arms, as I held her close, kissing her hungrily. But there rose in her eyes that look I knew so well, that remote clear look as if she had gone far away even though I held her beautiful body so close, and was now on some snowy mountain regarding me from a distance.

"I feel it quite clearly," she said to me. "It gives me a deep sympathy with what you feel, no doubt more strongly still. But what I feel, even what you feel, dearest, does not convince me that it is right. Until I am sure of that, of course I cannot do as you wish."

Ellador, at times like this, always reminded me of Epictetus. "I will put you in prison!" said his master. "My body, you mean," replied Epictetus calmly. "I will cut your head off," said his master. "Have I said that my head could not be cut off?" A difficult person, Epictetus.

What is this miracle by which a woman, even in your arms, may withdraw herself, utterly disappear till what you hold is as inaccessible as the face of a cliff?

"Be patient with me, dear," she urged sweetly. "I know it is hard for you. And I begin to see—a little—how Terry was so driven to crime."

"Oh, come, that's a pretty hard word for it. After all, Alima was his wife, you know," I urged, feeling at the moment a sudden burst of sympathy for poor Terry. For a man of his temperament—and habits—it must have been an unbearable situation.

But Ellador, for all her wide intellectual grasp, and the broad sympathy in which their religion trained them, could not make allowance for such—to her—sacrilegious brutality.

It was the more difficult to explain to her, because we three, in our constant talks and lectures about the rest of the world, had naturally avoided the seamy side; not so much from a desire to deceive, but from wishing to put the best foot foremost for our civilization, in the face of the beauty and comfort of theirs. Also, we really thought some things were right, or at least unavoidable, which we could readily see would be repugnant to them, and therefore did not discuss. Again there was much of our world's life which we, being used to it, had not noticed as anything worth describing. And still further, there was about these women a colossal innocence upon which many of the things we did say had made no impression whatever.

I am thus explicit about it, because it shows how unexpectedly strong was the impression made upon Ellador when she at last entered our civilization.

She urged me to be patient, and I was patient. You see I loved her so much that even the restrictions she so firmly established left me much happiness. We were lovers, and there is surely delight enough in that.

Do not imagine that these young women utterly refused "the Great New Hope," as they called it, that of dual parentage. For that they had agreed to marry us, though the marrying part of it was a concession to our prejudices rather than theirs. To them the process was the holy thing—and they meant to keep it holy.

But so far only Celis, her blue eyes swimming in happy tears, her heart lifted with that tide of race motherhood which was their supreme passion, could with ineffable joy and pride announce that she was to be a mother. "The New Motherhood" they called it, and the whole country knew. There was no pleasure, no service, no honor in all the land that Celis might not have had. Almost like the breathless reverence with which, two thousand years ago, that dwindling band of women had watched the miracle of virgin birth, was the deep awe and warm expectancy with which they greeted this new miracle of union.

All mothers in that land were holy. To them, for long ages, the approach to motherhood has been by the most intense and exquisite love and longing, by the Supreme Desire, the overmastering demand for a Child. Every thought they held in connection with the processes of maternity was open to the day, simple yet sacred. Every woman of them placed Motherhood not only higher than other duties, but so far higher that there were no other duties, one might almost say. All their wide mutual love, all the subtle interplay of mutual friendship and service, the urge of progressive thought and invention, the deepest religious emotion, every feeling and every act was related to this great central Power, to the River of Life pouring through them, which made them the bearers of the very Spirit of God.

Of all this I learned more and more; from their books, from talk, especially from Ellador. She was at first, for a brief moment, envious of her friend— a thought she put away from her at once and forever.

"It is better," she said to me. "It is much better that it has not come to me yet—to us, that is. For if I am to go with you to your country, we may have

257

'adventures by sea and land,' as you say [and as in truth we did], and it might not be at all safe for a baby. So we won't try again, dear, till it is safe—will we?"

This was a hard saying for a very loving husband.

"Unless," she went on, "if one is coming, you will leave me behind. You can come back, you know—and I shall have the Child."

Then that deep ancient chill of male jealousy of even his own progeny touched my heart.

"I'd rather have you, Ellador, than all the children in the world. I'd rather have you with me—on your own terms—than not to have you."

This was a very stupid saying. Of course I would! For if she wasn't there I should want all of her and have none of her. But if she went along as a sort of sublimated sister—only much closer and warmer than that, really—why I should have all of her but that one thing. And I was beginning to find that Ellador's friendship, Ellador's comradeship, Ellador's sisterly affection, Ellador's perfectly sincere love—none the less deep that she held it back on a definite line of reserve—were enough to live on very happily.

I find it quite beyond me to describe what this woman was to me. We talk fine things about women, but in our hearts we know that they are very limited beings—most of them. We honor them for their functional powers, even while we dishonor them by our use of it; we honor them for their carefully enforced virtue, even while we show by our own conduct how little we think of that virtue; we value them, sincerely, for the perverted maternal activities which make our wives the most comfortable of servants, bound to us for life with the wages wholly at our own decision, their whole business, outside of the temporary duties of such motherhood as they may achieve, to meet our needs in every way. Oh, we value them, all right, "in their place," which place is the home, where they perform that mixture of duties so ably described by Mrs. Josephine Dodge Daskam Bacon, in which the services of "a mistress" are carefully specified. She is a very clear writer, Mrs. J. D. D. Bacon, and understands her subject— from her own point of view. But—that combination of industries, while convenient, and in a way economical, does not arouse the kind of emotion commanded by the women of Herland. These were women one had to love "up," very high up, instead of down. They were not pets. They were not servants. They were not timid, inexperienced, weak.

After I got over the jar to my pride (which Jeff, I truly think, never felt— he was a born worshipper, and which Terry never got over—he was quite clear in his ideas of "the position of women"), I found that loving "up" was a very good sensation after all. It gave me a queer feeling, way down deep, as of the stirring of some ancient dim prehistoric consciousness, a feeling that they were right somehow—that this was the way to feel. It was like—coming home to mother. I don't mean the underflannels-and-doughnuts mother, the fussy person that waits on you and spoils you and doesn't really know you. I mean the feeling that a very little child would have, who had been lost—for ever so long. It was a sense of getting home; of being clean and rested; of safety and yet freedom; of love that was always there, warm like sunshine in May, not hot like a stove or a feather-bed—a love that didn't irritate and didn't smother.

I looked at Ellador as if I hadn't seen her before. "If you won't go," I said, "I'll get Terry to the coast and come back alone. You can let me down a rope. And if you will go—why you blessed Wonder-Woman—I would rather live with you all my life—like this—than to have any other woman I ever saw, or any number of them, to do as I like with. Will you come?"

She was keen for coming. So the plans went on. She'd have liked to wait for that Marvel of Celis's, but Terry had no such desire. He was crazy to be out of it all. It made him sick, he said, *sick*; this everlasting mother-mother-mothering. I don't think Terry had what the phrenologists call "the lump of philoprogenitiveness" at all well developed.

"Morbid one-sided cripples," he called them, even when from his window he could see their splendid vigor and beauty; even while Moadine, as patient and friendly as if she had never helped Alima to hold and bind him, sat there in the room, the picture of wisdom and serene strength. "Sexless, epicene, undeveloped neuters!" he went on bitterly. He sounded like Sir Almwroth Wright.

Well—it was hard. He was madly in love with Alima, really; more so than he had ever been before, and their tempestuous courtship, quarrels, and reconciliations had fanned the flame. And then when he sought by that supreme conquest which seems so natural a thing to that type of man, to force her to love him as her master—to have the sturdy athletic furious woman rise up and master him—she and her friends—it was no wonder he raged.

Come to think of it, I do not recall a similar case in all history or fiction. Women have killed themselves rather than submit to outrage; they have killed the outrager; they have escaped; or they have submitted—sometimes seeming to get on very well with the victor afterward. There was that adventure of "false Sextus," for instance, who "found Lucrese combing the fleece, under the midnight lamp." He threatened, as I remember, that if she did not submit he would slay her, slay a slave and place him beside her and say he found him there. A poor device, it always seemed to me. If Mr. Lucretius had asked him how he came to be in his wife's bedroom overlooking her morals, what could he have said? But the point is Lucrese submitted, and Alima didn't.

"She kicked me," confided the embittered prisoner—he had to talk to someone. "I was doubled up with the pain, of course, and she jumped on me and yelled for this old Harpy [Moadine couldn't hear him] and they had me trussed up in no time. I believe Alima could have done it alone," he added with reluctant admiration. "She's as strong as a horse. And of course a man's helpless when you hit him like that. No woman with a shade of decency—"

I had to grin at that, and even Terry did, sourly. He wasn't given to reasoning, but it did strike him that an assault like his rather waived considerations of decency.

"I'd give a year of my life to have her alone again," he said slowly, his hands clenched till the knuckles were white.

But he never did. She left our end of the country entirely; went up into the fir-forest on the highest slopes, and stayed there. Before we left he quite desperately longed to see her, but she would not come and he could not go. They watched him like lynxes. (Do lynxes watch any better than mousing cats, I wonder!)

Well—we had to get the flyer in order, and be sure there was enough fuel left, though Terry said we could glide all right, down to that lake, once we got started. We'd have gone gladly in a week's time, of course, but there was a great to-do all over the country about Ellador's leaving them. She had interviews with some of the leading ethicists—wise women with still eyes, and with the best of the teachers. There was a stir, a thrill, a deep excitement everywhere.

Our teaching about the rest of the world has given them all a sense of isolation, of remoteness, of being a little outlying sample of a country, overlooked and forgotten among the family of nations. We had called it "the family of nations," and they liked the phrase immensely.

They were deeply aroused on the subject of evolution; indeed, the whole field of natural science drew them irresistibly. Any number of them would have risked everything to go to the strange unknown lands and study; but we could take only one, and it had to be Ellador, naturally.

We planned greatly about coming back, about establishing a connecting route by water; about penetrating those vast forests and civilizing—or

260

exterminating the dangerous savages. That is, we men talked of that last—not with the women. They had a definite aversion to killing things.

But meanwhile there was high council being held among the wisest of them all. The students and thinkers who had been gathering facts from us all this time, collating and relating them, and making inferences, laid the result of their labors before the council.

Little had we thought that our careful efforts at concealment had been so easily seen through, with never a word to show us that they saw. They had followed up words of ours on the science of optics, asked innocent questions about glasses and the like, and were aware of the defective eyesight so common among us.

With the lightest touch, different women asking different questions at different times, and putting all our answers together like a picture puzzle, they had figured out a sort of skeleton chart as to the prevalence of disease among us. Even more subtly with no show of horror or condemnation, they had gathered something—far from the truth, but something pretty clear—about poverty, vice, and crime. They even had a goodly number of our dangers all itemized, from asking us about insurance and innocent things like that.

They were well posted as to the different races, beginning with their poison-arrow natives down below and widening out to the broad racial divisions we had told them about. Never a shocked expression of the face or exclamation of revolt had warned us; they had been extracting the evidence without our knowing it all this time, and now were studying with the most devout earnestness the matter they had prepared.

The result was rather distressing to us. They first explained the matter fully to Ellador, as she was the one who purposed visiting the Rest of the World. To Celis they said nothing. She must not be in any way distressed, while the whole nation waited on her Great Work.

Finally Jeff and I were called in. Somel and Zava were there, and Ellador, with many others that we knew.

They had a great globe, quite fairly mapped out from the small section maps in that compendium of ours. They had the different peoples of the earth roughly outlined, and their status in civilization indicated. They had charts and figures and estimates, based on the facts in that traitorous little book and what they had learned from us.

Somel explained: "We find that in all your historic period, so much longer than ours, that with all the interplay of services, the exchange of inventions and discoveries, and the wonderful progress we so admire, that in this widespread Other World of yours, there is still much disease, often contagious."

We admitted this at once.

"Also there is still, in varying degree, ignorance, with prejudice and unbridled emotion."

This too was admitted.

"We find also that in spite of the advance of democracy and the increase of wealth, that there is still unrest and sometimes combat."

Yes, yes, we admitted it all. We were used to these things and saw no reason for so much seriousness.

"All things considered," they said, and they did not say a hundredth part of the things they were considering, "we are unwilling to expose our country to free communication with the rest of the world—as yet. If Ellador comes back, and we approve her report, it may be done later—but not yet.

"So we have this to ask of you Gentlemen [they knew that word was held a title of honor with us], that you promise not in any way to betray the location of this country until permission—after Ellador's return."

Jeff was perfectly satisfied. He thought they were quite right. He always did. I never saw an alien become naturalized more quickly than that man in Herland.

I studied it awhile, thinking of the time they'd have if some of our contagions got loose there, and concluded they were right. So I agreed.

Terry was the obstacle. "Indeed I won't!" he protested. "The first thing I'll do is to get an expedition fixed up to force an entrance into Ma-land."

"Then," they said quite calmly, "he must remain an absolute prisoner, always."

"Anesthesia would be kinder," urged Moadine.

"And safer," added Zava.

"He will promise, I think," said Ellador.

And he did. With which agreement we at last left Herland.

With Her in Ourland

Chapter I

The Return

The three of us, all with set faces of high determination, sat close in the big biplane as we said good-bye to Herland and rose whirring from the level rock on that sheer edge. We went up first, and made a wide circuit, that my wife Ellador might have a view of her own beloved land to remember. How green and fair and flower-brightened it lay below us! The little cities, the thick dotted villages, the scattered hamlets and wide parks of grouped houses lay again beneath our eyes as when we three men had first set our astonished masculine gaze on this ultra-feminine land.

Our long visit, the kind care and judicious education given us, even though under restraint, and our months of freedom and travel among them, made it seem to me like leaving a second home. The beauty of the place was borne in upon me anew as I looked down on it. It was a garden, a great cultivated park, even to its wildest forested borders, and the cities were ornaments to the landscape, thinning out into delicate lace-like tracery of scattered buildings as they merged into the open country.

Terry looked at it with set teeth. He was embittered through and through, and but for Ellador I could well imagine the kind of things he would have said. He only made this circuit at her request, as one who said: "Oh, well—an hour or two more or less—it's over, anyhow!"

Then the long gliding swoop as we descended to our sealed motor-boat in the lake below. It was safe enough. Perhaps the savages had considered it some deadly witch-work and avoided it; at any rate, save for some dents and scratches on the metal cover, it was unhurt.

With some careful labor, Terry working with a feverish joyful eagerness, we got the machine dissembled and packed away, pulled in the anchors, and with well-applied oiling started the long disused motor, and moved off toward the great river.

Ellador's eyes were on the towering cliffs behind us. I gave her the glass, and as long as we were on the open water her eyes dwelt lovingly on the high rocky border of her home. But when we shot under the arching gloom of the forest she turned to me with a little sigh and a bright, steady smile.

"That's good-bye," she said. "Now it's all looking forward to the Big New World—the Real World—with You!"

Terry said very little. His heavy jaw was set, his eyes looked forward, eagerly, determinedly. He was polite to Ellador, and not impolite to me, but he was not conversational.

We made the trip as fast as was consistent with safety; faster, sometimes; living on our canned food and bottled water, stopping for no fresh meat; shooting down the ever-widening river toward the coast.

Ellador watched it all with eager, childlike interest. The freshness of mind of these Herland women concealed their intellectual power. I never quite got used to it. We are so used to seeing our learned men cold and solemn, holding themselves far above all the "enthusiasm of youth," that it is hard for us to associate a high degree of wisdom and intellectual power with vivid interest in immediate events.

Here was my Wife from Wonderland, leaving all she had ever known,—a lifetime of peace and happiness and work she loved, and a whole nation of friends, as far as she knew them; and starting out with me for a world which I frankly told her was full of many kinds of pain and evil. She was not afraid. It was not sheer ignorance of danger, either. I had tried hard to make her understand the troubles she would meet. Neither was it a complete absorption in me—far from it. In our story books we read always of young wives giving up all they have known and enjoyed "for his sake." That was by no means Ellador's position. She loved me—that I knew, but by no means with that engrossing absorption so familiar to our novelists and their readers. Her attitude was that of some high ambassador sent on an important and dangerous mission. She represented her country, and that with a vital intensity we can hardly realize. She was to meet and learn a whole new world, and perhaps establish connections between it and her own dear land.

As Terry held to his steering, grim and silent, that feverish eagerness in his eyes, and a curb on his usually ready tongue, Ellador would sit in the bow, leaning forward, chin on her hand, her eyes ahead, far ahead, down the long reaches of the winding stream, with an expression such as one could imagine on Columbus. She was glad to have me near her. I was not only her own, in a degree she herself did not yet realize, but I was her one link with the homeland. So I sat close and we talked much of the things we saw and more of what we were going to see. Her short soft hair, curly in the moist air, and rippling back from her bright face as we rushed along, gave the broad forehead and clear eyes a more courageous look than ever. That finely cut mobile mouth was firmly set, though always ready to melt into a tender smile for me.

"Now Van, my dear," she said one day, as we neared the coast town where we hoped to find a steamer, "Please don't worry about how all this is going to affect me. You have been drawing very hard pictures of your own land,

and of the evil behavior of men; so that I shall not be disappointed or shocked too much. I won't be, dear. I understand that men are different from women—must be, but I am convinced that it is better for the world to have both men and women than to have only one sex, like us. We have done the best we could, we women, all alone. We have made a nice little safe clean garden place and lived happily in it, but we have done nothing whatever for the rest of the world. We might as well not be there for all the good it does anyone else. The savages down below are just as savage, for all our civilization. Now you, even if you were, as you say, driven by greed and sheer love of adventure and fighting—you have gone all over the world and civilized it."

"Not all, dear," I hastily put in. "Not nearly all. There are ever so many savages left."

"Yes I know that, I remember the maps and all the history and geography you have taught me."

It was a never-ending source of surprise to me the way those Herland women understood and remembered. It must have been due to their entirely different system of education. There was very much less put into their minds, from infancy up, and what was there seemed to grow there— to stay in place without effort. All the new facts we gave them they had promptly hung up in the right places, like arranging things in a large well-planned, not over-filled closet, and they knew where to find them at once.

"I can readily see," she went on, "that our pleasant collective economy is like that of bees and ants and such co-mothers; and that a world of fathers does not work as smoothly as that. We have observed, of course, among animals, that the instincts of the male are different from those of the female, and that he likes to fight. But think of all you have *done!*"

That was what delighted Ellador. She was never tired of my stories of invention and discovery, of the new lands we had found, the mountain ranges crossed, the great oceans turned into highways, and all the wonders of art and science. She loved it as did Desdemona the wild tales of her lover, but with more understanding.

"It must be nobler to have Two," she would say, her eyes shining. "We are only half a people. Of course we love each other, and have advanced our own little country, but it is such a little one—and you have The World!"

We reached the coast in due time, and the town. It was not much of a town, dirty and squalid enough, with lazy half-breed inhabitants for the most part. But this I had carefully explained and Ellador did not mind it, examining everything with kind impartial eyes, as a teacher would

269

examine the work of atypical children.

Terry loved it. He greeted that slovenly, ill-built, idle place with ardor, and promptly left us to ourselves for the most part.

There was no steamer. None had touched there for many months, they said; but there was a sailing vessel which undertook, for sufficient payment, to take us and our motor-boat with its contents, to a larger port.

Terry and I had our belts with gold and notes; he had letters of credit too, while Ellador had brought with her not only a supply of gold, but a little bag of rubies, which I assured her would take us several times around the world, and more. The money system in Herland was mainly paper, and their jewels, while valued for decoration, were not prized as ours are. They had some historic treasure chests, rivaling those of India, and she had been amply supplied.

After some delay we set sail.

Terry walked the deck, more eager as the days passed. Ellador, I am sorry to say, proved a poor sailor, as was indeed to be expected, but made no fuss about her disabilities. I told her it was almost unescapable, unpleasant but not dangerous, so she stayed in her berth, or sat wrapped mummy fashion on the deck, and suffered in patience.

Terry talked a little more when we were out of her hearing.

"Do you know they say there's a war in Europe?" he told me.

"A war? A real one—or just the Balkans?"

"A real one, they say—Germany and Austria against the rest of Europe apparently. Began months ago—no news for a long time."

"Oh well—it will be over before we reach home, I guess. Lucky for us we are Americans."

But I was worried for Ellador. I wanted the world, my world, to look its best in her eyes. If those women, alone and unaided, had worked out that pleasant, peaceful, comfortable civilization of theirs, with its practical sisterliness and friendliness all over the land, I was very anxious to show her that men had done at least as well, and in some ways better—men and women, that is. And here we had gotten up a war—a most undesirable spectacle for an international guest.

There was a missionary on board, a thin, almost emaciated man, of the Presbyterian denomination. He was a most earnest person, and a great talker, naturally.

"Woe unto me," he would say, "if I preach not this gospel! And he preached it "in season and out of season."

Ellador was profoundly interested. I tried to explain to her that he was an enthusiast of a rather rigid type, and that she must not judge Christianity too harshly by him, but she quite re-assured me.

"Don't be afraid, my dear boy—I remember your outline of the various religions—all about how Christianity arose and spread; how it held together in one church for a long time, and then divided, and kept on dividing—naturally. And I remember about the religious wars, and persecutions, that you used to have in earlier ages. We had a good deal of trouble with religion in our first centuries too, and for a long time people kept appearing with some sort of new one they had had 'revealed' to them, just like yours. But we saw that all that was needed was a higher level of mentality and a clear understanding of the real Laws—so we worked toward that. And, as you know, we have been quite at peace as to our religion for some centuries. It's just part of us."

That was the clearest way of putting it she had yet thought of. The Herland religion was like the manners of a true aristocrat, a thing unborn and inbred. It was the way they lived. They had so clear and quick a connection between conviction and action that it was well nigh impossible for them to know a thing and not do it. I suppose that was why, when we had told them about the noble teachings of Christianity, they had been so charmed, taking it for granted that our behavior was equal to our belief.

The Reverend Alexander Murdock was more than pleased to talk with Ellador—any man would be, of course. He was immensely curious about her too, but even to impertinent questions she presented an amiable but absolute impermeability.

"From what country do you come, Mrs. Jennings;" he asked her one day, in my hearing. He did not know I was within earshot, however.

Ellador was never annoyed by questions, nor angry, nor confused. Where most people seem to think that there is no alternative but to answer correctly or to lie, she recognized an endless variety of things to say or not say. Sometimes she would look pleasantly at the inquirer, with those deep kind eyes of hers, and ask: "Why do you wish to know?" Not sarcastically, not offensively at all, but as if she really wanted to know why they wanted to know. It was generally difficult for them to explain the cause of their curiosity, but if they did; if they said it was just interest, a kindly human interest in her, she would thank them for the interest, and ask if they felt it about everyone. If they said they did, she would say, still with her quiet

271

gentleness: "And is it customary, when one feels interested in a stranger, to ask them questions? I mean is it a—what you call a compliment? If so, I thank you heartily for the compliment."

If they drove her—some people never will take a hint—she would remain always quite courteous and gentle, even praise them for their perseverance, but never say one word she did not choose to. And she did not choose to give to anyone news of her beloved country until such time as that country decided it should be done.

The missionary was not difficult to handle.

"Did you not say that you were to preach the gospel to all nations—or all people—or something like that?" she asked him. "Do you find some nations easier to preach to than others? Or is it the same gospel to all?"

He assured her that it was the same, but that he was naturally interested in all his hearers, and that it was often important to know something of their antecedents. This she agreed might be an advantage, and left it at that, asking him if he would let her see his Bible. Once he was embarked on that subject, she had only to listen, and to steer the conversation, or rather the monologue.

I told her I had overheard this bit of conversation, begging her pardon for listening, but she said she would greatly enjoy having me with her while he talked. I told her I doubted if he would talk as freely if there were three of us, and she suggested in that case that if I was interested I was quite welcome to listen as far as she was concerned. Of course I wasn't going to be an eavesdropper, even on a missionary trying to convert my wife, but I heard a good bit of their talk as I strolled about, and sat with them sometimes.

He let her read his precious flexible Oxford Bible at times, giving her marked passages, and she read about a hundred times as much as he thought she could in a given time. It interested her immensely, and she questioned him eagerly about it:

"You call this 'The Word of God'?"

"Yes," he replied solemnly. "It is His Revealed Word."

"And every thing it says is true?"

"It is Truth itself, Divine Truth," he answered.

"You do not mean that God wrote it?"

"Oh, no. He revealed it to His servants. It is an Inspired Book."

"It was written by many people, was it not?"

"Yes—many people, but the same Word."

"And at different times?"

"Oh yes—the revelation was given at long intervals—the Old Testament to the Jews, the New Testament to us all."

Ellador turned the pages reverently. She had a great respect for religion, and for any sincere person.

"How old is the oldest part?" she asked him.

He told her as best he could, but he was not versed in the latest scholarship and had a genuine horror of "the higher criticism." But I supplied a little information on the side, when we were alone, telling her of the patchwork group of ancient legends which made up the first part; of the very human councils of men who had finally decided which of the ancient writings were inspired and which were not; of how the Book of Job, the oldest of all, had only scraped in by one vote, and then, with rather a malicious relish, of that most colossal joke of all history—how the Song of Songs—that amorous, not to say salacious ancient love-lyric, had been embraced with the others and interpreted as a mystical lofty outburst of devotion with that "black but comely" light-o'-love figuring as The Church.

Ellador was quite shocked.

"But Van!—he ought to know that. You ought to tell him. Is it generally known?"

"It is known to scholars, not to the public as a whole."

"But they still have it bound in with the others—and think it is holy—when it isn't."

"Yes," I grinned, "the joke is still going on."

"What have the scholars done about it?" she asked.

"Oh, they have worked out their proof, shown up the thing—and let it go at that."

"Wasn't there any demand from the people who knew to have it taken out of the Bible?"

"There is one edition of the Bible now printed in all the separate books— a whole shelf full of little ones, instead of one big one."

"I should think that would be much better," she said, "but the other one is still printed—and sold?"

"Printed and sold and given away by hundreds of thousands—with The Joke going right on."

She was puzzled. It was not so much the real outside things we did which she found it hard to understand, but the different way our minds worked. In Herland, if a thing like that had been discovered, the first effort of all their wisest students would have been to establish the facts. When they were sure about it, they would then have taken the rather shameful old thing out of its proud position among the "sacred" books at once. They would have publicly acknowledged their mistake, rectified it, and gone on.

"You'll have to be very patient with me, Van dearest. It is going to take me a long time to get hold of your psychology. But I'll do my best."

Her best was something amazing. And she would have come to her final conclusions far earlier but for certain firm preconceptions that we were somehow better, nobler, than we were.

The Reverend Murdock kept at her pretty steadily. He started in at the beginning, giving her the full circumstantial account of The Temptation, The Fall, and The Curse.

She listened quietly, with no hint in her calm face of what she might be thinking. But when he came to the punishment of the serpent: "Upon thy belly shalt thou go, and dust shalt thou eat all the days of thy life," she asked a question.

"Will you tell me please—how did the serpent 'go' before?"

Mr. Murdock looked at her. He was reading in a deep sorrowful voice, his mind full of the solemn purport of the Great Tragedy.

"What was his method of locomotion before he was cursed?" asked Ellador.

He laid down the book in some annoyance. "It is believed that the serpent walked erect, that he stood like a man, that he was Satan himself," he replied.

"But it says: 'Now the serpent was more subtle than any of the beasts of the field,' doesn't it? And the picture you showed me is of a snake, in the tree."

"The picture is, as it were, allegorical," he replied. "It is not reverent to question the divine account like this."

She did not mind this note of censure, but asked further: "As a matter of fact, do snakes eat dust? Or is that allegorical too? How do you know which is allegorical and which is fact? Who decides?"

They had a rather stormy discussion on that point; at least the missionary was stormy. He was unable to reconcile Ellador's gentle courtesy with her singular lack of reverence for mere statements.

But our theological discussions were summarily ended, and Ellador reduced to clinging to her berth, by a severe storm. It was not a phenomenal hurricane by any means; but a steady lashing gale which drove us far out of our course, and so damaged the vessel that we could do little but drive before the wind.

"There's a steamer!" said Terry on the third day of heavy weather. And as we watched the drift of smoke on the horizon we found it was nearing us. And none too soon! By the time they were within hailing distance our small vessel ran up signals of distress, for we were leaking heavily, and we were thankful to be taken off, even though the steamer, a Swedish one, was bound for Europe instead of America.

They gave us better accommodations than we had had on the other, and eagerly took on board our big motor-boat and biplane—too eagerly, I thought.

Ellador was greatly interested in the larger ship, the big blond men, and in their talk. I prepared her as well as I could. They had good maps of Europe, and I filled in her outlines of history as far as I was able, and told her of the war. Her horror at this was natural enough.

"We have always had war," Terry explained. "Ever since the world began—at least as far as history goes, we have have had war. It is human nature."

"Human?" asked Ellador.

"Yes," he said, "human. Bad as it is, it is evidently human nature to do it. Nations advance, the race is improved by fighting. It is the law of nature."

Since our departure from Herland, Terry had rebounded like a rubber ball from all its influences. Even his love for Alima he was evidently striving to forget, with some success. As for the rest, he had never studied the country and its history as I had, nor accepted it like Jeff; and now he was treating it all as if it really was, what he had often called it to me, a bad dream. He would keep his word in regard to telling nothing about it; that virtue was his at any rate. But in his glad reaction, his delighted return, "a man in a world of men," he was now giving information to Ellador in his superior way, as if she was a totally ignorant stranger. And this war seemed

275

almost to delight him.

"Yes," he repeated, "you will have to accept life as it is. To make war is human activity."

"Are some of the soldiers women?" she inquired.

"Women! Of course not! They are men; strong, brave men. Once in a while some abnormal woman becomes a soldier, I believe, and in Dahomey—that's in Africa—one of the black tribes have women soldiers. But speaking generally it is men—of course."

"Then why do you call it 'human' nature?" she persisted. "If it was human wouldn't they both do it?"

So he tried to explain that it was a human necessity, but it was done by the men because they could do it—and the women couldn't.

"The women are just as indispensable—in their way. They give us the children—you know—men cannot do that."

To hear Terry talk you would think he had never left home.

Ellador listened to him with her grave gentle smile. She always seemed to understand not only what one said, but all the back-ground of sentiment and habit behind.

"Do you call bearing children 'human nature'?" she asked him.

"It's woman nature," he answered. "It's her work."

"Then why do you not call fighting 'man nature'—instead of human?"

Terry's conclusion of an argument with Ellador was the simple one of going somewhere else. So off he went, to enjoy himself in the society of those sturdy Scandinavians, and we two sat together discussing war.

Chapter II

War

For a long time my wife from Wonderland, as I love to call her, used to the utmost the high self-restraint taught by her religion, her education, the whole habit of her life. She knew that I should be grieved by her distresses, that I expected the new experiences would be painful to her and was watching to give what aid and comfort I could; and further she credited me with a racial sensitiveness and pride far beyond the facts.

Here again was one of the differences between her exquisitely organized people and ours. With them the majority of their interests in life were communal; their love and pride and ambition was almost wholly for the group, even motherhood itself was viewed as social service, and so fulfilled. They were all of them intimately acquainted with their whole history, that was part of their beautiful and easy educational system; with their whole country, and with all its industries.

The children of Herland were taken to all parts of the country, shown all its arts and crafts, taught to honor its achievements and to appreciate its needs and difficulties. They grew up with a deep and vital social consciousness which not one in a thousand of us could approach.

This kind of thing does not show; we could not see it externally, any more than one could see a good housewife's intimate acquaintance with and pride in the last detail of her *menage*. Further, as our comments on their country had been almost wholly complimentary (they had not heard Terry's!), we had not hurt this national pride; or if we had they had never let us see it.

Now here was Ellador, daring traveler, leaving her world for mine, and finding herself, not as we three had been, exiled into a wisely ordered, peaceful and beautiful place, with the mothering care of that group of enlightened women; but as one alone in a world of which her first glimpse was of hideous war. As one who had never in her life seen worse evil than misunderstanding, or accident, and not much of these; one to whom universal comfort and beauty was the race habit of a thousand years, the sight of Europe in its present condition was far more of a shock than even I had supposed.

She thought that I felt as she did. I did feel badly, and ashamed, but not a thousandth part as she would have felt the exposure of some fault in Herland; not nearly as badly as she supposed.

I was constantly learning from her to notice things among us which I had never seen before, and one of the most conspicuous of my new impressions was the realization of how slightly socialized we are. We are quite indifferent to public evils, for the most part, unless they touch us personally; which is as though the housewife was quite indifferent to having grease on the chairs unless she happened to spoil her own dress with it. Even our "reformers" seem more like such a housewife who should show great excitement over the greasy chairs, but none over the dusty floor, the grimy windows, the empty coal-bin, the bad butter, or the lack of soap. Special evils rouse us, some of us, but as for a clean, sanitary, effortless housekeeping—we have not come to want it—most of us.

But Ellador, lovely, considerate soul that she was, had not only the incessant shock of these new impressions to meet and bear, but was doing her noble best to spare my feelings by not showing hers. She could not bear to blame my sex, to blame my country, or at least my civilization, my world; she did not wish to cast reproach on me.

I was ashamed, to a considerable degree. If a man has been living in the pleasant atmosphere of perfect housekeeping, such as I have mentioned, and is then precipitated suddenly into foul slovenliness, with noise, confusion and ill-will, he feels it more than if he had remained in such surroundings from the first.

It was the ill-will that counted most. Here again comes the psychic difference between the women of Herland and us. People who grow up amid slang, profanity, obscenity, harsh contradiction and quarrelling, do not particularly note or mind it. But one reared in an atmosphere of the most subtle understanding, gracious courtesy, and a loving use of language as an art, is very sharply impressed if someone says: "Hold yer jaw, yer son of a —!," or even by a glowering roomful of silent haters.

That's what was heavy on Ellador all the time,—the atmosphere, the social atmosphere of suspicion, distrust, hatred, of ruthless self-aggrandizement and harsh scorn.

There was a German officer on this ship. He tried to talk to Ellador at first, merely because she was a woman and beautiful. She tried to talk to him, merely because he was a human being a member of a great nation.

But I, watching, saw how soon the clear light of her mind brought out the salient characteristics of his, and of how, in spite of all her exalted philosophy, she turned shuddering away from him.

We were overhauled by an English vessel before reaching our destination in Sweden, and all three of us were glad to be transferred because we could so reach home sooner. At least that was what we thought. The German officer was not glad, I might add.

Ellador hailed the change with joy. She knew more about England than about the Scandinavian countries, and could speak the language. I think she thought it would be—easier there.

We were unable to get away as soon as we expected. Terry indeed determined to enlist, or to join the service in some way, and they were glad to use him and his aeroplane. This was not to be wondered at. If Terry had the defects of his qualities he also had the qualities of his defects, and he did good work for the Allies.

Ellador, rather unexpectedly asked to stay awhile: "It is hard," she said, "but we may not come again perhaps, and I want to learn all I can."

So we stayed and Ellador learned. It did not take her long. She was a rapid reader, and soon found the right books. She was a marvellous listener, and many were glad to talk to her, and to show her things.

We investigated in London, Manchester, Birmingham; were entertained in beautiful country places; went motoring up into Scotland and in Ireland; visited Wales, and then, to my great surprise, she urged that we go to France.

"I want to see, to know," she said. "To really *know*—."

I was worried about her. She had a hard-set fixity of expression. Her unfailing gentleness was too firm of surface, and she talked less and less with me about social conditions.

We went to France.

She visited hospitals, looking at those broken men, those maimed and blinded boys, and grew paler and harder daily. Day by day she gathered in the new language, till soon she could talk with the people.

Then we ran across Terry, scouting about with his machine; and Ellador asked to be taken up—she wanted to see a battlefield. I tried to dissuade her from this, fearing for her. Even her splendid health seemed shaken by all she had witnessed. But she said: "It is my duty to see and know all I can. This is not, they tell me—exceptional? This—war?"

"Not at all," said Terry. "It's only bigger than usual, as most things are now. Why, in all our history there have only been about three hundred years without war."

She looked at him, her eyes widening, darkening. "When was that?" she said. "After Jesus came?"

Terry laughed. "Oh no," he said. "It wasn't any one time. It's three hundred years here and there, scattering. So you see war is really the normal condition of human life."

"So," she said. "Then I ought to see it. Take me up, please."

He didn't want to; said it was dangerous; but it was very hard to say no to Ellador, and she had her way. She saw the battle lines of trenches. She saw the dead men; she saw and heard the men not dead, where there had been recent fighting. She saw the ruins, ruins everywhere.

That night she was like a woman of marble, cold, dumb, sitting still by the window where she could rest her eyes on the far stars. She treated me with a great poignant tenderness, as one would treat a beloved friend whose whole family had become lepers.

We went back to England, and she spent the last weeks of our stay there finding out all she could about Belgium.

That was the breaking point. She locked the door of her room, but I heard her sobbing her heart out—Ellador, who had never in all her splendid young life had an experience of pain, and whose consciousness was mainly social. We feel these horrors as happening to other people; she felt them as happening to herself.

I broke the lock—I had to get to her. She would not speak, would not look at me, but buried her face in the pillow, shuddering away from me as if I, too, were a German. The great sobs tore her. It was, I suddenly felt, not like the facile tears of an ordinary woman, but like the utter breakdown of a strong man. And she was as ashamed of it.

Then I had enough enlightenment to see some little relief for her, not from the weight of horrible new knowledge, but from the added burden of her self-restraint.

I knelt beside her and got her into my arms, her head hidden on my shoulder.

"Dear," said I, "Dear—I can't help the horror, but at least I can help you bear it—and you can let me try. You see you're all alone here—I'm all you've got. You'll have to let it out somehow—just say it all to me."

She held me very close then, with a tense, frightened grip. "I want—I want—my Mother!" she sobbed.

Ellador's mother was one of those wise women who sat in the Temples, and gave comfort and counsel when needed. They loved each other more than I, not seeing them always together, had understood. Yet her mother had counseled her going, had urged it, for the sake of their land and its future.

"Mother! Mother! Mother!" she sobbed under her breath. "Oh—*Mother!* Help me bear it!"

There was no Mother and no Temple, only one man who loved her, and in that she seemed to find a little ease, and slowly grew quieter.

"There is one thing we know more about than you do," I suggested. "That is how to manage pain. You mustn't keep it to yourself—you must let it out—let the others help bear it. That's good psychology, dear."

"It seems so—unkind," she murmured.

"Oh, no, it's not unkind; it's just necessary. 'Bear ye one another's burdens,' you know. Also we have a nice proverb about marriage. 'It makes joy double and halveth trouble.' Just pile it on me, dearest—that's what a husband is for."

"But how can I say to you the things I feel? It seems so rude, so to reflect on your people—your civilization."

"I think you underrate two things," I suggested. "One is that I'm a human creature, even if male; the other that my visit to Herland, my life with you, has had a deep effect on me. I see the awfulness of war as I never did before, and I can even see a little of how it must affect you. What I want you to do now is to relieve the pressure of feeling which is hurting so, by putting it into words—letting it out. Say it all. Say the very worst. Say— 'This world is not civilized, not human. It is worse than the humble savagery below our mountains.' Let out, dear—I can stand it. And you'll feel better."

She lifted her head and drew a long, shuddering breath.

"I think you are right—there must be some relief. And here are You!" Suddenly she threw her arms around me and held me close, close.

"You *do* love me—I can feel it! A little—a very little—like mother love! I am so grateful!"

She rested in my arms, till the fierce tempest of pain had passed somewhat, and then we sat down, close together, and she followed my advice, seeking to visualize, to put in words, to fully express, the anguish which was upon her.

"You see," she began slowly, "it is hard for me to do this because I hate to hurt you. You must care so—so horribly."

281

"Stop right there, dear," I told her. "You overestimate my sensitiveness. What I feel is nothing at all to what you feel—I can see that. Remember that in our race-traditions war is a fine thing, a splendid thing. We have idealized war and the warrior, through all our history. You have read a good deal of our history by now."

She had, I knew, and she nodded her head sadly. "Yes, it's practically all about war," she agreed. "But I didn't—I couldn't visualize it."

She closed her eyes and shrank back, but I went on steadily: "So you see this is not—to us—wholly a horror; it is just more horrible than other wars on account of the infamous behavior of some combatants, and because we really are beginning to be civilized. Now this pain that you see is no greater than the same pain all the way back in history—always. And you are not being miserable about that, surely?"

No, she admitted, she wasn't.

"Very well," I hurried on, "we, the human race, outside of Herland, have been fighting one another for all the ages, and we are here yet; some of these military enthusiasts say because of war—some of the pacifists say in spite of it, and I'm beginning to agree with them. With you, Ellador, through you, and because of you, and because of seeing what human life can be, in your blessed country, I see things as I never did before. I'm growing."

She smiled a little at that, and took my hand again.

"You are the most important ambassador that ever was," I continued. "You are sent from your upland island, your little hidden heaven, to see our poor blind bleeding world and carry news of it to your people. Perhaps that vast storehouse of mother-love can help to set us straight at last. And you can't afford to *feel* our sorrow—you'd die of it. You must think—and talk it off, remorselessly, to me."

"You Amazing Darling!" she answered at last, drawing a deep breath. "You are right—wholly right. I'm afraid I have—a little—underrated your wisdom. Forgive me!"

I forgave her fast enough, though I knew it was an impossible offence, and she began to free her mind.

"First as to Christianity," she said. "That gave me great hopes—at first. Not the mythology of course, but the spirit; and when that missionary man enlarged on the spread of Christianity and its countless benefits I began to feel that here was a lovely thing it would do us good to know about— something very close to Motherhood."

"Motherhood," always reverently spoken, was the highest, holiest word they knew in Herland.

"But as I've read and talked and studied all these weeks, I do not find that Christianity has done one thing to stop war, or that Christian countries fight any less than heathen ones—rather more. Also they fight among themselves. Christianity has not brought peace on earth—not at all."

"No," I admitted, "it hasn't, but it tries to—ameliorate, to heal and save."

"That seems to me simply—foolish," she answered. "If there is a house on fire, the only true way to check the destruction is to put the fire out. To sit about trying to heal burned skin and repair burned furniture is—foolish."

"Especially when the repaired furniture serves as additional fuel for more fire," I added.

"You see it!" she exclaimed joyfully. "Then why don't you—but, I see—you are only one. You alone cannot change it."

"Oh no, I'm not alone in that," I answered cheerfully. "There are plenty more who see it."

"Then why—" she began, but checked herself, and paused a little, continuing slowly. "What I wish to get off my mind is this spectacle of measureless suffering which human beings are deliberately inflicting on one another. It would be hard enough to bear if the pain was unavoidable—that would be pure horror, and the eager rush to help. But here there is not only horror but a furious scorn—because they do not have to have it at all."

"You're quite right, my dear," I agreed. "But how are you going to make them stop?"

"That's what I have to find out," she answered gravely. "I wish Mother was here—and all the Over-Mothers. They would find a way. There must *be* a way. And you are right—I must not let myself be overcome by this—"

"Put it this way," I suggested. "Even if three quarters of the world should be killed there would be plenty left to refill, as promptly as would be wise. You remember how quickly your country filled up?"

"Yes," she said. "And I must remember that it is the race-progress that counts, not just being alive."

Then, wringing her hands in sudden bitterness, she added: "But this stops all progress! It is not merely that people are being killed. Half the world might die in an earthquake and not do this harm! It is the Hating I mind more than the killing—the perversion of human faculty. It's not humanity dying—it is humanity going mad!"

She was shivering again, that black horror growing in her eyes.

"Gently dear, gently," I told her. "Humanity is a large proposition. You and I have a whole round world to visit—as soon as it is safe to travel. And in the meantime I want to get you to my country as soon as possible. We are not at war. Our people are good-natured and friendly. I think you'll like us."

It was not unnatural for an American, in war-mad Europe, to think of his own land with warm approval, nor for a husband to want his wife to appreciate his people and his country.

"You must tell me more about it," she said eagerly. "I must read more too—study more. I do not do justice to the difference, I am sure. I am judging the world only by Europe. And see here, my darling—do you mind if we see the rest first? I want to know The World as far as I can, and as quickly as I can. I'm sure that if I study first for awhile, in England—they seem so familiar with all the world—that we might then go east instead of west, and see the rest of it before we reach America—leave the best to the last."

Except for the danger of traveling there seemed no great objection to this plan. I would rather have her make her brief tour and then return with me to my own dear country at the end, than to have her uneasy there and planning to push on.

We went back to a quiet place in England, where we could temporarily close our minds to the Horror, and Ellador, with unerring judgment, found an encyclopedic young historian with the teaching gift, and engaged his services for a time.

They had a series of maps—from old blank "terra incognita" ones, with its bounding ocean of ancient times, to the spread of accurate surveying which now gives us the whole surface of the earth. She kissed the place where her little homeland lay hidden—but that was when he was not looking.

The rapid grasp she made at the whole framework of our history would have astonished anyone not acquainted with Herland brains and Herland methods of education. It did astonish the young historian. She by no means set herself to learn all that he wanted to teach her; on the contrary she continually checked his flow of information, receiving only what she wanted to know.

284

A very few good books on world evolution—geological, botanical, zoological, and ethnic, gave her the background she needed, and such a marvel of condensation as Winwood Reade's *Martydom of Man* supplied the outline of history.

Her own clear strong uncrowded and logical mind, with its child-fresh memory, saw, held and related the facts she learned, with no apparent effort. Presently she had a distinct view of what we people have been up to on earth for the few ages of our occupancy. She had her estimate of time taken and of the rate of our increased speed. I had never realized how long, how immeasurably long and slow, were the years "before progress," so to speak, or the value of each great push of new invention. But she got them all clearly in place, and, rigidly refusing to be again agonized by the ceaseless wars, she found eager joy in counting the upward steps of social evolution.

This joy increased as the ages came nearer to our own. She became fascinated with the record of inventions and discoveries and their interrelative effects. Each great religion as it entered, was noted, defined in its special power and weakness, and its consequences observed. She made certain map effects for herself, "washing in" the different areas with various colors, according to the different religions, and lapping them over where they had historically lapped, as for instance, where the "mañana" of the Spaniard marks the influence following Oriental invasion, and where Buddhism produces such and such effects according to its reception by Hindu, Chinese, or Japanese.

"I could spend a lifetime in these details," she eagerly explained again, "but I'm only after enough to begin on. I must get them *placed*—so that I can understand what each nation is *for*, what they have done for one another, and for the world; which of them are going on, and how fast; which of them are stopping—or sinking back—and why. It is *profoundly* interesting."

Ellador's attitude vaguely nettled me, just a little, in that earlier consciousness I was really outgrowing so fast. She seemed like an enthusiastic young angel "slumming." I resented—a little—this cheerful and relentless classification—just as poor persons resent being treated as "cases."

But I knew she was right after all, and was more than delighted to have her so soon triumph over the terrible influence of the war. She did not, of course, wholly escape or forget it. Who could? But she successfully occupied her mind with other matters.

"It's so funny," she said to me. "Here in all your history books, the whole burden of information is as to who fought who—and when; and who 'reigned' and when—especially when. Why are your historians so morbidly anxious about the exact date?"

"Why it's important, isn't it?" I asked.

"From certain points of view, yes; but not in the least from that of the general student. The doctor wants to know at just what hour the fever rises, or declines; he has to have his 'chart' to study. But the public ought to know how fever is induced and how it is to be avoided. People in general ought to know the whole history of the of the world in general; and what were the most important things that happened. And here the poor things are required to note and remember that this king 'came to the throne' at such a date and died at such another—facts of no *historic* importance whatever. And as to the wars and wars and wars—and all these 'decisive battles of history'—" Ellador had the whole story so clearly envisaged now that she could speak of war without cringing—"why that isn't history at all!"

"Surely it's part of history, isn't it?" I urged.

"Not even part of it. Go back to your doctor's 'chart'—his 'history of the case.' That history treats of the inception, development, success or failure of the disease he is treating. To say that 'At four-fifteen p.m. the patient climbed into another patient's bed and bit him,' is no part of that record of tuberculosis or cancer."

"It would be if it proved him delirious, wouldn't it?" I suggested.

Ellador lifted her head from the chart she was filling in, and smiled enchantingly. "Van," she said, "I'm proud of you. That's splendid!

"It would then appear," she pursued, glancing over her papers, "as if the patent had a sort of intermittent fever—from the beginning; hot fits of rage and fury, when he is practically a lunatic, and cold fits, too," she cried eagerly, pursuing the illustration, "cold and weak, when he just lies helpless and cannot do anything."

We agreed that as a figure of speech this was pretty strong and clear, with its inevitable suggestion that we must study the origin of the disease, how to cure, and still better, prevent it.

"But there is a splendid record behind all that," she told me. "I can't see that your historians have ever seen it clearly and consecutively. You evidently have not come to the place where all history has to be consciously revised for educational purposes."

"Ours is more complex than yours, isn't it?" I offered. "So many different nations and races, you know?"

But she smiled wisely and shook her head, quoting after her instructor: "And history, with all her volumes vast, hath but one page.'

"They all tell about the same things," she said. "They all do the same things, and not one of them ever sees what really matters most—ever gives 'the history of the case' correctly. I truly think, dear, that we could help you with your history."

She had fully accepted the proposition I made that day when the Horror so overthrew her, and now talked to me as freely as if I were one of her sisters. She talked about men as if I wasn't one, and about the world as if it was no more mine than hers.

There was a strange exaltation, a wonderful companionship, in this. I grew to see life as she saw it, more and more, and it was like rising from some tangled thorny thicket to take a bird's eye view of city and farmland, of continent and ocean. Life itself grew infinitely more interesting. I thought of that benighted drummer's joke, that "Life is just one damn thing after another," so widely accepted as voicing a general opinion. I thought of our pathetic virtues of courage, cheerfulness, patience—all so ridiculously wasted in facing troubles which need not be there at all.

Ellador saw human life as a thing in the making, with human beings as the makers. We have always seemed to regard it as an affliction—or blessing—bestowed upon us by some exterior force. Studying, seeing, understanding, with her, I grew insensibly to adopt her point of view, her scale of measurements, and her eager and limitless interest. So when we did set forth on our round-the-world trip to my home, we were both fairly well equipped for the rapid survey which was all we planned for.

Chapter III

A Journey of Inspection

It was fortunate for Ellador's large purposes that her fat little bag of jewels contained more wealth than I had at first understood, and that there were some jewel-hungry millionaires left in the world. In India we found native princes who were as much athirst for rubies and emeralds as ever were their hoarding ancestors, and who had comfortable piles of ancient gold wherewith to pay for them. We were easily able to fill snug belts with universally acceptable gold pieces, and to establish credit to carry us wherever there were banks.

She was continually puzzled over our money values. "Why do they want these so much?" she demanded. "Why are they willing to pay so much for them?"

Money she understood well enough. They had their circulating medium in Herland in earlier years; but it was used more as a simple method of keeping accounts than anything else—like tickets, and finally discontinued. They had so soon centralized their industries, that the delay and inconvenience of measuring off every item of exchange in this everlasting system of tokens became useless, to their practical minds. As an "incentive to industry" it was not necessary; motherhood was their incentive. When they had plenty of everything it was free to all in such amounts as were desired; in scarcity they divided. Their interest in life was in what they were doing—and what they were going to do, not in what they were to get. Our point of view puzzled her.

I remember this matter coming up between Ellador and a solemn college professor, an economist, as we were creeping through the dangerous Mediterranean. She questioned and listened, saying nothing about her country—this we had long since found was the only safe way; for the instant demand: "Where is it?" was what we did not propose to answer.

But having learned what she could from those she talked with, and sped searchingly through the books they offered her, she used to relieve her mind in two ways; by talking with me, and by writing.

"I've simply got to," she told me. "I'm writing a book—in fact, I'm writing two books. One is notes, quotations, facts, and pictures—pictures—pictures. This photography is a wonderful art!"

She had become quite a devotee of said art, and was gathering material right and left, to show her people.

"We'll have to go back and tell them, you know," she explained, "and they'll be *so* interested, I shall have to go about lecturing, as you men did."

"I wish you'd go about lecturing to us," I told her. "We have more to learn than you have—of the really important matters in living."

"But I couldn't, you see, without quoting always from home—and then they'd want to know—they'd have a right to know. Or else they wouldn't believe me. No, all I can do is to ask questions; to make suggestions, perhaps, here and there; even to criticise a little—when I've learned a lot more, and if I'm very sure of my hearers. Meanwhile I've got to talk it off to you, you poor boy—and just write. You shall read it, if you want to, of course."

Her notes were a study in themselves.

Ships and shipping interested her at once, as something totally new, and her first access to encyclopedias had supplied background to what she learned from people. She had set down, in the briefest possible manner, not mere loose data as to vessels and navigation, but an outlined history of the matter, arranged like a genealogical tree.

There were the rude beginnings—log, raft, skin-boat, basket-boat, canoe; and the line of paddled or oared boats went on to the great carved war-canoes with outriggers, the galleys of Romans and Norsemen, the delicate birchbarks of our American Aborigines, and the neat manufactured ones on the market. A bare sentence covered it, and another the evolution of the sailing craft; then steam.

"Navigation is an exclusively masculine process," she noted. "Always men, only men. Oared vessels of large size required slave labor; status of sailors still akin to slavery; rigid discipline, miserable accommodations, abusive language and personal violence." To this she added in parenthesis: "Same holds true of armies. Always men, only men. Similar status, but somewhat better provision for men, and more chance of promotion, owing to greater danger to officers."

Continuing with ships, she noted: "Psychology: a high degree of comradeship, the habit of obedience—enforced; this doubtless accounts for large bodies of such indispensable men putting up with such wretched treatment. Obedience appears to dull and weaken the mind; same with soldiers—study further. Among officers great personal gallantry, a most exalted sense of duty, as well as brutal and unjust treatment of inferiors. The captain in especial is so devoted to his concept of duty as sometimes to prefer to 'go down with his ship' to being saved without her. Why? What social service is there in being drowned? I learn this high devotion is found also in engineers and in pilots. Seems to be a product of extreme responsibility. Might be developed more widely by extending opportunity."

She came to me with this, asking for more information on our political system of "rotation in office."

"Is that why you do it?" she asked eagerly. "Not so much as to get the work done better, as to make all the people—or at least most of them—feel greater responsibility, a deeper sense of duty?"

I had never put it that way to myself, but I now agreed that that was the idea —that it must be. She was warmly interested; said she knew she should love America. I felt sure she would.

There was an able Egyptologist on board, a man well acquainted with ancient peoples, and he, with the outline she had so well laid down during her English studies, soon filled her mind with a particularly clear and full acquaintance with our first civilizations.

"Egypt, with its One River; Asia Minor, with the Valley of the Two Rivers and China with its great rivers—" she poured over her maps and asked careful eager questions. The big black bearded professor was delighted with her interest, and discoursed most instructively.

"I see," she said. "I see! They came to places where the soil was rich, and where there was plenty of water. It made agriculture possible, profitable— and then the surplus—and then the wonderful growth—of course!"

That German officer, who had made so strong and disagreeable an impression while we were on the Swedish ship, had been insistent, rudely insistent, on the advantages of difficulty and what he called "disclipine." He had maintained that the great races, the dominant races, came always from the north. This she had borne in mind, and now questioned her obliging preceptor, with map outspread and dates at hand.

"For all those thousands of years these Mediterranean and Oriental peoples held the world—were the world?"

"Yes, absolutely."

"And what was up here?" she pointed to the wide vacant spaces on the northern coasts.

"Savages—barbarians—wild, skin-clad ferocious men, madam."

Ellador made a little diagram, a vertical line, with many ages marked across it.

"This is The Year One—as far back as you can go," she explained, pointing to the mark at the bottom. "And here we are, near the top—this is Now. And these Eastern peoples held the stage and did the work all the way up to—here, did they?"

"They certainly did, madam."

"And were these people in these northern lands there all the time? Or did they happen afterward?"

"They were there—we have their bones to prove it."

"Then if they were there—and as long, and of the same stock—you tell me that all these various clans streamed out, westward, from a common source, and became in time, Persians, Hindus, Pelasgians, Etruscans, and all the rest—as well as Celts, Slavs, Teutons?"

"It so held, roughly speaking." He resented a little her sweeping generalizations and condensations; but she had her own ends in view.

"And what did these northern tribes contribute to social progress during all this time?"

"Practically nothing," he answered. "Their arts were naturally limited by the rigors of the climate. The difficulties of maintaining existence prevented any higher developments."

"I see, I see." she nodded gravely. "Then why is it, in the face of these facts, that some still persist in attributing progress to difficulties, and cold weather."

This professor, who was himself Italian, was quite willing to question this opinion.

"That theory you will find is quite generally confined to the people who live in the colder climates," he suggested.

When Ellador discussed this with me, she went further. "It seems as if, when people say—'The World' they mean their own people," she commented. "I've been reading history as written by the North European races. Perhaps when we get to Persia, India, China and Japan, it will be different."

It was different. I had spent my own youth in the most isolated of modern nations, the one most ignorant of and indifferent to all the others; the one whose popular view of foreigners is based on the immigrant classes, and whose travelling rich consider Europe as a playground, a picture gallery, a museum, a place wherein to finish one's education. Being so reared, and associating with similarly minded persons, my early view of history was a great helter-skelter surging background to the clear, strong, glorious incidents of our own brief national career; while geography consisted of the vivid large-scale familiar United States, and a globe otherwise covered with more or less nebulous maps; and such political evolution as I had in mind consisted of the irresistible development of our own "institutions."

All this, of course, was my youthful attitude. In later studies I had added a considerable knowledge of general history, sociology and the like, but had never realized until now how remote all this was to me from the definite social values already solidly established in my mind.

Now, associating with Ellador, dispassionate and impartial as a visiting angel, bringing to her studies of the world, the triple freshness of view of one of different stock, different social development, and different sex, I began to get a new perspective. To her the world was one field of general advance. Her own country held the foreground in her mind, of course, but she had left it as definitely as if she came from Mars, and was studying the rest of humanity in the mass. Her alien point of view, her previous complete ignorance, and that powerful well-ordered mind she brought to bear on the new knowledge so rapidly amassed, gave her advantages as an observer far beyond our best scientists.

The one special and predominant distinction given to her studies by her supreme femininity, was what gave me the most numerous, and I may say, unpleasant surprises. In my world studies I had always assumed that humanity did thus and so, but she was continually sheering through the tangled facts with her sharp distinction that this and this phenomenon was due to masculinity alone.

"But Ellador," I protested, "why do you say—'the male Scandinavians continually indulged in piracy,' and 'the male Spaniards practiced terrible cruelties,' and so on? It sounds so—invidious—as if you were trying to make out a case against men."

"Why, I wouldn't do that for anything!" she protested. "I'm only trying to understand the facts. You don't mind when I say 'the male Phoenicians made great progress in navigation,' or 'the male Greeks developed great intelligence,' do you?"

"That's different," I answered. "They did do those things."

"Didn't they do the others, too?"

"Well—yes—they did them, of course; but why rub it in that they were exclusively males?"

"But weren't they, dear? Really? Did the Norse women raid the coasts of England and France? Did the Spanish women cross the ocean and torture the poor Aztecs?"

"They would have if they could!" I protested.

"So would the Phoenician women and Grecian women in the other cases—wouldn't they?"

I hesitated.

"Now my Best Beloved," she said, holding my hand in both hers and looking deep into my eyes—"Please, oh *please*, don't mind. The facts are there, and they are immensely important. Think, dearest. We of Herland have known no men—till now. We, alone, in our tiny land, have worked out a happy, healthy life. Then you came—you 'Wonderful Three.' Ah! You should realize the stir, the excitement, the Great Hope that it meant to us! We knew there was more world—but nothing about it, and you meant a vast new life to us. Now I come to see—to learn—for the sake of my country.

"Because, you see, some things we gathered from you made us a little afraid. Afraid for our children, you see. Perhaps it was better, after all, to live up there, alone, in ignorance, but in happiness, we thought. Now I've come—to see—to learn—to really understand, if I can, so as to tell my people.

"You *mustn't* think I'm against men, dear. Why, if it were only for your sake, I would love them. And I'm sure—we are all sure at home (or at least most of us are) that two sexes, working together, must be better than one.

"Then I can see how, being two sexes, and having so much more complex a problem than ours, and having all kinds of countries to live in—how you got into difficulties we never knew.

"I'm making every allowance. I'm firm in my conviction of the superiority of the bisexual method. It *must* be best or it would not have been evolved in all the higher animals. But—but you can't expect me to ignore facts."

No, I couldn't. What troubled me most was that I, too, began to see facts, quite obvious facts, which I had never noticed before.

Wherever men had been superior to women we had proudly claimed it as a sex-distinction. Wherever men had shown evil traits, not common to women, we had serenely treated them as race-characteristics.

So, although I did not enjoy it, I did not dispute any further Ellador's growing collection of facts. It was just as well not to. Facts are stubborn things.

We visited a little in Tunis, Algiers, and Cairo, making quite an excursion in Egypt, with our steamship acquaintance, whose knowledge was invaluable to us. He translated inscriptions; showed us the more important discoveries, and gave condensed accounts of the vanished civilizations.

Ellador was deeply impressed.

"To think that under one single city, here in Abydos, there are the remains of five separate cultures. Five! As different as can be. With a long time between, evidently, so that the ruins were forgotten, and a new people built a new city on the site of the old one. It is wonderful."

Then she turned suddenly on Signor Armini. "What did they die of?" she demanded.

"Die of? Who, madam?"

"Those cities—those civilizations?"

"Why, they were conquered in war, doubtless; the inhabitants were put to the sword—some carried away as slaves, perhaps—and the cities razed to the ground."

"By whom?" she demanded. "Who did it?"

"Why, other peoples, other cultures, from other cities."

"Do you mean other peoples, or just other men?" she asked.

He was puzzled. "Why, the soldiers were men, of course, but war was made by one nation against another."

"Do you mean that the women of the other nations were the governing power and sent the men to fight?"

No, he did not mean that.

"And surely the children did not send them?"

Of course not.

"But people are men, women and children, aren't they? And only the adult men, about one-fifth of the population, made war?"

This he admitted perforce, and Ellador did not press the point further.

"But in these cities were all kinds of people, weren't there? Women and children, as well as men?"

This was obvious, also; and then she branched off a little: "What made them want to conquer a city?"

"Either fear—or revenge—or desire for plunder. Oftenest that. The ancient cities were the centers of production, of course." And he discoursed on the beautiful handicrafts of the past, the rich fabrics, the jewels and carved work and varied treasures.

"Who made them," she asked.

"Slaves, for the most part," he answered.

"Men and women?"

"Yes—men and women."

"I see," said Ellador. She saw more than she spoke of, even to me.

In ancient Egypt she found much that pleased her in the power and place of historic womanhood. This satisfaction was short-lived as we went on eastward.

With a few books, with eager questioning of such experts as we met, and what seemed to me an almost supernatural skill in eliciting valuable and apposite information from unexpected quarters, my lady from Herland continued to fill her mind and her note-books.

To me, who grew more and more to admire her, to reverence her, to tenderly love her, as we traveled on together, there now appeared a change in her spirit, more alarming even than that produced by Europe's war. It was like the difference between the terror roused in one surrounded by lions, and the loathing experienced in the presence of hideous reptiles, this not in the least at the people, but at certain lamentable social conditions.

In visiting our world she had been most unfortunately first met by the hot horrors of war; and I had thought to calm her by the static nations, the older peoples, sitting still among their ruins, richly draped in ancient and interesting histories. But a very different effect was produced. What she had read, while it prepared her to understand the sequence of affairs, had in no case given what she recognized as the really important events and their results.

"I'm writing a little history of the world," she told me, with a restrained smile. "Just a little one, so that I can have something definite to show them."

"But how can you, dearest—in this time, with what data you have? I know you are wonderful—but a history of the world!"

"Only a little one," she answered. "Just a synopsis. You know we are used to condensing and simplifying for our children. I suppose that is where we get the 'grasp of salient features' you have spoken of so often. These historians I read now certainly do not have it."

She continued tender to me, more so if anything. Of two things we talked with pleasure: of Herland and my land, and always of the beauty of nature. This seemed to her a ceaseless source of strength and comfort.

"It's the same world," she said, as we leaned side by side on the rail at the stern, and watched the white wake run uncoiling away from us, all silver-shining under the round moon. "The same sky, the same stars, some of them, the same blessed sun and moon. And the dear grass—and the trees—the precious trees."

Being by profession a forester, it was inevitable that she should notice trees; and in Europe she found much to admire, though lamenting the scarcity of food-bearing varieties. In Northern Africa she had noted the value of the palm, the olive, and others, and had readily understood the whole system of irrigation and its enormous benefits. What she did not easily grasp was its disuse, and the immeasurable futility of the fellaheen, still using the shadoof after all these ages of progress.

"I don't see yet," she admitted, "what makes their minds so—so impervious. It can't be because they're men, surely. Men are not duller than women, are they, dear?"

"Indeed they are not!" I cried, rather stung by this new suggestion. "Men are the progressive sex, the thinkers, the innovators. It is the women who are conservative and slow. Even you will have to admit that."

"I certainly will if I find it so," she answered cheerfully. "I can see that these women are dull enough. But then—if they do things differently there are penalties, aren't there?"

"Penalties?"

"Why, yes. If the women innovate and rebel the least that happens to them is that the men won't marry them—isn't that so?"

"I shouldn't think *you* would call that a penalty, my dear," I answered.

"Oh, yes, it is; it means extinction—the end of that variety of woman. You seem to have quite successfully checked mutation in women; and they had neither education, opportunity, or encouragement in other variation."

"Don't say 'you,'" I urged. "These are the women of the Orient you are talking about, not of all the world. Everybody knows that their position is pitiful and a great check to progress. Wait till you see my country!"

296

"I shall be glad to get there, dearest, I'm sure of that," she told me. "But as to these more progressive men among the Egyptians—there was no penalty for improving on the shadoof, was there? Or the method of threshing grain by the feet of cattle?"

Then I explained, trying to show no irritation, that there was a difference in the progressiveness of nations, of various races; but that other things being equal, the men were as a rule more progressive than the women.

"Where are the other things equal, Van?"

I had to laugh at that; she was a very difficult person to argue with; but I told her they were pretty near equal in our United States, and that we thought our women fully as good as men, and a little better. She was comforted for a while, but as we went on into Asia, her spirit sank and darkened, and that change I spoke of became apparent.

Burmah was something of a comfort, and that surviving matriarchate in the island hills. But in our rather extended visit to India, guided and informed by both English and native friends, and supplied with further literature, she began to suffer deeply.

We had the rare good fortune to be allowed to accompany a scientific expedition up through the wonder of the Himalayas, through Tibet, and into China. Here that high sweet spirit drooped and shrunk, with a growing horror, a loathing, such as I had never seen before in her clear eyes. She was shocked beyond words at the vast area of dead country; skeleton country, deforested, deshrubbed, degrassed, wasted to the bone, lying there to burn in the sun and drown in the rain, feeding no one.

"Van, Van," she said. "Help me to forget the women a little and talk about the land! Help me to understand the—the holes in the minds of people. Here is intelligence, intellect, a high cultural development—of sorts. They have beautiful art in some lines. They have an extensive literature. They are old, very old, surely old enough to have learned more than any other people. And yet here is proof that they have never mastered the simple and obvious facts of how to take care of the land on which they live."

"But they still live on it, don't they?"

"Yes—they live on it. But they live on it like swarming fleas on an emaciated kitten, rather than careful farmers on a well-cultivated ground. However," she brightened a little, "there's one thing; this horrible instance of a misused devastated land must have been of one great service. It must have served as an object lesson to all the rest of the world. Where such an old and wise nation has made so dreadful a mistake—for so long, at least

297

no other nation need to make it."

I did not answer as fully and cheerfully as she wished, and she pressed me further.

"The world has learned how to save its trees—its soil—its beauty—its fertility, hasn't it? Of course, what I've seen is not all—it's better in other places?"

"We did not go to Germany, you know, my dear. They have a high degree of skill in forestry there. In many countries it is now highly thought of. We are taking steps to preserve our own forests, though, so far, they are so extensive that we rather forgot there was any end of them."

"It will be good to get there, Van," and she squeezed my hand hard. "I must see it all. I must 'know the worst'—and surely I am getting the worst first! But you have free education—you have every advantage of climate—you have a mixture of the best blood on earth, of the best traditions. And you are brave and free and willing to learn. Oh, Van! I am so glad it was America that found us!"

I held her close and kissed her. I was glad, too. And I was proud clear through to have her speak so of us. Yet, still—I was not as perfectly comfortable about it as I had been at first.

She had read about the foot-binding process still common in so large a part of China, but somehow had supposed it was a thing of the past, and never general. Also, I fancy she had deliberately kept it out of her mind, as something impossible to imagine. Now she saw it. For days and days, as we traveled through the less known parts of the great country, she saw the crippled women; not merely those serenely installed in rich gardens and lovely rooms, with big-footed slaves to do their bidding; or borne in swaying litters by strong Coolies; but poor women, working women, toiling in the field, carrying their little mats to kneel on while they worked, because their feet were helpless aching pegs.

Presently, while we waited in a village, and were entertained by a local magnate who had business relations with one of our guides, Ellador was in the women's apartment, and she heard it—the agony of the bound feet of a child. The child was promptly hushed, struck and chided; made to keep quiet, but Ellador had heard its moaning. From a woman missionary she got details of the process, and was shown the poor little shrunken stumps.

That night she would not let me touch her, come near her. She lay silent, staring with set eyes, long shudders running over her from time to time.

When it came to speech, which was some days later, she could still but faintly express it.

"To think," she said slowly, "that there are on earth men who can do a thing like that to women—to little helpless children!"

"But their men don't do it, dearest," I urged. "It is the women, their own mothers, who bind the feet of the little ones. They are afraid to have them grow up 'big-footed women.'"

"Afraid of what?" asked Ellador, that shudder passing over her again.

Chapter IV

Nearing Home

We stayed some little time in China, meeting most interesting and valuable people, missionaries, teachers, diplomats, merchants, some of them the educated English-speaking Chinese.

Ellador's insatiable interest, her exquisite courtesy and talent as a listener, made anyone willing to talk to her. She learned fast, and placed in that wide sunlit mind of hers each fact in due relation.

"I'm beginning to understand," she told me sweetly, "that I mustn't judge this—miscellaneous—world of yours as I do my country. We were just ourselves—an isolated homogeneous people. When we moved, we all moved together. You are all kinds of people, in all kinds of places, touching at the edges and getting mixed. And so far from moving on together, there are no two nations exactly abreast—that I can see; and they mostly are ages apart; some away ahead of the others, some going far faster than others, some stationary."

"Yes," I told her, "and in the still numerous savages we find the beginners, and the back-sliders—the hopeless back-sliders, in human progress."

"I see—I see—" she said reflectively. "When you say 'the civilized world' that is just a figure of speech. The world is not civilized yet—only spots in it, and those not wholly."

"That's about it," I agreed with her. "Of course, the civilized nations think of themselves as the world—that's natural."

"How does it compare—in numbers?" she inquired. "Let's look!"

So we consulted the statistics on the population of the earth, chasing through pages of classification difficult to sift, until we hit upon a little table: "Population of the earth according to race."

"That ought to do, roughly speaking," I told her. "We'll call the white races civilized—and lump the others. Let's see how it comes out."

It came out that the total of Indo-Germanic, or Aryan—White, for Europe, America, Persia, India and Australia, was 775,000,000; and the rest of the world, black, red, brown and yellow, was 788,000,000.

"Do you mean that the majority of mankind is still uncivilized?" she asked.

She didn't ask it unpleasantly. Ellador was never sarcastic or bitter. But the world was her oyster—to study, and she was quite impartial.

I, however, felt reproached by this cool estimate. "No indeed," I said, "you can't call China uncivilized—it is one of the very oldest civilizations we have. This is only by race you see, by color."

"Oh, yes," she agreed, "and race or color do not count in civilization? Of course not—how stupid I was!"

But I laid down the pencil I was using to total up populations, and looked at her with a new and grave misgiving. She was so world-innocent. Even the history she had so swiftly absorbed had not changed her, any more than indecent novels affect a child; the child does not know the meaning of the words.

In the light of Ellador's colossal innocence of what we are accustomed to call "life," I began to see that process in a wholly new perspective. Her country was but one; her civilization was one and indivisible; in her country the women and children lived as mothers, daughters, sisters, in general tolerance, love, education and service. Out of that nursery, school, garden, shop, and parlor, she came into this great scrambling world of ours, to find it spotted over with dissimilar peoples, more separated by their varying psychology than by geography, politics, or race; often ignorant of one another, often fearing, despising, hating one another; and each national group, each racial stock, assuming itself to be "the norm" by which to measure others. She had first to recognize the facts and then to disentangle the causes, the long lines of historic evolution which had led to these results. Even then it was hard for her really to grasp the gulfs which divide one part of the human race from the others.

And now I had the unpleasant task of disabusing her of this last glad assumption, that race and color made no difference.

"Dear," I said slowly, "you must prepare your mind for another shock—though you must have got some of it already, here and there. Race and color make all the difference in the world. People dislike and despise one another on exactly that ground—difference in race and color. These millions who are here marked 'Aryan or White' include Persians and Hindus, yet the other white races are averse to intermarrying with these, whose skins are indeed much darker than ours, though they come of the same stock."

"Is the aversion mutual?" she asked, as calmly as if we had been discussing insects.

I assured her that, speaking generally, it was; that the flatter-faced Mongolians regarded us as hawklike in our aquiline features; and that little African children fled screaming from the unnatural horror of a first-seen white face.

But what I was thinking about was how I should explain to her the race prejudice in my own country, when she reached it. I felt like a housekeeper bringing home company, discovering that the company has far higher and more exacting standards than herself, and longing to get home first and set the house in order before inspection.

We spent some little time in Japan, Ellador enjoying the fairy beauty of the country, with its flower-worshipping, sunny-faced people, and the plump happy children everywhere.

But instead of being content with the artistic beauty of the place; with that fine lacquer of smiling courtesy with which their life is covered, she followed her usual course of penetrating investigation. It needed no years of study, no dreary tables of figures. With what she already knew, so clearly held in mind, with a few questions each loaded with implications, she soon grasped the salient facts of Japanese civilization. Its conspicuous virtues gave her instant joy. The high honor of the Samurai, the unlimited patriotism of the people in general, the exquisite politeness, and the sincere love of beauty in nature and art—these were all comforting, and the free-footed women also, after the "golden lilies" of China.

But presently, piercing below all these, she found the general poverty of the people, their helplessness under a new and hard-grinding commercialism, and the patient ignominy in which the women lived.

"How is it, dear," she asked me, "that these keenly intelligent people fail to see that such limited women cannot produce a nobler race?"

I could only say that it was a universal failing, common to all races—except ours, of course. Her face always lighted when we spoke of America.

"You don't know how I look forward to it, dear," she said. "After this painful introduction to the world I knew so little of—I'm so glad we came this way—saving the best to the last."

The nearer we came to America and the more eagerly she spoke of it, the more my vague uneasiness increased. I began to think of things I had never before been sensitive about and to seek for justification.

Meanwhile Ellador was accumulating heart-ache over the Japanese women, whose dual duty of child-bearing and man-service dominated all their lives.

"It is so hard for me to understand, Van; they aren't people at all, somehow—just wives—or worse."

"They are mothers, surely," I urged.

"No—not in our sense, not consciously. Look at this ghastly crowding! Here's a little country, easy to grasp and manage, capable of supporting about so many people—not more. And here they are, making a 'saturated solution' of themselves." She had picked up that phrase from one of her medical friends, a vigorous young man who told her much that she was eager to know about the health and physical development of the Japanese. "Can't they see that there are too many?" she went on. "If a people increases beyond its means of support it has to endure miserable poverty— or what is that the Germans demand?—expansion! They have to have somebody else's country. How strangely dull they are!"

"But, my dear girl, please remember that this *is* life," I told her. "This *is* the world. This *is* the way people live. You expect too much of them. It is a law of nature to increase and multiply. Of course, Malthus set up a terrified cry about over-populating the earth, but it has not come to that yet, not near. Our means of subsistence increase with the advance of science."

"As to the world, I can see that; but as to a given country, and especially as small a one as this—what does become of them?" she asked suddenly.

This started her on a rapid study of emigration, in which, fortunately, my own knowledge was of some use; and she eagerly gathered up and arranged in her mind that feature of our history on which hangs so much, the migration and emigration of peoples. She saw at once how, when most of the earth's surface was unoccupied, people moved freely about in search of the best hunting or pasturage; how in an agricultural system they settled and spread, widening with the increase of population; how ever since they met and touched, each nation limited by its neighbors, there had been the double result of over-crowding inside the national limits, and warfare in the interests of "expansion."

"I can see now the wonderful advantage you have," she said eagerly. "Humanity got its 'second wind' with the discovery of the 'new world'— didn't it?"

It always delighted me to note the speed and correctness with which she picked up idioms and bits of slang. They were a novelty to her, and a constant delight.

"You had a big new country to spread out in, and no competitors—there were no previous inhabitants, were there?"

"Nothing but Indians," I said.

"Indians?"

"Yes, savages, like those in the forests below your mountain land, though more advanced in some ways."

"How did you arrange with them?" she asked.

"I hate to tell you, Ellador. You see you have—a little—idealized my country. We did not 'arrange' with those savages. We killed them."

"All of them? How many were there?" She was quite calm. She made no movement of alarm or horror, but I could see the rich color fade from her face, and her dear gentle mouth set in harder lines of control.

"It is a long story, and not a nice one, I'm sorry to say. We left some, hemming them in in spots called 'reservations.' There has been a good deal of education and missionary work; some Indians have become fully civilized—as good citizens as any; and some have intermarried with the whites. We have many people with Indian blood. But speaking generally this is one of our national shames. Helen Hunt wrote a book about it, called *A Century of Dishonor*."

Ellador was silent. That lovely far-off homesick look came into her eyes.

"I hate to disillusion you, dear heart," I said. "We are not perfect in America. I truly think we have many advantages over any other country, but we are not blameless."

"I'll defer judgment till I get there," she presently answered. "Let's go back to what we were discussing—the pressure of population."

Rather sadly we took it up again, and saw how, as long as warfare was the relief, nations continually boiled over upon one another; gaining more land by the simple process of killing off the previous owners, and having to repeat the process indefinitely as soon as the population again pressed against its limits. Where warfare was abandoned and a settled boundary established, as when great China walled itself in from marauding tribes, then the population showed an ingrowing pressure, and reduced the standard of living to a ghastly minimum. Then came the later process of peaceful emigration, by which the coasts and islands of the Pacific became tinged with the moving thousands of the Yellow Races.

She saw it all as a great panorama, an endless procession, never accepting a static world with the limitations of parti-colored maps, but always watching the movement of races.

"That's what ails Europe now, isn't it?" she said at last. "That's why those close-packed fertile races were always struggling up and down among one another, and making room, for awhile, by killing people?"

"That's certainly a good part of it," I agreed. "Every nation wants more land to accommodate its increasing population."

"And they want an increase of population in order to win more land—don't they?"

This, too, was plain.

"And there isn't any way out of it—on a limited earth—but fixed boundaries with suicidal crowding inside, or the 'fortunes of war?'"

That, too, was plain, unfortunately.

"Then why do not the women limit the population, as we did?"

"Oh, Ellador, Ellador—you cannot seem to realize that this world is not a woman's world, like your little country. This is a man's world—and they did not want to limit the population."

"Why not?" she urged. "Was it because they did not bear the children? Was it because they would rather fight than live in peace? What *was* the reason?"

"Neither of those," I said slowly. "The real reason is that neither men nor women have been able to see broadly enough, to think deeply enough, sufficiently to visualize these great racial questions. They just followed their instincts and obeyed their ancient religions, and these things happened without their knowing why."

"But the women!" protested Ellador. "Surely the women could see as simple a thing as that. It's only a matter of square miles; how many people to a mile can live healthfully and pleasantly. Are these women willing to have their children grow up so crowded that they *can't* be happy, or where they'll have to fight for room to live? I can't understand it."

Then she went determinedly to question a Japanese authority, to whom we were introduced by one of our friends, as to the status of women in Japan. She was polite; she was meek; she steeled herself beforehand to hear without surprise; and the authority, also courteous to a degree, gave her a brief outline with illustrative story and quotation, of the point of view from which women were regarded in that country.

She grasped it even more thoroughly than she had in India or China.

We left Japan for Home, via Hawaii, and for days she was silent about the subject. Then, as the wide blue sea, the brilliant days spinning by, the smooth magnificence of our progress comforted her, she touched on it

305

once more.

"I'm trying not to *feel* about these particularly awful things, and not to judge, even, till I know more. These things are *so*; and my knowing them does not make them any worse than they were before."

"You're a brave girl—and a strong one," I assured her. "That's the only way to do. I'm awfully sorry you had to have such a dose at first—this war, of all things; and then women in the East! I ought to have prepared you better."

"You could not have, dearest—it would have been impossible. No mere words could have made me visualize the inconceivable. And no matter how I came to it, slow or fast, the horror would have been the same. It is as impossible for me to make you see how I feel it now, as it would have been for you to make me feel it beforehand."

The voyage did her great good. She loved the sea, and gloried in the ships, doing her best to ignore the pitiful labor conditions of those who made the glory possible. Always she made friends—travelers, missionaries, business men, and women, wherever she found them. Yet, strangely enough, she seemed more at a loss with the women than with the men; seemed not to know, quite, how to approach them. It was not for lack of love and sympathy—far from it; she was eager to make friends with them. I finally worked out an explanation like this: She made friends with the men on the human side rather than attracting them by femininity; and as human beings they exchanged ideas and got on well together. The women were not so human; had a less wide outlook, less experience, as a rule. When she did get near enough to one of them for talk at all intimate, then came the ultra-feminine point of view, the different sense of social and moral values, the peculiar limitations of their position.

I saw this, as reflected by Ellador, as I had never seen it for myself before. What I did not understand, at first, was why she seemed to flag in interest and in patience, with the women, sooner than with the men. She never criticized them, but I could see a puzzled grieved look come over her kind face and then she would withdraw.

There were exceptions, marked ones. A woman doctor who had worked for years in China was going home for a long-needed vacation, and Ellador was with her day after day, "learning," she told me. And there was another, once a missionary, now a research worker in biology, who commanded her sincere admiration.

We came to the lovely Hawaiian Islands, quite rested and refreshed, and arranged to stay there awhile and enjoy the splendor of those sea-girt mountains. Here her eager social interest was again aroused and she supplied herself with the history of this little sample of "social progress" most rapidly. There were plenty to teach her, a few excellent books to read, and numbers of most self-satisfied descendants of missionaries to boast of the noble work of their fathers.

"This is very illuminating," she told me. "It is a—what's that nice word Professor Whiting used?—a microcosm—isn't it?"

By this time my dear investigator had as clear an idea of general human history as any one, not a specialist could wish; and had it in a very small note-book. While in England someone had given her Winwood Reade's wonderful *Martyrdom of Man*, as good a basis for historical study as could be asked; and all the facts and theories she had been collecting since were duly related to her general views.

"Here you have done it so quickly—inside of a century. Only 1820—and these nice gentle golden-colored people were living here by themselves."

"They weren't always gentle—don't idealize them too much!" I interrupted. "They had wars and quarrels, and they had a very horrid taboo religion—particularly hard on women."

"Yes—I know that—they weren't 'perfect, as we are,' as Professor Boynton used to say; but they were beautiful and healthy and happy; they were courteous and kind; and oh, how splendidly they could swim! Even the babies, they tell me."

"I've understood a child can swim earlier than it can walk—did they tell you that?"

"Yes—why not? But look here, my dear. Then came the missionaries and—interfered. Now these natives and owners of the land are only 15 per cent of the population, with 20 per cent of the deaths. They are dispossessed and are being exterminated."

"Yes," I said. "Well?"

Ellador looked at me. One could watch the expressions follow one another over her face, like cloud shadows and sunlight over a landscape. She looked puzzled; she evidently saw a reason. She became stern; then a further reason was recognized, and then that heavenly mother-look came over her, the one I had grown to prize most deeply.

But all she said was: "I love you. Van."

"Thank Heaven for that, my dear. I thought you were going to cast me out because of the dispossessed Hawaiians. *I* didn't do it—you're not blaming me, are you?"

"Did not—America—do it?" she asked, quietly. "And do you care at all?"

Then I embarked on one of those confined and contradictory explanations by which the wolf who has eaten the lamb seeks to show how unavoidable—if not how justifiable it all was.

"Do you feel like that about England's taking the Boers' country?" she asked gently.

I did not. I had always felt that a particularly inexcusable piece of "expansion."

"And your country it not packed very close yet—is it? Having so much—why did you need these?"

"We wanted to Christianize them—to civilize them," I urged rather sulkily.

"Do you think Christ would have had the same effect on them? And does civilization help dead people?"

She saw I was hurt, and stopped to kiss me. "Let's drop it, dear—I was wrong to press the point. But I've become so used to saying everything to you, just as if you were one of my sisters—I forget that things must look differently when one's own country is involved."

She said no more about the vanishing Hawaiians, but I began to look at them with a very different feeling from what I had ever had before. We had brought them syphilis and tuberculosis. The Chinese brought them leprosy. One of their lovely islands was now a name of horror from that ghastly disease, a place where noble Christians strive to minimize the evil—too late.

The missionaries, nobly purposed, no doubt, to begin with, had amassed great fortunes in land given to them by these careless children who knew so little of land ownership; and the children and grandchildren of the missionaries lived wealthy and powerful, proud of the "great work" of their forefathers, and apparently seeing no evil in the sad results. Perhaps they thought it was no matter how soon the natives died, so that they died Christians.

And the civilization we have brought them means an endless day of labor, long hours of grinding toil for other people's profit, in place of the clean ease and freedom of their own old life. Hard labor, disease, death; and the lasting consciousness of all this among their dwindling ranks; exclusion, social dissemination, industrial exploitation, approaching extermination—

it is no wonder their music is mournful.

I was glad to leave the lovely place; glad to put aside a sense of national guilt, and to see Ellador freshen again as the golden days and velvet nights flowed over us as we steamed toward the sunrise—and Home.

There were plenty of Californians on board, both wise and unwise, and I saw my wife, with a constantly increasing case and skill, extracting information from each and all she talked with. It is not difficult to extract information about California from a Californian. Not being one myself; and having more definite knowledge about my own country than I had had about most of the others we had visited, I was able to check off this triumphant flood of "boosting" with somewhat colder facts.

Ellador liked it. "It does my heart good," she said, "both to know that there is such a country on earth, and that people can care for it like that."

She particularly revelled in Ina Coolbrith's exquisite poem "California," so rich with tender pride, with vivid appreciation. Some devotee had the book with her, and poured forth a new torrent of praise over a fine list she had of "Californian authors."

This annoyed me rather more than real estate, climate, fruit or flowers; and having been somewhat browbeaten over Hawaii, I wanted to take it out of somebody else. I am not as good as Ellador; don't pretend to be. At moments like that I don't even want to be. So I said to this bubbling enthusiast: "Why do you call all these people 'Californian authors'?"

She looked at me in genuine surprise.

"Were they born there?" I inquired. "Are they native sons or daughters?"

She had to admit they were not, save in a few cases. We marked those who were—it was a most insufficient list.

"But they lived in California," she insisted.

"How long?" I asked. "How long a visit or residence does it take to make an author a 'Californian'—like Mark Twain, for instance? Is he 'a Connecticut author' because he lived more years than that in Connecticut, or 'a New York author' because he lived quite a while in New York?"

She looked much annoyed, and I was not a bit sorry, but went on ruthlessly: "I think California is the only state in the Union that is not content with its own crop—but tries to claim everything in sight."

Chapter V

My Country

In through the Golden Gate we steamed at last, one glorious morning; calm Tamalpais basking on the northern side, and the billowing city rising tumultuously on the southern, with the brilliant beauty of "The Fair" glowing on the water's edge.

I had been through before, and showed her through the glass as we passed, the Seal Rocks and the Cliff House with the great Sutro Baths beside it; and then the jewelled tower, the streaming banners of that wonder-city of a year.

It was in February. There had been rain, and now the luminous rich green of the blazing sudden spring was cloaking every sloping shore. The long bay stretched wide on either hand; the fair bay cities opposite embroidered the western shore for miles; San Francisco rose before us.

Ellador stood by my side, holding my arm with tense excitement. "Your country, dear!" she said. "How beautiful it is! I shall love it!"

I was loving it myself, at that moment, as I never had before.

Behind me was that long journey of us three adventurous explorers; our longer imprisonment, and then these travels of ours, through war-torn Europe, and the slow dark reaches of the Oriental civilization.

"It certainly looks good to me!" I told her.

We spent many days at the great Exposition, and others, later, at the still lovelier, smaller one at San Diego,—days of great happiness to both of us, and real pride to me. Later on I lost this feeling—replacing it with a growing discomfort.

I suppose everyone loves and honors his own country—practically everyone. And we Americans, so young a people, so buoyantly carried along on the flood of easy geographical expansion, so suddenly increased in numbers, not by natural growth of our own stock but by crowding injections of alien blood, by vast hordes of low-grade laborers whose ignorant masses made our own ignorant masses feel superior to all the earth—we Americans are almost as boastful as the still newer Federation of Germany.

I had thought myself a sociologist, an ethnologist, one able to judge fairly from wide knowledge. And yet, with all my knowledge, with all my lucid criticism of my country's errors and shortcomings, I had kept an unshaken inner conviction of our superiority.

Ellador had shaken it.

It was not that she had found any fault with the institutions of my beloved land. Quite the contrary. She believed it faultless—or nearly so. She expected too much. Knowing her as I now did, becoming more and more familiar with the amazing lucidity and fairness of her mind, with its orderly marshalling of well-knit facts and the swinging searchlight of perception which covered every point in her field of vision, I had a strange helpless sense of coming to judgment.

In Herland I had never fully realized the quality of mind developed by their cultural system. Some of its power and clarity was of course plain to us, but we could no more measure that mind than a child can measure its teacher's. I had lived with it now, watched it work, seen it in relation to others, to those of learned men and women of various nations. There was no ostentation about Ellador's intellectual processes. She made no display of learning, did not contradict and argue. Sometimes, in questions of fact, if it seemed essential to the matter under discussion, she would quote authority in opposition, but for the most part she listened, asking a few questions to satisfy herself as to the point of view of her interlocutor. I used to note with appreciative delight how these innocent, almost irrelevant questions would bring out answers, each one of which was a branching guide-post as to the mind of the speaker. Sometimes just two would show him to be capable of believing flat contradictions, or merely one would indicate a limitation of knowledge or an attitude of prejudice which "placed" the man at once. These were not "smart" questions, with a flippantly triumphant and all-too-logical demand at the end, leaving the victim confused and angry. He never realized what was being done to him.

"How do you have patience with these chumps?" I asked her. "They seem like children in your hands—and yet you don't hurt them a bit."

"Perhaps that is why," she answered gravely. "We are so used to children, at home—And when a whole country is always, more or less, teaching children—why it makes us patient, I suppose. What good would it do to humiliate these people? They all know more than I do—about most things."

"They may know more, about some things, but it's their mental processes that seem so muddy—so sticky—so slow and fumbling somehow."

"You're right there, Van. It impresses me very much. There is an enormous fund of knowledge in the minds of your people—I mean any of these people I have met, but the minds themselves are—to me—astonishing.

The Oriental mind is far more highly developed than the Occidental—in some lines; but as serenely unconscious of its limits as—as the other is. What strikes me most of all is the lack of connection between all this knowledge they have accumulated, and the way they live. I'm hoping to find it wholly different here. You Americans, I understand, are the people who do things."

Before I go on with Ellador's impressions of America I want to explain a little further, lest my native-born fellow-citizens resent too bitterly her ultimate criticisms. She perhaps would not have published those criticisms at all; but I can—now.

The sensitiveness I felt at first, the hurt pride, the honest pain, as my pet ideals inexorably changed color under that searchlight of hers, do what I would to maintain them in their earlier glory—all this is outgrown. I love my country, better than I ever did before. I understand it better—probably that accounts for the increased tenderness and patience. But if ever a country needed to wake up and look itself in the face, it is this one.

Ellador, in that amazing little pocket history she compiled, had set up the "order of exercises" in our development, and placed the nations in due sequence as contributors. Running over its neat pages, with the outline maps, the charts with their varied washes of color, showing this or that current of tendency and pressure of condition, one gathered at once a clear bird's eye view of what humanity had been doing all this time. She speculated sagely, with me, as to what trifling deflection of type, what variation in environment, was responsible for the divagation of races; especially those of quite recent common stock. But in the little book was no speculation, merely the simple facts.

Referring to it she could show in a few moments what special influences made Egypt Egypt, and differentiated Assyria from Chaldea. She shook her head sadly over those long early ages.

"They *were* slow to learn, weren't they?" she'd say; "Never seemed to put two and two together at all. I suppose that peculiar arrest of the mental processes was due first to mere social inertia, with its piled-up weight of custom, and then much more to religion. That finality, that 'believing', seemed to put an end to real thinking and learning."

"But, my dear," interposed, "they were learned, surely. The ancient priests had practically all the learning, and in the Dark Ages, the Church in Europe was all that kept learning alive at all."

"Do you mean 'learning' dear, or just 'remembering'?" she asked. "What did the Mediaeval Church 'learn'?"

This was a distinction I had never thought of. Of course what we have always called "learning" was knowing what went before—long before—and mostly what people had written. Still I made out something of a case about the study of alchemy and medicine—which she gravely admitted.

It remained true that the Church, any church, in any period, had set its face like a flint against the people's learning anything new; and, as we commonly know, had promptly punished the most progressive.

"It is a wonder to me," said Ellador, tenderly, "that you have done as well as you have—with all these awful handicaps. But you—America!—you have a different opportunity. I don't suppose you quite realize yourselves what a marvellous difference there is between you and every other people on earth."

Then she pointed out, briefly, how by the start in religious rebellion we had set free the mind from its heaviest shackles; by throwing off the monarchy and aristocracy we had escaped another weight; how our practically unlimited area and fluctuating condition made custom but a name; and how the mixture of races broke the current of heredity.

All this we had gone over on the steamer, sitting by the hour in our long chairs, watching the big smooth swells roll by, and talking of my country.

"You have reason to be proud," she would say. "No people on earth ever had such a chance."

I used to feel misgivings then, especially after Hawaii. I tried to arrange some satisfying defense for our treatment of the Asiatics, the Negroes, Mexico. I thought up all that I could to excuse the open evils that I knew—intemperance, prostitution, graft, lynching. I began to see more holes in the bright fabric of Columbia's robe than I had ever noticed before—and bigger ones. But at that I did not anticipate—.

We spent several weeks in California. I took her to see Shasta, the Yosemite, the cedars of Monterey, the Big Trees, the Imperial Valley. All through the country she poured out constant praises of the boundless loveliness of the land, the air, the sunshine, even the rain. Rain did not depress Ellador—she was a forester.

And she read, avidly. She read John Muir with rapture. "How I should have *loved* him!" she said. She read the brief history of the state, and some books about it—Ramona, for instance. She visited and talked with some leading Japanese—and Chinamen. And she read steadily, with a fixed non-committal face, the newspapers.

If I asked her anything about it all she would pour forth honest delight in

313

the flowers and fruit, the beauty and brightness of the land. If I pressed for more, she would say: "Wait, Van dear—give me time. I've only just come—I don't know enough yet to talk!"

But, I knowing how quickly she learned, and how accurately she related new knowledge to old, watched her face with growing dismay. In Europe I had seen that beautiful face pale with horror; in Asia, sicken with loathing; now, after going around the world; after reaching this youngest land, this land of hope and pride, of wealth and power, I saw that face I loved so well, set in sad lines of disappointment—fairly age before my eyes.

She was still cheerful, with me, still happy out of doors; and her heart rose as I had hoped it would among the mountains, on the far-spread lustrous deserts, in that wordless wonder, the Grand Canyon of the Colorado.

But as she read, as she sat thinking, I could see the light die out of her face and a depressing look creep over it; a look of agonized disappointment, yet of patience too—and a courageous deep determination. It was as if a mother had learned that her baby was an idiot.

. . . . .

As we drew eastward and the cities grew larger, nosier, blacker, her distress increased. She began to urge me to play games with her; to read aloud from books she loved; and especially to talk of Herland.

I was willing; more than willing. As I saw my country through her eyes— as I saw its effect on her—I became less and less inclined, indeed less able, to discuss with her it. But the tension grew; her suffering increased; until I told her as I had that terrible night in Europe, that she must talk to me about it.

"You see you will have to, whether you want to or not," I argued. "You cannot take all America to task about itself—you would get yourself disliked. Besides—if you don't want to tell them about your country—and if you pitch into theirs, they will insist on knowing where you come from, quite naturally. I can't bear to see you getting more and more distressed and saying nothing about it. Besides—it is barely possible that I might offer some palliation, or explanation, of some of the worst things."

"What do you consider the 'worst things'?" she asked casually enough.

But I was already wise enough to see at once that we might not agree on definition.

"Suppose we do this," I suggested. "Here are you, as extramundane as a

Martian. You are like an Investigating Committee from another world. Quite apart from my love for you, my sympathy with you, my admiration for you—yes, all serious and sincere, my dear—I do appreciate this unparalleled opportunity to get a real outsider's point of view.

"This is something that never happened before, you see; Marco Polo came nearest to it, perhaps, when he went poking into the Asiatic wonderland. But these old adventurers of ours, whatever their hardships, never took it so hard as you do. They enjoyed satisfying their curiosity; they always thought their own birthplace infinitely superior, and the more inferior they found other places the more they enjoyed it. Now with you—it seems to hurt your feelings most horribly. I wish you could somehow detach yourself from it—so that you could learn, and not suffer."

"You are quite right, dear boy—it is most unphilosophical of me. I suppose it is largely a result of our long period of—lovingness—at home, that things strike so harshly on my mind."

"And partly your being a woman, don't you think?" I urged. "You see yours is a feminine culture and naturally more sensitive, isn't it?"

"Perhaps that is it," she said, pondering. "The very first thing that strikes me in this great rich lovely land of yours is its *unmotherliness*. We are of course used to seeing everything taken care of."

"But surely, it was worse—far worse—in the other countries wasn't it?"

She smiled tenderly and sadly. "Yes, Van, it was—but here—well, doubtless I expected too much."

"But isn't there some comfort in the contrast?" I asked eagerly. "Here is not the petrified oppression, the degradation of women, that so sickened you in Asia; and here is not the wild brutality of war that so horrified you in Europe."

"No—not either of those," she slowly agreed. "But you see I had warning that Europe was at war, and had read about it a little. It was like going into a—a slaughter-house, for the first time.

"Then all I learned in my studies in Europe prepared me to find what I did find in Asia—Asia was in some ways better than I had been told—in some ways worse. But here!...Oh, Van!" That look of gray anguish had settled on her face again. She seized my arms, held me fast, searched my face as if I was withholding something. Big slow tears welled over and dropped. "This is the top of the tree, Van; this is the last young nation, beginning over again in a New World—a New World! Here was everything to make life richly happy—everything. And you had all the dreadful record of the

315

past to guide you, to teach you at least what not to do. You had courage; you had independence; you had intelligence, education, opportunity. And such splendid principles to start with—such high ideals. And then all kinds of people coming! Oh, surely, surely, surely this should be the Crown of the World!

"Why, Van—Europe was like a man with—with delirium tremens. Asia was like something gnarled and twisted with hopeless age. But America is a Splendid Child...with..." She covered her face with her hands.

I couldn't stand this. I was an American, and she was my wife. I took her in my arms.

"Look here, you blessed Herlander," I said, "I'm not going to have my country wiped off the map in disgrace. You must remember that all judgment is comparative. You cannot compare any other country with your country for two reasons; first your long isolation, and second that miraculous manlessness of yours.

"This world of ours has been in more or less intercourse and exchange for many more thousands of years than Herland has lived. We Americans were not a new created race—we were just English and Dutch and French and Scandinavian and Italian, and so on—just everybody. We brought with us our inherited tendencies, of course—all of them. And while we did make a clean break with some of the old evils, we had no revelation as to a perfect social method. You are expecting too much...

"Don't you see," I went on, for she said nothing, "that a Splendid Child may be a pretty bad child, sometimes, and may have the measles pretty hard—and yet not be hopeless?"

She raised her wet face from my shoulder and her own warm loving smile illuminated it once more.

"You're right, Van, you're wholly right," she agreed. "I was most unreasonable, most unwise. It is just a piece of the same world—a lot of pieces—mixed samples—on a new piece of ground. And it was a magnificent undertaking—I can see that—and you *are* young, aren't you? Oh, Van dear, you do make it easier."

I held her very close for awhile. This journey among strange lands had brought me one deep joy. Ellador had grown to need me as she never did in her own peaceful home.

"You see, dearest," I said, "you have a dual mission. You are to study all about the world and take your knowledge back with you—but all you need of it is to decide whether you'll come out and play with us or not—or let any more of us come in. Then you have what I, as a citizen of the rest of the world—rather the biggest part of it, consider a more important duty. If that Herland mind of yours can find out what ails us—and how we are to mend it; if your little country with its strange experiment can bring aid in solving the problems of the world—that is what I call a Historic Mission! How does that strike you, Mrs. Jennings?"

It was good to see her rise to it. That wonderful motherheart, which all those women had, seemed to shine out like a sunrise. I went on, delighted with my success.

"I'll just forget I'm an American," I said. "This country is The Child. I'm not its father or anything—I'm just a doctor, a hygienist, an investigator. You're another—and a bigger one. Now I understand that you find The Child is in a bad way—worse off than I thought it was. To judge from your expression, dear, on several occasions, you think it is a very dirty child, a careless child, a wasteful child, with a bad temper and no manners—am I right?"

"Not about the temper, dear. Pettish at times, but not vindictive, and very, very kind....Van...I think I've been too hard on The Child! I'm quite ashamed. Yes, we are two investigators—I'm so glad there are two!"

She stopped and looked at me with an expression I never saw enough of, that I used to long for in vain, at first; that look as if she *needed* me.

"No matter what we have in Herland," she said slowly, "we miss this—this united feeling. It grows, Van; I feel more and more as if—somehow or other—we were really *blended*. We have nothing just like it."

"No, you haven't—with all your Paradise. So let's allow some good things in your 'case', and particularly in this case of the bad child. And we'll pitch in and work out a diagnosis—won't we? And then prescribe."

We pitched in.

First she had insisted on knowing the whole country. We made a sort of spiral, beginning on the outside, and circulated south, east, north, west, and so over again; till we wound ourselves up in Topeka. By that time we had been in every state, in all the principal cities, and in many of those tiny towns which are more truly indicative of the spirit of the community than the larger ones.

When we were interested in a given place we would stay awhile—there was nothing to hurry us; and when Ellador showed signs of wear and tear there was always some sweet wild country to fly to, and rest. She sampled both sea-coasts, the Great Lakes, and some little ones, many a long winding river, mountains wooded and mountains bare; the restful plains, the shadowy cypress swamps.

Her prompt reaction to the beauty of the real country was always beneficial, and, to my great delight she grew to love it, and even to feel a pride in its vast extent and variety—just as I did. We both admitted that it was a most illegitimate ground for pride, but we both felt it.

As she saw more of the cities, and of the people, by mere usage she grew accustomed to what had grieved her most at first. Also I suggested a method which she gladly used, and found most comforting, in which we classified all the evils as "transient", and concerned ourselves merely with finding out how they came there and how to remove them.

"Some of these things you'll just outgrow," she said relievedly. "Some are already outgrown. America is not nearly so—cocky—as Dickens found her. She is now in an almost morbid attitude of self-distrust and condemnation—but she'll outgrow that too."

It was a great relief to me to have her push through that period of shocked disappointment so readily. But of course the vigor of her mental constitution made it possible for her to throw off a trouble like that more easily than we can do it.

She soon devised methods of her own of acquiring further information. In her capacity of a traveler, and recently come from the seat of war, to say nothing of the Orient, she found frequent opportunity for addressing women's clubs, churches and forums of various kinds, and so coming in touch with large bodies of people; and their reactions.

"I am learning to realize 'the popular mind'," she said. "I can already distinguish between the different parts of the country. And, oh, Van—" she laughed a little, caught her breath over, and added with an odd restraint: "I'm getting to know the—women."

"Why do you say it like that?" I inquired.

She looked at me in what I might describe as "forty ways at once." It was funny. There was such an odd mixture of pride and shame, of hope and disillusionment; of a high faith and a profound distrust.

"I can stand it," she protested. "The Child is by no means hopeless—in fact I begin to think it is a very promising child, Van. But, oh, how it does behave!"

And she laughed.

I was a little resentful. We were such good chums by this time; we had played together such a lot, and studied together so widely; we had such a safe foundation of mutual experience that I began to dare to make fun of my strange Princess now and then, and she took it most graciously.

"There's one thing I won't stand for," I told her solemnly. "You can call my country a desert, my people incompetent, dishonest, wasteful and careless to a degree; you can blackguard our agriculture, horticulture, aboriculture, floriculture, viticulture, and—and—["Apiculture," she suggested, with a serious face.]—you can deride our architecture and make trivial objections to the use of soot as a civic decoration; but there is one thing I, as an American Man, will not stand—you mustn't criticize our Women!"

"I won't," she said meekly, a twinkle in her eye. "I won't say one word about them, dear—until you ask me to!"

Whereat I knew that my doom was sealed once more. Could I rest without knowing what she thought of them?

Chapter VI

The Diagnosis

"How are you getting on with 'The Case,' Mrs. J.?" I asked Ellador one evening when she seemed rather discouraged. "What symptoms are worrying you most now?"

She looked at me with wide anxious eyes, too much in earnest to mind the "Mrs. J.," which usually rather teased her.

"It's an awfully important case, Van dear," she answered soberly, "and a serious one—very serious, I think. I've been reading a lot, had to, to get background and perspective, and I feel as if I understand a good deal better. Still—. You helped me ever so much by saying that you were not new people, just mixed Europeans. But the new country and the new conditions began to make you all into a new people. Only—."

"These pauses are quite terrifying," I protested. "Won't you explain your ominous 'still,' and sinister 'only'!"

She smiled a little. "Why the 'still' should have been followed by the amount which I did not understand, and the 'only'—." She stopped again.

"Well, out with it, my dear. Only what?"

"Only you have done it too fast and too much in the dark. You weren't conscious you see."

"Not conscious—America not conscious?"

"Not self-conscious, I mean, Van."

This I scouted entirely, till she added patiently: "Perhaps I should say nationally conscious, or socially conscious. You were plunged into an enormous social enterprise, a huge swift, violent experiment; the current of social evolution burst forth over here like a subterranean river finding an outlet. Things that the stratified crust of Asia could not let through, and the heavy shell of European culture could not either, just burst forth over here and swept you along. Democracy had been—accumulating, through all the centuries. The other nations forced it back, held it down. It boiled over in France, but the lid was clapped on again for awhile. Here it could pour forward—and it poured. Then all the people of the same period of social development wanted to come too, and did,—lots of them. That was inevitable. All that 'America' means in this sense is a new phase of social development, and anyone can be an American who belongs to it."

"Guess you are right so far, Mrs. Doctor. Go ahead!"

"But while this was happening to you, you were doing things yourselves, some of them in line with your real position and movement, some dead against it. For instance, your religion."

"Religion against what? Expound further."

"Against Democracy."

"You don't mean the Christian religion, do you?" I urged, rather shocked.

"Oh, no, indeed. That would have been a great help to the world if they had ever taken it up."

I was always entertained and somewhat startled by Ellador's detached view. She knew the same facts so familiar to us, but they had not the same connotations.

"I think Jesus was simply wonderful," she went on. "What a pity it was he did not live longer!"

This was a new suggestion to me. Of course I no longer accepted that pitiful old idea of his being a pre-arranged sacrifice to his own father, but I never deliberately thought of his having continued alive, and its possible effects.

"He is supposed to have been executed at about the age of thirty-three, was he not?" she went on. "Think of it—hardly a grown man! He should have had thirty or forty more years of teaching. It would all have become clearer, more consistent. He would have worked things out, explained them, made people understand. He would have made clear to them what they were to *do*. It was an awful loss."

I said nothing at all, but watched the sweet earnest face, the wise far-seeing eyes, and really agreed with her, though in my mind rose a confused dim throng of horrified objections belonging not to my own mind, but to those of other people.

"Tell me how you mean that our religion was against democracy," I persisted.

"It was so personal," she said, "and so unjust. There must have crept into it, in early times, a lot of the Buddhist philosophy, either direct or filtered, the 'acquiring merit' idea, and ascetism. The worst part of all was the idea of sacrifice—that is *so* ancient. Of course what Jesus meant was social unity, that your neighbor *was* yourself—that we were all one humanity— 'many gifts, but the same spirit.' He must have meant that—for that is so.

"What I mean by 'your religion' is the grade of Calvinism which dominated

321

young America, with the still older branches, and the various small newer ones. It was all so personal. *My* soul—*my* salvation. *My* conscience—*my* sins. And here was the great living working truth of democracy carrying you on in spite of yourselves—*E Pluribus Unum.*

"Your economic philosophy was dead against it too—that foolish *laissez-faire* idea. And your politics, though what was new in it started pretty well, has never been able to make much headway against the highest religious sanction, the increasing economic pressure, and the general drag of custom and tradition—inertia."

"You are somewhat puzzling, my fair Marco Polo," I urged. "So you mean to extol our politics, American politics?"

"Why of course!" she said, her eyes shining. "The principles of democracy are wholly right. The law of federation, the method of rotation in office, the stark necessity for general education that the people may understand clearly, the establishment of liberty—that they may act freely—it is splendidly, gloriously right! But why do I say this to an American!"

"I wish you could say it to every American man, woman, and child," I answered soberly. "Of course we used to feel that way about it, but things have changed somehow."

"Yes, yes," she went on eagerly. "That's what I mean. You started right, for the most part, but those high-minded brave old ancestors of yours did not understand sociology—how should they? It wasn't even born. They did not know how society worked, or what would hurt it the most. So the preachers went on exhorting the people to save their own souls, or get it done for them by imputed virtues of someone else—and no one understood the needs of the country.

"Why, Van! Vandyke Jennings! As I understand more and more how noble and courageous and high-minded was this Splendid Child, and then see it now, bloated and weak, with unnatural growth, preyed on by all manner of parasites inside and out, attacked by diseases of all kinds, sneered at, criticized, condemned by the older nations, and yet bravely stumbling on, making progress in spite of it all—I'm getting to just *love* America!"

That pleased me, naturally, but I didn't like her picture of my country as bloated and verminous. I demanded explanation.

"Do you think we're too big?" I asked. "Too much country to be handled properly?"

"Oh, *no!*" she answered promptly. "Not too big in land. That would have been like the long lean lines of youth, the far-reaching bones of a country gradually rounding out and filling in as you grow. But you couldn't wait to grow, you just—swelled."

"What on earth do you mean, Ellador?"

"You have stuffed yourself with the most ill-assorted and unassimilable mass of human material that ever was held together by artificial means," she answered remorselessly. "You go to England, and the people are English. Only three per cent of aliens, even in London, I understand. And in France the people are French—bless them! And in Italy, Italian. But here—it's no wonder I was discouraged at first. It has taken a lot of study and hard thinking, to see a way out at all. But I do see it. It was simply awful when I begun.

"Just look! Here you were, a little band of really promising people, of different nations, yet of the same general stock, and *like-minded*—that was the main thing. The real union is the union of idea; without that—no nation. You made settlements, you grew strong and bold, you shook off the old government. You set up a new flag, and then—!"

"Then," said I proudly, "we opened our arms to all the world, if that is what you are finding fault with. We welcomed other people to our big new country—'the poor and oppressed of all nations!'" I quoted solemnly.

"That's what I mean by saying you were ignorant of sociology," was her cheerful reply. "It never occurred to you that the poor and oppressed were not necessarily good stuff for a democracy."

I looked at her rather rebelliously.

"Why just study them," she went on, in that large sweeping way of hers. "Hadn't there been poor and oppressed enough in the past? In Chaldaea and Assyria and Egypt and Rome—in all Europe—everywhere? Why, Van, it is the poor and oppressed who make monarchy and despotism—don't you see that? "

"Hold on, my dear—hold on! This is too much. Are you *blaming* the poor helpless things for their tyrannical oppression?"

"No more than I blame an apple-tree for bearing apples," she answered. "You don't seriously advance the idea that the oppressor began it, do you? Just one oppressor jumping on the necks of a thousand free men? Surely you see that the general status and character of a people creates and maintains its own kind of government?"

"Y-e-es," I agreed. "But all the same, they are *human*, and if you give them proper conditions they can all rise—surely we have proved that."

"Give them proper conditions, and give them time—yes."

"Time! They do it in one generation. We have citizens, good citizens, of all races, who were born in despotic countries, all equal in our democracy."

"How many Chinese and Japanese citizens have you?" she asked quietly. "How are your African citizens treated in this 'equal' democracy!"

This was rather a facer.

"About the first awful mistake you made was in loading yourself up with those reluctant Africans," Ellador went on. "If it wasn't so horrible, it would be funny, awfully funny. A beautiful healthy young country, saddling itself with an antique sin every other civilized nation had repudiated. And here they are, by millions and millions, flatly denied citizenship, socially excluded, an enormous alien element in your democracy."

"They are not aliens," I persisted stoutly. "They are Americans, loyal Americans; they make admirable soldiers"

"Yes, and servants. You will let them serve you and fight for you—but that's all, apparently. Nearly a tenth of the population, and not part of the democracy. And they never asked to come!"

"Well," I said, rather sullenly. "I admit it—everyone does. It was an enormous costly national mistake, and we paid for it heavily. Also it's there yet, an unsolved question. I admit it all. Go on please. We were dead wrong on the blacks, and pretty hard on the reds; we may be wrong on the yellows. I guess this is a white man's country, isn't it? You're not objecting to the white immigrants, are you?"

"To legitimate immigrants, able and willing to be American citizens, there can be no objection, unless even they come too fast. But to millions of deliberately imported people, not immigrants at all, but victims, poor ignorant people scraped up by paid agents, deceived by lying advertisements, brought over here by greedy American ship owners and employers of labor—there are objections many and strong."

"But, Ellador—even granting it is you say, they too can be made into American citizens, surely?"

"They can be, but are they? I suppose you all tacitly assume that they are; but an outsider does not see it. We have been all over the country now, pretty thoroughly. I have met and talked with people of all classes and all races, both men and women. Remember I'm new to 'the world,' and I've just come here from studying Europe, and Asia, and Africa. I have the

324

hinterland of history pretty clearly summarized, though of course I can't pretend to be thorough, and I tell you, Van, there are millions of people in your country who do not belong to it at all."

She saw that I was about to defend our foreign born, and went on:

"I do not mean the immigrants solely. There are Bostonians of Beacon Hill who belong in London; there are New Yorkers of five generations who belong in Paris; there are vast multitudes who belong in Berlin, in Dublin, in Jerusalem; and there are plenty of native Sons and Daughters of the Revolution who are aristocrats, plutocrats, anything but democrats."

"Why of course there are! We believe in having all kinds—there's room for everybody—this is the 'melting-pot,' you know."

"And do you think that you can put a little of everything into a melting-pot and produce a good metal? Well fused and flawless? Gold, silver, copper and iron, lead, radium, pipe clay, coal dust, and plain dirt?"

A simile is an untrustworthy animal if you ride it too hard. I grinned and admitted that there were limits to the powers of fusion.

"Please understand," she urged gently. "I am not looking down on one kind of people because they are different from others. I like them all. I think your prejudice against the black is silly, wicked, and—hypocritical. You have no idea how ridiculous it looks, to an outsider, to hear your Southern enthusiasts raving about the horrors of 'miscegenation' and then to count the mulattos, quadroons, octoroons and all the successive shades by which the black race becomes white before their eyes. Or to see them shudder at 'social equality' while the babies are nourished at black breasts, and cared for in their most impressionable years by black nurses—their *children!*"

She stopped at that, turned away from me and walked to the opposite window, where she stood for some time with her hands clenched and her shoulders heaving.

"Where was I?" she asked presently, definitely dropping the question of children. "Black—yes, and how about the yellow? Do they 'melt'? Do you want them to melt? Isn't your exclusion of them an admission that you think some kinds of people unassimilable? That democracy must pick and choose a little?"

"What would you have us do?" I asked rather sullenly. "Exclude everybody? Think we are superior to the whole world?"

Ellador laughed, and kissed me. "I think *you* are," she whispered tenderly. "No—I don't mean that at all. It would be too great a strain on the imagination! If you want a prescription—far too late—it is this: Democracy is a psychic relation. It requires the intelligent conscious co-operation of a great many persons all 'equal' in the characteristics required to play that kind of a game. You could have safely welcomed to your great undertaking people of every race and nation who were individually fitted to assist. Not by any means because they were 'poor and oppressed,' nor because of that glittering generality that 'all men are born free and equal,' but because the human race is in different stages of development, and only some of the races—or some individuals in a given race—have reached the democratic stage."

"But how could we discriminate?"

"You mustn't ask me too much, Van. I'm a stranger; I don't know all I ought to, and, of course I'm all the time measuring by my background of experience in my own country. I find you people talk a good bit about the Brotherhood of Man, but you haven't seemed to think about the possibilities of a sisterhood of women."

I looked up alertly, but she gave a mischievous smile and shook her head. "You do not want to hear about the women, I remember. But seriously, dear, this is one of the most dangerous mistakes you have made; it complicates everything. It makes your efforts to establish democracy like trying to make a ship go by steam and at the same time admitting banks of oars, masses of sails and cordage, and mere paddles and outriggers."

"You can certainly make some prescription for this particularly dreadful state, can't you?" I urged. "Sometimes 'an outsider' can see better than those who are—being melted."

She pondered awhile, then began slowly: "Legitimate immigration is like the coming of children to you,—new blood for the nation, citizens made, not born. And they should be met like children, with loving welcome, with adequate preparation, with the fullest and wisest education for their new place. Where you have that crowded little filter on Ellis Island, you ought to have Immigration Bureaus on either coast, at ports so specified, with a great additional department to definitely Americanize the newcomers, to teach them the language, spirit, traditions and customs of the country. Talk about offering hospitality to all the world! What kind of hospitality is it to let your guests crowd and pack into the front hall, and to offer them neither bed, bread nor association? That's what I mean by saying that you are not conscious. You haven't taken your immigration seriously enough. The consequence is that you are only partially America, an American clogged and confused, weakened and mismanaged, for lack of political compatibility."

326

"Is this all?" I asked after a little. "You make me feel as if my country was a cross between a patchwork quilt and a pudding stone."

"Oh, dear, no!" she cheerfully assured me. "That's only a beginning of my diagnosis. The patient's worst disease was that disgraceful out-of-date attack of slavery, only escaped by a surgical operation, painful, costly, and not by any means wholly successful. The second is this chronic distension from absorbing too much and too varied material, just pumping it in at wild speed. The third is the most conspicuously foolish of all—to a Herlander."

"Oh—leaving the women out?"

"Yes. It's so—so—well, I can't express to you how *ridiculous* it looks. "

"We're getting over it," I urged. "Eleven states now, you know—it's getting on."

"Oh, yes, yes, it's getting on. But I'm looking at your history, and your conditions, and your loud complaints, and then to see this great mass of fellow-citizens treated as if they weren't there—it is unbelievable!"

"But I told you about that before we came," said I. "I told you in Herland—you knew it."

"I knew it, truly. But, Van, suppose anyone had told you that in Herland women were the only citizens—would that have prevented your being surprised?"

I looked back for a moment, remembering how we men, after living there so long, after "knowing" that women were the only citizens, still never got over the ever-recurring astonishment of *realizing* it.

"No wonder it surprises you, dear,—I should think it would. But go on about the women."

"I'm not touching on the women at all, Van. This is only in treating of democracy—of your country and what ails it. You see—"

"Well, dear? See what?"

"It is so presumptuous of me to try to explain democracy to you, an American citizen. Of course you understand, but evidently the country at large doesn't. In a monarchy you have this one allowed Ruler, and his subordinate rulers, and the people submit to them. Sometimes it works very well, but in any case it is something done for and to the people by someone they let do it.

"A democracy, a real one, means the people socially conscious and doing it themselves—doing it *themselves*! Not just electing a Ruler and subordinates and submitting to them—transferring the divine right of kings to the divine right of alderman or senators. A democracy is a game everybody has to play—*has* to—else it is not a democracy. And here you people deliberately left out half!"

"But they never had been 'in'; you know, in the previous governments."

"Now, Van—that's really unworthy of you. As subjects they were the same as men, and as queens they were the same as kings. But you began a new game—that you *said* must be 'by the people'—and so on, and left out half."

"It was—funny," I admitted, "and unfortunate. But we're improving. Do go on."

"That's three counts, I believe," she agreed. "Next lamentable mistake,— failure to see that democracy must be economic."

"Meaning socialism?"

"No, not exactly. Meaning what Socialism means, or ought to mean. You could not have a monarchy where the king was in no way different from his subjects. A monarchy must be expressed not only in the immediate symbols of robe and crown, throne and sceptre, but in the palace and the court, the list of lords and gentlemen-in-waiting. It's all part of monarchy.

"So you cannot have a democracy while there are people markedly differentiated from the others, with symbolism of dress and decoration, with courts and palaces and crowds of servitors."

"You can't except all the people to be just alike, can you?"

"No, nor even to be 'equal.' Some people will always be more valuable than others, and some more useful than others; but a poet, a blacksmith, and a dancing master might all be friends and fellow-citizens in a true democratic sense. Your millionaires vote and your day-laborers vote, but it does not bring them together as fellow citizens. That's why your little old New England towns and your fresh young western ones, have more of 'America' in them than is possible—could ever be possible—in such a political menagerie as New York, for instance."

"Meaning the Tiger?" I inquired.

"Including the Tiger, with the Elephant, the Moose and the Donkey— especially the Donkey! No—I do not really mean those—totems. I mean the weird collection of political methods, interests, stages of growth.

"New York's an oligarchy; it's a plutocracy; it's a hierarchy; it reverts to the clan system with its Irishmen, and back of that, to the patriarchy, with its Jews. It's anything and everything you like—but it's not a democracy."

"If it was, what would it do to prove it? Just what do you expect of what you call democracy? Don't you idealize it?" I asked.

"No." She shook her head decidedly. "I do not idealize it. I'm familiar with it, you see—we have one at home, you know."

So they had. I had forgotten. In fact I had not very clearly noticed. We had been so much impressed by their all being women that we had not done justice to their political development.

"It's no miracle," she said. "Just people co-operating to govern themselves. We have universal suffrage, you know, and train our children in the use of it before they come to the real thing. That far-seeing Mr. Gill is trying to do that in your public schools, I notice, and Mr. George of the Junior Republics. It requires a common knowledge of the common need, local self-management, recognizing the will of the majority, and a big ceaseless loving effort to make the majority wiser. It's surely nothing so wonderful, Van, for a lot of intelligent people to get together and manage their common interests."

It certainly had worked well in Herland. So well, so easily, so smoothly, that it was hardly visible.

"But the people who get together have got to be within reach of one another," she went on. "They've got to have common interests. What united action can you expect between Fifth Avenue and—Avenue A?"

"I've had all I can stand for one dose, my lady," I now protested. "From what you have said I should think your 'Splendid Child' would have died in infancy—a hundred years ago. But we *haven't* you see. We're alive and kicking—especially kicking. I have faith in my country yet."

"It is still able to lead the world—if it will," she agreed. "It has still all the natural advantages it began with, and it has added new ones. I'm not despairing, nor blaming, Van—I'm diagnosing, and pretty soon I'll prescribe. But just now I suggest that we change politics for tennis."

We did. I can still beat her at tennis—having played fifteen years to her one—but not so often as formerly.

Chapter VII

In Our Homes

If there was one thing more than another I had wanted to show Ellador it was our homes,—my home, of course, and others that I knew.

In all the peace and beauty of Herland there was nowhere the small lit circle of intimate love and mutually considered comfort which means so much to us. The love, the comfort, were everywhere, to be sure, but that was different. It was like reflected lighting instead of a lamp on the center table; it was like an evenly steam-heated house, instead of one with an open fire in each room. We had missed those fires, so warm to the front, so inadequate on the back, so inclusive of those who can sit near it, so exclusive of everyone else.

Now, as we visited far and wide, and as Ellador, in her new capacity as speaker to clubs and churches went farther and wider, she was becoming well acquainted with our American homes, it seemed to me.

But it did not satisfy her. She had become more and more the sociologist, the investigator.

"They are all alike," she said. "The people vary, of course, but the setting is practically the same. Why, Van—in all my visits, in so many states, in so many kind families, I've found the most amusing similarity in homes. I can find the bathroom in the dark; I know just what they'll have for breakfast; there seem to be only some eight or ten dinners or luncheons known."

I was a little nettled,—just a little.

"There is a limit to edible animals, if that's what you mean," I protested. "Beef and veal, mutton and lamb, pig,—fresh, salted and smoked—poultry and game. Oh, and fish."

"That's ten, and can be stretched, of course. No, I don't mean the basis of supplies. I mean only the lack of—of specialization in it all. You see the women have talked with me—eagerly. It really is pathetic, Van, the effort—effort—effort, to do what ought to be so easy. And the expense!"

"We know it is laborious, but most women hold it is their duty, dear. Of course, I agree with you, but most of our people don't, you see. And the men, I'm afraid, consider their own comfort."

"I only wish they did," she remarked, surprisingly. "But I'm studying the home not merely on the economic side; I'm studying it as a world institution—it's new to me, you see. Europe—Africa—Asia—the Islands—America—see here, dear, we haven't seen South America. Let's learn Spanish and go!"

Ellador spoke of learning a new language as if it were a dance, a brief and entertaining process. We did it, too; at least she did. I knew some Spanish already and polished it up with her new enthusiasm to help. It was not until observing her intellectual processes in our journeyings together that I had realized the potential energy of the Herland mind. Its breadth and depth, its calm control, its rationality, its fertility of resource, were apparent while we were there, but accustomed as I was to the common limitations of our own minds, to the narrow specialization with accompanying atrophy of other powers, to the "brain-fag" and mental breakdown, with all the deadly lower grades of feeble-mindedness and last gulf of insanity—I had not realized that these disabilities were unknown in Herland. A healthy brain does not show, any more than a sick one, and the airy strength of a bounding acrobat can hardly be judged if you see him in a hammock.

For this last year or two I was observing a Herland brain at work, assimilating floods of new impressions, suffering keen and severe emotional shocks, hampered by an inevitable nostalgia, and yet picking up languages in passing as one picks flowers by the roadside.

We made our trip to South America, with Spanish history carefully laid in beforehand, and learned what everyone of us ignorant United Statesians ought to know,—that "America" is a world-spanning double continent, not merely a patch on one, and that, if we do our duty by our brother countries, we may some day fill out legitimately that large high-sounding name of ours and really be The United States of America.

"I certainly have enough data now to be fair in my deduction," Ellador said, on our home trip. "It has been awfully interesting, visiting your world. And coming back to your country now, with wider knowledge and a background of experience, I think I can be fairer to it. So if you're ready, we'll go back to where we left off that day I jumped to South America."

She turned over her book of notes on the United States and looked at me cheerfully.

"Homes," she said, "The Home, The American Home—and the homes of all the rest of the world, past and present—"

I tucked the Kenwood rug closer about her feet, settled my own, and prepared to listen.

"Yes, ma'am. Here you and I, at great expense, have circled the habitable globe, been most everywhere except to Australasia and South Africa—spent a good year canvassing the U. S.—and if you're not ready to give us your diagnosis—*and* prescriptions—why, I shall lose faith in Herland!"

"Want it for the world—or just your country?" she asked serenely.

"Oh, well, give us both; you're capable of it. But not quite all at once—I couldn't take it in. America first, please."

"It's not so long," she began slowly. "Not if you generalize, safely. One could, of course, say that because the Jones children were let alone they spilled the ink, teased the dog, hurt the kitten, let the canary out, ate too much jam, soiled their clothes, pulled up the tulip bulbs, smeared the wallpaper, broke the china, tore the curtains—and so forth, and so forth, and so forth. And you could tell just how it happened in each case—that would take some time. Especially if you added a similar account of the Smith children and the Brown children and so on. But if you say: 'Neglected children are liable to become mischievous,' you've said it all."

"Don't be as short as that," I begged. "It would not be illuminating."

We spent many hours on the endless subject,—rich, fruitful hours, full of insight, simplification, and hope.

"I'm not so shocked as I was at first," she told me. "I've seen that Europe goes on being Europe even if each nation loses a million men—two million men. They'll grow again....I see that all this horror is no new thing to the world—poor world—poor, wretched, blind baby! But it's a sturdy baby for all that. It's *Here*—it has not died...

"What seems to be the matter, speaking very generally, is this: People have not understood their own works—their social nature, that is. They have not understood—that's all."

"Stupid? Hopelessly stupid?" I asked.

"Not at all—not in the least—but here's the trouble: their minds were always filled up beforehand with what they used to believe. Talk about putting new wine in old bottles—it's putting old wine in new bottles that has kept the world back.

"You can see it all the way long," she pursued. "New life, continually arising, new condition, but always the old, older, oldest ideas, theories, beliefs. Every nation, every race, hampered and hag-ridden by what it used to think, used to believe, used to know. And all the nice, fresh, eager, struggling children forcibly filled up with the same old stuff. It is pretty terrible, Van. But it's so—funny—that I can stand it. In one way human misery is a joke—because you don't have to have it!

"Then you people came over to a New Continent and started a New Country, with a lot of New Ideas—yet you kept enough old ones to drown any country. No wonder you've splashed so much—just to keep above water."

I didn't say much. I wanted her to work it out, gradually. She was letting me see her do it. Of course, in this record I'm piecing together a great many talks, a great many ideas, and I'm afraid leaving out some. It was no light matter she had undertaken, even for a Herlander.

"This family and home idea is responsible for a great part of it," she said. "Not, as I find you quite generally believe, as a type and pattern of all that is good and lovely, but as a persistent primitive social group, interfering with the development of later groups. If you look at what you ought to have evolved by this time, it becomes fairly easy to see what is the matter.

"Take your own case—with its wonderful new start—a clean slate of a country, and a very good installation of people to begin with. A good religion, too, in essence, and a prompt appreciation of the need of being generally educated. Then your splendid political opening—the great wave of democracy pouring out into expression. Room for all, wealth for all. What should have been the result—easily? Why, Van—the proudest Yankee, Southerner, Westerner, that ever lived doesn't begin to estimate what your people might have done!

"What they have done is a good deal —but, Oh—what they might have done! You see, they didn't *understand* democracy. They began to play, but they didn't know the game. It was like a small child, running a big auto. Democracy calls for the conscious intelligent co-ordinate action of all the people. Without it, it is like a partly paralyzed king.

"First you left out half the people—an awful mistake. You only gradually took in the other half. You saw dimly the need of education, but you didn't know what education was—'reading, writing, and arithmetic' are needed, even in monarchies. You needed special education in the new social process.

"Democracy calls for the understanding, recognition, and universal practise of social laws,—laws which are "natural," like those of physics and chemistry; but your religion—and your education, too—taught Authority—not real law. You couldn't make a good electrician on mere authority, could you? He has to understand, not merely obey. Neither can you so make the citizens of a democracy. Reverence for and submission to authority are right in monarchies—wrong in democracies. When Demos is King he must learn to act for himself, not to do as he is told.

"And back of your Christian religion is the Hebrew; back of that—The Family. It all comes down to that absurd root error of the proprietary family."

We were easily at one in this view, but I had never related it to America's political shortcomings before.

"That old Boss Father is behind God," she went on calmly. "The personal concept of God as a father, with his special children, his benign patronage, his quick rage, long anger, and eternal vengeance—" she shivered, "it is an ugly picture.

"The things men have thought about God," she said slowly, "are a ghastly proof of the way they have previously behaved. As they have improved, their ideas of God have improved slowly.

"When Kings were established, they crystallized the whole thing, in plain sight, and you had Kings a very long time, you see—have them yet. Kings and Fathers, Bosses, Rulers, Masters, Overlords—it is all such a poor preparation for democracy. Fathers and Kings and the Hebrew Deity are behind you and above you. Democracy is before you, around you; it is a thing to do...

"You have to learn it by trying—there is no tradition, and no authority. It calls for brave, careful, continuous, scientific experiment, with record of progress, and prompt relinquishment of failures and mistakes. It is open in front, and in motion—democracy is a going concern." (How a foreigner does love an idiom or a bit of slang! Even this Herland angel was not above it.)

"Now, you in young America had left off the King idea, for the most part. But you had the King's ancestor—the Father, the Absolute Boss, and you had a religion heavily weighted with that same basic concept. Moreover, as Protestants, book-worshippers, in default of a King, you must needs make a written ruler for yourselves, and that poor, blind, blessed baby, Democracy, promptly made itself a Cast-Iron Constitution—and crawled under it."

That was something to chew on. It was so. It was undeniably so. We had done just that. We had been so anxious for "stability"—as if a young living thing could remain "stable"—the quality of stones.

"You grew, in spite of it. You had to. The big wild land helped, the remoteness and necessity for individual action and continual experiment. The migration of the children helped."

"Migration of the children! What on earth do you mean, Ellador?"

"Why, haven't you noticed? Hardly any of your children stay at home any more than they can help, any longer than they can help. And as soon as they are able they get off—as far as they can. They may love the old homestead—but they don't stay in it."

This was so, too.

"You see that steadily lightens up this old mistake about Authority. It is the change to the laboratory system of living—finding out how by doing it."

"It does not seem to me that there is much 'authority' left in the American home," I urged. "All the immigrants complain of just that."

"Of course they do. Your immigrants, naturally, understand democracy even less than you do. You have all of you set the word 'Freedom' over the most intricately co-ordinated kind of political relation. You see the Authority method is so simple. 'It is an order!'—and you merely do it—no thought, no effort—no responsibility. God says so—the King or the captain says so—the Book says so—and back of it all, the Family, the Father-Boss. What's that nice story: 'Papa says so—and if he says so, it is so, if it ain't so!'"

"But, Ellador—really—there is almost none of that in the American family; surely you must have seen the difference?"

"I have. In the oldest countries the most absolute Father-Boss—and family worship—the dead father being even more potent than the live ones. Van, dear—the thing I cannot fully understand is this reverence people have for dead people. Why is it? How is it? Why is a man who wasn't much when he was alive anything more when he is dead? You do not really believe that people are dwindling and deteriorating from age to age, do you?"

"That is precisely what we used to believe," I told her, "for the greater part of our history—for all of it really—the evolution idea is still less than a century old—in popular thought."

"But you Americans who *are* free, who *are* progressive, who *are* willing to change in most things—why do you still talk about what 'your fathers' said and did—as if it was so important?"

"It's because of our recent birth as a nation, I suppose," I answered, "and the prodigious struggle those fathers of ours made—the Pilgrim Fathers, the Church fathers, the Revolutionary fathers—and now our own immediate fathers in the Civil War."

"But why is it that you only reverence them politically—and perhaps, religiously! Nobody quotes them in business methods, in art, or science, or medicine, or mechanics. Why do you assume that they were so permanently wise in knowing how to govern a huge machine-run, electrically-connected, city-dominated nation, which they were unable even to imagine? It's so foolish, Van."

It is foolish. I admitted it. But I told her, perhaps a little testily, that I didn't see what our homes had to do with it.

Then that wise lady said sweet, kind, discriminating things about us till I felt better, and came back with smooth clarity to the subject.

"Please understand, dear, that I am *not* talking about marriage—the beauty and joy and fruitful power of this dear union are a growing wonder to me. You know that—!"

I knew that. She made me realize it, with a praising heart, every day.

"No, this monogamous marriage of yours is distinctly right—when it is a real one. It is the making a business of it that I object to."

"You mean the women kept at housework?"

"That's part of it—about a third of it. I mean the whole thing: the men saddling themselves for life with the task of feeding the greedy thing, and the poor children heavily stamped with it before they can escape. That's the worst—"

She stopped at that for a little. So far she had not entered on the condition of women, or of children, in any thorough way. She had notes enough—volumes.

"What I'm trying to establish is this," she said slowly, "the connection between what seem to me errors in your social fabric, and the natural result of these in your political action. The family relation is the oldest—the democratic relation is the newest. The family relation demands close, interconnected love, authority and service. The democratic relation demands universal justice and good will, the capacity for the widest co-ordinate action in the common interest, together with a high individual responsibility. People have to be educated for this—it is not easy. Your homes require the heaviest drain on personal energy, on personal loyalty, and leave a small percentage either of feeling or action for the State."

"You don't expect everyone to be a statesman, do you?"

"Why not? Everyone must be—in a democracy."

"But we should not make better citizens if we neglected our homes, should we?"

"Does it make a man a better soldier if he stays at home—to protect his family? Oh, Van, dear, don't you see? These poor foolish fighting men are at least united, co-ordinated, making a common effort for a common cause. They are—or think they are—protecting their homes together."

"I suppose you mean socialism again," I rather sulkily suggested, but she took it very sweetly.

"We isolated Herlanders never heard of Socialism," she answered. "We had no German-Jewish economist to explain to us in interminable, and, to most people, uncomprehensible prolixity, the reasons why it was better to work together for common good. Perhaps 'the feminine mind' did not need so much explanation of so obvious a fact. We co-mothers, in our isolation, with a small visible group of blood relations (without any Father-Boss) just *saw* that our interests were in common. We couldn't help seeing it."

"Stop a bit, Sister," said I. "Are you insinuating that Mr. Father is at the bottom of the whole trouble? Are you going to be as mean as Adam and lay all the blame on him?"

She laughed gleefully. "Not quite. I won't curse him. I won't suggest ages of hideous injustice to all men because of the alleged transgression of one man. No, it is not Mr. Father I am blaming, nor his fatherhood—for that is evidently the high crown of physiological transmission." (Always these Herland women bowed their heads at what they called the holy mystery of fatherhood, and always we men were—well—not completely pleased.)

"But it does seem clear," she went on briskly, "that much mischief has followed from too much father. He did put himself forward so! He thought he was the whole thing, and motherhood—Motherhood!—was quite a subordinate process."

I always squirmed a little, in the back of my mind, at this attitude. All their tender reverence for fatherhood didn't seem in the least to make up for their absolutely unconscious pride in motherhood. Perhaps they were right—

"The dominance of him!" she went on. "The egoism of him! 'My name!'— and not letting her have any. 'My house—my line—my family'—if she had to be mentioned it was on 'the spindle side,' and when he is annoyed with her—what's that man in Cymbeline, Mr. Posthumous, wishing there was some way to have children without these women! It is funny, now, *isn't* it, Van?"

"It certainly is. Man or not, I can face facts when I see them. It is only too plain that 'Mr. Father' has grossly overestimated his importance in the part.

"Don't you think the American husband and father is a slight improvement on the earlier kind?" I modestly inquired. At which she turned upon me with swift caresses, and delighted agreement.

"That's the beauty and the wonder of your country, Van! You are growing swiftly and splendidly in spite of yourselves. This great thing you started so valiantly is sweeping you along with it, educating and developing as it goes. Your men are better, your women are freer, your children have more chance to grow than anywhere on earth."

"That's good to hear, my dear," I said with a sigh of relief. "Then why so gloomy about us?"

"Suppose everybody was entitled to a yearly income of five thousand dollars. Suppose most people averaged about five cents. Suppose a specially able, vigorous and well placed group had worked it up to $50...Why, Van—your superiority to less fortunate peoples is not worth mentioning compared to your inferiority to what you ought to be."

"Now we are coming to it," I sighed resignedly. "Pitch in, dear—give it to us—only be sure and show the way to help it."

She nodded grimly. "I will do both as well as I can. Let us take physical conditions first: With your numbers, your intelligence and mechanical ingenuity, your limitless materials, the United States should by now have the best roads on earth. This would be an immediate and progressive economic advantage, and would incidentally go far to solve other 'problems,' as you call your neglected work, such as 'unemployment,' 'the negro question,' 'criminality,' 'social discontent.' That there are not good roads in Central Africa does not surprise nor annoy me. That they are lacking in the United States is—discreditable!"

"Granted!" said I hastily. "Granted absolutely—you needn't stop on *that* point."

"That's only one thing," she went on serenely. "Here you are, a democracy—free—the power in the hands of the people. You let that group of conservatives saddle you with a constitution which has so interfered with free action that you've forgotten you had it. In this ridiculous helplessness—like poor old Gulliver—bound by the Lilliputians—you have sat open-eyed, not moving a finger, and allowed individuals—mere private persons—to help themselves to the biggest, richest, best things in the country. You know what is thought of a

338

housekeeper who lets dishonest servants run the house with waste and robbery, or of a King who is openly preyed upon by extortionate parasites—what can we think of a Democracy, a huge, strong, young Democracy, allowing itself to become infested with such parasites as these? Talk of blood-suckers! You have your oil-suckers and coal-suckers, water-suckers and wood-suckers, railroad-suckers and farm-suckers—this splendid young country is crawling with them—and has not the intelligence, the energy, to shake them off."

"But most of us do not believe in Socialism, you see," I protested.

"You believe in it altogether too much," she replied flatly. "You seem to think that every step toward decent economic health and development has been appropriated by Socialism, and that you cannot do one thing toward economic freedom and progress unless you become Socialists!"

There was something in this.

"I admit the Socialists are partly to blame for this," she went on, "with their insistent claims, but do you think it is any excuse for a great people to say: 'We have all believed this absurd thing because they told us so?'"

"Was it our—stupidity—that shocked you so at first?" I ventured.

She flashed a bright look at me. "How brilliant of you, Van! That was exactly it, and I hated to say so to you. How *can* you, for instance, let that little bunch of men 'own' all your anthracite coal, and make you pay what they choose for it? You, who wouldn't pay England a little tax on tea! It puzzled me beyond words at first. Such intelligence! Such power! Such pride! Such freedom! Such good will! And yet such Abyssmal Idiocy! That's what brought me around to the home, you see."

"We've wandered a long way from it, haven't we?"

"No—that's just the point. You should have, but you haven't. Don't you see? All these changes which are so glaringly necessary and so patently easy to make, require this one ability—*to think in terms of the community*...you only think in terms of the family. Here are men engaged in some absolutely social enterprise, like the railroad business, in huge groups, most intricately co-ordinated. And from the dividend-suckers to the road-builders, every man thinks only of his *Pay*,—of what he is to get out of it. 'What is a railroad?' you might ask them all. 'An investment,' says the dividend-sucker. 'A means of speculation,' says the Sucker-at-Large. 'A paying business," says the Corporate-Owner. 'A thing that pays salaries,' says the officer. 'A thing that furnishes jobs,' says the digger and builder."

"But what has all this to do with the Home?"

"It has this to do with it," she answered, slowly and sadly. "Your children grow up in charge of home-bound mothers who recognize no interest, ambition, or duty outside the home—except to get to heaven if they can. These home-bound women are man-suckers; all they get he must give them, and they want a good deal. So he says: 'The world is mine oyster,'— and sets his teeth in that. It is not only this relentless economic pressure, though. What underlies it and accounts for it all is the limitation of idea! You think Home, you talk Home, you work Home, where you should from earliest childhood be seeing life in terms of the community...You could not get much fleet action from a flotilla of canoes—with every man's first duty to paddle his own, could you....?"

"What do you want *done?*" I asked, after awhile.

"Definite training in democratic thought, feeling and action, from infancy. An economic administration of common resources under which the home would cease to be a burden and become an *unconscious* source of happiness and comfort. And, of course, the socialization of home industry."

Chapter VIII

More Diagnosis

Our study of American problems went on now with persistence. Ellador was as busy, as patient, as inexorably efficient as an eminent surgeon engaged in a first-class operation. We studied together, she wrote carefully, from time to time, and read me the results—or part of them. And we talked at all hours, not only between ourselves, but with many other persons, of all kinds and classes.

"I've seen the ruined lands that were once so rich," she said one day, "and the crowded lands now being drained by a too thick population. (Those blind mothers! Can't they once think of what is going to happen to their children?)

"But here I see land in plenty, carelessly skimmed and left, or not even skimmed, just lying open to the sun, while your squeezed millions smother in the cities.

"You are used to it, to you it is merely a fact—accepted without question. To an outsider, it seems as horribly strange as to see a people living in cellars thick and crawling, while great airy homes stand empty above.

"My study is mainly to get at your state of mind, to understand, if possible, what mysterious ideas and convictions keep you so poor, so dirty, so crowded, so starved, so ill-clothed, so unhealthy, so unhappy, when there is no need of it."

"Now look here, Ellador! That's rather strong, isn't it? You surely don't describe the American people that way."

Then she produced another of those little groups of assorted statistics she was so fond of. She gave the full wealth of the country—as at present administered, and showed that it ought to give nearly $2,000 to each of us. "That is per capita, you see, Van, not per family. For a family of five, that would be nine or ten thousand—not a bad nest egg, besides what they earn."

Then she showed me the estimate made by our latest scientific commission of inquiry, that "fully one-half of our wage earners do not receive incomes sufficient to maintain healthful conditions of living." A World Almanac was at hand, and she pointed out on page 228 the summary of manufactures.

"Here you have enough to show how people live in this splendid country, Van. See here—'Average number of wage earners 6,615,046. Wages,

$3,427,038,000'—which, being divided, gives to each $518 plus—less than $520 a year, Van. Less than $10 a week—to keep a family—average family, five; $104 a year, $2 a week apiece for Americans to live on. And you know what food and rent costs. Of course they are not healthy—how could they be?"

I looked at the figures, uncomfortably. She gave me a few more.

"Salaried employees average $1,187 plus—that's a bit more than twice as much. About $4.40 a week, apiece, for Americans to live on."

"How much do you want them to have?" I asked a little irritably; but she was sweetly patient, inquiring, "How much would you be willing to live on—or how little, rather? I don't mean luxuries; I mean a decent, healthy life. Think you could do it on $4.40? Think you could do it on less than $6 say? Rent, board, clothing, car fares?"

Now I had spent a few months during my youth, living on a modest salary of $10 a week, and remembered it as a period of hardship and deprivation. There was $6 a week for board, 60 cents for carfare, 90 cents for my modest 15-cent lunches, 70 cents for tobacco—it left $1.80 for clothing and amusements, if any. I had thought it hard enough at that time to endure life on $10 a week for one. It had never occurred to me that the working man had to keep five on it. And here were six million of them who did, it appeared, and a lot of clerks who were only twice as well off.

"Ten dollars a week, for each person is little enough for decent living in this country, isn't it, Van? That would call for $50 a week for a family of five—$2,600 a year."

"But, my dear girl, the business would not stand it! You ask impossibilities!" I protested. She turned to her figures again.

"Here is the 'value added by manufacture'!" she said. "That must be what these workers produce, isn't it? $8,530,261,000. Now we'll take out these wages—it leaves $5,103,223,000. Then we'll take out the salaries, that leaves $4,031,649,000. Where does that go? Here is a four-billion dollar item—for services—whose?

"It must be those proprietors and firm members—only 273,265 of them—let's see, out of that four billion they get nearly $16,000 a year each. Don't you think it is a little—remarkable, Van? These services are valued at fourteen times as much as those of the salaries of employees and thirty times as much as the workers?"

"My dear girl," I said, "You have the most wonderful mind I ever lived with—ever met. And you know more than I do about ever so many things.

342

But you haven't touched economics yet? There are laws here which you take no notice of."

And I told her of the iron law of wages, the law of supply and demand, and others. She listened, giving careful attention.

"You call them 'laws,'" she said, presently, "are they laws of nature?"

"Why, yes," I agreed slowly, "of human nature acting under economic conditions."

"Surely the economic conditions are those of soil, climate, materials available, the amount and quality of strength, intelligence, scientific and mechanical development."

"Why, of course; but also there are these I have mentioned."

"Do you mean to tell me that it is a 'law of nature' for men to arrange their working and paying so that half the people shall be unhealthy? Do you really believe for a minute that this has to be so?"

But I was not prepared to repudiate all my education in economics at once, and doggedly pointed out, "It is a law of human nature."

Then she smiled at me with cheerful derision. I am glad to say that Ellador had risen above the extreme horror and pain of her first year among us, and was able to smile at what used to bring distress.

"It must be male human nature," quoth she, "we have no such 'law' in Herland."

"But you are all sisters," I said rather lamely.

"Well, you are all sisters and brothers—aren't you? Of course, Van, I know the difference. You have had your long history of quarrels and hatred, of inimical strange races, of conquest and slavery. It looks to me as if the contempt of the rich for the poor was a lineal descendant of that of the conqueror for the vanquished. A helpless enemy, a slave, a serf, an employee, and the state of mind coming along unchanged. But the funny part of it is that in this blessed land, with more general good will and intelligence than I have found anywhere, you should have allowed this old foolishness to hang on so long.

"Now, Van, dear, don't you see how foolish it is? This is a democracy. To be efficient, that demands a competent electorate, doesn't it?"

"Why, we know that," I answered, with some heat. "Those forefathers of ours that you so scoff at knew that much. That's why we have our great system of free public education—from kindergarten to college."

"And in 1914," said Ellador, turning to that handy volume again, "you had a public school primary enrollment of 17,934,982. A drop in high school enrollment down to 1,218,804—only one out of seventeen to get that far; and another drop to a college enrollment of 87,820. That free public education does not seem to go far does it?"

"But most of these children have to go to work early—they cannot take the time for more education, even if they could afford it."

"Does going to work early make them better citizens?"

"I dare say it does—some of the college graduates aren't any too good."

She shook her head at this, and confronted me with more figures. The college graduates certainly made a pretty good showing, and the terrible dregs, as she called the criminals and paupers, were not as a rule well educated.

"Do look at it reasonably, Van. I'm not trying to be unpleasant and I know I am ignorant of this 'economics' you talk of. But I'm looking as a stranger, of average intelligence, and with the additional advantage of an entirely different background at your country. You have natural advantages as good as earth affords. You have plenty of room. You have good racial stocks in large variety. You have every element of wealth. You have a good many true principles to go on. And yet—in the time you have been at it—in a hundred and forty years, you have built up the most crowded cities on earth, robbed, neglected and wasted the soil, made politics a thing of shame, developed private wealth that is monstrous and general poverty that is—disgraceful."

There was some silence after this.

It was extremely unpleasant. It was quite true.

"I know it is better here than in Europe," she went on, "I know that, with all your imperfections and errors you are better off than Germany—poor, mistaken Germany, so authoritatively perfect that she became proud; so proud that she became hateful, so hateful that it will take generations before the world can forgive her. You are not lost, Van—not a bit of it. But surely you can see that it is as I say?"

I could. Who couldn't?

"It is very easy for me to show what could be done, how easily and how soon. In ten years' time you could see an end of poverty, in twenty of crime, in thirty of disease. This whole great land could be as fair and clean and healthy and happy as my own—and vastly richer in products. Even

344

richer in happiness—with this heaven of married love to crown all else!"

She took my hand at the end and was still for a little.

"But for the most part—you don't have that," she continued evenly. "Van, I've been reading. I've been talking with doctors and many wise persons, and, it seems to me, dear, that you don't appreciate marriage."

I had to grin at that. This Herlander, who never saw a man till a few years ago, and had only married one of them. Moreover, I recalled, with a momentary touch of bitterness, that we were not "married people" at present—not in the usual sense. And then I was ashamed. I had accepted my bargain, such as it was, with open eyes; I had had all this time of unbroken, happy love, living so near a beautiful woman who gave me comfort and rest and calmness in some mysterious, super-sexual way, and keeping always the dear hope of a further fulfilment.

We had had no misunderstandings, no quarrels, and while I own that at first there had been periods of some unease for me, they were as nothing to our larger joy. It was as if, in clean vigor and activity, I was on an expedition with a well-loved sister—a sister dearer and sweeter than all the world, and with that background of a still happier future.

From this I looked at the world about me, seeing it as I had never seen it before, as it was. All the eager, fresh young boys and girls, all the happy, hopeful lovers, the marriages, and then, how painful a proportion of miserable failures. It was not only the divorces, not only the undivorced ill-doing; but the low order of happiness among so many.

That was what Ellador had in mind, with her fine sense of personal relationship. She did not know as much as I of the deeper gulf; what she meant was the dreary level.

"You make fun of it, you know," she went on. "It's a joke, a question for discussion—'Is Marriage a Failure?'—it is being discussed by many, ignored, made the subject of cheap talk."

"There are many who feel this," I answered her. "There is great effort to check the divorce evil, to preserve the sanctity of marriage."

Another thing my Ellador had learned, I think from being in America, was a spice of mischief. It became her well. With a mind as keen and powerful as hers, lack of humor would have been a serious loss.

"Have they tried benzoate—to preserve the sanctity of marriage?" she inquired. "Or is it enough to be hermetically sealed—under pressure—at the boiling point?"

I'm not much of a cook, nor is she for that matter, but I could smile at that, too.

"Without going into the marriage question at present, I wish you would go on with your Herland view of economics," I told her. "It looks to me as if you wanted to adopt socialism at once. And that's out of the question—most of us don't believe in it."

"Most of you don't seem to understand it, it seems to me," she answered. "If you mean by socialism, the principles of socialism—yes, that is the way we manage in Herland. The land is ours, visibly. We never divided it up into little bits as you people have. What we raised on it and out of it was ours, too, visibly—when there was little, we had little—children first, of course—and now that there is a balanced plenty why, of course, every one has enough."

"Had you no selfish women? No ambitious women? No super-women trying to get ahead of the others?"

"Why of course we had; still have some few."

"Well—how did you manage them?"

"Why that is what government is for isn't it?" she replied. "To preserve justice, to prevent the selfish and ambitious from injuring the others, to see to it that production is increased and distribution fairly carried on."

"We say that government is the best that governs least," I told her.

"Yes, I've heard that. Do any of you really believe it? Why do you believe it? How can you?"

"But look at Germany!" I cried; "there you see what comes of too much government."

"I wish you would look at Germany—every other nation might study Germany with great improvement," she replied, a little hotly. "Just because Germany has gone criminally insane, that is no reason for underrating all the magnificent work she has done. The attitude of some people toward Germany is like that of your lynchers. Nations that do wrong are not to be put to death with torture, surely! Like individual criminals, they need study—help—better conditions. I think Germany is one of the most glorious, pathetic, awful examples of—of the way our world works," she concluded solemnly.

"They wouldn't thank you for calling them pathetic," I said.

"No; I know they wouldn't. Their weakest spot is their blind pride. I find

346

all of your nations are proud—it's easy to see why."

"Well—if you see it easily, do tell us."

"Why, it's one of your laws of nature," she explained, with a twinkle in her eye. "You know something of perspective? The farther a thing is away from you the smaller it is, the less well you can see it, the less you are able to understand it, and by the 'law of nature' you look down upon it! That was the reason when nations were really far apart and separate. Now that you are all so close together you should have long since come to see and know and understand and work together—that means love, you know. But to prevent that are two big, unnecessary, foolish things. One is ignorance—the common ignorance which takes the place of distance. The man next door is as strange as the man in the antipodes—if you don't know him.

"The nations of the earth don't try to understand each other, Van. Then as a positive evil you have each built up for yourselves an artificial wall of brag and boastfulness. Each nation ignores the other nations and deliberately teaches its helpless children that It alone is the greatest and best—

"Why, Van—" The tears always came when she touched upon children, but this time they vanished in a flashing smile.

"Children!" she said. "Anything more like the behavior of a lot of poor, little, underbred children it would be hard to find. Quarrelsome, selfish, each bragging that he can 'lick' the others—oh, you poor dears! How you do need your mother! And she's coming at last."

"I suppose you think she will solve these economic problems forthwith."

"Why not, Van? Look here, dear—why can't you people see that—" (Here she spoke very slowly as if she were writing some A, B, C's very large on a blackboard.) "There is nothing to prevent human beings in this historic period from being healthy, beautiful, rich, intelligent, good—and happy."

"That's easy to say, my dear," I remarked, rather glumly. "I wish it was true."

"Why isn't it true?" she demanded. "Do you think Satan prevents you, or God, or what? Don't you see—can't you see? God's on the side of all the growing good of life. God's with you—what's against?"

"I suppose it is only ourselves," I agreed; "but that's something. Of course I know what you mean. We could, conceivably, do and be all that you say, but there's an 'if—an 'if' as big as all the world. If we knew what to do,

347

and IF we would act together."

"That is not half such an obstacle, as you think, Van. You know enough now easily to set everything going in the right direction. It doesn't have to be done by hand, you know. It does itself, give it a chance. You know what to do for one baby, to give it the best chance of health, full growth and happy usefulness, don't you?"

"Well, yes; we do know that much," I admitted.

"Very well then, do it for all of them, and you lift the whole stock; that's easy. You know how good roads, waterways and efficient transportation build up the wealth of a community. Very well. Have them everywhere."

She was splendid in her young enthusiasm—that keen, strong face, all lit and shining with love for the naughty world and wise suggestions for its betterment. But I could not catch the fire.

"I don't want to dash your hopes, my dear," I told her gently. "You are, in a sense, correct; even I could make a plan that would straighten things out quite a bit. The difficulty is to get that plan accepted by the majority. No king is going to do it, and in a democracy you have to convince more than half the people; that's slow work."

She sat silent, looking out of our high hotel window, and thinking of what I said.

"It isn't as if our minds were empty," said I, "we don't think we're ignorant. We think we know it all. Only the wise are eager to learn, I'm afraid, and for everything you tell the people as truth there are no end of other teachers to tell them something else. It's not so easy as it looks. There's more excuse for us than would appear at first sight."

. . . . .

We had made special studies as we traveled about, of different industries and social conditions. Now we plunged more deeply into economics, politics and the later researches of sociology and social psychology. Ellador became more and more interested. Again and again she wished for the presence and help of certain of her former teachers in Herland.

"How they would love it," she said. "They wouldn't be tired or discouraged. They'd just plunge in and find a way to help in no time. Even I can see something."

From time to time she gave me the benefit of the things she saw.

"The reason we had so little trouble is that we had no men, I'm sure of that.

348

The reason you have made so much progress is because you have had men, I'm sure of that, too. Men are splendid, but—" here was a marked pause, "the reason you had so much trouble is not because of the men, but because of this strange dissociation of the men and women. Instead of the smooth, helpful interrelationship, you have so much misery. I never knew—of course not, how could I?—that there could be such misery. To have two kinds of people, evidently adapted for such perfect co-ordinate action— once in a while you see it, even now—and then to have them hurt and degrade one another so."

Another time she propounded this suggestion:

"Can't some of your big men, and women, of course, work out an experiment station in methods of living—an economic and social unit, you know—to have for reference, to establish facts, as you do in other things?"

"What do you mean?" I asked her. "Compulsory eugenics and a co-operative colony?"

"Don't tease me, Van. I'm not as foolish as that. No, what I mean is something like this. Take a given piece of ground, most anywhere, and have it surveyed by competent experts to see how much it could produce under the best methods known. Then see how many persons it would take to do the necessary work to ensure that production. Then see by what arrangements of living those persons could be kept healthful and happy at the least expense. For that unit you'd have something to go on—some definite proof of what the country could do."

"You leave out the human side of the problem, my dear. We have so many different causes for living where and how and as we do. Our people are not pawns on a chessboard; they can't be managed to prove theories."

It was no wonder that Ellador, for all her wonderful clarity of vision, her exceptionable advantage of viewpoint, should become somewhat overwhelmed in our sociological morass. The very simplicity and ease of living to which she was accustomed made her see a delusive simplicity and ease in attempting to solve our problem.

"How about the diagnosis?" I suggested. "Suppose we merely consider symptoms awhile. What strikes you most forcibly in the way of symptoms?"

"Physically?"

"Yes, physically, first."

"As to the land—neglect, waste, awful, glaring waste," she answered promptly. "It makes me sick. It makes me want to cry. As a mere wilderness, of course, it would be interesting, but as a wilderness with a hundred million people in it, and such able people, I don't know whether it is more laughable or horrible. As to the water, neglect and waste again, and hideous, suicidal defilement.

"As to means of communication—" words failed her. "You know how I feel about your roads, and the city streets are worse. One would think to see the way you rip up and lay down in your cities that an organized group of human habitations had never been built before. Such childish experiments. Over and over and over. Why a city, Van, is no new thing. It can be foreseen and planned for. That was done in ancient Egypt, in Assyria, and today, with all you know, with the whole past to learn from— Van, as I come into your cities, by rail, and see the poor, miserable, dirty, unhealthy things it makes me feel almost as badly as those European battlefields. They are at least trying to kill one another; you are doing it unconsciously. A city should be the loveliest thing. Why you remember— oh, Van!"

For the moment homesickness overcame her. I did remember. From that first low flight of ours, soaring across that garden land, that fruitful park and pleasure ground, with its little villages, so clean, so bright in color, so lovely in arrangement, lying here and there among the green, all strung together by those smooth, shaded roads and winding paths. From that bird's-eye view to my later, more intimate knowledge, I recalled them with deep admiration and with a painful envy. They had no slums—not in all Herland; they had no neglected, dirty places; they had no crowded tenements; they lived in houses, and the houses were in gardens, and their manufacturing, storing and exchanging—all the larger business of life was carried on in buildings, if possible even more lovely than their dwelling houses. It could be done—I had seen it.

"I don't wonder you cry, my dear."

Chapter IX

"This is the most fascinating study," Ellador announced one day. "At home we are so smoothly happy, so naturally growing, that it's almost unconscious. Here, if you have not happiness, you have a call on all your sympathy, all your energy, all your pride—you have such a magnificent Opportunity.

"I've gone deeper into my diagnosis, dear," she continued, "and have even some prescriptions. Be patient while I generalize a little more. You see this 'case' has so many diseases at once that one has to discriminate a bit.

"Here is the young new-made country, struggling out of the old ones to escape their worst diseases, breaking loose from monarchy, from aristocracy, and feudalism with its hereditary grip on land and money, on body and soul, and most of all, from that mind-crushing process of Enforced Belief which had kept the whole world back so long.

"Note—"she interpolated. "It is easy to see that as man progresses in social relation he needs more and more a free strong agile mind, with sympathetic perception and understanding and the full power of self-chosen action. The Enforced Belief in any religion claiming to be Final Truth cripples the mind along precisely those lines, tending to promote a foolish sense of superiority to other believers or disbelievers; running to extremes of persecution; preventing sympathy, perception, and understanding, and reducing action to mere obedience.

"There," she said cheerfully. "If America had done nothing but that— establish the freedom of thought and belief—she would have done world-service of the highest order."

"The Greeks allowed it, didn't they? And the Romans?" I offered.

"If they did it was 'a lost art' afterward," she replied. "Anyhow you did it later, and you have gone on doing it—splendidly.

"Then, in establishing the beginning of a democracy you performed another great service. This has not progressed as successfully, first because of its only partial application, second because you did not know it needed to be earnestly studied and taught—you thought you had it once and for all just by letting men vote, and third because it has been preyed upon by both parasites and diseases. In the matter of religion you threw off an evil restriction and let the mind grow free—a natural process. In the matter of government you established a social process, one requiring the utmost knowledge and skill. So it is no wonder the result has been so poor.

351

"Prescription as to government:

"A. Enfranchisement of all adult citizens. You have started on this.

"B. Special training—and practice—in the simpler methods and principles of democratic government as far as known, for all children, with higher courses and facilities for experiment and research for special students. You are beginning to do this already.

"C. Careful analysis and reports on the diseases of democracy, with applied remedies, and as careful study of the parasites affecting it—with sharp and thorough treatment. Even this you are beginning."

"A little severe on the parasites, aren't you?" I asked.

"It is time you were severe on them, Van. I'm no Buddhist—I'm a forester. When I see trees attacked by vermin, I exterminate the vermin if I can. My business is to raise wood, fruit, nuts—not insects."

"Except of course when the mulberry tree is sacrificed to the silk worms," I suggested, but she merely smiled at me.

"You need to transfer to your democracy the devotion you used to have for your kings," she went on. "To kill a common man was murder—to kill a king was regicide. You have got to see that for one man to rob another man is bad enough; for a man to rob the public is worse; but to rob the public *through the government* is a kind of high treason which—if you still punished by torture—would be deserving of the most excruciating kind. As it is you have allowed the practice to become so common that it is scarcely condemned at all—you do not even call it robbery; you call it 'graft'—or 'pork'—or a 'plum tree'—or some such polite term."

Of course I knew all this—but I never had felt it as anything particularly dreadful.

"Don't you see," she went on. "The government is the social motor system. By means of it society learns, as a baby learns, to check some actions and to make others. If your government is sick, you are paralyzed, weakened, confused, unable to act.

"In practical instance your city governments are frequently corrupt from the policemen up. Therefore when, with infinite labor, the public feeling has been aroused to want something done, you find that the machinery to do it with won't work. What you do not seem to realize at all is that the specific evil you seek to attack is not nearly so serious as the generic evil which makes your whole governmental system so—so—"

"Groggy," I suggested with a wry smile.

"Yes—that's about it. As weak and slow and wavering as a drunken man."

"Remedy," I demanded, "remedy?"

"Why that comes under 'C' in those I just gave," she said. "It needs full study and careful experiment to decide on the remedies. But here is what might be done at once: A report be made which should begin with a brief survey of the worst cases of governmental corruption in other countries, past and present. Not only in general, but with specific instances, people called by name with their crimes clearly shown. What such and such a person cost his country. How such decisive battles were lost because of such crippling disorders in the government. Parallel made between conspicuous traitors already recognized and this kind. Report now brought to our own country with both summary and instances. Our waterways described, what has been done, legitimately, to improve them, and what has been done, illegitimately, to hinder, pervert, and prevent right government action. History of our River and Harbor Bills given, and brought down to date, with this last huge 'steal' now accomplished—and not even rebuked! Names should be given—and names called! The congressmen and senators concerned, and the beneficiaries in the localities thus nefariously fattened.

"This kind of thing could be put simply and briefly so that the children could understand. They should be taught, early and steadily, how to judge the men who corrupt the very vitals of their country. Also how to judge the lazy shirks who do not even vote, much less study how to help the country."

"It needs—it needs a new kind of public opinion, doesn't it?" I ventured.

"Of course it does, but new public opinion has to be made. It takes no great genius to recognize a thief and a traitor, once he is shown up; but yours are *not* shown up."

"Why, Ellador—I'm sure there's a lot about this in the papers—"

She looked at me—just looked at me—and her expression was like that of an over-ripe volcano, firmly suppressed.

"For Heaven's sake! Let it out, Ellador. Say it quick and say it all—what's the matter with the papers!"

She laughed. Fortunately she could laugh, and I laughed with her.

"I couldn't say it all—under ten volumes," she admitted, "but I'll say some of it. This is a special department—I must begin again.

"This whole matter of societies, parasites and diseases is intensely

353

interesting. We in Herland, being normal, have not realized our society much, any more than a healthy child realizes her body."

I noticed that Ellador and her sisters always said "she" and "her" as unconsciously as we say "he" and "his." Their reason, of course, is that all the people are shes. Our reason is not so justifiable.

"But the rest of the world seems to be painfully conscious of its social body—without being able to help it much. Now you know there are diseases and diseases, some much preferable to others. In their degree of danger they vary much, and in what they are dangerous to. One might better have a very sick leg than an even partly sick heart or brain. Rheumatism for instance is painful and crippling, but when it reaches the heart it becomes fatal. Some creatures cannot have certain diseases for lack of material; one does not look for insanity in an angleworm, or neurasthenia in a clam.

"Society, as it has developed new functions, has developed new diseases. The daily press is one of the very newest social functions—one of the very highest —one of the most measureless importance. That is why the rheumatism of the press is worse than rheumatism of the farm, or the market."

"Rheumatism of the press?"

"Yes—that's a poor figure perhaps. I mean any serious disease is worse there than in some lower or less important function. Look at the whole thing again, Van. Society, in the stage of democracy, needs to be universally informed, mutually sympathetic, quick and strong to act. For this purpose it must introduce machinery to develop intelligence, to supply information, to arouse and impart feeling, to promote prompt action. The schools are supposed to train the intelligence, but your press is the great machine through which the democracy is informed, aroused, and urged to act. It is the social sensorium. Through it you see and hear and feel—collectively. Through it you are incited to act—collectively. It is later and by that much higher than the school and the church. It is the necessary instrument of democracy."

"Admitted, all admitted. But isn't that our general belief, dear, though perhaps not so clearly put?"

"Yes, you seem to think a great deal of your press—so much so that you cannot see, much less cure, its diseases."

"Well—you are the doctor. Pitch in. I suppose you know there are many and fierce critics of 'our sensational press' and 'our venal press.'"

"Oh yes, I have read some of the criticisms. They don't touch it."

"Go on, and touch it yourself, Sister—I'm listening."

She was too serious to be annoyed at my light manner.

"It's like this," she said slowly. "This great new function came into being in a time when people were struggling with what seemed more important issues,—were, perhaps. In Europe it has become, very largely, a tool of the old governments. Here, fearing that, it has been allowed to become the tool of individuals, and now of your plutocratic powers. You see you changed your form of government but failed to change your ideas and feelings to go with it. You allow it to go on over your heads as if it were a monarchy and none of your business. And you jealously refuse to give it certain necessary tools, as if it were a monarchy and would misuse them. What you have got to learn is to keep your government the conscious determined action of the majority of the people, and see that it has full power. A democracy is *self*-government, the united self of the people. Is that self control the best that self-controls the least?"

"Do you want a government-owned press?" I inquired. "We see that in Europe—and do not like it."

"You mean a monarchy-controlled press, do you not? No, I do not mean anything like that. You should have a press with democratic control, surely, and that means all the people, or at least the majority of them. What you have now is a press controlled by starkly mercenary motives of individuals, and the more powerful purposes of your big 'interests.'"

"What are you going to *do*—that's what I want to know. Lots of people criticize our press, but no one seems able to suggest the better method. Some propose endowment; we must have freedom of expression."

"You mustn't expect too much of me, Van. I can see the diseases easier than the cures, of course. It seems to me that you could combine perfect freedom of opinion, comment, idea, with the most authoritative presentation of the facts."

"Do you think a government-run paper could be trusted to give the facts correctly?"

"If it did not there would be heavier charges against it than could be survived over election. What you have not recognized yet is the social crime of misrepresenting the facts. Your papers lie as they please."

"We have our libel laws—"

"I didn't say libel—I said lie. They lie, on whichever side they belong, and there is no penalty for it."

I laughed, as an American would. "Penalty for lying! Who's going to throw the first stone?"

"Exactly. That's the awful part of it, Van. Your people are so used to public lying that you don't mind. You are paralyzed, benumbed, calloused, to certain evils you should be keenly alive to. There are plenty of much less dangerous things you make far more noise about. You see the press is suffering from a marked confusion of function. It makes all its proud claims for freedom and protection as an 'expression of public opinion,' as 'a medium of information,' and then makes its main business the cheapest kind of catering to prejudices, and to a market—the market of the widest lowest popular taste for literary amusement. Why does 'the palladium of your liberties' have to carry those mind-weakening, soul-degenerating 'comics'? They are neither information nor opinion—only bait."

"The people would not buy the papers if they were not amusing."

"What people would not? Wouldn't you?"

"Oh, I would, of course; I want to know the news; I mean the lower classes."

"And these 'lower classes,' so low that they take no interest in the news of the day and have to be given stuff suited to imbeciles, imbeciles with slightly criminal tastes—are they a large and permanent part of your democracy?"

"You mean that we ought to put out decent papers and see that the people are educated up to them?"

"Why not?"

I was trying to see why not, but she went on:

"If your papers were what they ought to be, they could be used in the schools, should be so used. Every boy and girl in the high school should take the Current Events course. Each day they should be required to read the brief clear summary of *real* news which would not be a long task, and required to state what seemed to them most important, and why.

"This array of 'crimes and casualties' you print is not *news*—it is as monotonous as the alphabet. All that needs is a mere list, a bulletin from the sick chamber of society, interesting only to the specialist. But the children should be taught to see the world move—every day; to be interested, to feel responsible. People educated like that wouldn't need to be baited with foul stuff to read the papers."

For the life of me I couldn't see anything the matter with this. If we can trust our government with the meteorological reports why not with the social ones?

"The best brains, the best backing, the whole country watching," she continued,—"papers that gave the news—and people who could read them. Then your comment and opinion could be as free as it pleased—on the side. Anybody could publish all of that she wanted to. But why should private opinion be saddled on the public facts, Van?"

"All right; diagnosis accepted with reservations; remedy proposed too suspiciously simple. But go ahead—what else ails us? With every adult enfranchised, the newspapers reliable, our natural resources properly protected, developed and improved—would that do for a starter?"

"Not while half the people do not earn enough to be healthy."

I groaned. "All right. Let's get down to it. Bring on your socialism. Do you want it by evolution, or revolution, or both?"

She was not deceived by my mock pathos. "What is your prejudice against socialism, Van? Why do you always speak as if it were—slightly ridiculous?"

I considered for a moment, thoughtfully.

"I suppose it is on account of my college education, and the kind of people I've lived with most," I answered.

"And what is your own sincere view of it?"

That had to be considered too.

"Why—I suppose the theory is right enough," I began, but she stopped me to ask:

"What is the theory—as you see it?"

Then I was obliged to exhibit my limitations, for all I could produce was what I had heard other people say about it, what I could remember of various articles and reviews, mostly adverse, a fruitless excursion into the dogmatic mazes of Marx, and a most unfavorable impression of certain socialist papers and pamphlets I had seen.

"That's about what I find everywhere," she was good enough to say. "That is your idea of it; now, very honestly, what is your feeling about it—say it right out, please."

So without waiting to be careful and to see if my feelings bore any relation to my facts, I produced a jumble of popular emotions, to the effect that Socialism was a lazy man's paradise; that it was an effort of the underdog to get on top, that it was an unfair "evening down" of the rewards of superior ability with those of the inferior; that it was a class movement full of hatred and injustice, that nobody would be willing "to do the dirty work," and that "such a world wouldn't be worth living in, anyhow."

Ellador laughed merrily, both at this nondescript mass of current misconception, and at my guilty yet belligerent air, as who should say: "It may be discreditable, but that's the way I feel."

She sobered soon enough, and looked far past me—through me. "It's not you, Van dear," she said. "It's America talking. And America ought to be ashamed of itself. To have so little vision! To be so gullible! To believe so easily what the least study would disprove! To be so afraid of the very principles on which this nation rests!"

"This nation rests on the principle of individual liberty—not on government ownership," I protested.

"What individual liberty has the working man?" she countered. "What choice of profession has his ill-born, ill-fed, ill-clothed, ill-taught child? The thing you call 'free competition' is long past—and you never saw it go. You see ideas stay fixed in peoples' minds long after the facts have changed. Your industrial world is in a state of what Ghent called 'feudalism'—and he was right. It is like Europe under the robber barons, and your struggling trade unions are like the efforts of the escaping serfs in that period. It only takes a little history and economics to see the facts. The perplexing part of the problem, to me, is the dullness of the popular mind. You Americans are an intelligent people, and a somewhat educated people, but you can't seem to see things."

"Are we any blinder than other people, my lady? Do they recognize these glaring facts any better than we do?"

Ellador sat still a moment, running over her fresh clear view of the world, past and present.

"No," she said. "No other people is any better—in all ways—except New Zealanders perhaps. Yet ever so many countries are wiser in some particulars, and you—with all your advantages—haven't sense enough to see it. Oh I know you'll say the others don't see it either, but you ought to. You are *free*—and you are able to act when you do see. No, Van—there's no excuse for you. You had supreme advantages, you made a brave start, you established a splendid beginning, and then you sat back and bragged about your ancestors and your resources—and your prospects—and let the vermin crawl all over you."

Her eyes were grave, her tone solemn, her words most offensive.

"Look here, Ellador, why will you use that term. It's very disagreeable."

"What else can you call these people who hang like clusters of leeches on the public treasury, who hop like fleas to escape the law, who spin webby masses of special legislation in which to breed more freely, who creep and crawl on every public work that is undertaken, and fatten undisturbed on all private business? What do you call your 'sidewalk speculators' in theater-tickets, for instance—but vermin? Just to steal a ticket and go to see the play would be a clean manly thing to do compared to this. They are small ones, openly disgusting, yet you do nothing but grumble a little.

"To turn from little to big I want to know what you call your sleeping-car extortionists? What is the size limit of vermin, anyhow? I suppose if a flea was a yard long he would be a beast of prey wouldn't he?"

"You certainly are—drastic, my dear girl. But what have you got against the sleeping cars? I've always thought our service was pretty good."

She shook her head slowly, regarding me with that motherly patient expression.

"The resignation of the American public to its devourers is like that of— of a sick kitten. You remember that poor little lean thing we picked up, and had to drop, quick, and brush ourselves? Why, Van Jennings—don't you even know you are being *robbed*, to the bone, by that sleeping-car company? Look here, please—"

Then she produced one of those neat little sheets of figures I had so learned to respect. Most damaging things, Ellador's figures.

"Twelve double berths to a car, beside the 'stateroom,' or rooms which I won't count; twenty-four passengers, who have already bought a ticket on which they are entitled to transportation with accommodations in the day-coach. Usual price $5.00 for twenty-four hours. For this $5.00 the passenger receives by day a whole seat instead of a half one—unless there is a day crowd and then extra seats are cheerfully sold to other victims—I have seen sleeping-cars crowded to standing! By night he has a place to lie down—three by three by six, with a curtain for privacy."

"Well, but he is being carried on his journey all the time," I urged.

"So he is in the day-coach or chair-car. This money is not for transportation—that's paid for. It is for special accommodation. I am speaking of the kind of accommodation, and what is extorted for it. The night arrangements are what you know. Look at the price."

"Two dollars and a half isn't so much," I urged, but she pursued relentlessly.

"Wouldn't you think it was much, here, in this hotel, for a space of that size?"

I looked about me at the comfortable room in the first-class hotel where we were then lodged, and thought of the preceding night, when we had had our two berths on the car. Here was a room twelve by fourteen by ten. There were two windows. There was a closet and a bathroom. There was every modern convenience in furniture. There was a wide, comfortable bed. My room adjoined it, equally large and comfortable.

"This is $2.00 for twenty-four hours," she remarked. "That was $5.00."

"Sleeping cars are expensive to build," I remarked feebly.

"More expensive than hotels?" she asked. "The hotel must pay ground rent, and taxes."

"The sleeping cars are not always full," I urged.

"Neither are the hotels—are they?"

"But the car has to be moved—"

"Yes, and the railroad company pays the sleeping car for being moved," she triumphed.

I wanted to say something about service; tried to, but she made merry over it.

"They have one conductor for their string of sleepers, and as to porters— we mostly pay them, you know."

I did know, of course.

"This is how I have figured it," said Ellador. "Of course I don't know the exact facts about their business, and they won't tell, but look at it this way: Suppose they average twenty passengers per car—staterooms and all—at $5.00 a day; that's $100.00 a day income, $36,500.00 a year per car. Now they pay the porter about $30.00 a month, I understand, or less, leaving the public to do the rest. Each car's fraction of the conductor's wages wouldn't be more than $20.00, I should think; there's $50.00 a month, $600 a year for service. Then there is laundry work and cleaning—forty sheets— pillow-cases—towels—flat-work rates of course; and renovating at the end of the journey. I don't believe it comes to over—say $800.00 a year.

Then there is insurance, depreciation, repairs—"

"Look here, Ellador, where did you get up these technicalities? Talking with business men, I suppose—as usual?"

"Yes, of course," she agreed. "And I'm very proud of them. Well—I'll allow $1,600.00 a year for that. That is $3,000.00 for their running expenses. And remember they are paid something for running—I don't know how much. That leaves $33,500.00. I will magnanimously leave off that $3,500.00—for times when they carried fewer passengers—call it a clear income of $30,000.00 a year. Now that is 10 per cent of $300,000.00. You don't honestly suppose that one sleeping car costs three hundred thousand dollars—do you, Van?"

I did not. I knew better. Anybody knows better.

"If it costs $100,000 to build and fit a sleeping car," she went on calmly, "then they could charge about $1.75 for their berths, and still 'make money,' as you call it. If ten per cent is a legitimate 'profit,' I call the extra twenty per cent a grinding extortion. What do you call it?"

"Up to date I never called it anything. I never noticed it."

She nodded. "Exactly. You people keep quiet and pay three times what is necessary for the right to live. You are bled—sucked—night and day, in every direction. Now then, if these blood-suckers are beasts of prey—fight them, conquer them. If they are vermin—Oh, I know you don't like the word—but Van, what is your estimate of people who are willing to endure—vermin?"

Chapter X

Going about with Ellador among familiar conditions, and seeing things I never dreamed were there, was always interesting, though sometimes painful. It was like carrying a high-powered light into dark places. As she turned her mind upon this or that feature of American life it straightway stood out sharply from the surrounding gloom, as the moving searchlight of a river boat brings out the features of the shore.

I had known clever women, learned women, even brilliant women, a few. But the learned ones were apt to be bit heavy, the clever ones twinkled and capered like spangled acrobats, and the brilliant ones shone, indeed, like planets among stars, but somehow did not illuminate much.

Ellador was simple enough, modest enough. She was always keeping in mind how little she knew of our civilization, but what she saw she saw clearly and was able to make her hearers see. As I watched her, I began to understand what a special strength it was not to have in one's mind all the associate ideas and emotions ours are so full of. She could take up the color question, for instance, and discuss it dispassionately, with no particular sentiment, one way or the other. I heard her once with a Southern sociologist, who was particularly strong on what he called "race conflict."

He had been reading a paper at some scientific meeting which we attended, a most earnest paper, full of deep feeling and some carefully selected facts. He spoke of the innate laziness of the negro race, their inborn objection to work, their ineducability—very strong on this—but his deepest horror was "miscegenation." This he alluded to in terms of the utmost loathing, hardly mitigated by the statement that it was impossible.

"There is," he averred, "an innate, insuperable, ineradicable, universal race antipathy, which forever separates the negro from the white."

Ellador had her chance at him afterward, with quite a group about, and he was too polite or insufficiently ingenious to escape. First she asked him what was the market price of a good, ablebodied negro before the war; if it was not, as she had read, about a thousand dollars. To this he agreed unsuspectingly. She inquired, further, if there had not been laws in the slave States forbidding the education of negroes, and if there were not laws still forbidding their intermarriage with whites. To this he agreed also; he had to. Then she asked whether the sudden emancipation of the negro had not ruined many rich men; if the major part of the wealth of the South had not been in slaves and the products of their labor. Here again could be no denial.

"But," she said, "I do not understand, yet. If negroes can not or will not work, why was one worth a thousand dollars? And how could the owners have accumulated wealth from their inefficiency? If they could not learn anything, why was it necessary to make laws forbidding their education; and if there is this insuperable antipathy separating the races, why are the laws against miscegenation needed?"

He was quite naturally incensed. There were a good many of his previous hearers about, some of them looking quite pleased, and he insisted rather stormily that there was this deep-seated antipathy, and that every Southerner, at least, knew it.

"At what age does it begin?" she asked him. He looked at her, not getting the drift of her question.

"This innate antipathy," she pursued gently. "I have seen the Southern babies clinging to their black nurses most affectionately. At what age does the antipathy begin?"

He talked a good bit then, with much heat, but did not seem to meet the points she raised, merely reiterating much of what he had said before. Then she went on quite calmly.

"And your millions of mulattos—they appear, not only against the law, but against this insuperable antipathy?"

This seemed to him so unwomanly of her, that he made some hasty excuse and got away, but his position was upheld by another man, for a moment. His little speech was mainly emotion, there are such hot depths of feeling on this subject in the children of slave owners that clear reasoning is naturally hard to find. This man made a fine little oration, with much about the noble women of the South, and how he, or any man, would lay down his life to protect them against the faintest danger of social contact with the colored race, against the abomination of a proposal of marriage from a black man.

"Do you mean," said Ellador slowly, her luminous eyes on his, "that if black men were free to propose to white women, the white women would accept them?"

At this he fairly foamed with horror. "A white woman of the South would no sooner marry a black man than she would a dog."

"Then why not leave it to the women?" she inquired.

Neither of these men were affected, save in the way of deep annoyance, by Ellador's gentle questions, but many of her hearers were, and she,

363

turning that searchlight of hers on the subject, later announced to me that it seemed rather a long but by no means a difficult problem.

"About ten million negroes, counting all the mulattos, quadroons, octaroons and so on, to about ninety million whites," she said. "As a mere matter of interbreeding, following the previous habits of the white men, it could be worked out mathematically—how long it would take to eliminate the negro, I mean."

"But suppose there remains a group of negroes, that have race pride and prefer to breed true to the stock," I suggested. "What then?"

"If they are decent, orderly and progressive, there is no problem, surely. It is the degraded negro that is so feared. The answer to that is easy. Compulsory and efficient education, suitable employment at fair wages, under good conditions—why, don't you see, dear," she interrupted herself to say, "the proof that it is not impossible is in what has been accomplished already. Here you white people wickedly brought over the ocean a great lot of reluctant black ones, and subjected them to several generations of slavery. Yet in those few generations these previously savage people have made noble progress."

She reeled off to me a list of achievements of the negro race, which I found surprising. Their development in wealth, in industry, in the professions, even the arts, was, considering the circumstances, astonishing.

"All you have to do is to improve the cultural conditions, to increase the rate of progress. It's no problem at all."

"You are a wonder," I told her. "You come out of that little far away heaven of yours, and dip into our tangle of horror and foolishness, and as soon as the first shock is over, you proceed to administer these little doses of wisdom, as if a mere pill or two would set the whole world straight."

"It would," said Ellador, "if you'd take it."

"Do you mean that seriously?" I demanded.

"I do. Why not? Why, Van—you've got all the necessary ingredients for peace and happiness. You don't have to wait a thousand years to grow. You're *here*. It's just a little matter of—behaving differently."

I laughed. "Exactly, my dear. And in Herland, so far as I make out, you behave accordingly to your perceptions and decisions. Here we don't."

"No," she admitted, grudgingly, "You don't, not yet. But you *could*" she persisted, triumphantly. "You could in a minute, if you wanted to."

I ducked this large proposition, and asked her if she had an answer to the Jewish race question as simple as that of the negro.

"What's the question?" she countered.

"I suppose there's more than one question involved," I answered slowly, "but mine would be: why don't people like Jews?"

"I won't be severe with your question, Van, though it's open to criticism. Not all people feel this race prejudice. And I'll tell you frankly that this is a bigger wide spread. It has deeper roots than the other. It's older. I've looked into it—a little?"

I grinned. "Well, you young encyclopaedia, what did you discover?"

"I soon discovered that the very general dislike to this one people is not due to the religious difference between them and Christians; it was quite as general and strong, apparently, in very ancient times."

"Do you think it is a race feeling, then, an 'insuperable, ineradicable,' etc., antipathy."

"No," she said, "there are other Semitic and allied races to whom there is no general objection. I don't think it can be that. I have several explanations to suggest, of varying weight. Here's one of them. The Jews are the only surviving modern people that have ever tried to preserve the extremely primitive custom of endogenous marriage. Everywhere else, the exogenous habit proved itself best and was generally accepted. This people is the only one which has always assumed itself to be superior to every other people and tried to prevent intermarriage with them."

"That's twice you've said 'tried,'" I put in. "Do you mean that they have not succeeded?"

"Of course they haven't," she replied, cheerfully. "When people endeavor to live in defiance of natural law, they are not as a rule very successful."

"But, they boast the purity of their race—"

"Yes, I know they do, and other people accept it. But, Van, dear, surely you must have noticed the difference between, say, the Spanish and the German Jews, for instance. Social contract will do much in spite of Ghettos, but it hardly alters the color of the eyes and hair."

"Well, my dear, if it is not religion, nor yet race, what is it?"

"I have two other suggestions, one sociologic, one psychic. The first is this: In the successive steps of social evolution, the Jewish people seem not to have passed the tribal stage. They never made a real nation.

Apparently they can't. They live in other nations perforce."

"Why perforce?" I interrupted.

"Well, if they don't die, they have to live somewhere, Van. And unless they go and set up a new nation in a previously uninhabited country, or on the graves of the previous inhabitants, they have to live in other nations, don't they?"

"But they were a nation once," I urged.

"In a way,—yes. They had a piece of land to live on and they lived on it, as tribes, not as one people. According to their own account, ten out of twelve of these tribes got lost, somehow, and the others didn't seem to mind. No—they could not maintain the stage of social organization rightly called a nation. Their continuing entity is that of a race, as we see in far lesser instance in gypsies. And the more definitely organized peoples have, not a racial, but a sociological aversion to this alien form of life, which is in them, but not of them."

"But, Ellador, do not the modern Jews make good citizens in whatever country they are in?"

"They do, in large measure, wherever they are allowed," she agreed; "and both this difference and the old marriage difference would long ago have been outgrown but for the last one—the psychic one."

"Do you mean what that writer in *Blackwoods* said about Spain: 'There seems to be something Spanish in the minds of Spaniards which causes them to act in a Spanish manner?'"

She laughed. "All of that, Van, and a lot more." She stopped, looking away toward the far horizon. "I never tire of the marvel and interest of your mixed humanity" she resumed. "You see we were just *us*. For two thousand years we have been one stock and one sex. It's no wonder we can think, feel, act as one. And it's no wonder you poor things have had such a slow, tumultuous time of it. All kinds of races, all kinds of countries, all kinds of conditions, and the male sex to manage everything. Why, Van, the wonder is that before this last world-quake of war, you could travel about peaceably almost anywhere, I understand. Surely that ought to prove, once and for all how safe and quiet the world might be."

"But about the Jews?" I urged at last.

"Oh, yes. Well, dear, as I see it, people are moving on to a wide and full mutual understanding, with peace, of course, free trade and social intercourse and intermarriage, until everyone is what you call civilized.

Against this process stood first total ignorance and separation. Then opposing interests. Then opposing ideas. To-day it is ideas that do the most damage. Look at poor Europe. Every interest calls them together but their different mental content holds them apart. Their egregiously false histories, their patriomanias, their long-nursed hatreds and vengeances—oh it is pathetic."

"Yes—and the Jews?"

"Oh dear me, Van, they're only one people. I get so interested in the world at large that I forget them. Well, what the Jews did was to make their patriomania into a religion."

I did not get that and said so.

"It was poorly put," she admitted. "They couldn't be patriomaniacs without a fatherland, could they? But it was the same feeling at a lower stage, applied only to the race. They thought they were 'the chosen people'—of God."

"Didn't other races think the same thing? Don't they yet?" I urged.

"Oh in a way, they do—some of them. Especially since the Jews made a Bible of it. You see, Van, the combination was peculiar. The special talent of this race is in literary expression. Other races had their sorrows but could not utter them. Carthage had no Jeremiah; nor has Armenia."

She saw that I was impressed by this point.

"You have Greece in its sculpture, its architecture and its objective literature. Even Greek history is a story told by an artist, a description. Rome lives in its roads, I have read, as well as its arts and its power of social organization. Rome, if it could have survived its besetting sins, was a super-nation, the beginning of a real world people. Egypt, India,—they all have something, but none of them concentrated on literature as the Jews did, having no other social expression."

"Why Ellador, don't you call their religion anything? Haven't they lifted the world with great religious concepts?"

She smiled at me, that gentle warm, steady smile of hers. "Forgive an outsider, please. I know that the Christian religion rests on the Jewish books, and that it hard indeed to see around early teachings. But I have read your Bible carefully, and some little of the latest study and criticism upon it. I think the Christian races have helped the Jews to overestimate their religion."

"You've never said much about our various religions, my fair foreigner.

What do you really think about them?"

This she pondered carefully.

"It's a large subject to try to comment on in a few words, but I can say this—they are certainly improving."

I had to laugh. This was such faint praise for our highest institution.

"How do you measure them, O casual observer?"

"By their effect upon the people, of course. Naturally, each set of believers holds its own to be the All True, and as naturally that is impossible. But there is enough truth and enough good will in your religions if you would only use them, instead of just believing them."

"And do you not think, especially considering the time of its development, that the Jewish concept of one God, the Jewish ethical ideal, was a long step upward?"

"It was a step, certainly, but, Van, they did not think their God was the only one. He was just Theirs. A private tribal God, openly described as being jealous of the others. And as to their ethics and the behavior of the people—you have only to read their own books to see how bad it was. Van, no religion can be truly good where the initial doctrines are false, or even partly false. That utterly derogatory concept of a God who could curse all humanity because of one man's doing what he knew he would, a God so petty as to pick out one small people for no better reason than that they gave him some recognition, and to set his face against all the rest of his equally descended 'children'—can't you see how unethical, how morally degrading, such a religion must be?"

"It was surely better than others at the time," I insisted.

"That may be, but the others of that period have mercifully perished. They weren't so literary. Don't you see, by means of their tremendous art this people have immortalized their race egotism and their whole record of religious aspirations, mistakes and failures, in literature. That is what has given them their lasting place in the world. But the effect of this primitive religion, immortalized by art, and thrust upon the world so long, has been far from good. It has well-nigh killed Christianity, from its cradle. It has been the foundation of most of those hideous old wars and persecutions. With quotations from that Hebrew 'voice of God' the most awful deeds have been committed and sanctioned. I consider it in many ways a most evil religion."

"But we have, as you say, accepted it; so it does not account for the general dislike for which you were offering explanations."

"The last explanation was the psychic one," she went on. "What impresses me here is this: The psychic attitude of this people presents to all the other inhabitants of the world a spirit of concentrated pride. It rests first on the tribal animus, with that old endogenous marriage custom; and then on this tremendous literary-religious structure. One might imagine generations of Egyptians making their chief education a study of the pyramids, sphynxes and so on, or generations of Greeks bringing up their children in the ceaseless contemplation of the Acropolis, or the works of their dramatists; but with the Jews, as a matter of fact, we do see, century after century of education in their ancient language, in their ancient books, and everlasting study and discussion of what remote dead men have written. This has given a peculiar intensity to the Jewish character—a sort of psychic inbreeding; they have a condensed spirit, more and more so as time passes, and it becomes increasingly inimical to the diffused spirit of modern races. Look at the pale recent imitation of such a spirit given in Germany. They have tried in a generation or two to build up and force upon their people an intense national spirit, with, of course, the indwelling egotism essential to such an undertaking. Now, suppose all German national glory rested on a few sacred books; their own early writings imposed upon the modern world; and suppose that German spirit, even now so offensive to other nations, had been concentrated and transmitted for thousands of years. Do you think people would like them?"

I was silent a bit. Her suggestions were certainly novel, and in no way resembled what I had heard before, either for or against this "peculiar people."

"What's the answer?" I said at last. "Is it hopeless?"

"Certainly not. Aren't they born babies, with dear little, clean, free minds? Just as soon as people recognize the evil of filling up new minds with old foolishness, they can make over any race on earth."

"That won't change 'race characteristics,' will it?"

"No, not the physical ones," she answered. "Intermarriage will do that."

"It looks to me as though your answer to the Jewish question was—leave off being Jews. Is that it?"

"In a measure it is," she said slowly. "They are world-people and can enrich the world with their splendid traits. They will keep, of course, their high race qualities, their special talents and virtues, by a chosen, not an enforced, selection. Some of the noblest people are Jews, some of the

369

nicest. That can't be denied. But this long-nursed bunch of ancient mistakes—it is high time they dropped it. What is the use of artificially maintaining characteristics which the whole world dislikes, and then complaining of race prejudice? Of course, there is race prejudice, a cultural one; and all the rest of you will have to bring up your children without that. It is only the matter of a few generations at most."

This was a part of the spirit of Herland to which I was slow in becoming accustomed. Their homogeneous, well-ordered life extended its social consciousness freely, ahead as well as backwards; their past history was common knowledge, and their future development even more commonly discussed. They planned centuries ahead and accomplished what they planned. When I thought of their making over the entire language in the interests of childhood, of their vast field of cultural literature, of such material achievements as their replanting all their forests, I began to see that the greatness of a country is not to be measured by linear space, in extent of land, nor arithmetically by numbers of people, nor shallowly by the achievements of the present and a few left-overs, but by the scope of its predetermined social advance.

As this perception grew within me, it brought first a sense of shame for all the rest of the world, and even more intensely for my own country, which had such incomparable advantages. But after a little, instead of shame, which is utter waste, I began to see life as I never had before: as a great open field of work; in which we were quite free to do as we would. We have always looked at it as a hopeless tangle of individual lives, short, aimless threads, as blindly mixed as the grass stems in a haystack. But collectively, as nations, taking sufficient time, there was nothing we could not do. I told her of my new vision, and she was dumbly happy—just held my hand, her eyes shining.

"That's how to stand the misery and failure, isn't it?" I said. "That's how not to be discouraged at the awfulness of things; and the reason you take up these separate 'questions' so lightly is that none of them mean much alone. The important thing is to get people to think and act together."

"There's nothing on earth to hinder them, Van, dear, except what's in their heads. And they can stop putting it in, in the babies, I mean, and can put it out of their own, at least enough to get to work. They are beginning, you know."

She spoke most encouragingly, most approvingly, of the special efforts we were making in small groups or as individuals to socialize various industries and functions, but with far more fervor of the great "movements."

"The biggest of all, and closest related, are your women's movement and labor movement. Both seem to be swiftly growing stronger. The most inclusive forward-looking system is Socialism, of course. What a splendid vision of immediate possibilities that is. I can not accustom myself to your not seeing it at once. Of course, the reason is plain: your minds are full of your ancient mistakes, too; not so much racial and religious, as in beliefs of economic absurdities. It is so funny!"

It always nettled me a little to have her laugh at us. That she should be shocked and horrified at the world I had expected; that she should criticize and blame; but to have her act as though all our troubles were easily removable, and we were just a pack of silly fools not to set about it—this was irritating.

"Well, dear," she pursued pleasantly, "doesn't it look funny to you, like a man sleeping cold with good blankets at the foot of his bed; like Mr. Tantalus, quite able to get what he wanted, if he would only reach?"

"If what you said was so—" I began.

"And why isn't it, dear?"

"The trouble is, I think, in your psychology. You, as a free-minded Herlander, can not seem to see how helpless we are in our minds. All these ages of enforced belief have done something to us, I tell you. We can't change all in a minute."

"The worst thing that has been done to you is to fill your poor heads with this notion that you cannot help yourselves. Tell me, now, what is there to hinder you?"

"You had better be studying as to what does hinder us," I answered, "and explain it so that we can do something. We mean well. We are fairly well educated. We are, as you say, rich enough and all that. But we, up to date, seem unable to get together on any line of concerted action toward better living."

"I have been studying just that, Van, ever since I first came. Of course after I saw how things were, that was the only thing to do."

"Well?" I said, and again, "Well?"

She sat considering, turning over some books and papers that lay on the table beside her. A lovely picture she made, unique among the women of this land, she had the smooth rounded freedom of body we see in noble statues, and whatever her new friends tried to make her wear, she insisted upon a dress of such simplicity as did not contradict her natural lines and movements. Her face had changed, somewhat, in our two years of travel and study; there was a sadness in it, such as it never wore in Herland, such as I never seen in anyone while there; and for all her quiet courtesy, her gentle patience, her scientific interest and loving kindness, there was a lonely look about her, as of some albatross in a poultry yard.

To me she was even more tender and delicately sympathetic than in our first young happiness. She seemed to be infinitely sorry for me, though carefully refraining from expressing it. Our common experiences, our studying and seeing so much together, had drawn us very close, and for my own part I had a curious sense of growing detachedness from the conditions about me and an overwhelming attachment to her which transcended every other tie. It seemed as if my love for her as a human being, such love as a brother, a sister, a friend might feel, was now so much greater than my love of her as a woman, my woman, that I could not miss that fulfilment much while so contented in the larger relation.

I thought of the many cases I had known where the situation was absolutely reversed, where a man loved a woman solely because of sex desire, without ever knowing her nature as a person, without even wanting to.

I was very happy with Ellador.

Chapter XI

It was inevitable that my wife should take a large interest in Feminism. With that sweeping swiftness of hers she read a dozen or so of the leading —and misleading—books on the subject; spent some time in library work looking over files of papers and talked with all manner of people we met who had views on the matter. Furthermore, she thought about it.

As I grew more and more accustomed to seeing Ellador think, or at least to seeing the results of that process, I was sharply struck with the lack of thinking among people in general. She smiled sociably when I mentioned it.

"Why, yes, dear, that is largely what is the matter. You do not train your children to think—you train them not to. Your men think hard in narrow lines, just little pushing lines of their special work, or how to get richer, and your women—"

"Oh, come, let's have it!" I cried despairingly. "Whatever else you say or don't say you are always thinking about the women; I can fairly hear your brain click. And I'll tell you honestly, my dear, that I don't believe you can hurt me now, no matter how hard you hit them—or the men. It certainly has been a liberal education to live with you. Also I've had my time in Herland to show me the difference. I confess that as I now see this life of ours the women shock me, in some ways, more than the men. And I've been doing some reading as well as you, even some thinking. I suppose one thing that has made you so reticent about this is that you can't criticize the women without blaming the men. Perhaps it will encourage you if I begin to do the blaming."

She mildly said that perhaps it would seem more magnanimous, so I started in and found the case worse when stated at length than I had seen it in glimpses.

"Of course, there is no getting around Lester Ward," I began slowly. "No one can study biology and sociology much and not see that on the first physiological lines the female is the whole show, so to speak, or at least most of it. And all the way up she holds her own, even into early savagery, till Mr. Man gets into the saddle. How he came to do it is a mastery that I don't believe even you can explain."

"No," she agreed, "I can't. I call it 'The Great Divergence.' There is no other such catastrophic change in all nature—as far as I've been able to gather."

What Ellador had "gathered" in two years was perhaps not equal in detailed knowledge to the learning of great specialists, but she had a marvellous gift for selecting the really important facts and for arranging them. That was the trick—she did something with what she knew—not merely stored it.

"Well, he did take the reins, somehow," I resumed, "and we began our historic period, which is somewhat too large to be covered in an hour—by me. But in all this time, as far as I can make out, he has never been even fair to women, and has for the most part treated her with such an assortment of cruelty and injustice as makes me blush for my sex."

"What made you think so, Van? What first?"

"Why Herland first," I answered promptly. "Seeing women who were People and that they were People *because* they were women, not in spite of it. Seeing that what we had called 'womanliness' was a mere excess of sex, not the essential part of it at all. When I came back here and compared our women with yours—well, it was a blow. Besides, if I'd had no other evidence *You* would have shown me—just living with you, my Wonder Darling."

She looked at me with shining eyes, that look that was more than wife, more than mother, the illimitable loving Human look.

"What I have learned from you, Dearest; from our companionship without the physical intimacy of sex, is this; that Persons, two Persons who love each other, have a bigger range of happiness than even two lovers. I mean than two lovers who are not such companions, of course. I do not deny that it has been hard, very hard, sometimes. I've been disagreeable to live with—"

"Never!" she interpolated.

"—but somehow the more I loved you the less it troubled me. Now I feel that when we do reach that union, with all our love, with all the great mother purpose that is in your heart and the beginning of a sense of father purpose in mine, I'm sure that it will be only an incident in our love, our happiness, not the main thing."

She gave a long soft sigh of full content, still listening.

"All this makes me see the—limitations of our women," I continued, "and when I look for a reason there is only the conduct of men toward them. Cruelty? Why, my dear, it is not the physical cruelty to their tender bodies; it is not the shame and grief and denial that they have had to bear; those are like the 'atrocities' in warfare—it is the war itself which is wrong. The petted women, the contented women, the 'happy' women—these are perhaps the worst result."

374

"It's wonderful how clearly you see it," she said.

"Pretty plain to see," I went on. "We men, having all human power in our hands, have used it to warp and check the growth of women. We, by choice and selection, by law and religion, by enforced ignorance, by heavy overcultivation of sex, have made the kind of woman we so made by nature, that that is what it was to be a woman. Then we heaped our scornful abuse upon her, ages and ages of it, the majority of men in all nations still looking down on women. And then, as if that was not enough—really, my dear, I'm not joking, I'm ashamed, as if I'd done it myself—we, in our superior freedom, in our monopoly of education, with the law in our hands, both to make and execute, with every conceivable advantage—we have blamed women for the sins of the world!"

She interrupted here, eagerly—"Not *all* of you, Van dear! That was only a sort of legend with some people. It was only in the Jewish religion you think so much of that the contemptible lie was actually stated as a holy truth—and even God made to establish that unspeakable injustice."

"Yes, that's true, but nobody objected. We all accepted it gladly—and treated her accordingly. Well, sister—have I owned up enough? I guess you can't hurt my feelings any with anything you say about men. Of course, I'm not going into details, that would take forever, but just in general I can see what ails the women—and who's to blame for it."

"Don't be too hard on Mr. Man," she urged gently. "What you say is true enough, but so are other things. What puzzles me most is not at all that background of explanation, but what ails the women *now*. Here, even here in America, *now*. They have had some education for several generations, numbers of them have time to think, some few have money—I cannot be reconciled to the women, Van!"

She was so unusually fierce about it that I was quite surprised at her. I had supposed that her hardest feeling would be about men. She saw my astonishment and explained.

"Put yourself in my place for a moment, Van. Suppose in Herland we had a lot of—subject men. Blame us all you want to for doing it, but look at the men. Little creatures, undersized and generally feeble. Cowardly and not ashamed of it. Kept for sex purposes only or as servants; or both, usually both. I confess I'm asking something difficult of your imagination, but try to think of Herland women, each with a soft man she kept to cook for her, to wait upon her and to—'love' when she pleased. Ignorant men mostly. Poor men, almost all, having to ask their owners for money and tell what they wanted it for. Some of them utterly degraded creatures, kept

375

in houses for common use—as women are kept here. Some of them quite gay and happy—pet men, with pet names and presents showered upon them. Most of them contented, piously accenting kitchen work as their duty, living by the religion and laws and customs the women made. Some of them left out and made fun of for being left—not owned at all—and envying those who were! Allow for a surprising percentage of mutual love and happiness, even under these conditions; but also for ghastly depths of misery and a general low level of mere submission to the inevitable. Then in this state of degradation fancy these men for the most part quite content to make monkeys of themselves by wearing the most ridiculous clothes. Fancy them, men, with men's bodies, though enfeebled, wearing open-work lace underclothing, with little ribbons all strung through it; wearing dresses never twice alike and almost always foolish; wearing hats—" she fixed me with a steady eye in which a growing laughter twinkled—"wearing such hats as your women wear!"

At this I threw up my hands. "I can't!" I said. "It's all off. I followed you with increasing difficulty, even through the lace and baby ribbon, but I stop there. Men wear such hats! Men! I tell you it is unthinkable!"

"Unthinkable for such men?"

"Such men are unthinkable, really; contemptible, skulking, cowardly spaniels! They would deserve all they got."

"Why aren't you blaming the women of Herland for treating them so, Van?"

"Oh!" said I, and "Yes," said I, "I begin to see, my dear Herlander, why you're down on the women."

"Good," she agreed. "It's all true, what you say about the men, nothing could be blacker than that story. But the women, Van, the women! They are not dead! They are here, and in your country they have plenty of chance to grow. How can they bear their position, Van; how can they stand it another day? Don't they know they are *Women*?"

"No," said I slowly. "They think they are—women."

We both laughed rather sadly.

Presently she said, "We have to take the facts as we find them. Emotion does not help us any. It's no use being horrified at a—hermit crab—that's the way he is. This is the woman man made—how is she going to get over it?"

"You don't forget the ones who have gotten over it, do you? And all the splendid work they are doing?"

"I'm afraid I did for a moment," she admitted. "Besides—so much of their effort is along side lines, and some of it in precisely the wrong direction."

"What would you have them do?"

"What would you have those inconceivable men of Herland do?" she countered. "What would you say to them—to rouse them?"

"I'd try to make them realize that they were *men*," I said. "That's the first thing."

"Exactly. And if the smooth, plump, crazily dressed creatures answered 'A true man is always glad to be supported by the woman he loves' what would you say to that?"

"I should try to make him realize what the world really was," I answered slowly, "and to see what was a man's place in it."

"And if he answered you—a hundred million strong—'A man's place is in the home!'—what would you say then?"

"It would be pretty hard to say anything—if men were like that."

"Yes, and it is pretty hard to say anything when women are like that—it doesn't reach them."

"But there is the whole women's movement—surely they are changing, improving."

She shook off her mood of transient bitterness. "My ignorance makes me hard, I suppose. I'm not familiar enough with your past history, recent past history, I mean, to note the changes as clearly as you do. I come suddenly to see them as they are, not knowing how much worse it has been. For instance, I suppose women used to dress more foolishly than they do now. Can that be possible?"

I ran over in my mind some of the eccentricities of fashion in earlier periods and was about to say that it was possible when I chanced to look out of the window. It was a hot day, most oppressively hot, with a fiercely glaring sun. A woman stood just across the street talking to a man. I picked up my opera glass and studied her for a moment. I had read that "the small waist is coming in again." Hers had come. She stood awkwardly in extremely high-heeled slippers, in which the sole of the foot leaned on a steep slant from heel to ball, and her toes, poor things, were driven into the narrow-pointed toe of the slipper by the whole sliding weight of the body above. The thin silk hose showed the insteps puffing up like a pincushion

377

from the binding grip of that short vamp.

Her skirts were short as a child's, most voluminous and varied in outline, hanging in bunches on the hips and in various fluctuating points and corners below. The bodice was a particolored composition, of indiscreet exposures, more suitable for a ballroom than for the street.

But what struck me most was that she wore about her neck a dead fox or the whole outside of one.

No, she was not a lunatic. No, that man was not her keeper. No, it was not a punishment, not an initiation penalty, not an election bet.

That woman, of her own free will and at considerable expense, wore heavy furs in the hottest summer weather.

I laid down the glass and turned to Ellador. "No, my dear," said I gloomily. "It is not possible that women ever could have been more idiotic in dress than that."

We were silent for a little, watching that pitiful object with her complacent smile as she stood there on those distorted feet, sweating under her load of fur, perfectly contented and pleased with herself.

"Some way," said Ellador slowly, "it makes me almost discouraged about the woman's movement. I'm not, of course, not really. I do know enough to see that they are far better off than a hundred years ago. And the laws of life are on their side, solid irresistible laws. They are women after all, and women are people—are *the* people, really, up to a certain point. I must make more allowances, must learn to see the gain in some ways even where there is none in others. Now that—that tottering little image may be earning her own living or doing something useful....What's worst of all, perhaps, is the strange missing of purpose in those who are most actively engaged in 'advancing.' They seem like flies behind a window, they bump and buzz, pushing their heads against whatever is in front of them, and never seem really to plan a way out....No, there's one thing worse than that—much worse. I wouldn't have believed it possible—I can hardly believe it now."

"What's this horror?" I asked. "Prostitution? White slavery?"

"Oh, no," she said, "those things are awful, but a sort of natural awfulness, if I may say so; what a scientific observer would expect of the evil conditions carried to excess. No—this thing is—*unnatural!* I mean—the Antis."

"Oh—the Anti-Suffragists?"

"Yes. Think of the men again—those poor degraded men I was imagining. And then think of some of them struggling for freedom, struggling long and hard, with pathetically slow progress, doing no harm in the meantime, just talking, arguing, pleading, petitioning, using what small money they could scrape together to promote their splendid cause, their cause that meant not only their own advantage, but more freedom and swifter progress for all the world. And then think of some other of those pet men, not only misunderstanding the whole thing, too dull or too perverse even to see such basic truth as that, but actually banding together to oppose it— !

"Van, if you want one all-sufficient and world-convincing proof of the degradation of women, you have it in the anti-suffragist!"

"The men are backing them, remember," I suggested.

"Of course they are. You expect the men to oppose the freeing of women, they naturally would. But the women, Van—the women themselves—it's unnatural."

With a sick shudder she buried her face in her hands for a moment, then straightened up bravely again, giving that patient little sigh of dismissal to the subject. I was silent and watched her as she sat, so strong, so graceful, so beautiful, with that balanced connection in line and movement we usually see only in savages. Her robe was simple in form, lovely in color, comfortable and becoming. I looked at her with unfailing pleasure always, never having to make excuses and reservations. All of her was beautiful and strong.

And I thought of her sisters, that fair land of full grown women, all of whom, with room for wide personal distinction, were beautiful and strong. There were differences enough. A group of thorough-bred race horses might vary widely in color, size, shape, marking and individual expression; yet all be fine horses. There would be no need of scrubs and cripples to make variety. And I looked again out of our window, at the city street, with its dim dirtiness, its brutal noise and the unsatisfied, unsatisfying people going so hurriedly about after their food, crowding, pushing, hurrying like hungry rats; the sordid eagerness of the men, the shallow folly of the women. And all at once there swept over me a great wave of homesickness for Herland.

Ellador was never satisfied merely to criticize; she must needs plan some way out, some improvement. So, laying aside her discouragement, she plunged into this woman question with new determination and before long came to me in loving triumph.

"I was wrong, Van, to be so harsh with them; it was just my Herland background. Now I have been deliberately putting myself in the woman's place and measuring the rate of progress—as of a glacier. And it's wonderful, really wonderful. There was the bottom limit—not so very far back—some savages still keeping to it—merely to live long enough to bear a daughter. Then there's the gain, this way in one land and that way in another, but always a gain. Then this great modern awakening which is now stirring them all over the world. By keeping my own previous knowledge of women entirely out of my mind and by measuring your really progressive ones to-day against their own grandmothers—that movement I was so scornful about now seems to me a sunburst of blazing improvement. Of course they 'bump and buzz' in every direction, that is mere resilience—haven't they been kept down in every direction? They'll get over that as they grow accustomed to real liberty.

"It would be inconceivable that they should have been so unutterably degraded for so long and not show the results of it, the limitations. Instead of blaming them I should have been rejoicing at the wonderful speed with which they have surged forward as fast as any door was opened, even a crack. I have been looking at what might be called the unconscious as apart from the conscious woman's movement, and it comforts me much."

"Just what do you mean?"

"I mean the women's clubs, here in this country especially; and largest of all the economic changes; the immense numbers who are at work."

"Didn't they always work? The poor ones, that is?"

"Oh, yes, at home. I mean human work."

"Wage earning?"

"That, incidentally, as a descriptive term; but it would be different grade of work, even without that."

"So I've heard people say, some people. But what is there superior in doing some fractional monotonous little job like bookkeeping, for instance, as compared with the management and performance of all the intimate tasks in a household?"

I was so solemn about this that she took me seriously, at least for a moment.

"It isn't the difference between a bookkeeper and a housekeeper that must be considered; it is the difference between an organized business world that needs bookkeeping and an unorganized world of separate families with no higher work than to eat, sleep and keep alive."

Then she saw me grin and begged pardon, cheerfully. "I might have known you were wiser than that, Van. But, oh, the people I've been talking to! The questions they ask and the comments they make! Fortunately we do not have to wait for universal conviction before moving onward."

"If you could have your way with the women of this country and the others what would you make them do?" I asked.

She set her chin in her hand and meditated a little. "What they are doing, only more of it, for one thing," she answered presently, "but, oh, so much more! Of course they have to be taught differently, they need new standards, new hopes, new ideals, new purposes. That's the real field of work, you see, Van, in the mind. That is what was so confusing to me at first. You see the difference in looks between your women and our women is as one to a thousand compared to the differences between their mental content.

"Your conditions are so good, the real ones, I mean, the supplies, the materials, the abilities you have, that at first I underrated the difficulties. Inside you are not as advanced as outside, men or women. You have such antique minds! I never get used to it. You see we, ever so long ago, caught up with our conditions; and now we are always planning better ones. Our minds are ahead of our conditions—and yet we live pretty comfortably."

"And how are our women going to catch up?"

"They have to make a long jump, from the patriarchal status to the democratic, from the narrowest personal ties to the widest social relation, from first hand labor, mere private service of bodily needs, to the specialized, organized social service of the whole community. At present this is going on, in actual fact, without their realizing it, without their understanding and accepting it. It is the mind that needs changing."

"I suppose it seems a trifling matter to you to change the working machinery of twenty million homes—that's what it amounts to—doesn't it?"

"How long does it take to do up twenty million women's hair?" she inquired. "No longer than it does one—if they all do it at once. Numbers don't complicate a question like this. What could be done in one tiny village could be done all over the country in the same time. I suppose I do underestimate the practical difficulties here on account of our having settled all those little problems. The idea of your still not being properly fed!—I can't get used to it."

Then I remembered the uniform excellence of food in Herland; not only all that we ourselves had enjoyed, but that I never saw in any shop or market any wilted, withered, stale or in any way inferior supplies.

"How did you manage that?" I asked her. "Did you confiscate all the damaged things? Was there a penalty for selling them?"

"Does one of your housekeepers confiscate her damaged food? Is there any penalty for feeding her family with it?"

"Oh, I see. You only provided enough to keep fresh."

"Exactly. I tell you numbers don't make any difference. A million people do not eat any more—apiece—than a dozen at one table. We feed our people as carefully and as competently as you try to feed your families. You can't do as well because of the inferiority of materials."

This I found somewhat offensive, but I knew it was true.

"It's so simple!" she said wearily. "A child could see it. Food is to *eat*, and if it is not good to eat it is not food. Here you people use food as a thing to play with, to buy and sell, to store up, to throw away, with no more regard for its real purpose than—"

"Than the swine with pearls before him," I suggested. "But you know those economic laws come in—"

She laughed outright.

"Van, dear, there is nothing in all your pitiful tangled life more absurd than what you so solemnly call 'economics.' Good economics in regard to food is surely this: to produce the best quality, in sufficient quantity, with the least expenditure of labor, and to distribute it the most rapidly and freshly to the people who need it.

"The management of food in your world is perhaps the most inexplicably foolish of anything you do. I've been up and down the streets in your cities observing. I've been in the hotels and restaurants far and wide and in ever so many homes. And I confess, Van, with some mortification, that there is no one thing I'm more homesick for than food."

"I am getting discouraged, if you are not, Ellador. As compared with a rational country like yours, this is rather a mess. And it looks so hopeless. I suppose it will take a thousand years to catch up."

"You could do it in three generations," she calmly replied.

"Three generations! That's barely a century."

"I know it. The whole outside part of it you could do inside of twenty years; it is the people who will take three generations to remake. You could improve this stock, say, 5 per cent in one, 15 in two and 80 per cent in three. Perhaps faster."

"Are not you rather sanguine, my dear girl?"

"I don't think so," she answered gravely. "People are not *bad* now; they are only weighed down with all this falsehood and foolishness in their heads. There is always the big lifting force of life to push you on as fast as you will let it. There is the wide surrounding help of conditions, such conditions as you even now know how to arrange. And there is the power of education—which you have hardly tried. With these all together and with proper care in breeding you could fill the world with glorious people—soon. Oh, I wish you'd do it! I *wish* you'd do it!"

It was hard on her. Harder even than I had foreseen. Not only the war horrors, not only the miseries of more backward nations and of our painful past, but even in my America where I had fondly thought she would be happy, the common arrangements of our lives to which we are so patiently accustomed, were to her a constant annoyance and distress.

Through her eyes I saw it newly and instead of the breezy pride I used to feel in my young nation I now began to get an unceasing sense of what she had called "an idiot child."

It was so simply true, what she said about food. Food is to eat. All its transporting and preserving and storing and selling—if it interferes with the eating value of the food—is foolishness. I began to see the man who stores eggs until they are reduced to the grade called "rots and spots" as an idiot and a malicious idiot at that. Vivid and clear rose in my mind the garden-circled cities of Herland, where for each group of inhabitants all fresh fruits and vegetables were raised so near that they could be eaten the day they were picked. It did not cost any more. It cost *less*, saving transportation. Supplies that would keep they kept—enough from season to season, with some emergency reserves; but not one person, young or old, ever had to eat such things as we pay extortionately for in every city.

Nothing but women, only mothers, but they had worked out to smooth perfection what now began to seem to me to be the basic problem in human life.

How to make the best kind of people and how to keep them at their best and growing better—surely that is what we are here for.

Chapter XII

As I look over my mass of notes, of hastily jotted down or wholly reconstructed conversations, and some of Ellador's voluminous papers, I am distressingly conscious of the shortcomings of this book. There is no time now to improve it, and I wish to publish it, as a little better than no report at all of the long visit of my wife from Herland to the world we know.

In time I hope, if I live, and if I come back again, to make a far more competent study than this. Yet why trouble myself to do that? She will do it, I am sure, with the help of her friends and sisters, far better than I could.

I had hoped that she could go blazing about our world, lecturing on the wonders and beauties of Herland, but that was all dropped when they decided not to betray their strange geographical secret—yet. I am allowed to print the previous account of our visit there—even that will set explorers on their track; but she did not wish to answer specific questions while here, nor to refuse to answer.

They were quite right. The more I see of our world, the surer I am that they are right to try to preserve their lovely country as it is, for a while at least.

Ellador begs that I explain how inchoate, how fragmentary, how disproportionate, her impressions necessarily were.

"The longer I stay," she said, "the more I learn of your past and understand of your present, the more hopeful I feel for you. Please make that very clear." This she urged strongly.

The war did not discourage her, after a while. "What is one more—among so many?" she asked, with a wry smile. "The very awfulness of this is its best hope; that, and the growing wisdom of the people. You'll have no more, I'm sure; that is, no more except those recognized as criminal outbreaks, and punitive ones; the receding waves of force as these turbulent cross-currents die down and disappear.

"But, Van, dear, whatever else you leave out, be sure to make it as strong as you can about the women and children."

"Perhaps you'd better say it yourself, my dear. Come, you put in a chapter," I urged. But she would not.

"I should be too abusive, I'm afraid," she objected; "and I've talked enough on the subject—you know that."

She had, by this time, gone over it pretty thoroughly. And it is not very difficult to give the drift of it—we all know the facts. Her position, as a Herlander, was naturally the maternal one.

"The business of people is, of course, to be well, happy, wise, beautiful, productive and progressive."

"Why don't you say 'good,' too," I suggested.

"Don't be absurd, Van. If people are well and happy, wise, beautiful, productive and progressive, they must incidentally be good; that's being good. What sort of goodness is it which does not produce those effects? Well, these 'good' people need a 'good' world to live in, and they have to make it; a clean, safe, comfortable world to grow in.

"Then, since they all begin as children, it seems so self-evident that the way to make better people and a better world is to teach the children how."

"You'll find general agreement so far," I admitted.

"But the people who train children are, with you, the mothers," she pursued, "and the mothers of your world have not yet seen this simple truth."

"They talk of nothing else," I suggested. "They are always talking of the wonderful power and beauty of motherhood, from the most ancient morality to Ellen Key."

"Yes, I know they talk about it. Their idea of motherhood, to what it ought to be, is like a birchbark canoe to an ocean steamship, Van. They haven't seen it as a whole—that's the trouble. What prevents them is their dwarfed condition, not being people, real, world-building people; and what keeps them dwarfed is this amazing relic of the remote past—their domestic position."

"Would you 'destroy the home,' as they call it, Ellador?"

"I think the home is the very loveliest thing you have on earth," she unexpectedly replied.

"What do you mean, then?" I asked, genuinely puzzled. "You can't have homes without women in them, can you? And children?"

"And men," she gravely added. "Why, Van—do not men have homes, and love them dearly? A man does not have to stay at home all day, in order to love it; why should a woman?"

Then she made clear to me, quite briefly, how the home should be to the woman just what it was to a man, and far more to both, in beauty and comfort, in privacy and peace, in all the pleasant rest and dear companionship we so prize; but that it should not be to him a grinding weight of care and expense, or an expression of pride; nor to her a workshop or her sole means of personal expression.

"It is so pathetic," she said, "and so unutterably absurd, to see great city-size and world-size women trying to content themselves and express themselves in one house; or worse, one flat. You know how it would be for a man, surely. It is just as ridiculous for a woman. And your city-size and world-size men are all tied up to these house-size women. It's so funny, Van, so painfully funny, like a horse harnessed with an eohippus."

"We haven't got to wait for Mrs. Eohippus to catch up to Mr. Horse, I hope?"

"You won't have to wait long," she assured me. "They are born equal, your boys and girls; they have to be. It is the tremendous difference in cultural conditions that divides them; not only in infancy and youth; not only in dress and training; but in this wide gulf of industrial distinction, this permanent division which leaves one sex free to rise, to develop every social power and quality, and forcibly restrains the other to a labor-level thousands of years behind. It is beginning to change, I can see that now, but it has to be complete, universal, before women can do their duty as mothers."

"But I thought—at least I've always heard—that it was their duty as mothers which kept them at home."

She waved this aside, with a touch of impatience. "Look at the children," she said; "that's enough. Look at these girls who do not even know enough about motherhood to demand a healthy father. Why, a—a—sheep would know better than to mate with such creatures as some of your women marry.

"They are only just beginning to learn that there are such diseases as they have been suffering and dying from for all these centuries. And they are so poor! They haven't any money, most of them; they are so disorganized—unorganized—apparently unconscious of any need of organization."

I mentioned the growth of trade unions, but she said that was but a tiny step—useful, but small; what she meant was Mother Union...

"I suppose it is sex," she pursued, soberly. "With us, motherhood is so simple. I had supposed, at first, that your bi-sexual method would mean a better motherhood, a motherhood of two, so to speak. And I find that men have so enjoyed their little part of the work that they have grown to imagine it as quite a separate thing, and to talk about 'sex' as if it was wholly distinct from parentage. Why, see what I found the other day"— and she pulled out a copy of a little yellow medical magazine, published by a physician who specializes in sex diseases, and read me a note this doctor had written on "Sterilization," wherein he said that it had no injurious effect on sex.

"Just look at that!" she said. "The man is a doctor—and thinks the removal of parental power is no loss to 'sex'! What men—yes, and some women, too—seem to mean by sex is just their preliminary pleasure....When your women are really awake and know what they are for, seeing men as the noblest kind of assistants, nature's latest and highest device for the improvement of parentage, then they will talk less of 'sex' and more of children."

I urged, as genuinely as I could, the collateral value and uses of sex indulgence; not the common theories of "necessity," which any well-trained athlete can deny, but the more esoteric claims of higher flights of love, and of far-reaching stimulus to all artistic faculty: the creative impulse in our work.

She listened patiently, but shook her head when I was done.

"Even if all those claims were true," she said, "they would not weigh as an ounce to a ton beside the degradation of women, the corruption of the body and mind through these wholly unnecessary diseases, and the miserable misborn children. Why, Van, what's 'creative impulse' and all its 'far-reaching stimulus' to set beside the stunted, meager starveling children, the millions of poor little sub-ordinary children, children who are mere accidents and by-products of this much-praised 'sex'? It's no use, dear, until all the children of the world are at *least* healthy; at *least* normal; until the average man and woman are free from taint of sex-disease and happy in their love—lastingly happy in their love—there is not much to boast of in this popular idea of sex and sex indulgence.

"It can not be changed in a day or a year," she said. "This is evidently a matter of long inheritance, and that's why I allow three generations to get over it. But nothing will help much till the women are free and see their duty as mothers."

"Some of the 'freest' women are urging more sex freedom," I reminded her. "They want to see the women doing as men have done, apparently."

"Yes, I know. They are almost as bad as the antis—but not quite. They are merely a consequence of wrong teaching and wrong habits; they were there before, those women, only not saying what they wanted. Surely, you never imagined that all men could be unchaste and all women chaste, did you?"

I shamefacedly admitted that that was exactly what we had imagined, and that we had most cruelly punished the women who were not.

"It's the most surprising thing I ever heard of," she said; "and you bred and trained plenty of animals, to say nothing of knowing the wild ones. Is there any case in nature of a species with such a totally opposite traits in the two sexes?"

There wasn't, that I knew of, outside of their special distinctions, of course.

All these side issues she continually swept aside, all the minor points and discussable questions, returning again and again to the duty of women.

"As soon as the women take the right ground, men will have to follow suit," she said, "as soon as women are free, independent and conscientious. They have the power in their own hands, by natural law."

"What is going to rouse them, to make them see it?" I asked.

"A number of things seems to be doing that," she said, meditatively. "From my point of view, I should think the sense of maternal duty would be the strongest thing, but there seem to be many forces at work here. The economic change is the most imperative, more so, even, than the political, and both are going on fast. There's the war, too, that is doing wonders for women. It is opening the eyes of men, millions of men, at once, as no arguments ever could have."

"Aren't you pleased to see the women working for peace?" I asked.

"Immensely, of course. All over Europe they are at it—that's what I mean."

"But I meant the Peace Movement."

"Oh, that? Talking for peace, you mean, and writing and telegraphing. Yes, that's useful, too. Anything that brings women out into social relation, into a sense of social responsibility, is good. But all that they say and write and urge will not count as much as what they *do*.

"Your women will surely have more sense than the men about economics," she suggested. "It does not seem to me possible for business women to mishandle food as men do, or to build such houses. It is all so— unreasonable: to make people eat what is not good, or live in dark, cramped little rooms."

"You don't think they show much sense in their own clothes?" I offered, mischievously.

"No, they don't. But that is women as they are, the kind of women you men have been so long manufacturing. I'm speaking of real ones, the kind that are there underneath, and sure to come out as soon as they have a chance. And what a glorious time they will have—cleaning up the world! I'd almost like to stay and help a little."

Gradually it had dawned upon me that Ellador did not mean to stay, even in America. I wanted to be sure.

"Like to stay? Do you mean that you want to go back—for good?"

"It is not absolutely clear to me yet," she answered. "But one thing I'm certain about. If I live here I will not have a child."

I thought for a moment that she meant the distress about her would have some deleterious effect and prevent it; but when I looked at her, saw the folded arms, the steady mouth, the fixed determination in her eyes, I knew that she meant "will not" when she said it.

"It would not be right," she added, simply. "There is no place in all your world, that I have seen or read of, where I should be willing to raise a child."

"We could go to some lovely place alone," I urged; "some island, clean and beautiful—"

"But we should be 'alone' there. That is no place for a child."

"You could teach it—as they do in Herland," I still urged.

"I teach it? I? What am I, to teach a child?"

"You would be its mother," I answered.

"And what is a mother to teach a solitary little outcast thing as you suggest? Children need the teaching of many women, and the society of many children, for right growth. Also, they need a social environment—not an island!"

"You see, dear," she went on, after a little, "in Herland everything teaches. The child sees love and order and peace and comfort and wisdom everywhere. No child, alone, could grow up so—so richly endowed. And as to these countries I have seen—these cities of abomination—I would die childless rather than to bear a child in this world of yours."

In Herland to say "I would die childless" is somewhat equivalent to our saying "I would suffer eternal damnation." It is the worst deprivation they can think of.

"You are going to leave me!" I cried. It burst upon me with sudden bitterness. She was not "mine," she was a woman of Herland, and her heavenly country, her still clear hope of motherhood, were more to her than life in our land with me. What had I to offer her that was comparable to that upland paradise?

She came to me, then, and took me in her arms—strong, tender, loving arms—and gave me one of her rare kisses.

"I'm going to stay with you, my husband, as long as I live—if you want me. Is there anything to prevent your coming back to Herland?"

As a matter of fact, there was really nothing to prevent it, nothing I might leave behind which would cost me the pain her exile was costing her; and especially nothing which could compensate for losing my wife.

We began to discuss it, with eager interest. "I don't mean to forsake this poor world," she assured me. "We can come back again—later, much later. My mind is full of great things that can be done here, and I want to get all the wisdom of Herland at work to help. But let us go back now, while we are young, and before this black, stupid confusion has—has hurt me any worse. Perhaps it is no harm, that I have suffered so. Perhaps our child will have a heart that aches for all the world—and will do more than any of us to help it. Especially if it is—a Boy."

"Do you want a boy, darling?"

"Oh, do I not! Just think—none of us, ever, in these two thousand years, has had one. If we, in Herland, can begin a new kind of men!"

"What do you want of them?" I said, teasingly. "Surely you women alone have accomplished all that the world needs, haven't you?"

"Indeed, no, Van. We haven't begun. Ours is only a—a sample: a little bit of a local exhibit. If what we have done is the right thing, then it becomes our clearest duty to spread it to all the world. Such a new life as you have opened to us, Van, you Splendid Man!"

"Splendid Man! Splendid! I thought you thought we were to blame for all the misery in the world? Just look at the harm we've done!"

"Just look at the good you've done, too! Why, my darling, the harm you have done is merely the result of your misunderstanding and misuse of Sex; and the good you have done is the result of the humanness of you, the big, noble humanness that has grown and grown, that has built and lifted and taught the world in spite of all the dragging evil. Why, dear, when I see the courage, the perseverance, the persistent growth you men have shown, cumbered as you have been from the beginning by the fruits of your mistakes, it seems as if you were almost *more* than human."

I was rather stunned by this. No man who had seen Herland and then come back to our tangled foolishness, waste and pain, could be proud of his man-made world. No man who had solidly grasped the biological facts as to the initial use of his sex, and his incredible misuse of it, could help the further shame for the anomalous position of the human male, completely mistaken, and producing a constant train of evils.

I could see it all plainly enough. And now, to have her talk like this!

"Remember, dear, that men never *meant* to do it, or any part of it," she tenderly explained. "The trouble evidently began when nobody knew much; it became an ironclad 'custom' even before religion took it up, and law. Remember, too, that the women haven't died—they are here yet, in equal numbers. Also, even the unjust restrictions have saved them from a great deal of suffering which the men met. And then nothing could rob them of their inheritance. Every step the men really made upward lifted the women, too. And don't forget Love, ever. That has lived and triumphed even through all the lust and slavery and shame."

I felt comforted, relieved.

"Besides," she went on, "you men ought to feel proud of the real world work you have done, even crippled as you were by your own excessive sex, and by those poor, dragging dead-weights of women you had manufactured. In spite of it all, you have invented and discovered and built and adorned the world. You have things as far along as we have, even some things better, and many sciences and crafts we know nothing about. And you've done it alone—just men! It's wonderful."

In spite of all the kindness and honest recognition she showed, I could not help a feeling of inner resentment at this tone. Of course, we three men had been constantly impressed with all that they had done in Herland— just women, alone—but that she thought it equally wonderful for men to do it was not wholly gratifying.

She went on serenely.

"We had such advantages, you see. Being women, we had all the constructive and organizing tendencies of motherhood to urge us on and, having no men, we missed all that greediness and quarreling your history is so sadly full of. Also, being isolated, we could just grow—like a sequoia in a sheltered mountain glade.

"But you men, in this mixed, big world of yours, in horrid confusion of mind and long ignorance, with all those awful religions to mix you up and hold you back, and with so little real Happiness—still, you have built the world! Van, dear, it shows how much stronger humanity is than sex, even in men. All that I have had to learn, you see, for we make no distinction at home—women are people, and people are women.

"At first I thought of men just as males—a Herlander would, you know. Now I know that men are people, too, just as much as women are; and it is as one person to another that I feel this big love for you, Van. You are so nice to live with. You are such good company. I never get tired of you. I like to play with you, and to work with you. I admire and enjoy the way you do things. And when we sit down quietly, near together—it makes me so happy, Van!"

. . . . .

There were still a few big rubies in that once fat little bag she so wisely brought with her. We made careful plans, which included my taking a set of thorough lessons in aviation and mechanics; there must be no accidents on this trip. By a previous steamer we sent the well-fitted motorboat that should carry us and our dissembled aeroplane up that long river.

Of baggage, little could be carried, and that little, on Ellador's part, consisted largely of her mass of notes, all most carefully compressed, and done on the finest and lightest paper. She also urged that we take with us the lightest and newest of encyclopaedias. "We can leave it in the boat, if necessary, and make a separate trip," she suggested. Also photographs she took, and a moving picture outfit with well-selected films. "We can make them, I'm sure," she said; "but this one will do to illustrate." It did.

After all, her requirements did not weigh more than the third passenger whom we might have carried.

The river trip was a growing joy; day after day of swift gliding through those dark, drooping forests and wide, reedy flats; and when at last we shot out upon the shining silver of that hidden lake, and she saw above her the heights of Herland—my calm goddess trembled and cried, stretching her arms to it like a child to its mother.

But we set swiftly to work on our aeroplane, putting it all soundly together and fastening in the baggage, and then sealed up the tight sheathed boat like a trim cocoon.

Then the purr of our propeller, the long, skating slide on the water, and up—and up—in a widening spiral, Ellador breathless, holding fast to the supports, till we topped the rocky rim, rose above the forest, her forest—

and sailed out over the serene expanse of that fair land.

"O, let's look," she begged; "let's look at the whole of it first—it's the whole of it that I love!" So we swept in a great circle above, as one might sweep over Holland: the green fields, blossoming gardens, and dark woods, spread like a model of heaven below us, and the cities, the villages—how well I remembered them, in their scattered loveliness, rich in color, beautiful in design, everywhere fringed and shaded by clean trees, lit and cheered by bright water, radiant with flowers.

She leaned forward like a young mother over her sleeping child, tender, proud, gloating.

"No smoke!" she murmured; "no brutal noise, no wickedness, no disease. Almost no accidents or sickness—almost none." (This in a whisper, as if she were apologizing for some faint blemish on the child.)

"Beauty!" she breathed. "Beauty! Beauty!—everywhere. Oh, I had forgotten how beautiful it was!"

So had I. When I first saw it I was still too accustomed to our common ugliness to really appreciate this loveliness.

When we had swung back to the town where we had lived most, and made our smooth descent in a daisied meadow, there were many to meet us, with my Well-remembered Somel, and, first and most eager, Jeff and Celis, with their baby.

Ellador seized upon it as eagerly as her gentle tenderness would allow, with reverent kisses for the little hands, the rosy feet. She caught Celis to her arms and held her close. She even kissed Jeff, which he apparently liked, and nobody else minded. And then—well, if you live in a country of about three million inhabitants, and love them all; if you have been an envoy extraordinary—very extraordinary, indeed—to a far-off, unknown world, and have come back unexpectedly—why, your hands are pretty full for a while.

. . . . .

We settled back into the smooth-running Herland life without a ripple. No trouble about housing; they had always a certain percentage of vacancies, to allow for freedom of movement. No trouble about clothes; those perfect garments were to be had everywhere, always lovely and suitable. No trouble about food; that smooth, well-adjusted food supply was available wherever we went.

No appeals for deserving charity—no need of them. Nothing to annoy and

393

depress, everything to give comfort and strength; and under all, more perceptible to me now than before, that vast, steady, onmoving current of definite purpose, planning and working to make good better and better best.

The "atmosphere" in the world behind us is that of a thousand mixed currents, pushing and pulling in every direction, controverting and opposing one another.

Here was peace—and power, with accomplishment.

Eagerly she returned to her people. With passionate enthusiasm she poured out, in wide tours of lecturing, and in print, her report of world conditions. She saw it taken up, studied, discussed by those great-minded over-mothers of the land. She saw the young women, earnest eyed, of boundless hope and high purpose, planning, as eager missionaries plan, what they could do to spread to all the world their proven gains. Reprints of that encyclopaedia were scattered to every corner of the land, and read swiftly, eagerly, to crowding groups of listeners. There began to stir in Herland a new spirit, pushing, seeking, a new sense of responsibility, a larger duty.

"It is not enough," they said, "that we should be so happy. Here is the whole round world—millions and hundreds of millions of people—and all their babies! Not in a thousand years will we rest, till the world is happy!"

And to this end they began to plan, slowly, wisely, calmly, making no haste; sure, above all, that they must preserve their own integrity and peace if they were to help others.

. . . . .

When Ellador had done her utmost, given all that she had gathered and seen the great work growing, she turned to me with a long, happy sigh.

"Let's go to the forest," she said. And we went.

We went to the rock where I had first landed and she showed me where three laughing girls had been hidden. We went to the tree where they had slipped away like quicksilver. We went to a far-off, quiet place she knew, a place of huge trees, heavy with good fruit, of smooth, mossy banks, of quiet pools and tinkling fountains. Here, unexpected, was a little forester house, still and clean, with tall flowers looking in at the windows.

"I used to love this best of all," she said. "Look—you can see both ways."

It was on a high knoll and, through the great boughs, a long vista opened to a bright sunlight in the fields below.

The other side was a surprise. The land dropped suddenly, fell to a rocky brink and ended. Dark and mysterious, far beyond, in a horizon-sweeping gloom of crowding jungle, lay—the world.

"I always wanted to see—to know—to help," she said. "Dear—you have brought me so much! Not only love, but the great new spread of life—of work to do for all humanity.

"And then—the other new Hope, too,—perhaps—perhaps—a son!"

And in due time a son was born to us.

The End

Made in the USA
Monee, IL
06 September 2024

65225983R00239